Mediating Policy

Among the most serious consequences of the 2008 global financial collapse and sovereign debt crisis were a series of unprecedented international bailouts for Greece, Ireland, and Portugal between 2010 and 2011.

This book analyses the development policies of Greece, Ireland, and Portugal between 1990 and 2008, before the Eurozone crisis. It identifies national-level differences between the policy strategies and outcomes that have characterized recent developments in the Greek, Irish, and Portuguese political economies. In addition, it provides an explanation for these differences that takes into account variations in political institutions and state–society relations. In doing so, it locates an explanation for policy divergence in the presence or absence of the policy-making institutions and processes that make up a 'zone of mediation'. Overall, it argues there is significant variation in the extent to which Ireland, Portugal, and Greece have adapted their developmental goals and strategies in order to address the labour market challenges posed by the post-industrial era.

This book will be of key interest to students and scholars of European politics and studies, comparative political economy, public policy/policy studies, and democracy studies.

Kate Nicholls is Senior Lecturer in Social Sciences and Public Policy at AUT University, New Zealand.

Routledge advances in European politics

1 **Russian Messianism**
Third Rome, revolution, Communism and after
Peter J.S. Duncan

2 **European Integration and the Postmodern Condition**
Governance, democracy, identity
Peter van Ham

3 **Nationalism in Italian Politics**
The stories of the Northern League, 1980–2000
Damian Tambini

4 **International Intervention in the Balkans since 1995**
Edited by Peter Siani-Davies

5 **Widening the European Union**
The politics of institutional change and reform
Edited by Bernard Steunenberg

6 **Institutional Challenges in the European Union**
Edited by Madeleine Hosli, Adrian van Deemen and Mika Widgrén

7 **Europe Unbound**
Enlarging and reshaping the boundaries of the European Union
Edited by Jan Zielonka

8 **Ethnic Cleansing in the Balkans**
Nationalism and the destruction of tradition
Cathie Carmichael

9 **Democracy and Enlargement in Post-Communist Europe**
The democratisation of the general public in fifteen Central and Eastern European countries, 1991–1998
Christian W. Haerpfer

10 **Private Sector Involvement in the Euro**
The power of ideas
Stefan Collignon and Daniela Schwarzer

11 **Europe**
A Nietzschean perspective
Stefan Elbe

12 **European Union and E-Voting**
Addressing the European Parliament's internet voting challenge
Edited by Alexander H. Trechsel and Fernando Mendez

13 **European Union Council Presidencies**
A comparative perspective
Edited by Ole Elgström

14 **European Governance and Supranational Institutions**
Making states comply
Jonas Tallberg

15 **European Union, NATO and Russia**
Martin Smith and Graham Timmins

16 **Business, the State and Economic Policy**
The case of Italy
G. Grant Amyot

17 **Europeanization and Transnational States**
Comparing Nordic central governments
Bengt Jacobsson, Per Lægreid and Ove K. Pedersen

18 **European Union Enlargement**
A comparative history
Edited by Wolfram Kaiser and Jürgen Elvert

19 **Gibraltar**
British or Spanish?
Peter Gold

20 **Gendering Spanish Democracy**
Monica Threlfall, Christine Cousins and Celia Valiente

21 **European Union Negotiations**
Processes, networks and negotiations
Edited by Ole Elgström and Christer Jönsson

22 **Evaluating Euro-Mediterranean Relations**
Stephen C. Calleya

23 **The Changing Face of European Identity**
A seven-nation study of (supra) national attachments
Edited by Richard Robyn

24 **Governing Europe**
Discourse, governmentality and European integration
William Walters and Jens Henrik Haahr

25 **Territory and Terror**
Conflicting nationalisms in the Basque country
Jan Mansvelt Beck

26 **Multilateralism, German Foreign Policy and Central Europe**
Claus Hofhansel

27 **Popular Protest in East Germany**
Gareth Dale

28 **Germany's Foreign Policy Towards Poland and the Czech Republic**
Ostpolitik revisited
Karl Cordell and Stefan Wolff

29 **Kosovo**
The politics of identity and space
Denisa Kostovicova

30 **The Politics of European Union Enlargement**
Theoretical approaches
Edited by Frank Schimmelfennig and Ulrich Sedelmeier

31 **Europeanizing Social Democracy?**
The rise of the party of European socialists
Simon Lightfoot

32 **Conflict and Change in EU Budgetary Politics**
Johannes Lindner

33 **Gibraltar, Identity and Empire**
E.G. Archer

34 **Governance Stories**
Mark Bevir and R.A.W. Rhodes

35 **Britain and the Balkans**
1991 until the present
Carole Hodge

36 **The Eastern Enlargement of the European Union**
John O'Brennan

37 **Values and Principles in European Union Foreign Policy**
Edited by Sonia Lucarelli and Ian Manners

38 **European Union and the Making of a Wider Northern Europe**
Pami Aalto

39 **Democracy in the European Union**
Towards the emergence of a public sphere
Edited by Liana Giorgi, Ingmar Von Homeyer and Wayne Parsons

40 **European Union Peacebuilding and Policing**
Michael Merlingen with Rasa Ostrauskaite

41 **The Conservative Party and European Integration since 1945**
At the heart of Europe?
N.J. Crowson

42 **E-Government in Europe**
Re-booting the state
Edited by Paul G. Nixon and Vassiliki N. Koutrakou

43 **EU Foreign and Interior Policies**
Cross-pillar politics and the social construction of sovereignty
Stephan Stetter

44 **Policy Transfer in European Union Governance**
Regulating the utilities
Simon Bulmer, David Dolowitz, Peter Humphreys and Stephen Padgett

45 **The Europeanization of National Political Parties**
Power and organizational adaptation
Edited by Thomas Poguntke, Nicholas Aylott, Elisabeth Carter, Robert Ladrech and Kurt Richard Luther

46 **Citizenship in Nordic Welfare States**
Dynamics of choice, duties and participation in a changing Europe
Edited by Bjørn Hvinden and Håkan Johansson

47 **National Parliaments within the Enlarged European Union**
From victims of integration to competitive actors?
Edited by John O'Brennan and Tapio Raunio

48 **Britain, Ireland and Northern Ireland since 1980**
The totality of relationships
Eamonn O'Kane

49 **The EU and the European Security Strategy**
Forging a global Europe
Edited by Sven Biscop and Jan Joel Andersson

50 **European Security and Defence Policy**
An implementation perspective
Edited by Michael Merlingen and Rasa Ostrauskaitė

51 **Women and British Party Politics**
Descriptive, substantive and symbolic representation
Sarah Childs

52 **The Selection of Ministers in Europe**
Hiring and firing
Edited by Keith Dowding and Patrick Dumont

53 **Energy Security**
Europe's new foreign policy challenge
Richard Youngs

54 **Institutional Challenges in Post-Constitutional Europe**
Governing change
Edited by Catherine Moury and Luís de Sousa

55 **The Struggle for the European Constitution**
A past and future history
Michael O'Neill

56 **Transnational Labour Solidarity**
Mechanisms of commitment to cooperation within the European Trade Union Movement
Katarzyna Gajewska

57 **The Illusion of Accountability in the European Union**
Edited by Sverker Gustavsson, Christer Karlsson, and Thomas Persson

58 **The European Union and Global Social Change**
A critical geopolitical-economic analysis
József Böröcz

59 **Citizenship and Collective Identity in Europe**
Ireneusz Pawel Karolewski

60 **EU Enlargement and Socialization**
Turkey and Cyprus
Stefan Engert

61 **The Politics of EU Accession**
Turkish challenges and Central European experiences
Edited by Lucie Tunkrová and Pavel Šaradín

62 **The Political History of European Integration**
The hypocrisy of democracy-through-market
Hagen Schulz-Forberg and Bo Stråth

63 **The Spatialities of Europeanization**
Power, governance and territory in Europe
Alun Jones and Julian Clark

64 **European Union Sanctions and Foreign Policy**
When and why do they work?
Clara Portela

65 The EU's Role in World Politics
A retreat from Liberal Internationalism
Richard Youngs

66 Social Democracy and European Integration
The politics of preference formation
Edited by Dionyssis Dimitrakopoulos

67 The EU Presence in International Organizations
Edited by Spyros Blavoukos and Dimitris Bourantonis

68 Sustainability in European Environmental Policy
Challenge of governance and knowledge
Edited by Rob Atkinson, Georgios Terizakis and Karsten Zimmermann

69 Fifty Years of EU–Turkey Relations
A Sisyphean story
Edited by Armagan Emre Çakir

70 Europeanization and Foreign Policy
State diversity in Finland and Britain
Juha Jokela

71 EU Foreign Policy and Post-Soviet Conflicts
Stealth intervention
Nicu Popescu

72 Switzerland in Europe
Continuity and change in the Swiss political economy
Edited by Christine Trampusch and André Mach

73 The Political Economy of Noncompliance
Adjusting to the single European market
Scott Nicholas Siegel

74 National and European Foreign Policy
Towards Europeanization
Edited by Reuben Wong and Christopher Hill

75 The European Union Diplomatic Service
Ideas, preferences and identities
Caterina Carta

76 Poland within the European Union
New awkward partner or new heart of Europe?
Aleks Szczerbiak

77 A Political Theory of Identity in European Integration
Memory and policies
Catherine Guisan

78 EU Foreign Policy and the Europeanization of Neutral States
Comparing Irish and Austrian foreign policy
Nicole Alecu de Flers

79 Party System Change in Western Europe
Gemma Loomes

80 The Second Tier of Local Government in Europe
Provinces, counties, départements and Landkreise in comparison
Hubert Heinelt and Xavier Bertrana Horta

81 **Learning from the EU Constitutional Treaty**
Democratic constitutionalism beyond the nation-state
Ben Crum

82 **Human Rights and Democracy in EU Foreign Policy**
The cases of Ukraine and Egypt
Rosa Balfour

83 **Europeanization, Integration and Identity**
A social constructivist fusion perspective on Norway
Gamze Tanil

84 **The Impact of European Integration on Political Parties**
Beyond the permissive consensus
Dimitri Almeida

85 **Civic Resources and the Future of the European Union**
Victoria Kaina and Ireneusz Pawel Karolewski

86 **The Europeanization of National Foreign Policies towards Latin America**
Lorena Ruano

87 **The EU and Multilateral Security Governance**
Sonia Lucarelli, Luk Van Langenhove and Jan Wouters

88 **Security Challenges in the Euro-Med Area in the 21st Century**
Mare nostrum
Stephen Calleya

89 **Society and Democracy in Europe**
Oscar W. Gabriel and Silke Keil

90 **European Union Public Health Policy**
Regional and global trends
Edited by Scott L. Greer and Paulette Kurzer

91 **The New Member States and the European Union**
Foreign policy and Europeanization
Edited by Michael Baun and Dan Marek

92 **The Politics of Ratification of EU Treaties**
Carlos Closa

93 **Europeanization and New Member States**
A comparative social network analysis
Flavia Jurje

94 **National Perspectives on Russia**
European foreign policy in the making
Maxine David, Jackie Gower and Hiski Haukkala

95 **Institutional Legacies of Communism**
Change and continuities in minority protection
Edited by Karl Cordell, Timofey Agarin and Alexander Osipov

96 **Sustainable Development and Governance in Europe**
The evolution of the discourse on sustainability
Edited by Pamela M. Barnes and Thomas C. Hoerber

97 **Social Networks and Public Support for the European Union**
Elizabeth Radziszewski

98 **The EU's Democracy Promotion and the Mediterranean Neighbours**
Orientation, ownership and dialogue in Jordan and Turkey
Ann-Kristin Jonasson

99 **New Democracies in Crisis?**
A comparative constitutional study of the Czech Republic, Hungary, Poland, Romania and Slovakia
Paul Blokker

100 **Party Attitudes Towards the EU in the Member States**
Parties for Europe, parties against Europe
Nicolò Conti

101 **The European Union and Occupied Palestinian Territories**
State-building without a state
Dimitris Bouris

102 **Portugal in the European Union**
Assessing twenty-five years of integration experience
Laura C. Ferreira-Pereira

103 **Governance and European Civil Society**
Governmentality, discourse and NGOs
Acar Kutay

104 **The EU, Migration and the Politics of Administrative Detention**
Edited by Michela Ceccorulli and Nicola Labanca

105 **Political Representation in the European Union**
Democracy in a time of crisis
Edited by Sandra Kröger

106 **New Approaches to EU Foreign Policy**
Edited by Maciej Wilga and Ireneusz Pawel Karolewski

107 **Democracy, Law and Religious Pluralism in Europe**
Secularism and post-secularism
Edited by Ferran Requejo and Camil Ungureanu

108 **Contemporary Spanish Foreign Policy**
Edited by David Garcia and Ramon Pacheco Pardo

109 **Reframing Europe's Future**
Challenges and failures of the European construction
Edited by Ferenc Miszlivetz and Jody Jensen

110 **Italy's Foreign Policy in the 21st Century**
A contested nature?
Edited by Ludovica Marchi, Richard Whitman and Geoffrey Edwards

111 **The Challenge of Coalition Government**
The Italian case
Edited by Nicolò Conti and Francesco Marangoni

112 **The Nordic Countries and the European Union**
Still the other European community?
Edited by Caroline Howard Grøn, Peter Nedergaard and Anders Wivel

113 **Mediating Policy**
Greece, Ireland, and Portugal Before the Eurozone Crisis
Kate Nicholls

114 **The European Parliament and its International Relations**
Edited by Stelios Stavridis and Daniela Irrera

Mediating Policy

Greece, Ireland, and Portugal before the Eurozone crisis

Kate Nicholls

Routledge
Taylor & Francis Group
LONDON AND NEW YORK

First published 2015
by Routledge
2 Park Square, Milton Park, Abingdon, Oxon OX14 4RN

and by Routledge
711 Third Avenue, New York, NY 10017

First issued in paperback 2017

Routledge is an imprint of the Taylor & Francis Group, an informa business

British Library Cataloguing in Publication Data
A catalogue record for this book is available from the British Library

Library of Congress Cataloging in Publication Data
Nicholls, Kate,
Mediating policy : Greece, Ireland, and Portugal before the Eurozone crisis / Kate Nicholls.
pages cm. – (Routledge advances in European politics)
Includes bibliographical references and index.
Greece–Economic policy–1974– 2. Ireland–Economic policy.
3. Portugal–Economic policy. 4. Greece–Economic conditions–1974–
5. Ireland–Economic conditions–1949– 6. Portugal–Economic conditions–1974– I. Title.
HC240.N527 2015
338.94–dc23 2014038937

ISBN 13: 978-1-138-50489-9 (pbk)
ISBN 13: 978-1-138-79404-7 (hbk)

Typeset in Times New Roman
by Wearset Ltd, Boldon, Tyne and Wear

For Paul, and for Enda, who we will take to the Aran Islands and ride bicycles with some day very soon

Contents

Figures

Tables

Acknowledgements

This book, like so many these days, began life as a doctoral dissertation while I was a student at the University of Notre Dame. During my time there, I was assisted by a number of organizations, receiving research funding from the New Zealand government in the form of a Bright Futures Scheme (Top Doctoral Award), which was administered at the time by the Foundation for Research, Science and Technology/Tertiary Education Commission. The Kellogg Institute for International Studies at the University of Notre Dame awarded a Seed Money Grant (2003), a Tinker/Kellogg Travel Grant (2004), and a Dissertation Year Fellowship (2005–2006). I had financial support directly from the Department of Political Science during my first and final years. I also received a 2005 European Union Studies Association (United States) Haas Fund Award, which helped with travel costs in Southern Europe. My dissertation committee at Notre Dame, comprising Frances Hagopian, Robert Fishman, Anthony Messina, and Andrew Gould, of course did a tremendous amount to shape the first draft of this book, so to speak. When it came to adding data through further research in Greece and reframing the project into its current form, I received a three-year start-up grant from the National University of Singapore, which was nice enough to employ me for four years upon graduation. I particularly acknowledge the support of Professor Terry Nardin at NUS who encouraged me in various ways to complete this book project, even if that has taken a little longer than first anticipated.

During my field research trip in 2005, the institutional support given by the Geary Institute at the University College Dublin was invaluable, as was the advice, both very early and later on in the research project, of Niamh Hardiman at UCD and Séan Ó Riain at the National University of Ireland, Maynooth. In Portugal, the Centro de Investigaçao e Estudos de Sociologia at ISCTE (Instituto Superior de Ciências do Trabalho e da Empresa) provided similar helpful assistance, and the Portuguese academics and research staff who helped arrange this visit and offered much good advice during my stay include António Firmino da Costa, Carmo Gomes, Maria dos Dores Guerreiro, Fernando Luís Machado, Luís de Sousa, and Alan Stoleroff. In addition I wish to thank Virgínia Ferreira at the University of Coimbra for giving her views, and Fernando Maurício of the CGTP (Confederação Geral dos Trabalhadores Portugueses) for help with translation of an important interview. On a more personal note, Andrés Malamud and

Helena Carreira, also both at ISCTE, gave an especially good introduction to Portuguese academia and all sorts of other advice during my first visit to the country in 2004, while a very big *obrigada* is due to Pedro and Manuela Rala for hosting and touring us.

In Greece, the most difficult place for an outsider to make inroads into the complexities and conflicts of political life, I would not have got very far at all without the help of Professor Dimitri Sotiropoulos, nor without the enthusiasm and attempts to give me connections provided by Athene Lambrinidou. On my return to the country for a second round of data collection, in the midst of an economic crisis and a substantial amount of tear gas in 2010, Nikolas Koskoros provided invaluable research assistance. Nikolas experienced first-hand some of the difficulties in gaining access to policy-makers in his native country: 'If there is anyone important enough that she would want to bother talking to them, they don't have time; only the unimportant people who don't know anything about policy would have any time'. Thanks also to Nikolas and his family for a very entertaining evening discussing comparative protest rituals across several continents, dogs included.

Above all, thanks goes to my partner, sometimes in work and always in life, Paul Buchanan, to whom this book is dedicated. Paul has been there every single step of the way on this project, not always physically, but always ready to argue state–society relations with me.

1 A tale of three crises

Same symptoms, different underpinnings

Since late 2008, the news coming out of Europe's southern and western fringe has been overwhelmingly dominated by economic crisis and its resulting political fallout and social misery. Public debt on the periphery of the Eurozone mushroomed in the wake of the 2008 Global Financial Crisis (GFC), cascading into a series of events surrounding a round of unprecedented international bailouts for Greece, Ireland, and Portugal between 2010 and 2011. From 2007 to 2010, public debt spiralled well out of control in Greece and Ireland, from 112.9 to 147.3 per cent of Gross Domestic Product (GDP) in the former's case and more than tripling in the latter's. Portugal's level of debt, while not quite as serious, had also reached just over 103 per cent of GDP over the same period (OECD, 2011a: Table 3.1). Meanwhile, the larger economies of Spain and Italy similarly teetered on the brink of requiring rescue packages, with levels of Italian debt approaching those of Greece by 2010–2011, while the Spanish economy took a dive along a number of important dimensions in 2012. In all five countries, commitments to reducing sovereign debt, either as the direct result of the bailouts or as the result of efforts to avoid international intervention, led to the implementation of severe austerity measures including dramatic cuts to pension pay-outs and the slashing of public sector wages. The consequences of these events have been multidimensional, including the fall of several governments across the region since 2009 and rising levels of social dislocation and protest in response to increased unemployment, poverty rates, and a general feeling that the costs of the debt crisis are not being distributed particularly evenly across society.

Much has been written in the popular press as well as by economists about the 'causes' of the European sovereign debt crisis. In particular, attention has been paid to the failing of the European Monetary Union (EMU) experiment, which harmonized monetary but not fiscal policy in its member states, to include Greece, Ireland, and Portugal. In addition to these structural deficiencies, the response of the European Union (EU) to first the GFC and then the emerging sovereign debt crisis has also been criticized from a number of angles (Prausello, 2012). Analysis of national-level policy failings has concentrated on the immediate causes of rising debt itself, although the fact that the reasons for the national-level debt crisis diverge sharply across these three national cases is frequently glossed over by the international media. In other words, government spending per se is most often blamed for the crisis, with much less attention paid to the other side of this equation, namely reduced government revenues, let alone the stark differences between the roots of the crisis in each peripheral state. Put in bolder terms, the common perception that 'spending too much on social programmes and entitlements', or even 'European social democracy', lies at the root of the crisis is quite a distortion of the truth of the matter. Furthermore, the recurring reference to Portugal, Ireland, Greece, and Spain as the 'PIGS' of Europe (or PIIGS with the addition of Italy) in the English-speaking press during the years of crisis not only carried highly derogatory overtones, but lumped together this set of countries in a way that is unhelpful for understanding the specific causes of their woes. The present chapter of this book works against these unwarranted stereotypes by outlining the divergent underpinnings of the Eurozone debt crisis as it unfolded in the three smaller peripheral countries that received international bailouts between 2010 and 2011.

As a work of comparative politics, however, this book does not only seek to identify national-level differences in terms of the policy strategies and outcomes that have characterized Greek, Irish, and Portuguese developments in political economy in recent times. It also seeks to provide an explanation for this divergence in outcome that takes into account the *political* causes of crisis across the three countries. This explanation, which centres on basic features of state–society relations that vary markedly across the periphery of the Eurozone, and, more specifically, on the presence or absence of a robust 'zone of mediation' in each case, is fully fleshed out in the following chapters of this book. Yet before moving on to an analysis of the politics underpinning Greek, Irish, and Portuguese policy failures (and some significant successes), a better understanding of the nature of the debt crisis itself as it actually emerged in each of these three countries is required. Furthermore, as Chapter 2 explores in much more detail, the three tales of debt crisis presented below also hint at the very different developmental trajectories followed by the three countries over several decades.

The divergent underpinnings of crisis in the Eurozone

The GFC, usually traced to declining property prices and the sub-prime mortgage crisis in the United States that came to a head in 2007, ushering in the 'Great Recession', had a varying impact across the developed world. Some regions were able to weather the storm better than others. Notably, East Asia, and countries heavily dependent on East Asian success such as Australia and New Zealand, fared somewhat better due to what turned out to be superior Asian financial regulations and practices. The United States managed to avoid the recession deepening into a full-blown depression through large stimulus packages, but at the expense of gradually rising public debt, levels of unemployment far above those enjoyed since the early 1990s, and heightened political polarization. Several European economies, notably Germany, also came out of the crisis with a new-found respect for the German slow-but-steady growth model, traditionally high national savings rate, and generally cautious economic policy approach.

The crisis, however, exposed and deepened existing developmental and policy flaws across Europe's western and southern periphery. In Ireland, the GFC hastened the end of Ireland's construction boom, demonstrated the dangers of lax financial regulation, and uncovered a series of somewhat unhealthy relationships between bankers, property developers, and politicians. In Greece, the crisis highlighted a myriad of economic and political problems, including: the basic underdevelopment of the Greek economy, reliant as it has been in recent times on low technology-intensive growth concentrated in the retail and service sectors and with a still very large informal economy; a weak private and innovative sector contrasting with a large public sector; a distorted, expensive, and reform-avoidant pension system; and rampant tax evasion among other forms of corruption. By contrast, the evolving debt crisis underlined Portugal's status as a late-developing country of the European periphery that has, since the mid-1970s, frequently relied on public debt in order to rapidly catch up with European developmental standards. Recent events have exposed the country's position as a rather weak and dependent marginalised economy, since arguably the international bailout occurred in this case as the result of contagion, investor fears, and international pressure to take the bailout package rather than absolute necessity. The remainder of this chapter elaborates a little more on these divergent underpinnings of economic crisis in Ireland, Greece, and Portugal, before moving on to outline the main argument made in this book, along with the theoretical and methodological approach it takes.

Ireland

During the 1990s, Ireland reversed its historical status as the 'sick man' of Western Europe to become its so-called 'Celtic Tiger', exhibiting extraordinary economic growth rates based on high levels of foreign direct investment. This growth levelled off somewhat during the 2000s, but Irish success was celebrated right up until the impact of the GFC exposed cracks in the country's economic development model. Analysts have tried to present Ireland's post-1987 economic recovery, then boom, as less of a 'miracle' and result of luck, than as the consequence of a number of long-term policy strategies finally paying off.[1] Among these is the decision to pursue an outward-looking, investment-oriented strategy as early as 1958, focusing on tax breaks for overseas companies in particular. From the late 1980s the number of especially North American owned foreign companies taking advantage of these policies, as well as of Ireland's relatively young and well educated but comparatively cheap labour force, certainly increased.

The role of Ireland's technically inclined higher education strategy in all of this is discussed extensively in Chapter 4 of this book. Other factors clearly include the support received from the EU's Structural Funds and its associated cohesion policies, and the pursuit of a mixed economic development strategy that combined orthodox stabilization measures with expanded state planning in the field of industry policy and active labour market programmes. How much the recovery, especially in its early years, can also be traced to 'fiscal contraction' is something of a debate in the literature (Barry, 1995; Bradley *et al.*, 1993). The adoption of centralized wage bargaining, helping to control inflation, is also believed to have assisted in the recovery, and the broader implications of this for Irish policy-making patterns is a major theme of this book.

Ireland's stunning economic performance during the 1990s and into the 2000s meant that the country changed extremely rapidly over a comparatively short period of time. Dislocating consequences of growth included rises in the cost of living, driven especially by housing costs, and infrastructural inadequacies, especially in roads and public transport. Nevertheless, on the eve of its banking crisis, Ireland was generally considered a much more modernized and arguably happier place than it was twenty years before. The issue of housing, however, is particularly worth underlining, because, along with deficiencies in financial regulation, it lies at the heart of the predicament in which the country found itself in 2008. Given Ireland's historically low-income, underdeveloped economic status, the country entered the 1990s with one of the lowest housing supplies in the developed world. A decade or so later, however, this had completely changed. Rising income levels helped fuel an unprecedented housing boom, witnessing an increase in stock from 1.2 million dwellings in 1991 to 1.9 million in 2008 and construction accounting for the highest proportion of total employment, at 13.3 per cent, in the OECD.[2]

The construction boom itself was made possible on the supply side by the easy availability of loans, particularly to large-scale developers, facilitated by Ireland's relatively laissez-faire approach to financial regulation, putting it in line with other, predominantly English-speaking, what the political economy literature terms 'Liberal' Market Economies (Hall and Soskice, 2001). Thus, what made the Irish housing bubble – and its burst – distinctively different from that of the United States in particular, is that instead of the problem being chiefly located in the 'sub-prime' market where, due to the failing economy and rising interest rates, individual home-owners could no longer afford to pay their mortgages, the Irish crisis was due to large-scale developers suddenly no longer having a market for their houses. Banking loans to developers had in fact overtaken those of loans to households by 2007 (OECD, 2011b: 78). An over-supply issue combined with a decline in consumption sent many of these development companies into bankruptcy, leading in turn to the Irish banking crisis.

The proximate cause of Ireland's sovereign debt crisis was the near-collapse of Ireland's six major banks, for which the burst of the housing bubble and the worldwide economic downturn led to a 'liquidity' problem. In short, the rapid expansion of the banking sector combined with a lack of supervision and oversight meant that it had been loaning money that it did not really have and was unable to honour demands for withdrawals once the financial crisis hit. Believing that the only way to avoid a major depression was to recapitalize the banks, in September 2008 the Irish Government announced that it would guarantee the

Bank of Ireland, the Anglo-Irish Bank, the Allied Irish Bank, Irish Nationwide, the Education Building Society, and Irish Life and Permanent. This was followed in October by bailouts of €3.5 billion each for the first two banks that found themselves in danger of insolvency, the Allied Irish Bank and the Bank of Ireland, then in early 2009 by the nationalisation of the Anglo-Irish Bank. By 2010, the country had to turn outwards for assistance, accepting a bailout package of €85 billion in November, which amounted to over 50 per cent of Ireland's GDP for that year. Of that total €17.5 billion was sourced from Ireland's own National Pension Reserve Fund, while the remainder was drawn from the 'troika' of the European Commission's European Financial Stability Mechanism, the International Monetary Fund (IMF) and the European Financial Stability Fund (EFSF), and bilateral loans from the United Kingdom, Sweden, and Denmark (Lane, n.d).

By the end of 2013, Ireland had met all targets in terms of repaying that loan, entailing the raising of €5.3 billion in taxes and the reduction of public spending by €9.6 billion, but at enormous social cost, including an unemployment rate of around 12 per cent, a far cry from the steady 4 per cent of the early–mid 2000s. In many respects, however, this sorry state of affairs pales in comparison with that of Greece, which by 2013 was nowhere close to paying back its loan, despite having had it restructured several times, and had unemployment rates of around 30 per cent.

Greece

Whereas the Irish debt crisis is relatively easy to pinpoint as fundamentally a banking crisis stemming from a burst housing bubble, the causes of Greece's woes are much more multifaceted. On one level, the story is simply one of too much state spending versus a failure to expand its tax base. On the other hand, the tale is much more complex, involving blatant government corruption overlaid on basic developmental deficiencies stemming from the fact that in many respects the Greek economy still exhibits features that are characteristic of the developing rather than the developed world. Economic modernization in Greece did not really begin until the 1950s. Since then it has been relatively rapid, but belated development has bequeathed contemporary Greece an economy, and associated labour market structure, that put it at odds with Western European developmental norms. These include: a continued reliance on agriculture, despite the shift to industry and more especially services that has occurred since 1950; a very large informal or shadow economy; comparatively low female workforce participation; very high unemployment rates amongst the educated; an extremely high rate of workers employed in very small, especially family, businesses and a high level of self-employment; and a high incidence of unregulated home- or piece-working, much of which is considered to be highly exploitative.

During the 1990s Greece had drawn praise (and occasional astonishment) from its fellow EU members for managing to meet the EMU convergence criteria, which included strict limits on both government debt and inflation.

By 2004, however, the Greek government was forced to admit that it had falsified its accounts in order to make it *appear* to have met this set of criteria, specifically by masking the level of public debt genuinely held. By 2009 the state revealed an annual budget deficit of 12.7 per cent of GDP, which was twice that announced previously. This caused Greece's international credit rating to plummet and a series of government austerity measures to be introduced. In the first half of 2010, the recently elected government of George Papandreou implemented the Stability and Growth Programme designed to reduce the deficit to 2.8 per cent of GDP by 2012, froze public sector wages, then implemented three successive austerity packages. In early May, the first 'troika' bailout totalling €110 billion was granted to Greece, followed by a second rescue package negotiated between July 2011 and February 2012. Despite widespread privatization and ongoing austerity measures, Greece was still heavily in debt in 2014. All of this has come not only at enormous social cost, but also with intensified political polarization and crisis. The years between 2010 and 2014 witnessed intensive strike action across the economy; the 2011 collapse of the Pan-Hellenic Socialist (PASOK) government and the appointment of an un-elected 'interim prime minister'; a snap election in early 2012, out of which a workable coalition government was not able to be formed, entailing a second general election that year; and falling support for the two main establishment political parties, PASOK and New Democracy, and the consequent rise of both the comparatively new Coalition of the Radical Left (SYRIZA) and a number of extreme right-wing social movements, including the neo-fascist Golden Dawn.

The Greek sovereign debt crisis contrasts with the Irish not only in terms of its depth, political consequences, and inability to meet targets designed to put the country back on track, but also in its underpinnings. Whereas the Irish economy had been regarded as more or less a success during the 1990s and 2000s, while at the same time acknowledging the imbalances caused by the construction sector outstripping growth in parts of the economy, such problems were much deeper in the Greek case. A number of analysts have pointed out that the Greek public debt that spiralled out of control in the late 2000s was preceded by at least a decade of growth in levels of private debt. GDP growth appeared very strong in the years before the crisis, at an average of around four per cent, but this was largely based on growth in domestic consumption. Household debt grew very sharply in the 2000s, and, while this propped up an apparently strong retail sector, this was not matched by the development of 'knowledge-led' industries. Compared to other EU and OECD countries, the Greek economy is dominated by very small businesses, low levels of foreign direct investment, and a very low-tech export sector that is reliant on shipping and tourism.[3] Jobs in the private sector, particularly for young people including university graduates, were notoriously underpaid even before the crisis, so that nuclear and extended families had been overly reliant on comparatively well paid public sector jobs. This 'unofficial' subsidizing of the private sector can then be added to the 'official' rise in government expenditure on social transfers that occurred between 1999 and 2009.[4]

Added to these basic issues, which speak to Greece's recent past as a rather peripheral and underdeveloped economy, is what has been referred to as the country's lack of 'reform capacity' (Featherstone, 2011), or the inability to address long-standing fundamental problems and imbalances in the design of economic and social policy. These include an extremely expensive pension system that also lacks much in terms of coverage, widespread tax evasion in both the formal and large informal sector, and over-regulation across many different spheres of economic activity. Various institutional, political, and even cultural factors have been pinpointed as obstacles to reform. Chief among these is the tradition of political-party patronage, building on a general political culture of clientelism that has politicized the public service, explaining not only the distorted public sector pay and pension system, but also something about the inability to override entrenched societal interests when it comes to deregulation, re-regulation, or other strategies for addressing obvious inefficiencies. This is a theme that is developed further in this book.

Portugal

Portugal was the third Eurozone country in succession to receive a bailout, but there is less of a sense of immediate crisis leading up to this than in either the Irish or Greek cases. Rather, the 'crisis' in this case was a slow-burning one. In Portugal there was no housing bubble, no banking collapse, nor the sudden and extraordinary increase in the level of public debt experienced in Greece. In fact, some have argued that the bailout itself was unnecessary (Fishman, 2011). According to this line of analysis, even though there were underlying long-term and structural problems that fed into the debt 'crisis' of 2010, Portugal came under intense pressure to accept a loan chiefly as the result of a jittery international financial market. In short, Portugal can be viewed more as a victim of contagion and tightening access to global capital markets, in contrast to both Ireland and Greece. Following the events in Ireland and Greece discussed above, international concern about debt levels across Southern Europe began to mount, and, by mid-2010, Portugal's credit rating had been significantly downgraded by Moody's Investors Service. This placed pressure on the Portuguese Government to introduce a series of austerity measures in order to reduce public debt, beginning with tax increases and public sector wage cuts in September of that year. Further pressure from overseas rating agencies resulted in Portugal requesting assistance from the IMF and the EFSF, leading to a €78 million bailout package being approved in May 2011. In order to meet the target of a reduction in debt from 9.8 per cent of GDP in 2010 to 3 per cent in 2013 as per the bailout agreement, further wage cuts, tax rises, and privatisation measures were implemented over the next few years, with one of the most significant social costs being a rise in unemployment to around 15 per cent in a country that had enjoyed comparatively low unemployment rates in comparison to its Southern European neighbours over several decades. By April 2014, however, Portugal was set to successfully exit the bailout programme, putting the country in a much better position vis-à-vis Greece.

Even if one accepts, however, that the Portuguese bailout had more to do with international pressure than acute economic crisis, a number of problematic features of the Portuguese economy and political management of it certainly underpinned an increase in public debt experienced during the 2000s. Portugal had entered the 1970s as arguably the most underdeveloped country in Western Europe. It had become both economically and politically isolated under the Salazar–Caetano dictatorship of 1926–1974 and, unlike neighbouring Spain which also experienced a lengthy period of pseudo-fascism, had not significantly developed a manufacturing base. The 1974 'Revolution of the Carnations' brought an end to the dictatorship, but it also ushered in a decade of serious instability in Portugal. Communist and social democratic forces struggled over the future political direction of the country, while the Revolution itself, accompanied as it was by widespread social mobilization, disrupted agricultural and industrial production. Portugal thus did not begin to fully integrate into the European (and global) economy until the 1980s, and at that time had much further to go than Greece in terms of catching up to Western European levels of economic and social development. As Chapter 6 details thoroughly, Portugal has been somewhat successful at playing this catch-up game in at least some respects. In particular, it has been able to massively expand educational participation since the 1980s. However, some facets of underdevelopment clearly remain, and some of these Portugal shares with Greece. Notably, Portugal still relies on small-scale manufacturing, much of which ties in to its still important agricultural base, while the country lags behind in terms of developing 'knowledge-based' high-tech industries and services.

The Portuguese state's intensive effort to overcome such a difficult recent past has come at a cost. Portugal has suffered consistently high levels of public debt since the 1970s, to the point where budget deficits have been normalized as part of the way the state does its business. Public debt levels did begin to increase beyond the Portuguese version of normal from the late 1990s, at which point, similarly to Greece, private consumption and debt levels also began to escalate. To make things worse, economic growth remained almost static during the same period, so that at least one academic analyst warned as early as 2006 that the Portuguese economy was 'in serious trouble' (Blanchard, 2007).

In fact, one could argue that the Portuguese debt 'crisis', such as it was, began *before* the 2008 GFC. In 2005, the parliament reached a situation of policy deadlock over the passing of measures designed to address a budget deficit of 5.9 per cent, almost twice that allowed under the Eurozone Stability and Growth Pact, the rectification of which resulted in a wave of austerity measures and corresponding strike action that year. While this smaller crisis pales in comparison to the Eurozone Crisis five years later, it certainly created a great deal of political tension in Portugal at the time. Among the reasons given for the Portuguese pattern of slow (or even stagnant) growth combined with high levels of public debt were: despite the aforementioned growth in educational levels, a comparatively undereducated workforce, given that this expansion took place from an extremely debased threshold; low productivity levels; a concentration of economic activity in low-wage, low-technology industries, many of which had recently been opened to competition from newly industrializing countries; and bureaucratic and legal inefficiencies, despite a large-scale public sector reform programme.[5]

The argument ahead

This book seeks to further underline not only Irish, Greek, and Portuguese structural and developmental divergence, but also some of the important differences in terms of political institutions and public policy-making traditions that underpin this divergence. The objective is thus explicitly not to explain the debt crisis per se, but, among other things, to highlight the fact that the Eurozone crisis has been played out on an extremely uneven playing field. The developmental challenges faced by the three 'bailout' countries and their ability to meet these challenges during the 1990s and 2000s varied enormously, meaning the roots of, not to mention their ability to recover from, the sovereign debt crisis also varies. Not only are there important differences between Ireland, Greece, and Portugal in the extent to which they have embraced the challenges of economic modernization and catching up with Western European developmental averages, but there is a need to explain this variation in national experiences. The following chapters develop the argument that at least part of this explanation can be found in the nature of state–society relations as they are reflected in policy-making institutions and processes, the quality of which differs markedly across the three countries analysed. In a nutshell, the robustness of Ireland's 'zone of mediation' compares favourably with Greece's, and to a slightly lesser and qualitatively different extent, Portugal's.

It is frequently argued, albeit often implicitly, that developmental differences between countries 'explain themselves' in the sense that very rarely do states change their status as core, semi-peripheral, or peripheral states in the global economy. With the notable exception of the East Asian 'Tigers', countries in modern times generally find it difficult to carve out a 'pathway from the periphery', charging ahead in developmental terms while previously richer states fall behind (Haggard, 1990). Backing this up, social scientists have provided ample evidence that developmental hierarchies have remained more or less unchanged since the late eighteenth century (Mahoney, 2010). Yet this general explanation does not help us very much in seeking to explain diverging Irish, Greek, and Portuguese fortunes over the course of the last few decades because exactly this type of developmental 'switching' has in fact occurred, at least when discussing these three countries in relation to one another.

The first half of the 1970s provides the earliest reasonable starting point for the present analysis for two reasons: Ireland joined the EU while Greece and Portugal began their incorporation into the Western mainstream by abandoning, along with Spain, dictatorship and political isolation in favour of democracy and eventual European integration. At this point in time, Ireland was still extremely economically backward; even if the country had adopted many of the reforms that would later be credited with turning the country into the Celtic Tiger of the 1990s, these were far from paying off yet. Greece, at times, most notably during the 1960s, had been considered something of a developmental darling, exhibiting high growth rates assisted by not insignificant contributions and support from the United States and the United Kingdom as well as the booming Greek shipping industry. By contrast, Portugal lagged even further behind Ireland and the rest of Southern Europe in developmental terms. By the eve of the GFC and the European sovereign debt crisis, this situation, if not entirely reversed, looked quite different. Ireland had surged ahead during the 1990s, becoming a fully modern liberalized economy, despite all the dangers associated with doing so discussed above. Portugal in this sample had the furthest to come in many respects, yet had caught up and in some senses overtaken Greece, which had fallen behind on many indicators. Many specific aspects of this story are taken up in the following chapters.

In addition to this set of interesting contrasts, this book engages in a direct comparison of these three countries, refraining from extending its analysis to Spain and Italy, following the logic of a very similar research design. The comparison between Greece, Ireland, and Portugal is appropriate because, as smaller countries with highly centralized political systems and additional similar features such as histories of reliance on agricultural-based economic development and traditions of political clientelism, they share many features that cause us to suspect that they might respond in similar ways. Yet because they are also all small, they are often overlooked in analyses of national adaptation to contemporary developmental challenges in favour of the larger players. Furthermore, studies of public policy 'Europeanization' tend to dominate contemporary academic analyses of policy challenges across Europe as a whole.[6] Even when Southern Europe is the focus of such studies, it is much more common to compare Portugal with Spain, and Italy with Germany or the UK, whereas Greece is often overlooked entirely or considered too much of an outlier to compare to any other country.[7] A controlled comparison of this set of smaller and understudied countries is important, not least when we turn to the specific theme of labour market challenges as a basis for assessing the extent to which individual countries have adjusted their policy goals and strategies to meet twenty-first century needs, as this book soon does. Furthermore, smaller countries in contemporary times face additional challenges when it comes to labour market development in particular, often lacking the pool of high-skilled labour needed to fuel high-wage, knowledge-based economic growth, and increasingly relying on immigration in order to meet those needs.

In order to narrow the focus of this enquiry and make national differences especially transparent, this book focuses on three specific policy arenas that relate to the state's ability to shape labour market outcomes, or, more precisely, the ability of the state to influence population structure along with what sort of skills the working population possesses. This state capacity has been increasingly recognized as being central to a high-wage, high-skill, 'knowledge-based' development strategy that also seeks to ensure that the fruits of development are distributed more evenly than they have been in the past. Influencing labour market outcomes not only involves such aspects of state activity as industrial relations legislation or industrial policy itself, conceptualized here as the 'core' or 'first tier' of a labour market support structure, but through incorporating labour market concerns into a 'second tier' of state activity in the labour market arena. Constituting the three policy-area case studies on which this book is based, higher education and immigration policies and policies aimed at the reconciliation of family and working life are conceptualized here as part of the labour market support structure's second tier. Together, these arenas of state activity provide a good focus for weighing up differences in the extent to which development strategies have diverged across Greece, Ireland and Portugal, as well as a basis for explaining why such variation exists.

The following chapters argue, and provide evidence to back up the argument, that, despite their similarities, there is significant and important variation in the extent to which Ireland, Portugal, and Greece have adapted their developmental goals and strategies around the labour market challenges posed by the post-industrial era. Ireland appears to have adjusted the most and has benefited more than the two other countries compared here, vigorously pursuing an economic strategy centred on knowledge-based growth, especially through its education system. With economic successes over the course of the past decade and a half leading to a tightened labour market, immigration policy and policies for work–life balance have also been increasingly viewed as part of the labour market support structure, with goals of minority integration and gender equity also adding to the policy debate. On the other hand, Greece has had the most difficulty in responding to the set of labour market challenges analysed here. The gap between the policy strategies suggested by the requirements of the post-industrial economy and the reality of the national-level development strategies is most acute in this case. Portugal, in many ways the most interesting national case study in the set, falls somewhere in between. Portuguese policy initiatives in at least one of these areas, namely work–life balance, is relatively advanced and progressive in comparative terms, and certainly in comparison to other Southern European cases. The main question driving this investigation, then, is how can this variation, mostly between states, but also in some instances, *within* states, be explained? If it is not simply prior developmental legacies that explain developmental divergence, what does?

This book argues that in order to meet the economic and social development strategies of the twenty-first century, especially with respect to the construction of labour market support structures, incorporating new sets of goals and values across many areas of public policy, some crucially important changes had to have occurred at the level of national politics, and, more specifically, in the way that the state deals with interest groups. The core observation is that there is a strong relationship between the extent to which Ireland, Portugal, and Greece have reoriented their economic and social development strategies around new sets of goals and values, and the extent to which each country has developed new policy-making processes and institutions that are capable of mediating between the interests of the state and key societal groups. Such processes and institutions must be capable of delicately balancing two quite different characteristics: consultation and incorporation. When it comes to fundamentally reorienting a country's development strategy under conditions of political democracy, genuine consultation matters because interest groups are also often experts in their field. Their grass-roots knowledge of the policy problems in question is an important component in developing a coherent and effective solution to that problem. On the other hand, as the broader literature notes and is discussed fully in Chapter 3, fundamentally reorienting national development strategies often also requires overriding entrenched social group interests. This means that consultative policy-making usually also needs to fill an incorporative function; trade-offs between the state and interest groups and between key interest groups over policy details are made in order to prevent such groups from opposing the overall direction of the policy shift.

Intermediary policy-making processes and institutions that adequately combine consultative and incorporative characteristics are arguably important for *any* democratic regime attempting to reorient national development goals and strategies, because the cooperation and consent of key societal interest groups is necessary and because grass-roots expertise is useful. Yet it can also be argued that the prior existence or adoption of such a policy-making tradition is especially crucial to the particular phase of economic development that medium- to high-income countries found themselves in during the 1990s and 2000s. Reorienting development strategies around a high-wage, high-skill, technology intensive, knowledge-based and crucially, increasingly diversified, basis of economic competition, often involves a greater range of policy areas and, consequently, societal interest groups. Moreover, the construction of consultative and incorporative processes and institutions has particular salience for Greece, Ireland, and Portugal as countries undergoing the process of European integration. Not only does the EU sometimes prescribe specific policy measures that member states must adopt, the regional organization also tends to promote a certain type of politics, namely one based on consultation, negotiation, consensus building, and compromise. For formerly 'peripheral' countries such as Ireland, Portugal, and Greece, this mode of policy formulation is generally quite new, if not in some instances entirely alien.

At first glance, the location of an explanation for variation in the extent to which these three countries have responded effectively to the labour market challenges posed by the post-industrial era in the degree to which each state has proved capable of constructing new policy-making institutions that balance genuine consultation and interest group incorporation might appear especially narrow. Yet it is important to note that the capability to construct such processes and institutions is highly dependent on previously existing national policy-making traditions. Furthermore, not only are these policy-making traditions embedded in much broader patterns of state–society relations, but these broader patterns are reflective of specific features of recent political, and especially democratic, developments in each national case. Even though it is assumed here that Greece, Ireland, and Portugal all have some desire to adapt their policy goals around the labour market requirements of a post-industrial development strategy, their prior histories of democratic development and especially state–society relations as reflected in policy-making processes and institutions provide the main explanation for variation in the extent to which they have been able to do so. Legal traditions and both formal and informal institutional development are central to these histories, and provide the main facilitators of or barriers to the development of new institutions that effectively balance consultative and incorporative characteristics. In addition, not only the depth of democratization but also the path taken to contemporary democracy plays a large part in shaping policy-making traditions in each case.

Taking each of the national cases in turn, Ireland is the country in the sample that has adjusted its policy outcomes the most, as well as being the country that has developed the strongest consultative and incorporative policy-making processes and institutions. Ireland is advantaged in this respect because it has a longer democratic tradition than the other two cases, inheriting forms of consultative policy-making such as Green and White Paper public submission processes and commissions of enquiry in particular, from British rule. Yet until recently, many of Ireland's political processes were comparatively elitist, with some interest groups being privileged much more than others when it came to accessing the state. More recently, however, policy-making processes have becoming increasingly liberalized, moving away from a political tradition dominated by a single political party and its populist coalition toward a consultative and incorporative tradition that involves a wider variety of interest groups and importantly, takes place at multiple sites throughout the political system.

By contrast, the Greek public policy-making tradition is the least consultative and the least incorporative out of the three national cases analysed here. Despite more than three decades of democratization, politics and policy remain mostly an elite game. While there is plenty of civil society and interest group activity in Greece, there is above all a missing link between civil society and the state. This lack of a 'zone of mediation' in which policy compromise can be reached had, and continues to have, profound implications for Greek policy with respect to labour market challenges in particular. Portugal, as the country in the sample with the most mixed set of policy outcomes, also has in many ways the most complex policy-making tradition. There is no consistent tradition of consultative policy-making in this case, but there is a long-standing tendency toward the adoption of incorporative mechanisms that has its roots in the 'stable' corporatist Salazar–Caetano dictatorship but which has arguably survived Portugal's post-1974 transition to democracy.

Plan of the book

This book is divided into seven chapters. Chapter 2 provides an extended discussion of the labour market policy implications of the developmental crossroads that most middle- to high-income countries find themselves in. The dynamics of these challenges are captured in a series of often used but also often underdefined concepts such as the 'knowledge economy', 'competitive advantage' or even, more recently, 'flexicurity'. This chapter briefly deconstructs some of this terminology, spelling out what such notions mean for countries such as Ireland, Portugal, and Greece as they face the developmental challenges of the twenty-first century. Given that this set of countries is handicapped by a history of underdevelopment and, in particular, a lack of social investment over a long period of time, formerly 'peripheral' EU member states such as these have inherited undereducated workforces, fewer women in paid work than is the case elsewhere in Europe, and little basis for understanding how immigration policy might be used to attract the specific classes of skilled workers that the country needs. Those specific elements of a high-wage, high-skill labour market strategy are discussed extensively in the second part of the chapter, eventually providing a framework for the analysis of higher education, immigration, and policies for work–family balance to be adopted in the case study analyses.

Chapter 3 develops an explanatory framework centred on the emergence of policy-making institutions and processes that effectively balance consultative and incorporative functions. It finds some backing for arguing for the importance of such institutions in the existing literature but finds that much of this literature is limited to the discussion of industrial policy or labour relations and that consideration of such policy-making processes and institutions across a broader range of policy areas is required in order to deepen and generalize the analysis. The chapter then moves on to an extended discussion of how the concept of an institutional policy-making process that is both consultative and incorporative can be operationalized. What does such incorporative and consultative policy-making look like and how do we know when we have found it? It then begins to apply the explanatory framework to the case studies by identifying bases for the development of these specific types of institution in Ireland, Portugal, and Greece. Special attention is given to the impact of regime change and transformation on state–society relations, and the extent to which this has been institutionalized in legal, policy, and policy-making procedures. General patterns that later apply across the three case studies can be identified.

This book does not attempt to give a comprehensive explanation for explaining why and how policy-making traditions change, since the main focus is on proving why and how they matter in the specific cases under discussion. Yet some attention to this question is required. Chapter 3 thus also underlines why policy-making traditions are so *difficult* to change. Elements of elitism and legalism resistant to consultative policy-making survived even a revolution in the Portuguese case. Where policy traditions do change, they tend to do so over the long-term in response to gradually building demands for new forms of political representation on the part of societal interests. That occurred in the Irish case, even if the catalyst for change was an acute economic crisis that threatened to expand into the social and political spheres after 1987. Meanwhile, Greece's failure to construct a policy-making tradition lies not only in its inheritance of a number of 'authoritarian legacies' from the pre-democratic period, but also the impact of a new set of 'democratic transition legacies', including a lack of willingness or ability to compromise on core policy issues on the part of societal interest groups as well as a missing set of institutional mechanisms for inducing such compromise.

Chapters 4 to 6 take each of the national case studies in turn, concentrating on the relationship and interaction between policy outcomes in each of the three policy areas selected and the corresponding emergence or absence of consultative and incorporative policy-making institutions in each of the nine sub-national case studies. In that sense, the methodology employed is one of 'process-tracing', in which the cause (policy-making institutions and processes) and effect (policy outcomes) are tracked over time in order to tease out the full implications and gain better understanding of a causal relationship by observing and scrutinizing as far as is practically possible the *mechanisms* and *chain of events* at play suggested by a theory over the course of a historical sequence of events, rather than simply assessing the effects of a presumed cause (Collier, 2011; George and Bennett, 2005). The process-tracing method has the greatest affinity with qualitative and within-case analysis, which in the case of this research means detailing, then later theoretically abstracting from, the nine policy case studies analysed. Specifically, the discussion is based on national government, EU, and OECD policy documentation along with a large number of analyses drawn from the secondary literature. In addition, this document-based research is supplemented by a series of interviews conducted with government officials as well as policy stakeholders during 2005 in each of the three countries under investigation, as well as a second set of interviews conducted in Greece in early 2010. Special consideration is given to the experiences of those who have been 'incorporated' into state initiated policy-making networks in order to gauge the quality of these institutions and processes, something that is especially difficult to determine from published sources.

What emerges from the case study discussions is a more or less consistent pattern of state–society relations, as reflected in policy-making institutions and processes that are distinctive to each of the three nation-states. Since these patterns are country-specific rather than peculiar to the policy arena in question across the three national cases, the nature of the policy problem in question, which inevitably does often vary between national contexts, cannot fully explain outcomes. Because policy shifts are over a period of at least two decades in each case, neither can the actions of individual governments or political parties explain the emergence of such patterns. While individual governments are often responsible for pushing through reforms at a much greater pace than previous governments, and can in fact be responsible for taking the initiative for establishing consultative and incorporative policy-making processes themselves, the case study discussions illustrate the fact that general patterns of state–society relations tend to survive changes in executive and legislature.

The general finding is that by overlaying new forms of consultative policy-making institutions on pre-existing ones, Ireland has best adjusted its development strategies around twenty-first century policy challenges, even if state responses have been far from perfect. Greece is the country to which the consultative and incorporative policy-making tradition is most alien, and the use of consultative and incorporative institutions in order to bridge the gap between relevant interest groups and the political elite is largely absent. As a result, immigration, higher education, and work–family reconciliation policies have been least reformulated in response to contemporary labour market challenges. The mixed nature of Portuguese responses to labour market challenges posed by twenty-first century development needs is attributable to a relatively strong incorporative tradition but one that lacks robust processes of consultation with independent interest groups across all policy areas. That means that the modernization and adjustment of policy goals and values occurs very unevenly, with some aspects of policy better informed by interest group and stakeholder participation in policy-making than others. Finally, the conclusion to this book summarizes the case study findings, underlining in particular what makes each policy-making tradition and its impact on policy outcomes unique. It then offers some further reflections on the relationship between democracy, development strategies, and recovering from the Eurozone debt crisis.

Notes

1 For discussion on the following factors see ó Gráda and O'Rourke (1995); Barry (1999); and Nolan *et al.* (2000).
2 This data is from, and an excellent discussion is found in, Whelan (2010).
3 On these issues see Lapavitsas *et al.* (2010); and Kouretas and Vlamis (2010).
4 Half of the rise in government spending during this period can be attributed to social transfers (OECD 2011b: 35).
5 For a review of the literature that cites these particular underlying factors see Reis (2013). On the Portuguese public sector reform process see OECD (1996).
6 Two especially important works here are Cowles *et al.* (2001), and Featherstone and Radaelli (2003).
7 On the Iberian comparison, see Royo (2002), and Royo and Manuel (2003). Single-country studies of Greece, often pointing out the country's apparent exceptionalism in a European context, include Featherstone and Papadimitriou (2008); Lavdas (1997); Petmesidou and Mossialos (2006); and Sotiropoulos (1996).

References

Barry, Frank, "The Irish Recovery 1987–1990: An Economic Miracle?", Policy Paper N.PP91/5, (Dublin: Centre for Economic Research, University College Dublin, 1995).

Barry, Frank, ed., *Understanding Ireland's Economic Growth* (Basingstoke: Macmillan, 1999).

Blanchard, Olivier, "Adjustment within the Euro: The Difficult Case of Portugal", *Portuguese Economic Journal* 6, 1 (2007), 1–21.

Bradley, John, Karl Whelan, and Jonathan Wright, *Stabilization and Growth in the EC Periphery: A Study of the Irish Economy* (Aldershot: Avebury, 1993).

Collier, David, "Understanding Process Tracing", *PS: Political Science and Politics* 44, 4 (2011), 823–30.

Cowles, Maria Green, James Caporaso, and Thomas Risse, eds, *Transforming Europe:*

Europeanization and Domestic Change (Ithaca, NY and London: Cornell University Press, 2001).

Featherstone, Kevin, "The Greek Sovereign Debt Crisis and EMU: A Failing State in a Skewed Regime", *Journal of Common Market Studies* 49, 2 (2011), 193–217.

Featherstone, Kevin and Dimitris Papadimitriou, *The Limits of Europeanization: Reform Capacity and Policy Conflict in Greece* (Basingstoke, UK: Palgrave, 2008).

Featherstone, Kevin and Claudio M. Radaelli, *The Politics of Europeanization* (Oxford: Oxford University Press, 2003).

Fishman, Robert M., "Portugal's Unnecessary Bailout", *New York Times* (12 April 2011).

George, Alexander L. and Andrew Bennett, *Case Studies and Theory Development in the Social Sciences* (Cambridge, MA: MIT Press, 2005).

Haggard, Stephan, *Pathways from the Periphery: The Politics of Growth in the Newly Industrializing Countries* (Ithaca, NY: Cornell University Press, 1990).

Hall, Peter, and David Soskice, *Varieties of Capitalism: The Institutional Foundations of Comparative Advantage* (Oxford: Oxford University Press, 2001).

Kouretas, Georgias P. and Prodomos Vlamis, "The Greek Crisis: Causes and Implications", *Panoeconomicus* 4 (2010), 391–404.

Lane, Philip R., 'The Irish Crisis', *World Financial Review.* Available at www.worldfinancialreview.com/?p=874 (n.d). Accessed 14 February 2014.

Lapavitsas, Costas, Annina Kaltenbrunner, Duncan Lindo, J. Michell, Juan Pablo Painceira, Eugenia Pires, Jeff Powell, Alexis Stenfors, and Nuno Telas, 'Eurozone Crisis: Beggar Thyself and Thy Neighbour', *Journal of Balkan and Near Eastern Studies* 12, 4 (2010), 321–73.

Lavdas, Kostas A., *The Europeanization of Greece: Interest Politics and the Crises of Integration* (Basingstoke, UK: Macmillan, 1997).

Mahoney, James, *Colonialism and Postcolonial Development: Spanish America in Comparative Perspective* (Cambridge: Cambridge University Press, 2010).

Nolan, Brian, Philip J. O'Connell, and Christopher T. Whelan, eds, *Bust to Boom? The Irish Experience of Growth and Inequality* (Dublin: Institute of Public Administration, 2000).

OECD, *Putting Citizens First: Portuguese Experience in Public Management Reform.* Public Management Occasional Papers N.13 (Paris: Organisation for Economic Cooperation and Development, 1996).

OECD, *Government at a Glance* (Paris: Organisation for Economic Cooperation and Development, 2011a).

OECD, *Economic Surveys: Ireland* (Paris: Organisation for Economic Cooperation and Development, 2011b).

Ó Gráda, Cormac and Kevin O'Rourke, "Economic Growth: Performance and Explanations", in J.W. O'Hagan, ed., *The Economy of Ireland: Policy and Performance of a Small European Country* (Basingstoke, UK: Macmillan, 1995), 198–227.

Petmesidou, M., and E. Mossialos, eds, *Social Policy Developments in Greece* (Aldershot, UK: Ashgate, 2006).

Prausello, Franco, ed., *The Eurozone Experience: Monetary Integration in the Absence of a European Government* (Milan: Franco Angeli, 2012).

Reis, Ricardo, "The Portuguese Slump and Crash and the Eurozone Crisis", *Brookings Papers on Economic Activity* (Spring 2013).

Royo, Sebastián, *A New Century of Corporatism? Corporatism in Southern Europe –Spain and Portugal in Comparative Perspective* (Westport, CT: Praeger, 2002).

Royo, Sebastián and Paul Christopher Manuel, eds, *Spain and Portugal in the European Union: The First Fifteen Years* (London and Portland: Frank Cass, 2003).
Sotiropoulos, Dimitri A., *Populism and Bureaucracy: The Case of Greece Under PASOK* (Notre Dame, IN: University of Notre Dame Press, 1996).
Whelan, Kevin, "Policy Lessons from Ireland's Latest Depression", *The Economic and Social Review,* 41, 2 (2010), 225–54.

2 Labour market challenges for Greece, Ireland, and Portugal

Since at least the early 1990s, most developed countries have found themselves at a crossroads: maintaining existing living standards while making the transition to a post-industrial development strategy has proven to be challenging. Even before the post-2001 oil shocks followed by the GFC that began in 2007, carving out a national pathway to a high-wage, high-skilled economic growth strategy in an increasingly globalized world has turned out to be problematic task for many countries. Yet the starting assumption of this book's analysis is that during the 1990s a broad consensus emerged on the type of development strategy that post-industrial countries should pursue and that this consensus was best reflected in the widespread adoption of concepts such as the 'knowledge economy', 'competitive advantage', or, more recently and in the European context, 'flexicurity'. This does not mean that this author believes that these concepts carry with them the best prescription for what policy-makers *should* do; rather, these became core concepts among policy-making circles in the 1990s and early 2000s. While there was significant debate within individual states over which policies were best suited to achieving successful outcomes, arguably a general shared understanding emerged over what those outcomes should be. Furthermore, while the post-2008 global recession put balancing national budgets (to include slashing public spending and the erosion of public sector employment protections in some instances) at the forefront of the policy agenda, addressing the underlying causes of economic stagnation and formulating national responses around the requirements of the 'knowledge economy' are likely to make their way back onto the policy agenda over the longer term.

Because concepts such as the 'knowledge economy', 'competitive advantage' or more latterly 'flexicurity' are used much more often than they are defined, this chapter begins by mapping out these concepts in a broad sense, explaining the relevance of these terms for the scope of this book and the centrality of labour markets achieving knowledge-based outcomes. I then move on to an analysis of family, higher education, and immigration policies as important, although by no means the only, elements of a labour market support structure capable of sustaining the shift to a high-wage, high-skill, knowledge-based growth strategy. In the process, I also introduce the reader to the national case studies by comparing some objective indicators of how Greece, Ireland, and Portugal have measured up with respect to their work–life balance, higher education, and labour-based immigration policies. An overview of each country's approach to each policy area is presented, details of which are analysed much more fully in Chapters 4 to 6.

The promise of the 'knowledge economy'

During the 1990s, there was a veritable explosion in the use of the concept of the 'knowledge economy', even if the term had first been adopted in policy discourse decades earlier.[1] In particular, the promise of the knowledge economy captured the imagination of a number of international organizations, notably the OECD and the World Bank (OECD, 1996; Stiglitz, 1999; World Bank, 1998).[2] At its most basic, the concept refers to the need for developed, increasingly post-industrial countries to retain their competitive edge by investing, promoting, and encouraging those sectors of the economy that rely on 'knowledge' as the main component of their success. The supply of skilled labour, and hence the construction of support structures that play a key role in producing that skilled labour supply, are central to the idea of a knowledge-based economy, as well as this book. Education and training have always been important drivers of economic growth in the industrialized world, but the demands on post-industrial workers in terms of their 'knowledge' and, importantly, range of skills are considered to be greater as the result of the post-industrial shift. Workers in the knowledge economy are supposed to be skilled in information and computer technology, thus in some senses highly specialized, but also flexible and possessing a great deal of general and 'tacit' knowledge that is difficult to acquire.[3] Flexibility and generalizability are also central to the vision because the idea of the knowledge economy is tied to that of globalization. Since globalization has intensified competition between countries (and increasingly with the rise of the newly industrialized economies, regions of the world), post-industrial economies need to avoid the tendency towards low-paid, low-skilled, service-sector growth that has come about as the result of the shift of industrial decline, out-sourcing, off-shoring, and the consequent end of the policy commitment to full employment in many wealthier societies.

A closely related concept to that of the knowledge economy is the notion of 'competitive advantage'. Whereas the logic of comparative advantage dictated that countries rely on their 'natural' resources and abilities to gain from trade in the global economy, competitive advantage suggests that developmental success relies on gaining a competitive advantage through higher-quality inputs, to include a more highly skilled, a more flexible, and a more productive labour force (Porter, 1990). In other words, firms – and countries – can overcome natural disadvantages in terms of resources by concentrating on other aspects of their productive capabilities. In public policy terms, both the promise of the knowledge economy and the logic of competitive advantage point states in a similar direction when designing frameworks around meeting the labour market challenges of the early twenty-first century. The *quality* of labour, rather than simply its cost, is of special significance to a knowledge-based strategy for economic growth. Furthermore, the logic of knowledge-based growth strategies points towards certain sectors of the economy that governments should concentrate on expanding, as well as certain policy mechanisms that need to be adopted in order to expand these sectors. In terms of the economic sectors identified by policy-makers convinced of the promise of the knowledge economy, 'technology intensive' industries such as computing, biotechnology, and aerospace engineering are all singled out for intensive development. In terms of the policy mechanisms employed to promote such sectors, increased investment in, or, at the very least, stimulation of the information and communications infrastructure; research and development; and education at all levels, with a focus on computer-usage as well as science and technical skills, are prioritized. Policy-makers have also emphasized that a knowledge economy requires something frequently referred to as a knowledge *society*, characterized by a free flow of ideas; robust networks forged between producers, consumers, and researchers, in which these ideas can be exchanged; and a high level of knowledge about and access to information technology among the general population.

The idea of a transition not only to a knowledge economy but also a knowledge society has led some to claim that a fundamental, almost civilizational, shift has taken or is about to take place. Some of this is contained in the aforementioned visions of a number of World Bank and OECD officials during the 1990s, in which reference to the emergence of an entirely new phase of capitalism was frequently made. Some academics have gone further. Manuel Castells, for example, argues that the information and communications technology shift is symptomatic of a long-term shift to what he terms 'the network society', representing nothing less than a whole new stage of human development (Castells, 1996). Peter Drucker (1993) has similarly presented the knowledge society as taking us all not only to a new stage of capitalism, but somehow *beyond* capitalism: knowledge has 'sidelined' both labour and capital. Others, however, point out that there is a real danger in embracing the knowledge economy/society as a panacea for the inequalities and conflicts associated with capitalist development. Aside from the fact that the knowledge economy in no way seeks to alter basic relations of production, the belief that the rising tide of high-tech industries will automatically 'raise all boats equally' belies the fact that there are likely to be losers in the knowledge economy. Some marginalized groups are ill equipped to participate in the knowledge society and are unlikely to be able to catch up due to a lack of access to or lack of interest in accessing computing and information technologies in particular. Other problems include a continued mismatch between the skills required by companies and the 'knowledge' of available workers; coordination problems matching workers to jobs even where there is no actual mismatch; and the underlying threat of outsourcing as late-late-industrializing countries catch up in terms of technical ability, at a cheaper labour cost (Brown and Hesketh, 2004; Craig and Gunn, 2010). Arguably, the shift to the knowledge economy in fact has the potential to deepen inequalities within wealthier societies, as some workers are brought into the fold of the technology-intensive sector while others languish on the margins in sectors of the service economy that do not genuinely require the skills associated with the knowledge economy.

This book takes the perspective that whether the shift to the knowledge economy further deepens or helps ameliorate distributional inequalities depends very much on the extent to which individual states adopt policy frameworks that deliberately incorporate goals of social inclusion. If knowledge-economy policies are designed with the twin objectives of economic growth *and* a broad-based sharing in the benefits of that economic growth in mind, the new phase of capitalism envisaged by national and international actors during the 1990s is *potentially* a kinder one. Part of such a strategy involves the construction of labour market support structures that embrace the needs of entire national populations, not simply the labour market requirements of key industries. Yet the extent to which national governments have combined these goals in their pursuit of the knowledge economy has varied enormously. Because, at least in some respects, states in Europe have tried to incorporate goals of social inclusion into their knowledge-economy policies, and because Greece, Portugal, and Ireland have been subject to this 'Europeanizing' influence, I briefly consider the European variant on the pursuit of a high-skill, high-wage, knowledge-based approach to economic and social development before addressing the issue of knowledge economy-supporting labour market structures specifically. While this book does not take the view that European integration has been the only, or even the main, influence on policy outcomes in Greece, Ireland, or Portugal over the past two decades, the 'Europeanizing' influence on these three countries cannot be ignored.

European-level policy debate during the 1990s and 2000s centred on exactly some of the concerns highlighted above. The overall goal was to orient regional and national development plans around the idea of the 'knowledge economy', but at the same time that goals of social inclusion were met (Rodrigues, 2003; Room, 2005). This also gave rise to the notion of 'flexicurity', which began as a concept promoted by the Danish government in the 1990s before gradually making an influence on EU discourse (Keune, 2008; Madsen, 2004; Wilthagen and Tros, 2004). Flexicurity emphasizes the need for labour market flexibility to be combined with a robust social security system, active labour market policies, and an emphasis on life-long learning and is thus more clearly linked to preserving the welfare states than non-European versions of the knowledge-based economy may be prone to doing.

Three basic elements of the European version of a knowledge-based strategy can be further summarized. First, in order to maintain high income levels, important for the tax base required by European countries since they favour larger welfare states, EU members need to develop 'knowledge-based' industries alongside their burgeoning service sectors. This has been more difficult for European players such as Greece, Ireland, and Portugal due to their status as formerly 'peripheral' European economies, but all European countries face competition in the technology sectors from such countries as Taiwan, South Korea, and, increasingly, China, India, and Brazil. Second, the European model has had a greater self-conscious commitment to integrating marginalized social groups and ensuring income equality than is found elsewhere. This is not to say that these goals are always achieved, or that they are not increasingly difficult to achieve under conditions of budgetary constraint, as the literature on reforming welfare states in Europe acknowledges.[4] Rather, a great deal of policy debate and action around this topic does take place. Third, with obvious consequences for the second core feature just discussed, the basis of European integration has always been economic, aimed at promoting free trade at least within the region, so that goals of social equality and peace must be met within the confines of a basically liberal and open economic framework. There is no intrinsic reason why these goals are incompatible: the experiences of the Northern European social democracies have traditionally shown how corporatist labour relations and extensive state involvement in income redistribution can be combined with open trade policies (Katzenstein, 1985).

Labour market issues have gradually become central to the debate over the European variant of an economic and social development strategy for the twenty-first century, not least because sluggish European growth over the last two decades has also been combined with unemployment rates which have been persistently higher than the United States and elsewhere (Bermeo, 2001). An important reflection of these concerns, combined with a focus on knowledge-based growth, has been a policy programme known as the Lisbon Strategy. A cornerstone of European development policy between 2000 and 2010, this aimed at increasing productivity and stimulating job creation in order to deliver improved living standards in the region. While the Strategy was criticized on the grounds that it was too broad in scope, it singled out five specific policy areas for development: product and capital market reforms; investment in the knowledge-based economy; labour market reforms; social policy reforms; and, added later, environmental reforms (Council of the European Union, 2005: 9). Reform programmes at the national state level were supposed to be constructed around specific European-level targets: directly relevant to the development of policy for reconciling family and working life discussed shortly, the Lisbon Strategy includes a target of raising female workforce participation rates from 54 to 60 per cent by 2010 (Boeri *et al.*, 2005: 2). A similar approach has been adopted in the subsequent Europe 2020 Strategy, although the timeframe of this later set of commitments falls outside the scope of this book. However, what is most important to note is that attention to the state's role in promoting particular types of labour market outcomes, tied to concepts of innovation, flexibility, and knowledge-based growth, has been placed at the centre of the analysis.

Labour market dynamics in Ireland, Greece, and Portugal

For most of its history as an independent state, the Republic of Ireland suffered from underdevelopment, dependency, and a failure to industrialize, despite efforts to the contrary. The problem of a lack of employment opportunities beyond what was offered in the comparatively inefficient agricultural sector and nascent local industries was traditionally offset by mass emigration, a fact that will be returned to in Chapter 4 and which was also the case in both Portugal and Greece. The population continuously declined until around 1960, despite a high birth rate and efforts at industrialization under the first Fianna Fáil government.[5] During the 1970s through to the mid-1980s, however, the country began a plunge into what seemed to be a permanent economic crisis. The greatest labour market challenge during this era was how to combat the severe and long-term fact of unemployment that had set in since the early 1970s, and its related impact on poverty levels in the country. At the point when government-initiated crisis talks were held between state and 'social partners' in 1987, the unemployment rate stood at just under 20 per cent.[6] Of course, official unemployment rates do not report the percentage of the potential workforce that chooses not to engage in paid work and therefore the overall number of economically inactive adults. Importantly in Ireland, only a small percentage of women, and married women in particular, traditionally took up paid work outside the home up until the 1990s.

Ireland's 'miracle' economic recovery after 1987 was accompanied by massive employment growth, even if it took several years for this to make a serious impact on unemployment rates. By 1995, the unemployment rate was reduced to 12.2 per cent, above desired levels but reduced over the past decade (OECD, 1997: 65). A decade after that, Ireland had achieved one of the lowest unemployment rates in the developed world, remaining stable at around 4.5 per cent between 2000 and 2005. The benefits of economic growth, however, are best reflected in data related to employment creation, especially since new groups that had previously not been counted as 'unemployed' were now entering the workforce for the first time. Employment growth was especially strong in the new, foreign investment-led industries of computer technology and pharmaceuticals, as well as in the service sector, and the greatest boom years were to be found in the mid-1990s. Between 1989 and 1997, employment grew by 23 per cent overall – 32.4 per cent in the service sector and 25.7 per cent in industry – and fell by 17.3 per cent in the farming sector (Tansey, 1998: 36). Although the fast pace of economic growth led to increased wage dispersion and a widening income gap, absolute poverty levels were actually reduced (Nolan, 2003).

It should be noted that employment growth included a large percentage of jobs that were part-time in nature, something that contrasts sharply with the Southern European cases and significant for policies for work–life balance and also raising questions about job security, job quality, and underemployment. Also, in direct contrast with its long history of outward migration, Ireland experienced labour shortages in some sectors of the economy during the 2000s, which stimulated an immigration wave, especially from the newest members of the EU. At a policy-making level, the greatest concern was how to continue the expansion of knowledge-based employment opportunities based on indigenous capital and continued improvements in labour productivity rather than direct overseas investment, since Ireland now faced much competition in this area from regions

Table 2.1 Irish labour market indicators, 1995–2008

Year	*Employment rate (percentage of population aged 15–64)*		*Unemployment rate*		*Total workforce with at least upper-level secondary school education*	*Part-time employment as percentage of total workforce*
	Male	*Female*	*Total*	*Aged under 25*		
1995	67.1	41.6	12.3	19.5	45.2	12.1
1996	67.5	43.2	11.7	18.2	47.3	11.6
1997	69.1	45.9	9.9	15.4	50.0	12.3
1998	72.1	49.0	7.5	11.3	49.3	16.7
1999	74.5	52.0	5.7	8.6	–	16.8
2000	76.3	53.9	4.2	6.8	54.9	16.8
2001	76.6	54.9	4.0	7.3	57.6	16.6
2002	75.4	55.4	4.5	8.5	59.2	16.6
2003	75.2	44.7	4.7	9.1	60.3	17.0
2004	75.9	56.5	4.5	8.9	62.2	16.9
2005	76.9	58.3	4.3	8.6	63.0	–
2006	83.4*	63.3*	4.5	8.7	75.7	–
2007	83.0*	64.4*	4.7	9.1	75.7	17.7
2008	80.4*	64.0*	6.4	13.3	73.5	18.6

Source: Eurostat.

Note
* Percentage of population aged 20–64.

of the world in which labour was much cheaper (Clinch *et al.*, 2002). That concern was particularly prevalent in 2001–2002, although the threat of recession and an end to job growth that was predicted during this period did not in fact eventuate. A reversal of fortunes in terms of employment and unemployment did not occur until the following decade as a result of the banking crisis and subsequent austerity measures.

Meanwhile, Greece emerged from the 1940s, which had been dominated by the upheavals of foreign occupation and civil war, economically devastated and socially dislocated. The period of occupation not only ensured that industrial production across most sectors of the economy ground to a halt, but also led to widespread starvation and mortality, making this arguably the last 'Third World-like' famine experienced in Europe (Hionidou, 2006). The series of centre-right governments that dominated Greece during the post-war period aimed to shift the country away from reliance on agriculture through an industrialization programme and state investment in infrastructure. Agriculture itself was singled out for investment in the 1960s, with increased attention paid to modernizing that sector. This resulted in strong growth through much of the recovery period, although it should be noted what a low threshold the country was 'growing' from and that much of the growth was state-led. Although the recovery had started by the early 1950s, initial employment opportunities were scarce. As in both the Irish and Portuguese cases, the potential problem of unemployment that emerged once people began to move away from their family farms and into the cities was resolved through mass emigration. Also, as in the two other cases, emigration and underemployment in agriculture probably masked the true level of unemployment and under-employment during the 1950s and 1960s. Two other developments that were highly significant for later labour market developments were the concentration of urban growth in and around Athens and the rise of the service sector as the basis for future economic growth, more so than manufacturing.[7]

As in the case of the rise of military regimes in Latin America during the 1960s and 1970s, Greece's military coup of 1967 was preceded by several years of 'leftist' government, in this case of George Papandreou's Centre Union. Yet the colonels' regime did not attempt to implement a structural adjustment project, but instead pursued a much more mixed economic strategy, including massive public sector investment that stimulated growth between 1968 and 1974, but at the expense of a ballooning public debt. When a recession hit the country in 1974, the military left behind an economy in trouble that would weigh down many of the developmental efforts of the new democratic regime. The period between 1974 until at least 1990 is thus often portrayed as one long economic crisis for Greece. As in other OECD countries, stagflation had set in by the early 1970s, and one major task of the first democratic government, headed by Konstantinos Karamanlis and the newly formed New Democracy party, was to address the problem of inflation. Stabilization measures were also imposed under the PASOK government of the mid-1980s, but that decade was marked much more decisively by a slowdown in economic growth, a decline in GDP, continued inflationary pressures, and an expansion of the public sector.

Although a short-lived New Democracy government was elected on a structural adjustment platform in 1990, the serious task of 'modernizing' the economy was left to the post-Papandreou PASOK government of Costas Simitis, who led the party from 1996 to 2004 (Oltheten *et al.*, 2003; Papagoulatos, 2000). The major motivation for the austerity measures imposed during this period was the need to conform to the EMU criteria, which Greece eventually achieved. Tight monetary and fiscal discipline was accompanied by apparently strong economic growth but also by greater income inequality and continuously high unemployment. Later developments, notably those surrounding the 2010 debt crisis, also revealed that very little of this growth was 'knowledge' based.

Greece's labour market performance has been generally regarded as poor for most of the post-1974 democratic period under discussion. Unemployment has been high, averaging at over 10 per cent of the working age population between 1995 and 2005. Although many European countries have had similar recent experiences of high unemployment, several features of the Greek experience are particularly worth noting. First, the unemployment rate has remained steadily high, especially in comparison with Ireland, which has shown major improvement over time, and with Portugal, which has been able to maintain quite a low rate. Second, the rate of female workforce participation did increase during the late 1970s and early 1980s, but so did female unemployment. Female

Table 2.2 Greek labour market indicators, 1995–2008

Year	*Employment rate (percentage of population aged 15–64)*		*Unemployment rate*		*Total workforce with at least upper-level secondary school education*	*Part-time employment as percentage of total workforce*
	Male	*Female*	*Total*	*Aged under 25*		
1995	72.5	38.1	9.2	28.5	42.6	4.8
1996	72.7	38.7	9.6	31.0	44.3	5.3
1997	72.1	39.3	9.8	30.8	45.7	4.6
1998	71.7	40.5	10.8	29.9	47.7	6.0
1999	71.1	41.0	12.0	31.5	50.1	6.1
2000	71.5	41.7	11.2	29.1	51.6	4.6
2001	71.4	41.5	10.7	28.0	52.1	4.1
2002	72.2	42.9	10.3	26.8	53.9	4.4
2003	73.4	44.3	9.7	26.8	55.7	4.1
2004	73.7	45.2	10.5	26.9	59.0	4.6
2005	74.2	46.1	9.8	26.0	60.0	4.8
2006	80.3*	51.2*	9.0	25.0	63.9	5.7
2007	80.4*	51.6*	8.4	22.7	62.8	5.6
2008	80.4*	52.5*	7.8	21.9	63.3	5.6

Source: Eurostat.

Note
* Percentage of population aged 20–64.

unemployment grew by an average annual rate of 15.3 per cent between 1981 and 1986, compared to a rate of 9.1 for men (Didika-Logiadou, 1993: 185). That the Greek labour market does not appear to serve women very well is reflected in low contemporary rates of female workforce participation in comparison to many other OECD countries, a problem discussed extensively below. Third, with particular relevance for the analysis of higher education policy that follows, the rate of unemployment among young people has been and is extremely high, and more so amongst the educated. In 2005, the youth unemployment rate was 26 per cent in Greece, 16.1 per cent in Portugal, and 8.6 per cent in Ireland. Four, long-term unemployment has been a particular problem of its own, consistently representing around 50 per cent of the unemployed (Charalambis *et al.*, 2004).

What explains poor labour market performance in Greece? As in the Spanish and occasionally the Portuguese cases, labour market 'rigidities' in the form of stringent employment protections are often blamed (Burtless, 2001; Demekas and Kontolemis, 1997). The problem with this explanation is that many of these protections only apply to a fraction of Greece's labour force, bringing into question the extent to which they really matter. As the discussion of family and welfare policy below will illustrate, rights in Greece at least in the field of labour and social security law, are strongly fragmented along occupational lines. Public sector workers and professionals have more rights than other occupational groups; it was not until 1990 that part-time workers were awarded the set of basic labour protections afforded full-time employees. In addition, there are a number of informal ways in which the labour market is indeed more flexible than formal protections might suggest (Petmesidou, 2001: 78). Greece has a particularly large informal sector, the largest in the OECD in fact, estimated in 2000 to be at least 28.5 per cent of GDP compared to 22.5 per cent in Portugal and 15.7 per cent in Ireland (Schneider, 2002: 13; see also Schneider and Enste, 2000). Other ways in which flexibility is built into the country's labour market structure include the use of (often) unpaid family labour in agriculture and small businesses. Labour force survey data suggests that this describes the position of one out of eight workers in Greece, six times the rate found in Portugal (Burtless, 2001: 478).

Some of these typically 'Southern European' labour market features are also to be found in Portugal. While the Portuguese economy remained underdeveloped and became increasingly stagnant under the Salazar dictatorship, unemployment did not start to become a significant social problem until the 1970s. Several factors account for this, the first being that true levels of underemployment were masked by Portugal's reliance on agriculture, which tends to report farmers as employed even if they are barely operating at a subsistence level. In addition, not only was unemployment avoided through emigration, but during the 1960s the colonial army absorbed many of the young men who might have been unemployed otherwise. This situation was reversed after 1974 once the decolonization policy was rapidly implemented. Not only did the army return home, but so did many migrants from the colonies and eventually many economic migrants returned from Europe and North America since Portugal had managed to redemocratize. Adding even further to the pressures of absorbing so much extra labour was a steadily increasing number of women seeking work during the 1970s; an extra burden on young job-seekers since new employment laws tended to protect those already with jobs; and a general reduction in agricultural and industrial production as the result of the political upheavals of the revolution (Lúcio, 1993: 17–18).

Given the increased number of individuals to find jobs for in addition to the sudden withdrawal of foreign investment and other disruptions that took place in the wake of the revolution, it is simply amazing that unemployment levels did not surge higher than they did during the transition to democracy. One estimate is that the unemployment rate rose from 3.1 per cent in 1973 to 14.4 per cent in 1976 before declining to about 12.8 per cent in 1977 (Corkill, 1993: 37). The fact that it was not any higher is usually attributed to the growth of public sector employment during the political transition period, including wide-scale nationalizations of certain industries and companies. One calculation finds that the number of individuals employed by the state more than doubled between 1968 and 1979, from 155,200 to 313,000, increasing again to 442,000 in 1983 (Graham, 1993: 99).

Portugal's ability to cope with the economic challenges of the late 1970s and early 1980s even as well as it did was at the cost of a burgeoning balance of

Table 2.3 Portuguese labour market indicators, 1995–2008

Year	*Employment rate (percentage of population aged 15–64)*		*Unemployment rate*		*Total workforce with at least upper-level secondary school education*	*Part-time employment as percentage of total workforce*
	Male	*Female*	*Total*	*Aged under 25*		
1995	73.5	54.4	7.3	16.5	21.9	7.5
1996	73.9	54.9	7.3	16.7	21.8	8.7
1997	75.5	56.5	6.8	15.1	22.0	9.9
1998	75.9	58.2	5.1	10.7	17.8	11.2
1999	75.8	59.4	4.5	9.1	19.1	11.1
2000	76.5	60.5	4.0	8.8	19.4	10.8
2001	77.0	61.3	4.0	9.4	20.2	11.3
2002	76.5	61.4	5.0	11.6	20.7	11.4
2003	75.0	61.4	6.3	14.5	22.8	11.8
2004	74.2	61.7	6.7	15.3	25.2	11.2
2005	73.4	61.7	7.6	16.1	26.5	11.5
2006	79.2*	66.3*	8.6	20.4	67.8	11.3
2007	79.1*	66.3*	8.9	20.6	68.3	12.1
2008	79.4*	67.0*	8.5	20.5	69.6	11.9

Source: Eurostat.

Note
* Percentage of population aged 20–64.

payments crisis and a huge public debt. By 1983, this spilled over into an economic recession, the social effects of which continued to be offset by public employment, even if by this stage some workers were not always being paid on time given the financial circumstances the state found itself in (Stoleroff, 2001: 79). Privatization of many of the nationalized sectors began in 1987 in conjunction with a general structural adjustment project implemented by the centre-right Social Democratic Party (PSD). Employment growth occurred in the late 1980s and early 1990s, after which another recession led to an overall employment decrease, led by the service sector as well as small-scale manufacturing for export (Lúcio, 1993). Both of these sectors increasingly made use of female labour, a factor that is discussed extensively in Chapter 6.

Portugal is considered something of an exception when it comes to the ability to sustain a comparatively low unemployment rate, at least by European standards, over the past two decades. This appears all the more remarkable when it is recognized that the country has hardly experienced a magnificent general growth record since the late 1980s, despite the surge in employment creation that followed shortly after Portugal's European integration in 1986. In Ireland, the gradual decline in unemployment levels since 1987 is correlated with impressive employment growth and a stunning expansion of GDP. The Portuguese economy, by contrast, seems to suffer badly from periodic boom and bust cycles. The Portuguese economy only grew by an average rate of 0.85 per cent between

2001 and 2004, including an actual shrinkage occurring in 2003, compared to average growth rates of a little over 4 per cent between 1997 and 2000. The corresponding data for Ireland is an average growth rate of 10.1 per cent between 1997 and 2000, falling to an average rate of 5.1 per cent between 2001 and 2004, the slowdown due in part to Irish dependence on the United States and the slowdown experienced in that country after 2001. The Greek economy grew by an average of 4.6 per cent per year in the latter period and 3.7 per cent in the former.[8]

Explanations for Portuguese successes in maintaining relatively high employment levels despite periodic economic difficulties often centre on comparisons with Spain, given that the two countries share similar wage-setting agreements among other things (Blanchard and Jimeno, 1995; Bover *et al.*, 2000). A common explanation is that Spain's labour market is more rigid, especially in terms of wages – meaning mostly that wages are lower in Portugal than in Spain. It is true that, despite formal 'inflexibility' such as stringent job security laws, the Portuguese labour market is flexible in a number of other ways. Comparatively low wages constitute one form of flexibility; so do the use of short-term contracts, used increasingly by employers from the mid-1980s, and the use of child and illegal migrant labour. Yet many of these conditions also exist elsewhere in Southern Europe, especially in Greece, and unemployment levels have been consistently much worse in Greece. The weakness of explanations centred on labour market rigidities, which arguably do not differ as much across Southern Europe as the economics literature likes to make out, has led others to focus on broader political factors and especially on the interventionist role of the Portuguese state after 1974. These include the extension of credit to small businesses, initially under a largely nationalized banking sector (Fishman, 2003), and, more recently, active labour market programmes. More generally, it is proposed that the sequencing of privatization of state services, well after the transition to democracy began, meant that a cutback in state employment only occurred after enterprises located in the industrial and service sectors were sufficiently developed to begin contributing to employment growth.

A major problem Portugal now faces is that many of these 'new' services and industries, some of which are still heavily tied to an inefficient agricultural sector, are no longer sustainable given competition from Eastern Europe and Asia. Staple Portuguese products have suffered either a loss of market or the growth of competition in recent years, including cork, fisheries, clothing and footwear. Furthermore, a growth strategy based chiefly on low-wage competition is not going to provide an adequate basis for meeting the expectations of an increasingly consumerist society whose reference point is Western Europe and not the 'developing' or 'peripheral' world. This is slowly leading towards the development of new industries structured around the concept of 'the innovation society', yet Portugal has much further than most European countries to go in making this concept a reality. As Chapter 6 discusses in much detail, levels of education in Portugal still lag far behind those in their Western and Southern European counterparts. Despite efforts to improve education levels, an 'information underclass' (Corkill, 1999: 179) can be clearly identified.[9] This translates into the emergence of a very limited number and range of 'knowledge based' local industries and the lack of a clear strategy about how to shift away from continued Portuguese reliance on an underdeveloped agricultural sector, struggling industries, and a growing low-wage service sector.

Some components of a two-tiered labour market support structure

This book seeks to explain the variation in the extent to which Greece, Ireland, and Portugal embraced a high-wage, high-skill, 'knowledge-based' development strategy for the twenty-first century between 1990 and 2008 by analysing their responses to a series of labour market challenges, namely in the fields of family, higher education, and immigration policy. As the discussion so far has demonstrated, the state's role in shaping labour market outcomes – specifically, the skills-level and adaptability of the workforce – is also central to the idea of the knowledge economy. Policies aimed at reconciling family and working life along with higher education and immigration policies form what can be referred to as a secondary tier of a labour market support structure (see Figure 2.1). While very interesting in themselves, this research does not focus on what are classically referred to as active labour market programmes, which aim squarely at easing citizens from labour market inactivity to activity, and are usually administered directly by departments or ministries of labour or employment. Although these programmes are extremely important to labour market outcomes,

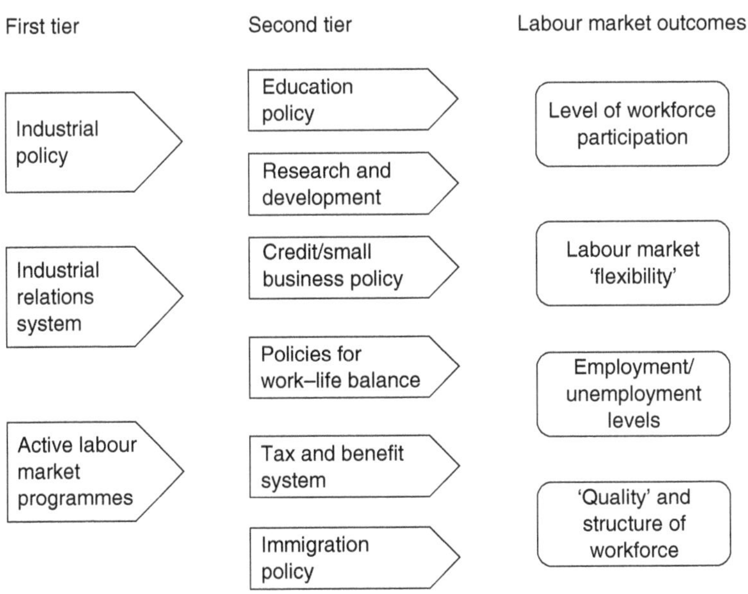

Figure 2.1 A two-tiered labour market support structure.

the policy areas selected here, as part of the outer ring of a labour market support structure, are more important for the purposes of this research project because they involve the interests of a diverse array of political actors and interests, not always related to labour market concerns. While the agencies responsible for the formation of family, higher education and training, and immigration policies often do take labour market issues into consideration, they must also often balance these against other and sometimes competing economic and social goals.

Three additional main criteria have led to the selection of these particular three policy areas. First, explaining variation means that policy areas must be selected over which these countries can and do have a range of policy options, especially since this particular group of countries is not only subject to international pressures for policy convergence but is also subject to the forces of Europeanization. European integration means that there are some policy arenas over which member states do not have a great deal of choice, and the regional body's influence may be either direct or indirect across the policy spectrum. It would not be terribly interesting or theoretically useful to thus select policy areas over which Greece, Ireland, and Portugal appear relatively uniform simply by virtue of their membership of the EU. Agriculture and fisheries are still extremely important industries for Greece, Ireland, and Portugal, for example, but EU member states have very little flexibility over these policy areas. Family policy, higher education, and immigration policies, on the other hand, are still primarily the responsibility of individual member nations, even if the EU occasionally shows interest in 'harmonizing' aspects of immigration policy in particular (Givens and Luedtke, 2004; Gubbay, 1999). Aspects of family and education policy are influenced but not determined by such EU activity as the regulation of working time; efforts to forge regional-level social bargaining that include the negotiation of anything from work-based childcare programmes to 'education for life' strategies for the purposes of retraining workers in a changing economy; and formal frameworks for social inclusion.

Second, looking ahead to the explanatory framework outlined in Chapter 3, the policy areas need to be important or central enough to be able to reflect something general about the nature of state–society relations, reflected in the development of incorporative and consultative institutions in each of the three countries under consideration. Policy areas that are not very important and in which there appears to be little societal interest will be especially subject to discretionary funding or the personal whims of individual policy makers, limiting their ability to reflect general patterns of state action across the case studies. As discussed further in the following chapter, the research project on which this book is based has been partly influenced by previous work that looks at the role of the state in promoting specific development strategies, and the patterns of state–society relations associated with the 'developmental' role of modern capitalist states. However, studies in this field tend to focus almost entirely on industrial policy as a key area for promoting economic growth (Evans, 1995). Yet industrial policy itself is often only one important element of state projects that seek to reorient economic development in a changing global political economy. Thus, this book differs from most work in comparative political economy that focuses on either industrial policy (the state's direct or indirect role in promoting specific types of economic development) or the state's management of the relationship between organized business and labour.

Third and related, studies that look at the role of the state and broad patterns of state–society relations in order to explain national choices between development strategies centre almost exclusively on the relationship between the state and organized labour and business. By contrast, this book makes a deliberate effort to examine the state's relationship with a broader range of groups. Is there something common or general in the way that the state deals with different types of interest groups, or are some groups obviously privileged (or excluded) over others? Some of the groups that are important to the development of family policy include business and labour unions, but the relationship between the state and women's lobby groups, childcare workers, and established churches, for example, are also important to analyse. In the field of higher education policy, clearly defined interest groups include student unions, university administrations, and private educational establishments. The views and interests of immigrant rights organizations and existing ethnic communities, alongside organized labour and business, are obviously important for states to take into account when designing the legal framework governing immigration.

The decision to concentrate on three policy areas across three countries, delivering a sample of nine case studies, is conditioned by the need to balance issues of manageability where qualitative methods are adopted, as is done here, against the need to increase the number of cases where possible, especially in order to increase the level of variation on the dependent variable (Geddes, 1990; King *et al.*, 1994: 208–30). Since this type of research is necessarily carried out using qualitative data such as interviews, published and unpublished policy recommendations, and legislation, students of comparative political economy are usually prompted to limit their selection of cases to a small number of countries, or an extremely limited number of policy issues, or both. Quantitative data is generally much more useful for measuring policy outcomes rather than how and why policy was actually made. However, the sample has been increased to as many as nine distinct cases so that general patterns of similarity can be observed within countries at the same time as patterns of difference between the three countries can be identified. The choice of policy areas, however, was not guided by a belief that that these three policy areas are necessarily the *most* important influences on labour market outcomes, let alone the most crucial elements of an overall successful economic strategy. Rather, together they act as a good lens through which to assess general claims about the importance of policy-making processes and institutions that are capable of balancing functions of consultation and incorporation.

Family policy

The centrality of family policy to influencing labour market outcomes was only explicitly recognized by states as well as academic analysts relatively recently, and, arguably, belatedly. Until the 1990s, the debate over the state's role in promoting particular types of family structure and organization was framed in terms of 'women's rights', especially to engage in paid work and determine how many children they will raise, which is sometimes set against either issues of 'children's rights' and welfare or fears about the 'breakdown' of the nuclear family. Increasingly, however, governments of developed countries, especially in Western Europe during the 1990s and, more recently, East Asia, have become concerned about declining birth rates and aging populations and are thus framing family policy in economic terms. Currently, women in many of these countries need to choose between having children (or, perhaps more accurately, having larger families or having children earlier in life) and engaging in paid work. The problem for governments is how state intervention might permit families, but especially individual women, to do both, meeting the twin policy objectives of increasing the birth rate and increasing economic productivity, without neglecting child welfare. Counter-intuitively, the 'work–family trade-off' is even more acute in countries that have strong family-oriented cultural beliefs and practices and yet provide a lower level of direct state support to families, including nations with 'conservative' welfare regimes such as Greece, Ireland, and Portugal. Traditionally, it was presumed that increased female participation in the paid workforce was linked to the declining birth rates experienced by advanced industrial nations, but recent data, especially from Europe, suggests that variations in the birth rate have much more to do with the extent to which states devote resources to easing the tension between paid work and raising families (Ahn and Mira, 2002; Bongaarts, 2002; Bettio and Villa, 1998; Brewster and Rindfuss, 2000; Esping-Andersen, 1996, 1999, 2002; Kalwij, 2010; Thévenon and Gautier, 2011).

Family policy may be 'direct' or 'indirect', meaning that deliberate attempts can be made to influence family size and parental workforce participation but also that many government policies have non-deliberate and unintended consequences in this field (Kamerman and Kahn, 1978). In addition, of the three policy areas considered here, responsibility for this one is the most diffused. Both policy analysts and family policy activists tend to argue that better policy would result from having a single administrative body coordinating state action in the field, but this is rare. Many different factors operate to influence the work–child trade-off, including access to contraception and abortion, local cultural beliefs and practices, indirect effects of the tax system, as well as deliberate government policies aimed at reducing the costs of this trade-off. While family policy is a much larger field than policies for work–life balance, this analysis will be limited to an assessment of the extent to which the state has deliberately responded to the challenge of creating a work–family balance in Greece, Ireland, and Portugal in order to influence future labour market structure.

The analysis that follows takes into account six key policy mechanisms by which states may encourage individuals and families to balance child-rearing against workforce participation. The first is taxation, where different regimes encourage or discourage the take-up of part-time work in particular. The tax code also interacts with other policy mechanisms, sometimes in unforeseen ways. The conventional wisdom is that if taxes are individualized and no tax benefits are granted for privately paid child-care, for example, this will both 'force' potential parents into full-time paid work and reduce their incentives to have children, because the family income will drop dramatically if one wage-earner, more often the female partner, decides to stay at home (Dingeldey, 2001). Alternatives to tax individualization include systems that compulsorily base levels on a couple's income. Tending to discourage workforce participation on the part of the second income-earner, such a regime can be found in Ireland. More likely to encourage part-time workforce participation, many family policy activists prefer the 'one and a half' family income model of income splitting for tax purposes, found in France among other European countries. In countries such as Greece, tax benefits or write-offs often increase according to the number of children in a family. This appears as a crude and often not very effective way of encouraging families to have more children.

A second policy mechanism that has received a considerable amount of attention at the European level and throughout the OECD in general is childcare, and research shows that the availability and affordability of childcare can be the most decisive factor influencing women's economic decision-making (Erhel and Guergoat-Lariviere, 2013). This can be provided directly by the state or indirectly by non-profit organizations, by the informal or family sector, or by the private sector outside or inside family homes, although the state usually has some oversight even in the case of the latter. Increased state involvement in the provision of childcare, or at least the funding of it, has become common in Europe, and with that involvement has come increasing concerns about the quality and quantity of care available. Specific measures include the number of places made available in the public child-care system (where it exists) and the extent to which the state indirectly or directly subsidizes the private and voluntary sectors.

Third, advanced industrial states have supported families since the early twentieth century through direct cash payments to either the mother or the 'head of the household', generally referred to as a child or family benefit (Ginsborg, 2000). Child benefits may be means-tested or universal, can vary according to the number of children in a household, and can provide a good lens on a state's overall approach to family policy. Given Ireland's pro-natalist albeit often 'hands-off' policy tradition, a 'children's allowance' has been paid on a non-means tested basis for third and subsequent children since 1944 (Curry, 1998: 24). Increasingly, many countries, including Portugal and Ireland in this case study comparison, have moved away from child benefit as a universal entitlement and have instead used it as means-tested poverty relief measure. Again, family policy frameworks with a bias toward supporting 'large families' might pay higher rates for third and subsequent children. This is the case in Greece.

A fourth key policy area is maternity leave and benefits. Though these are theoretically separate schemes, they must be considered together because the availability of benefits often influences the take-up of leave from paid work. If maternity leave is guaranteed by law, and yet this leave is unpaid and there are no maternity benefits or very limited state pay-outs to compensate for lost wages, women may choose not to take up their statutory rights. Similarly, but worth considering separately as a fifth mechanism for reconciling family and working life, is paternity leave legislation. The rate of paternity leave take-up is also strongly linked to whether or not the law guarantees that fathers are paid during their period of leave, usually by their employers. Portugal has been particularly proactive, not only compared with the other Southern European countries and Ireland, but also with the rest of the OECD on this score. As the Portuguese experience also shows, implementing parental leave legislation often requires a fundamental cultural shift surrounding traditional gender roles related to the care of children.

Finally, flexi-time, the availability of part-time work, and reduced working days are a sixth way by which states can reduce the costs of the work–family trade-off. Unlike the other five indicators, the difficulty for policy formulation here is that the use of flexi-time and other time-related measures is generally the subject of employment contracts, rather than enacted into law, but even so the state may actively encourage such strategies without codifying them in law. Moves in this direction are often reflected in social pacts or other types of signed agreements, where they exist. Ireland, for example, has built such voluntary 'family-friendly' initiatives into social partnership agreements. Encouragement of part-time work, in particular, is much more difficult in both Greece and Portugal since both countries abide by the 'Southern European model' of welfare provision. This model combines universal healthcare with other benefits such as retirement income that are strongly linked to an individual's occupation rather than distributed universally. There is also a greater emphasis on the provision of welfare by the family rather than the state. Benefits are generally tied to engagement in full-time work over an extended period of time, with Greece considered the near ideal-type, Portugal deviating furthest from it and Italy and Spain lying somewhere in between (Ferrera, 1996; see also Flaquer, 2000 and Martin, 1997).

The case study analyses presented in Chapters 4 to 6 assess the extent to which state and non-state political elites in Ireland, Portugal, and Greece increasingly view family policies as part of the second tier of a labour market support structure for twenty-first century economic and social development. As these chapters will show, there is considerable variation in the extent to which each of the three national cases has begun to reconceptualise family policy in this manner, and, correspondingly, the extent to which each of the six specific policy mechanisms discussed above has been employed with the aim of reducing the tension between work and family life in mind. Before discussing the case study material in detail and presenting an explanation for why there has been policy divergence across the countries considered, it is worth reviewing some objective data related to this issue area. Table 2.4 contains a number of family policy

Table 2.4 Family policy indicators

		Ireland	*Portugal*	*Greece*	*OECD average*
1 Fertility rate	1990	2.12	1.56	1.39	1.86
	2006	1.90	1.36	1.41	1.65
2 Maternal employment rate compared to female employment rate (2007)	Female employment rate (ages 25–49)	69.5	76.5	61.6	69.5
	Maternal employment rate (child under 16)	57.5	76.4	58.7	65.3
3 Enrolment rates of children in formal childcare or early education services (2006)	Ages 0–3	25.2	43.6	18.2	–
	Ages 3–5	49.4	78.9	47.3	–
4 Weeks of maternity leave, equivalent to 100 per cent of pay (2006–2007)		18.2	17	17	12.8
5 Weeks of paternity leave, equivalent to 100 per cent of pay (2006–2007)		0.0	2.0	0.4	–
6 Flexi-time provisions					
Proportion of companies that allow employees to accumulate hours for longer periods of leave		10	3	1	–
Possibility of varying the start and end of daily work, but no accumulation of hours		25	12	18	–
7 Total public spending on family (cash, services, and tax measures) as percentage of GDP (2003)		2.60	1.80	1.30	2.41

Source: OECD Family Database. Indicator 1, chart SF4.4; indicator 2, chart LM2.1; indicator 3, chart PF11.1; indicator 4, chart PF7.1; indicator 5 chart, PF7.1; indicator 6, LMF10.1. Indicator 7 from OECD (2007), chart 4.1.

indictors, especially related to issues of work–life balance, across the three national cases of interest here. These indictors not only partially reflect prior patterns of state intervention in this policy arena, but also illustrate the specific circumstances in which each country must construct policies for work–life balance. They do not precisely reflect the six key policy mechanisms above but, rather, reflect the impact of policies in each of these policy spheres.

Turning first to the Irish case, the country experienced a surge of women entering the paid workforce during the economic boom period of the 1990s. Employment growth during this decade was largely fuelled by return migration, then women entering the labour force for the first time, followed by, chronologically speaking, foreign migration (Fahey *et al.*, 2000; Tansey, 1998). This meant that, by the late 2000s, Ireland had a female workforce participation rate equal to that of the OECD average, although not as high as that of Portugal or of many Northern European countries. Part of the reason for this continued lag is that the gap between female and maternal employment rates is still pronounced, reflecting the fact that many mothers of young children opt to stay at home. This in turn can be explained by a combination of prevailing cultural attitudes that mothers should not be 'forced' to work outside the home, as well as continuing gaps in the availability and affordability of childcare in particular. In terms of fertility rates, Ireland continues to have one of the highest birth rates in the developed world, outstripped only by Iceland, the United States, Turkey, and Mexico, out of thirty OECD countries, in 2006. As Chapter 4 fully illustrates, Ireland still lags well behind most Western European countries in terms of the array of child and parental services and benefits made available by the state. This is due to the very recent shift that the country has made from being one that actively discourages women from engaging in paid work, towards one in which female workforce participation is increasingly expected. In addition, a number of targeted family welfare benefits and programmes were not expanded in Ireland until the 1990s. The somewhat belated attention given to issues of work–life balance, however, does mean that Ireland appears more generous than the two Southern European states on at least two dimensions: the total amount spent on family services as a percentage of GDP was twice that of Greece in the early 2000s, and Irish companies appear more resistant to the extension of flexi-time arrangements than do either Portuguese or Greek businesses.

For the past two decades, Greece has stood out among European countries, along with Italy and Spain, as combining an especially low female workforce participation rate with a low birth rate. While Table 2.4 reports Greece's 2006 fertility rate as being slightly higher that Portugal's, it not only remains below OECD and European averages, but there are also several additional reasons to be cautious about this trend. After reaching a low of 1.26 in 2001, the turnaround only began in 2004 and 2006 was in fact the first year that Greece's rate overtook Portugal's. Furthermore, the increase in birth rates may be more indicative of Greece's high rate of migration, discussed below, rather than government policy success as such. Most significantly, however, Greece has a particularly low female workforce participation rate, with only four OECD countries – Italy,

Mexico, Turkey, and Malta – trailing behind. This has remained an underlying trend for some time, in contrast to the way in which Irish women surged into the paid workforce during the 1990s. Taking into account women aged between fifteen and sixty four, a slightly different measure from that used in Table 2.1, Ireland's female workforce participation rate grew by 22.2 percentage points between 1991 and 2000, while Greece's increased only slightly, by 4.6 (Eurostat, 2003). As Chapter 5 fully illustrates, Greek family policy has generally been targeted only at a small group of families with 'many children', meaning that most families, given the prevalence of two-child, two-parent nuclear families in the country, receive little direct support for reconciling family and working life. Moreover, trends of declining fertility have been consistently framed as a 'population' or even 'cultural' crisis, rather than by the notion of work–life balance, per se.

Portugal is an interesting case when it comes to the development of policies for work–life balance, especially in a Southern European context, because high rates of female workforce participation have been maintained, especially from the early 1980s, without much direct support for families from the state. While there has historically been very little state intervention to help individuals and families ease the tension between working and family life, the majority of women engage in full-time paid work, with participation rates almost matching those of the Nordic countries. This can be explained by a mixture of idiosyncratic local factors, including the historical entry of women into the workforce as the result of labour shortages caused by the African colonial wars in the 1960s; the state's commitment to gender equality, legally enshrined in the 1974 post-revolutionary constitution; and the fact that the structure of the labour market in Portugal, as in the rest of Southern Europe, is hostile to part-time work (Fishman, 2003, 2010; Ferreira, 1998). Despite this high participation rate, during the 1990s fertility rates remained slightly above those of Italy, Greece, and Spain. This may also reflect an effort, especially on the part of the Socialist Government elected in 1996, to increase the support for work–life balance, especially through the expansion of childcare services, which is clearly reflected in the above table, and increasingly generous parental (including paternal) leave policies. It is worth noting, however, that everything Portuguese governments have done in this field has been built on a very low base, given the country's very late-developing welfare state.

Higher education

Education policies are rarely studied by political scientists, yet there is politics at play here as much as there is in any other policy arena. Not only are there non-state actors with deeply entrenched interests involved, but education policies are profoundly shaped by ideological shifts and long-term political and cultural changes. Investment in education, technical training, and research and development is clearly central to a high-wage, high-skill, knowledge-based economic strategy. State education strategies may have many components and education policy touches on a number of different areas of state activity, from the provision of primary school education to the retraining of older workers. Because it is impossible to cover all of this here, the focus is narrowed to higher or third-level education and training. While research and development policy, in which higher education institutions sometimes play a key role, is the explicit focus of students of the 'knowledge economy', the labour market focus of this book steers the analysis more towards the broader educational role played by these institutions. More specifically, the interest is in (1) the extent to which the university system has been reoriented towards vocational training or maintains a more traditional role, and (2) the extent to which the non-university sector has been expanded to meet new needs through such measures as 'life-long learning' programmes, job re-training, and the establishment of technical colleges or similar institutions. The focus is less on apprenticeship training schemes and other forms of secondary-level education both inside and outside the traditional school system since these are not usually considered part of higher education provision.

There are a number of mechanisms by which states may reorient the higher education system toward meeting new economic needs. Most notably, states may enact legislation or reallocate funding to various parts of the education system. It is helpful, however, to break the analytical framework down into four main dimensions in order to focus and guide the case study discussions which lie ahead. These are (1) action the state takes in order to balance technical training against non-technical education; (2) whether or not the state uses private provision in order to meet new needs; (3) how and to what extent higher education is funded by the state; (4) and how funding and other measures aim to increase participation in education, usually referred to as 'access' policies. Running through these four dimensions are also three enduring concerns – ensuring quality, increasing quantity, and the issue of institutional autonomy – which are often in conflict with one another.

One of the most overarching and difficult problems is how to balance technical and non-technical education. At its most philosophical (and ideological) level is the age-old debate over whether education is for education's sake, personal fulfilment and the enlightenment of society as a whole, or whether, in a tough modern world, education is about providing for the labour market. In the European context, both goals are valued, although many would argue that labour market, increasingly utilitarian, concerns are winning the day in the wake of the Lisbon Strategy.[10] Most European countries gradually turned to technical education as early as the 1950s, by which time traditional apprenticeship schemes and trade schools seemed no longer capable of meeting modern needs. States can achieve an appropriate balance between technical and non-technical education by a number of different means, but a crucial decision is whether to encourage the establishment of technical institutions parallel to the university system or to somehow force universities to provide technically oriented education and the general transferable skills emphasized by theorists of the knowledge economy. The latter strategy often runs up against the traditionally fiercely protected autonomy of universities, at least in democratic circumstances. Frequently, both strategies are pursued, creating debate over the proper function of 'the university' and whether new types of institution can apply for university status. One way to avoid some of these conflicts is to create or encourage the technical sector as a separate and parallel, functionally differentiated, set of institutions that do not compete with the universities so much as cater to different types of student. While countries often try to avoid creating a hierarchy between the university and non-university sector here, this is usually unavoidable. Referred to as a 'binary' approach, this can be more or less self-consciously pursued on the part of the state, and more or less successfully.

A second important distinction is between public and private institutions, which can cut across both the technical and university sectors. Traditionally, the state has played a major role in funding higher education in much of Western Europe because of the lack of private funding sources, setting the region apart from the United States in particular. However, the need for new technical and vocational training to respond to the needs of the market and to the need to increase participation rapidly without great expense to the state has led to a larger role for the private sector in some cases. On the third question of funding, it is important to focus on who funds education, to what levels, and on what basis. While public funding levels are usually a good indicator of state support for higher education in general, the basis of funding is also important because it has a major impact on the types of course offered. If, for example, universities are funded on the basis of how many students they can attract, or per student, there is a danger that the quality of degrees and other courses will be reduced in order to make course requirements lighter and more entertaining. Alternatively, research-output based funding may cause teaching programmes to be increasingly oriented toward the interests of researchers, and standards for measuring research output might be manipulated to favour the 'hard' sciences over other subjects. If overall levels of state funding are decreased, providers may have to turn to private donations for extra support, and private funding in turn may bring with it new teaching and research agendas.

Fourth, access policies regulate which and how many students enter the higher education system. On the one hand, access policies are about ensuring more equitable social outcomes by assisting students who, because of socio-economic background, age, ethnicity or disability, need extra help gaining entry to and completing higher education. Not only are funding structures important here, through the use of scholarship, student benefits and the like, but so are admittance systems, which in all three cases analysed here are highly centralized, causing potential difficulties for ensuring equality of access. On the other hand, access is also an issue tied strongly to labour market concerns. Encouraging mature students to participate in third-level education might be important for equity reasons, but it is also important for an economy increasingly based on new technical skills. In Ireland, access policies have become more important in an era of labour and skills shortages created by economic growth, but the debate in Greece and Portugal, for reasons discussed in the following chapters, is much more muted.

For Greece, Ireland, and Portugal at least, Europeanization – along with globalization more generally – raises an additional concern about quality assurance. The main mechanism for ensuring quality across technical and university, public and private sectors, is the qualifications system. The system can be used to control degree and diploma content and can provide a way of 'registering' (or accrediting) and 'deregistering' institutions and programmes even in highly variegated and privatized systems such as the Portuguese. However, national degree structures and accreditation regimes in Europe have recently come under pressure to harmonize, prompting increasing concerns about quality control. The 1999 Bologna Declaration, designed to bring national degree structures into line with the three-year undergraduate, two year Masters' and separate Doctoral degrees identified most readily with the English speaking nations outside North America. Quality concerns arise because the aim of the process is to make degrees and courses more easily transferable among EU member states, so that students may study abroad, transfer, and have their degrees recognized more easily when applying for jobs overseas.

The mix of strategies adopted by Greece, Ireland, and Portugal delivers quite different results in terms of funding, number of students in education, and the subjects they study. Using data compiled from the OECD's *Education at a Glance,* Ireland generally appears to provide the highest-quality higher education out of the three countries analysed here. Over the past two decades, Ireland has spent more than the OECD average on higher education, and significantly more than either Portugal or Greece. Since the 1960s, the Irish state has put great effort into expanding higher education, first through the development of new institutions and infrastructure, and later through the dedication of increased resources in order to improve the quality of teaching and research. Higher education policy has centred on a long-term self-conscious strategy on the part of policy-makers to develop and maintain a 'binary' higher education system, differentiating between technical and university education. The ability to supply technically trained, highly skilled workers helped fuel multinational-led job creation, especially during the 1990s, witnessed by the fact that Ireland has a much greater concentration of science graduates than the two Southern European countries.

Most analyses of Greek education policy since redemocratization in 1974 focus not only on the elite and restricted nature of the university sector in particular, but also the extremely low quality levels offered across the higher education system as a whole (Gavroglu, 1981; OECD, 1982 and 1987). Table 2.5 shows that, overall, Greek access rates to higher education are now similar to those of Ireland and Portugal. There is, however, a greater concentration in polytechnic, rather than university-type education, with only 23 per cent gaining access to this latter form of education out of high school. In fact, access to university education was severely restricted before 2000, with many Greeks continuing an intergenerational pattern of gaining university education elsewhere in Europe or in North America, given the tight restrictions placed on the number of places available. While the entrance criteria have been loosened since 2000,

Table 2.5 Higher education indicators

		Ireland	*Portugal*	*Greece*	*OECD average*
1 Expenditure on higher education institutions as a percentage of GDP, from both public and private sources (2000)		1.5	1.0	0.8	1.3
2 Graduation rates in tertiary education (2007)*		45.0	42.6	17.7	38.7
3 Entry rates to tertiary education (2007)	Tertiary A**	44	64	23	56
	Tertiary B	21	1	43	15
4 Ratio of students to teachers in higher education (2007)		16.5	13.2	26.3	15.3
5 Science graduates among 25–34 year olds in employment, per 100,000		2,239	2,000	1,089	1,709

Source: OECD (2009), tables B.2.1; A3.1; A.2.4; D.2.2; A.3.7, respectively.

Notes

* Graduation rates from Tertiary A institutions only.

** Tertiary A programmes are of three years full-time equivalent minimum study and are largely theory-based, being designed to provide sufficient qualifications for entry to advanced research programmes and professions that require a high level of skills. Tertiary B programmes are typically shorter in nature, although with a minimum of two years full-time equivalent study, and focus on practical, technical, or occupational skills.

higher education in Greece has suffered from low quality standards for several decades, at least in comparison with much of Europe. While efforts have been made to expand the non-university sector since the 1980s, technical education is seen as vastly inferior to university education, and there is a significant problem matching training to labour market needs: Greece has an extraordinarily high percentage of unemployed graduates. This is underscored by the low number of technically trained graduates: witness the very low number of science graduates reported in Table 2.5. Additional data in the same table also speaks to the issue of low quality higher education. The ratio of students to teachers is twice that of Portugal's, and drop-out rates and rates of students who fail to finish courses within a five or six-year period are extraordinarily high. While Indicator 3 does not exactly measure drop-out rates, it does show that a comparatively small percentage of the university-age cohort manages to complete their programme in any given year.

As in Ireland, Portugal has also greatly expanded participation in higher education, since the mid-1980s in this case. However, the means by which this expansion has been achieved has differed greatly from the Irish. A two-pronged approach involved the establishment of several new public universities and a network of polytechnic institutions, but, more significantly, the stimulation of the private sector to increase participation levels. Government policy directed at stimulating the development of private institutions involved altering the access system to higher education; changing rules to allow professors to work in both the public and private sectors simultaneously; and the provision of subsidies to private providers. The privatization strategy has been credited with delivering better than expected outcomes in terms of participation in education, although, as Table 2.5 illustrates, first degrees tend to be highly theoretical in focus (Tertiary A courses), rather than technically-focused (Tertiary B). Even so, Portugal produces a relatively high number of science graduates, and, on one other measure of quality at least, has a lower than average student–teacher ratio. This mix of results is also reflected in ongoing concerns about some of the consequences of the privatization strategy. While stimulating the private sector may have helped expand participation in higher education, serious concerns have often been raised not only about the quality of education provided by many private institutions, but also about the inability of the private sector in particular to respond to labour market needs. In addition, despite the rapid expansion of educational participation since the late 1980s, Portugal spends less than average on higher education, at just 1 per cent of GDP. In terms of expenditure on higher education per student, excluding research and development, in 2007 Portugal spent US$7,208, lower than the OECD average of $8,455, and lower than the EU-19 average of $7,592, a total which includes a number of Central and Eastern European low spenders (OECD, 2009: 188).

Immigration

Family and higher education policies are at best medium- to long-term solutions to labour market challenges caused by demographic imbalances and skills shortages. Immigration policy, by contrast, can have almost immediate effects and attracting skilled labour from overseas may be the best option where higher education and training policy fails or has not yet taken effect (OECD, 2002: 103–7). Likewise, governments may have to resort to immigration in order to increase the ratio of working-age to dependent members of the population. Yet the importation of labour might take one of two directions, depending on the particular development strategy adopted by each state and the sorts of pressure placed on governments to either encourage or discourage particular types of migrant. Cheap migrant labour has often been used in Western Europe during periods of economic expansion and labour shortage in order to undertake work in the service or manufacturing sectors that Europeans do not want to perform, such as in the growth years that followed the Second World War. In this case, migrant labour may be legal or illegal, and this work may be formal or informal in nature. Alternatively, highly skilled migrants may fill skills shortages resulting from rapid economic growth or change, failed education policies, or the simple lack of skills diversity often experienced by relatively small countries such as Greece, Ireland, and Portugal. Although the focus here is on labour migration, this aspect of a nation's immigration policy is often hard to disentangle from others. If policy toward asylum seeking is extremely restrictive, economic refugees might simple enter the country illegally and yet still perform an economic function. However, issues of refugee resettlement and the integration of migrants in general remain outside the scope of this research, even though it receives much attention in the literature.

While the regional harmonization of immigration policies is a desired goal of the EU, a great deal of variation across Europe remains (Collinson, 1993; Geddes, 2000; Lahav, 2004; Lahav and Messina, 2005). All three of the nations considered here have traditionally been countries of migration rather than immigration, a tradition that has been reversed in recent years. Ireland allowed a limited number of European refugees to add diversity to the country in the wake of the Second World War (Tracy, 2000), but no significant policy changes occurred until the nation's recent economic boom created demand for specific categories of skilled and unskilled labour as well as the increased possibility of illegal migration. Both Greece and Portugal have comparatively high levels of illegal migration, Greece due to the porous nature of its borders and geographic location as the meeting ground between Eastern, Western, and Southern Europe and the Middle East, and Portugal because of the ongoing legacy of South American and more particularly African colonial ties. Policy responses in the two Southern European cases have included attempts to combat illegal migration by both tightening border controls and establishing new processes to permit legal migration, but the skill levels attracted by these legislative acts appear quite mixed. Portugal has moved somewhat further than Greece in forging a coherent and pro-active policy response rather than relying on reactive ad-hoc regularization schemes.

The case study chapters will analyse specific features of national immigration policy, including an assessment of the state institutions responsible for this area. Unlike family policy, immigration policy is usually the responsibility of one department or ministry in conjunction with the government of the day, although whether immigration policy is aligned with the work of a labour or a justice department can tell much about whether the issue is primarily seen as an economic issue or a legal or criminal problem. In Greece, immigration has been perceived primarily as a law and order issue and thus is overseen by the Ministry of Internal Order. Greek immigration policy is in fact extremely contradictory and fragmented, as Chapter 5 details. Interestingly, by contrast, Portugal has coped with the sometimes contradictory elements of immigration policy by splitting institutional responsibility between two legally separate government bodies. While the High Commission for Immigrants and Ethnic Minorities (*Alto Comissariado para a Imigração e Minorias Étnicas* or ACIME) presents the softer side of immigration policy, responsible for assisting migrants including illegal workers, the Foreigner and Border Service (*Serviço de Estrangeiros e Fronteiras* or SEF) is the harsher face, responsible for expelling illegals and other more technical matters.

Actual immigration policy is normally reflected in a limited number of acts and decrees. Of particular interest is the extent to which policies on labour migration, asylum seekers, and how to address the problem of illegal migration and trafficking are coordinated with one another and to what extent policy responses are framed with the nation's developmental requirements in mind. Studies of immigration often cite raw data on the numbers of legal and illegal migrants, but these are only partial indicators of 'policy' since levels of migration are also conditional on the 'push' factors that encourage individual migrants to leave their home countries in the first place. What is very important, in the case of this study, is an analysis not only of how many migrants enter the country in any given year, but on what basis and conditions they are permitted to enter, how long they are able to stay and what types of jobs they can accept or are encouraged to accept. What is key is whether mechanisms to induce low-skilled or high-skilled migrants or a mix of both are established and altered over time.

The adoption of organized systems to control directly the number of migrants entering a country is actually quite rare. Indirect measures appear to influence migration numbers more, although some policy advisors argue that, in an ideal world, individual nations would make a better effort to anticipate their own labour needs and control numbers accordingly (OECD, 2002). Options would include the adoption of a quota system, adjusted over time to meet labour shortages. More often, numbers are controlled by giving attention to the basis on which migrants are permitted. This influences not only the number of migrants indirectly, but also the types of migrant. Work permits, for example, might be allocated on a 'point system', which takes into account such factors as an individual's skill level, personal and business assets, and possibly their country of origin. Alternatively, migration might only be permitted once the individual has already secured employment, often only after an employer has proved that the job cannot be filled from the pre-existing labour pool.

Immigration is such a new policy problem in Ireland that policy responses were minimalist during the 1990s, with the most significant changes occurring since 2003. The country only became one of net inward migration in the mid-1990s. Returning migrants, lured by the economic boom, were followed by both an influx of asylum seekers from various parts of Africa and Europe and then an upsurge of arrivals from Central and Eastern Europe after 2000 as a result of EU expansion (Ruhs, 2003). During the 1990s, immigration policy remained framed by security concerns and governed by restrictive and outdated legislation dating from the 1930s (Quinn and Hughes, 2005). However, by the end of that decade, it became clear that issues of migrant integration and reshaping the immigration policy framework around new labour market requirements needed to become the new policy priorities. Up until 2003, Ireland allowed an essentially market-based approach to determine the number of work permits issued to migrants from non-EU member states, after which the system was incrementally tightened around skills-based migration. The result of having a more or less unrestricted approach to immigration during a period of intense economic growth is reflected in Table 2.6. Ireland has a relatively high number of foreign-born members of the population, at 11.0 per cent according to 2008 figures, but this is especially

Table 2.6 Immigration indicators

		Ireland	*Portugal*	*Greece*
1 Percentage of population aged over 15 that is foreign-born		11.0	6.7	10.8
2 Percentage of population over 15 with tertiary qualifications	Native	22.7	7.7	14.0
	Foreign-born	41.1	19.3	15.9
3 Percentage of foreign-born population over 15 working as professionals		38.1	21.3	11.2
4 Percentage of foreign-born population over 15 working in the agriculture and industry sectors		28.0	33.1	49.7

Source: OECD (2008), tables 0.1; 3.1; 6.1; and 7.1 respectively.

remarkable given the fact that most of these migrants have arrived since 1995. Yet, in contrast especially to the two Southern European cases discussed below, this foreign population is increasingly concentrated in highly skilled, well paid professions, especially in the service sector. Indicator 4 shows that less than a third of immigrants are employed in primary and secondary sectors of the economy, something that is further underlined by government statistics. Correspondingly, the percentage of migrants with tertiary education qualifications is relatively high, and almost twice that of the native-born population.

Similarly to Ireland and also Portugal, by the 1990s Greece found itself in the position of having become a new country of migration, having experienced a huge influx of migrants, especially from its Balkan neighbours, intensifying after 1989. Given its close geographical proximity to Eastern Europe, the country has a particularly acute problem with illegal migration. Unfortunately, this means that combating illegality has almost entirely dominated the Greek immigration policy debate, leaving even less room for the possibility of designing policies capable of attracting highly skilled migrants from further afield than is the case in Portugal. By the mid-1990s, Greece followed the rest of Southern Europe in opting for migrant regularization programmes rather than comprehensive immigration policy change. Two main legalization programmes occurred in 1998 and 2001, and, while representing a step forward from previous arguments that immigration did not exist, these programmes suffered from a number of problems of design as well as implementation (Baldwin-Edwards and Fakiolas, 1999; Fakiolas, 2003).

The consequences of these policies are clearly reflected in the relevant statistics. Greece has a relatively large foreign-born population, at around 10.8 per cent, which is especially high considering that Greece has not made deliberate efforts to recruit foreigners, nor has the kind of well-paid job opportunities in highly skilled sectors offered by countries such as Ireland. The proportion of highly qualified foreigners is similar to that of Portugal, but, much more tellingly, there is virtually no gap between the local and foreign-born population in this regard. A clear minority of foreign workers is employed in the professions, and almost half are concentrated in the agricultural and industrial sectors. In addition to the fact that there is no real attempt to recruit highly skilled foreign labour in order to contribute to knowledge-based industrial growth, there are consistent concerns about the human rights abuses that are regularly associated with the detention and expulsion of undocumented migrants in Greece. In general, then, migration continues to be viewed more as a security concern than a labour market issue.

In Portugal, a slow but steady trickle of migrants from Portuguese-speaking Africa and Brazil arrived during the 1980s, but immigration did not really become much of a political issue until the 1990s, when the fall of communism in Eastern Europe encouraged an entirely new immigration phenomenon. Since the Portuguese state during this period inherited a relatively restrictive immigration policy framework, vast numbers of these recent arrivals were undocumented. Thus, along with Spain, Italy, and Greece, the challenge posed to the Portuguese government during the 1990s was how best to deal with the problem of undocumented workers. In common with the rest of Southern Europe, an apparently more realistic approach to immigration policy was reflected in a series of one-off mass regularization programmes. The problem with the regularization option, however, is that it does nothing to actively attract highly skilled migrants to the country. In this respect, Portugal lags behind Ireland in conceptualizing immigration policy as part of a high-wage, high-skill development strategy.[11]

Something of this is reflected in the objective indicators outlined in Table 2.6. A relatively small proportion of Portugal's population is foreign born, and while foreign workers are more than twice as likely to have completed higher education qualifications than native-born Portuguese workers, this is still half as likely as in the case of foreign workers in Ireland. While only a third of foreign-born Portuguese workers are concentrated in the primary and secondary sectors of the economy, which is much lower than is the case in Greece, specific groups of immigrants are heavily concentrated in specific occupations, including the construction sector for Portuguese-speaking Africans, the restaurant sector in the case of Brazilians, and the cleaning sector for Eastern Europeans, notably Ukrainians (Fiolhais, 2003; Pires, 2002). All three of these job categories are also dominated by informal labour. None of this is to say, however, that skilled workers do not perform important functions in the Portuguese economy. In fact, workers filling transfer and short-term contracts in overseas companies with new Portuguese branches or bases provide an important channel for increasing the skills of local workers. Rather, the point is that by 2008 the Portuguese state had not yet developed a comprehensive policy framework for attracting foreign talent.

Looking ahead

This overview of work–life balance, higher education, and immigration policies in Ireland, Portugal, and Greece identifies both similarities in the challenges posed by forging policy responses to twenty-first century labour market challenges associated with the construction of the 'knowledge economy', as well as differences in the way that the three countries have responded to these challenges. The similarities lie in the common point these three countries started from in developmental terms, namely as relatively low-income countries located on the periphery of Europe. In the family policy field, of which policies for the reconciliation of family and working life are one part, all three countries began their 'catch up' to Western European developmental averages while coping with the legacies of having conservative, familialist, and minimalist welfare states. The traditional non-interventionist stance meant that a major shift has had to take place on the part of the state in particular, in order to reframe parts of family policy around new labour market requirements. In the case of higher education, expanding participation while reorienting institutions towards science and technology has been the major challenge. Ireland was poised, at the end of the 1980s, in a much better place to meet this challenge since it had begun a process of higher education expansion and reform in the 1960s, although given Ireland's status as a relatively poor country until the 1990s, the country shared with Greece and Portugal a problem of under-resourcing in this area. The two Southern European countries needed to prioritize participation, as large sectors of the population remained undereducated in the 1980s as a legacy of long-term underdevelopment and its associated levels of social inequality. In the case of immigration policy, all three countries share a status as 'new' countries of immigration following centuries-old traditions of outward migration.

Despite these common starting points, even the brief outlines given in this chapter show that there are significant differences in the extent to which each country has reoriented each of these three policy areas around 'knowledge based' economic and societal needs. The advantage of the research design adopted in this book is that it compares policy responses across these three policy areas, revealing that national patterns are more significant than policy-level patterns across the three countries: common starting points can be identified, especially in the cases of higher education policy and policies for work–life balance, but responses diverge significantly, especially during the 1990s and 2000s, the decades on which this analysis centres. The following chapters offer one explanation as to why national-level patterns predominate. As outlined in the introduction, that explanation lies in each country's policy-making tradition, which is deeply influenced by legacies of state–society interaction in each case. Specifically, I argue that having a robust 'zone of mediation', densely constituted by processes and institutions that effectively balance functions of interest group consultation and incorporation, assists states attempting to reorient their policy frameworks around new developmental projects. In the case of building a second-tier labour market support structure around a project as ambitious as the one promised by the knowledge economy, getting the delicate mix of consultative and incorporative functions right is particularly important. After explaining the theoretical basis for these claims in more detail, the next chapter illustrates how Ireland has been advantaged in that it has a relatively strong tradition of consultative and incorporative policy-making; how Greece has suffered from a very underdeveloped zone of mediation; and how the Portuguese experience of long-term authoritarian rule being displaced by 'revolutionary' state collapse has shaped a policy-making tradition that is more incorporative than it is consultative.

Notes

1 The genealogy of the concept is traced back to the 1960s in Kenway *et al.* (2006).
2 Useful secondary works on the topic include Hearn and Rooney, eds (2008); Powell and Snellman (2004); Rooney *et al.* (2003).
3 The concept of tacit knowledge became enormously popular in business studies alongside the rise of the notion of the knowledge economy. See Gertler (2003); Howells (2002); Johnson and Lundvall (2002); Lawson and Lorenz (1999).
4 The future of the 'European Social Model' is a subject of enormous debate (Hine and Kassim, 1998; Sapir, 2006; Taylor-Gooby, ed., 2004; Teague, 1999; Wincott, 2003). There is also a great deal of concern about the impact of European monetary union on European welfare states. See Dyson, ed. (2002); Fishman and Messina, eds (2006); Martin and Ross, eds (2004).
5 The connection between unemployment and emigration is spelled out in a number of sources related to immigration cited in Chapter 4, as well as Tansey (1998): 51–2.
6 Reported data varies, but the OECD put the official rate at 19.6 per cent in 1987. OECD (1987/88): 32.
7 A good discussion of the post-Civil War recovery strategy is provided in Jouganatos (1992): 9–54. For an extended discussion of Greece's ability to achieve strong growth rates at least until 1973, see Tsaliki (1991).
8 Data calculated from Eurostat (2006).
9 An extended and recent discussion of the problem with specific reference to Portugal is Conceição and Heitor (2005), and see also for a more technical discussion Teixeira (1999).
10 For this debate with reference to the knowledge economy agenda see Olssen and Peters (2005) and Peters (2001): 1–22.
11 Along these lines, Joao Casqueira Cardoso (2006) has argued that Portugal has not yet decided whether it really is a country of immigration.

References

Ahn, Namkee and Pedro Mira, "A note on the Changing Relationship between Fertility and Female Employment Rates in Developed Countries", *Journal of Population Economics* 15 (2002), 667–82.

Baldwin-Edwards, Martin and Rossetos Fakiolas, "Greece: The Contours of a Fragmented Policy Response", *South European Society and Politics* 3 (1999), 186–204.

Bermeo, Nancy, ed., *Unemployment in the New Europe* (Cambridge: Cambridge University Press, 2001).

Bettio, Francesca and Paola Villa, "A Mediterranean Perspective on the Breakdown of the Relationship between Participation and Fertility", *Cambridge Journal of Economics* 22 (1998), 137–71.

Blanchard, Olivier and Juan F. Jimeno, "Structural Unemployment: Spain versus Portugal", *The American Economic Review* 85, 2 (1995), 212–18.

Boeri, Tito, Daniela Del Boca, and Christopher Pissarides, eds, *Women at Work: An Economic Perspective* (Oxford: Oxford University Press, 2005).

Bongaarts, John, "The End of the Fertility Transition in the Developed World", *Population and Development Review* 28, 3 (2002), 419–43.

Bover, Olympia, Pilar García-Perea, and Pedro Portugal, "Labour Market Outliers: Lessons from Spain and Portugal", *Economic Policy* (October 2000), 380–428.

Brewster, Karin L. and Ronald R. Rindfuss, "Fertility and Women's Employment in Industrialized Nations", *Annual Review of Sociology* 26 (2000), 271–96.

Brown, Phillip and Anthony Hesketh, *The Mismanagement of Talent: Employability and Jobs in the Knowledge Economy* (New York: Oxford University Press, 2004).

Burtless, Gary, "The Greek Labor Market", in Ralph C. Bryant, Nicholas C. Garganas, and George S. Tavias, eds, *Greece's Economic Performance and Prospects* (Athens and Washington DC: Bank of Greece/The Brookings Institution, 2001), 453–98.

Cardoso, Joao Casqueira, "Immigration to Portugal", *Journal of Immigration and Refugee Studies* 4 (2006), 3–18.

Castells, Manuel, *The Rise of the Network Society* (Oxford: Blackwell, 1996).

Charalambis, Dimitris, Laura Maratou-Alipranti, and Andromachi Hadjiyanni, eds, *Recent Social Trends in Greece 1960–2000* (Montreal and Kingston: McGill-Queen's University Press, 2004), 261–77.

Clinch, Peter, Frank Convery, and Brendan Walsh, *After the Celtic Tiger: Challenges Ahead* (Dublin: The O'Brien Press, 2002).

Collinson, Sarah, *Europe and International Migration* (London: Royal Institute of International Affairs, 1993).

Conceição, Pedro and Manuel V. Heitor, *Innovation for All? Learning from the Portuguese Path to Technical Change and the Dynamics of Innovation* (Westport, CT: Praeger, 2005).

Corkill, David, *The Portuguese Economy since 1974 (*Edinburgh: Edinburgh University Press, 1993).

Corkill, David, *The Development of the Portuguese Economy: A Case of Europeanization* (London and New York: Routledge, 1999).

Council of the European Union, "The Economic Costs of Non-Lisbon: A Survey of the Literature on the Economic Impact of Lisbon-type Reforms", Commission Staff Working Paper (Brussels, 17 March 2005).

Craig, John and Andrew Gunn, "Higher Skills and the Knowledge Economy: The Challenge of Offshoring", *Higher Education Management and Policy* 22, 3 (2010), 1–7.

Curry, John, *Irish Social Services* 3rd edition (Dublin: Institute of Public Administration, 1998).

Demekas, Dimitris and Zenon Kontolemis, "Labour Market Performance and Institutions in Greece", *South European Society and Politics* 2, 2 (1997), 78–109.

Didika-Logiadou, Despina, "Labour Market Structure", in Armando Montanari ed., *Labour Market Structure and Development in Portugal, Spain, Italy, Greece and Turkey* (Napoli: Edizioni Scientifiche Italiane, 1993), 181–202.

Dingeldey, Irene, "European Tax Systems and their Impact on Family Employment Patterns", *Journal of Social Policy* 30, 4 (2001), 653–72.

Drucker, Peter F., *Post-Capitalist Society* (New York: HarperBusiness, 1993).

Dyson, Kenneth, ed., *European States and the Euro: Europeanization, Variation, and Convergence* (Oxford: Oxford University Press, 2002).

Erhel, Christine and Mathilde Guergoat-Lariviere, "Labour Market Regimes, Family Policies, and Women's Behavior in the EU", *Feminist Economics* 19, 4 (2013), 76–109.

Esping-Andersen, Gøsta, "Welfare States without Work: the Impasse of Labour Shedding and Familialism in Continental European Social Policy", in Gøsta Esping-Andersen, ed., *Welfare States in Transition: National Adaptations in Global Economics* (London: Sage, 1996).

Esping-Andersen, Gøsta, *Social Foundations of Postindustrial Economies* (Oxford: Oxford University Press, 1999).

Esping-Andersen, Gøsta, "A Child-Centred Social Investment Strategy", in Gøsta Esping-Andersen ed., *Why We Need A New Welfare State* (Oxford: Oxford University Press, 2002).

Eurostat, Online Database of Statistics. Available at http://epp.eurostat.ec.europa.eu/portal/page/portal/statistics/themes. Accessed 12 September 2014.

Evans, Peter, *Embedded Autonomy: States and Industrial Transformation* (Princeton, NJ: Princeton University Press, 1995).

Fahey, Tony, Helen Russell, and Emyr Smyth, "Gender Equality, Fertility Decline and Labour Market: Patterns Among Women in Ireland", in Brian Nolan, Philip J. O'Connell, and Christopher T. Whelan, eds, *Bust to Boom? The Irish Experience of Growth and Inequality* (Dublin: Institute of Public Administration, 2000), 244–67.

Fakiolas, Rossetos, "Regularising Undocumented Immigrants in Greece: Procedures and Effects", *Journal of Ethnic and Migration Studies* 29 (2003), 535–61.

Ferreira, Vírginia, "Positive Action and Employment Segregation", in Vírginia Ferreira, Teresa Tavares, and Sílvia Portugal, eds, *Shifting Bonds, Shifting Bounds: Women, Mobility and Citizenship in Europe* (Oeiras, Portugal: Celta Editoria, 1998), 271–335.

Ferrera, Maurizio, "The 'Southern Model' of Welfare in Southern Europe", *Journal of European Social Policy* 6, 1 (1996): 17–37.

Fiolhais, Rui, "Imigração e Marcado de Trabalho em Portugal", in Ministério da Segurança Social e o Trabalho/Departamento de Estudos Prospectiva e Planeamento, *Imigração e Mercado de Trabalho* (Lisbon: MSST/DEPP, 2003), 93–105.

Fishman, Robert M., 'Shaping, not Making, Democracy: The European Union and the Post-Authoritarian Political Transformations of Spain and Portugal,' in Sebastián Royo and Paul Christopher Manuel, eds., *Spain and Portugal in the European Union: The First Fifteen Years* (London and Portland: Frank Cass, 2003), 31–46.

Fishman, Robert M., "Rethinking the Iberian Transformations: How Democratization Scenarios Shaped Labor Market Outcomes", *Studies in Comparative International Development* 45 (2010), 281–331.

Fishman, Robert M. and Anthony M. Messina eds, *The Year of the Euro: The Cultural, Social and Political Impact of Europe's Common Currency* (Notre Dame, IN: University of Notre Dame Press, 2006).

Flaquer, Lluís, "Family Policy and Welfare State in Southern Europe" Working Paper No. 185 (Barcelona: Institut de Ciències Polítiques i Socials, 2000).

Gavroglu, Kostas, "Certain Features of Higher Education in Greece and the Failure to Reform It", *Journal of the Hellenic Diaspora* 8, 1–2 (1981), 95–108.

Geddes, Andrew, *Immigration and European Integration: Towards Fortress Europe?* (Manchester, UK: Manchester University Press, 2000).

Geddes, Barbara, "How the Cases You Choose Affect the Answers You Get: Selection Bias in Comparative Politics", *Political Analysis* 2 (1990), 131–49.

Gertler, Meric S., "Tacit Knowledge and the Economic Geography of Context, or The Undefinable Tacitness of Being (There)", *Journal of Economic Geography* 3 (2003), 75–99.

Ginsborg, Paul, "The Politics of the Family in Twentieth-Century Europe", *Contemporary European History* 9, 3, (2000).

Givens, Terri and Adam Luedtke, "The Politics of European Union Immigration Policy: Institutions, Salience, and Harmonization", *The Policy Studies Journal* 32, 1 (2004), 145–65.

Graham, Lawrence S., *The Portuguese Military and the State: Rethinking Transitions in Europe and Latin America* (Boulder, CO: Westview Press, 1993).

Gubbay, Jon, "The European Union Role in the Formation, Legitimation and Implementation of Migration Policy", in Gareth Dale and Mike Cole, eds, *The European Union and Migrant Labour* (Oxford and New York: Berg, 1999), 43–66.

Hearn, Greg and David Rooney, eds, *Knowledge Policy: Challenges for the 21st Century* (Cheltenham, UK: Edward Elgar 2008).

Hine, David and Hussein Kassim, *Beyond the Market: The EU and National Social Policy* (London and New York: Routledge, 1998).

Hionidou, Violetta, *Famine and Death in Occupied Greece, 1941–1944* (Cambridge: Cambridge University Press, 2006).

Howells, Jeremy R. L., "Tacit Knowledge, Innovation and Economic Geography", *Urban Studies* 39, 5–6 (2002), 871–84.

Johnson, Bjorn Edward Lorenz, and Bengt-Ake Lundvall, "Why All This Fuss About Codified and Tacit Knowledge?", *Industrial and Corporate Change* 11, 2 (2002), 245–62.

Jouganatos, George A., *The Development of the Greek Economy, 1950–1991. An Historical, Empirical and Econometric Analysis* (Westport, CT: Greenwood Press, 1992).

Kalwij, Adriaan, "The Impact of Family Policy Expenditure on Fertility in Western Europe", *Demography* 47, 2 (2010), 503–19.

Kamerman, Sheila B. and Alfred J. Kahn, eds, *Family Policy: Government and Families in Fourteen Countries* (New York: Columbia University Press, 1978).

Keune, Maarten, "Flexicurity: a Contested Concept at the Core of the European Labour Market Debate", *Intereconomics* (March/April 2008), 92–8.

Lahav, Gallya, *Immigration and Politics in the New Europe: Reinventing Borders* (Cambridge: Cambridge University Press, 2004).

Lahav, Gallya and Anthony M. Messina, "The Limits of a European Immigration Policy: Elite Opinion and Agendas within the European Parliament", *Journal of Common Market Studies* 43, 4 (2005), 851–75.

Lawson, Clive and Edward Lorenz, "Collective Learning, Tacit Knowledge and Regional Innovative Capacity", *Regional Studies* 33, 4 (1999), 305–17.

Lúcio, Maria Pulquéria C., "Labour Market Structure", in Armando Montanari, ed., *Labour Market Structure and Development in Portugal, Spain, Italy, Greece and Turkey* (Napoli: Edizoni Scientifiche Italiane, 1993), 17–34.

Katzenstein, Peter, *Small States in World Markets* (Ithaca, NY and London: Cornell University Press, 1985).

Kenway, Jane, Elizabeth Bullen, Johannah Fahey, with Simon Robb, *Haunting the Knowledge Economy* (Oxford, UK: Routledge, 2006).

King, Gary, Robert O. Keohane, and Sidney Verba, *Designing Social Inquiry: Scientific Inference in Qualitative Research* (Princeton, NJ: Princeton University Press, 1994).

Madsen, Per Kongshoj, "The Danish Model of 'Flexicurity': Experiences and Lessons", *Transfer: European Review of Labour and Research,* 10, 2 (2004), 187–207.

Martin, Andrew and George Ross, eds, *Euros and the Europeans: Monetary Integration and the European Model of Society* (Cambridge: Cambridge University Press, 2004).

Martin, Claude, "Social Welfare and the Family in Southern Europe", in Martin Rhodes, ed., *Southern European Welfare States: Crisis and Reform* (London: Frank Cass, 1997), 23–41.

Nolan, Brian, "Income Inequality during Ireland's Boom", *Studies: An Irish Quarterly Review* 92, 366 (2003), 132–50.
OECD, *Reviews of National Policies for Education: Greece* (Paris: Organisation for Economic Co-operation and Development, 1982).
OECD, *Reviews of National Policies for Education: Greece* (Paris: Organisation for Economic Cooperation and Development, 1987).
OECD, *Economic Surveys: Ireland* (Paris: Organisation for Economic Co-operation and Development, 1987/88).
OECD, *The Knowledge-Based Economy* (Paris: Organization for Economic Cooperation and Development, 1996).
OECD, *Economic Surveys: Ireland* (Paris: Organisation for Economic Co-operation and Development, 1997).
OECD, *Trends in International Migration* (Paris: Organisation for Economic Cooperation and Development, Continuous Reporting System on Migration, Annual Report, 2002).
OECD, *Education at a Glance* (2003 edition, web version, www.oecd.org).
OECD, Family Database. Available at www.oecd.org/social/soc/oecdfamilydatabase.htm. Accessed 1 June 2008.
OECD, *A Profile of Immigrant Populations in the 21st Century* (Paris: Organisation for Economic Cooperation and Development, 2008).
OECD, *Education at a Glance* (Paris: Organisation for Economic Cooperation and Development, 2009).
Olssen, Mark and Michael A. Peters, "Neoliberalism, Higher Education and the Knowledge Economy: From the Free Market to Knowledge Capitalism", *Journal of Education Policy* 20, 3 (2005), 313–45.
Oltheten, Elisabeth, George Pinteris, and Theodore Sougiannis, "Greece in the European Union: Policy Lessons from two Decades of Membership", *The Quarterly Review of Economics and Finance* 43, 5 (2003), 774–806.
Papagoulatos, George, "Economic Adjustment and Financial Reform: Greece's Europeanization and the Emergence of a Stabilization State", *South European Politics and Society* 5, 2 (2000), 191–214.
Peters, Michael, "National Education Policy Constructions of the 'Knowledge Economy': Towards a Critique", *Journal of Educational Enquiry* 2, 1 (2001), 1–22.
Petmesidou, Maria, "Employment and labor market policies in Southern Europe", in Martin Kohli and Mojca Novak, eds, *Will Europe Work? Integration, Employment, and Social Order* (London and New York: Routledge, 2001), 73–91.
Pires, Rui Pena, "Mudanças na Imigração: Uma Análise das Estatísticas sobre a População Estrangeira em Portugal, 1998–2001", *Sociologia, Problemas e Práticas* 39 (2002), 151–66.
Porter, Michael E., *The Competitive Advantage of Nations* (New York: The Free Press, 1990).
Powell, Walter W. and Kaisa Snellman, "The Knowledge Economy", *Annual Review of Sociology* 30 (2004), 199–220.
Quinn, Emma and Gerard Hughes, *Policy Analysis Report on Asylum and Migration: Ireland 2003 to Mid-2004* (Dublin: ESRI/European Migration Network, 2005).
Rodrigues, Maria João, *European Policies for a Knowledge Economy* (Cheltenham: Edward Elgar 2003).
Room, Graham, ed., *The European Challenge: Innovation, Policy Learning and Social Cohesion in the New Knowledge Economy* (Bristol, UK: The Policy Press, 2005).
Rooney, David, Greg Hearn, Thomas Mandeville, and Richard Joseph, *Public Policy in*

the Knowledge-Based Economies (Cheltenham, UK and Northhampton, MA: Edward Elgar, 2003).

Ruhs, Martin, "Emerging Trends and Patterns in the Immigration and Employment of Non-EU Nationals in Ireland: What the Data Reveal", Working Paper No.6 (Dublin: The Policy Institute, Trinity College, 2003).

Sapir, André, "Globalization and the Reform of European Social Models", *Journal of Common Market Studies* 44, 2 (2006), 369–90.

Schneider, Friedrich, "The Size and Development of the Shadow Economies of 22 Transition and 21 OECD Countries", Discussion Paper No. 514 (Bonn: Institute for the Study of Labour, June 2002).

Schneider, Friedrich and Dominik H. Enste, "Shadow Economies: Size, Causes, and Consequences", *Journal of Economic Literature* 38, 1 (2000), 77–114.

Stiglitz, Joseph E., "Knowledge as a Global Public Good", in Inge Kaul, Isabelle Grunberg, and Marc A. Stern, eds, *Global Public Goods: International Cooperation in the 21st Century* (New York and Oxford, UK: United National Development Programme/Oxford University Press, 1999), 308–25.

Stoleroff, Alan, "Unemployment and Trade Union Strength in Portugal", in Nancy Bermeo, ed., *Unemployment in the New Europe* (Cambridge: Cambridge University Press, 2001), 173–202.

Tansey, Paul, *Ireland at Work: Economic Growth and the Labour Market, 1987–1997* (Dublin: Oak Tree Press, 1998).

Taylor-Gooby, Peter, ed., *New Risks, New Welfare: The Transformation of the European Welfare State* (Oxford: Oxford University Press, 2004).

Teague, Paul, *Economic Citizenship in the European Union* (London and New York: Routledge, 1999).

Teixeira, Aurora, *Capital Humano e Capacidade de Inovação: Contributos para o Estudo do Crescimento Económico Português, 1960–1991* (Lisbon: Conselho Económico e Social, 1999).

Thévenon, Olivier and Anne H. Gautier, "Family Policies in Development Countries: A 'Fertility-Booster' with Side-Effects", *Community, Work and Family* 14, 2 (2011), 197–216.

Tracy, Marshall, *Racism and Immigration in Ireland: A Comparative Analysis* (Dublin: Department of Sociology, Trinity College, 2000).

Tsaliki, Persefoni V., *The Greek Economy: Sources of Growth in the Postwar Era* (New York: Praeger, 1991).

Wilthagen, Ton, and Frank Tros, "The Concept of 'Flexicurity': a New Approach to Regulating Employment and Labour Markets", *European Review of Labour and Research* 10, 2 (2004): 166–86.

Wincott, Daniel, "The Idea of the European Social Model: Limits and Paradoxes of Europeanization", in Kevin Featherstone and Claudio Radaelli, eds, *The Politics of Europeanization* (Oxford: Oxford University Press, 2003), 280–300.

World Bank, *Knowledge for Development.* World Development Report (New York: Oxford University Press, 1998).

3 Explaining policy divergence

This chapter provides a framework for explaining why there is significant variation in the extent to which Ireland, Portugal, and Greece have been able to embrace a labour market development strategy that adequately addresses the challenges of the twenty-first century. This explanation centres on the significance of processes and institutions designed to both consult and incorporate key interest groups into policymaking for shaping immigration, higher education, and family policy outcomes. The argument is that countries that have a dense zone of mediation, established through the construction of institutions and processes that bridge the gap between interest groups and the state, are best placed to successfully reorient their development strategies. Lying at the centre of this overall argument is a very simple observation: the way in which policy is made can and does determine the content of policy decisions. Furthermore, pre-existing patterns of state–society interaction, crystallized in national policymaking traditions, circumscribe the development of institutions and processes that effectively balance genuine consultation with interest group incorporation. The task of this chapter is thus to (a) explain the importance of institutions and processes that combine consultative and incorporative characteristics for countries wishing to reorient their economic and social development strategies in much more detail, and (b) identify bases for doing so in the Irish, Greek, and Portuguese cases. In the process, the concept of an institution or process that is both consultative and incorporative must be fully defined: what does one look like and how do we know when we have found one? The following discussion is divided into three main sections. The first section contains an extended discussion of why both genuine consultation and interest group incorporation are crucial for states attempting to fundamentally reorient their own national development strategies. Some arguments along these lines are identified in the existing literature, but further theoretical development is needed in order to explain why these specific types of institutions are especially relevant in the contemporary context. The second section then operationalizes the key concept at play, outlining what makes a policymaking institution or process capable of effectively balancing consultation against incorporation. The third section begins to apply this explanatory framework to the three national case studies, identifying the presence or absence of a consultative and incorporative policymaking tradition in each national case.

The importance of balancing consultation and incorporation

Readers familiar with European-level 'ways of doing things' might have already noted that the emphasis of this book on consultative and incorporative policy-making mimics that of the EU itself. The EU actively promotes forms of policy consultation and interest incorporation that it refers to as 'social partnership' or 'social dialogue' and adopts some of the features of the consensus building, neo-corporatist labour relations regimes of post-war Northern Europe. Neo-corporatism provides the most obvious model for this new layer of EU-sponsored institutions and processes. Like neo-corporatism, social dialogue is most fully developed at the European level with respect to the Employment and Social Affairs branch of the Commission's activities, where core business and labour representatives meet with central EU actors in order to negotiate policy decisions (Gorges, 1996). Yet this model has been extended to negotiation between relevant non-traditional 'social partners' in other spheres of EU activity, notably environmental policy, with the incorporation of environmental organizations into policy negotiation. Furthermore, the EU also actively encourages the adoption of similar forms of policy concentration at the national level, within member states. In part, this is because, for 'social partnership' to function well at the supra-national level, functioning 'social partners' must have representation and membership at the national and local levels. Including national representatives of interest groups into European-level social dialogue can also serve as a good way to transmit European preferences and values to the national level; interest group leaders can return to their home countries and use arguments to the effect that 'the EU supports our stance so you have to listen this time' in order to pressure national governments on certain policy issues.[1]

It is extremely important to underline, however, that the focus on the policy-making space or the 'zone of mediation' between civil society and the state employed in this book is justified not merely because of the importance that the EU attaches to the creation of institutions and processes designed to consult and incorporate societal interest groups. Rather, the main reason for this focus is that state–society relations of this type prove capable of helping to explain variation in the extent to which countries outside this sample, and outside Europe, have reoriented their development strategies around specific values and goals. In other words, the theoretical importance of consultative and incorporative policy-making is generalizable beyond the specific cases of Ireland, Portugal, and Greece and, furthermore, beyond the case of reorienting policy goals and values around the needs of a twenty-first century development strategy.

The following section draws on the wider literature in political science, political economy, and democratic theory in order to introduce some of these additional reasons for concentrating on consultative and incorporative institutions, focusing especially on the role that states play in promoting specific development strategies and the mechanisms they use in order to do this. Consultation and incorporation are two quite different aspects of interest group participation in policy formulation that, even though they are potentially in tension with one another, are equally central to the reorientation of national development strategies especially under conditions of political democracy. That latter part of the discussion is tied into a review of the characterizations of consultative and incorporative institutions that are presented by the literatures on public participation and particularly 'deliberative democracy' in policymaking on the one hand, and neo-corporatism on the other. Furthermore, at least in some important respects, the theoretical framework adopted in this chapter amounts to a conceptual transfer of some of the insights of the developmental state literature to a fully democratic context.

Between society and the state: mediating the reorientation of national development projects

In arguing that states self-consciously take on a developmental role, that they are capable of pushing social and economic development in new directions, and that they employ specific means in order to achieve this, the explanatory framework adopted here quite clearly taps into the well-established 'developmental state' literature.[2] This body of work identifies particular types of states that take on an unusually direct and extensive role in developing and redirecting their national economies around a particular set of development goals. These goals are usually centred on economic modernization and often involve large-scale national construction projects or the heavy concentration of resources into particular sectors of the economy. State 'developmentalism' has often been identified with authoritarianism, especially the growth of the East Asian 'tiger' economies of Singapore, South Korea, and Taiwan. The first of these cases remains under authoritarian rule and the latter two cases did not fully democratize until the late 1990s.[3] In fact, some versions of developmental state analysis explicitly identify earlier democratization with developmental delays, suggesting that a sustained period of authoritarianism might actually lay better foundations for subsequent industrial growth (Kohli, 2004). Yet developmental characteristics are also to be found in democratic states, and it might also be noted that most, if not all, states have at least some developmentalist tendencies. Not only can strongly interventionist states that were compatible with democracy be found in the post-colonial histories of nations from Australia and New Zealand to Nigeria or India, but arguably the Scandinavian countries do the same through the construction of consensus-building neo-corporatist mechanisms.

Especially relevant for the theoretical framework adopted here is the recent literature on democratic developmental states that rely less on coercion than on connectedness with social groups in order to guide economic development in a specific direction. Most notably, Peter Evans' work on the promotion of information technology-based development strategies in several newly industrializing countries finds that a delicate mix of 'embeddedness', where state agencies are well connected to the business class and especially organized entrepreneurial and investment groups, and autonomy, where the state acts as a coherent and relatively cohesive actor, explains national success in the field (Evans, 1995).

The innovation in Evans' work is the identification of state 'embeddedness' as part of the explanation for developmental success and that insight is taken into account here, but, given that the focus of this book extends well beyond the arena of industrial policy, I consider the relationship between the state and a much wider variety of groups to be important. Drawing on the concept of 'embedded autonomy' and directly related to the Irish case, Séan Ó Riain has argued that much of Ireland's post-1987 success, again with specific reference to industrial policy, can be attributed to the development of formal institutions that regulate the relationship between players in the industry and the state. Although the most clearly recognized example of these new institutions is the social partnership process, which is discussed extensively here below, he insists that there are many others. Reinforced by this layer of consultative and incorporative institutions, social partnership has become 'the institutional mechanism of public governance through almost all spheres of Irish public life' (Ó Riain, 2004: 10).

There is also a good argument to be made that consultative and incorporative policymaking is important, not simply for *any* democratic regime undertaking major shifts in economic and social development strategy, but in particular for states attempting to make the shift to a high-skill, high-wage, 'knowledge based' economy. One of the theoretical propositions underlying this analysis is that certain development strategies require particular forms of interest group politics. This is underlined especially well by comparing the political requirements of so-called 'neoliberal' policy reforms with those of a 'knowledge based' strategy. The former, implemented to varying degrees across various regions of the world principally from 1975 until the mid-1990s, often required the removal of certain economic guarantees, rights, and privileges that had been awarded to citizens during the expansionist phase of the post-Second World War welfare state. Key policy prescriptions identified with this reform programme included labour market 'flexibilization', including the removal of employment guarantees and the abandonment of the goal of full employment; the 'rolling back' or privatization of public services; and increased 'targeting' of welfare entitlements. Most crucially for the purposes of this argument, this scaling back of economic rights and privileges was also often accompanied by an erosion of interest group consultation. This was expressed explicitly in the public choice literature and by 'neoliberal' policy activists as the need to prevent interest group capture of the state, since this inevitably leads to rent-seeking and market 'distortions' (Buchanan and Tullock, 1962). In the words of one such reformer, policymakers must embark on a 'blitzkrieg' approach, in which deliberate efforts to bypass parliamentary debate and interest group consultation were to be made where possible (Douglas, 1993). By contrast, knowledge-based policy formulation and implementation is a comparably more 'constructive' phase of development, in which there is greater collaboration with, and incorporation of, 'knowledgeable' (or at least interested) stakeholders on the part of the state. To give just one illustrative example: whereas the privatization of second-level education through the introduction of a voucher system, a classic 'neo-liberal' policy prescription in the field, does not require the co-operation of individual teachers and their organizations, the introduction of a radically new technology curriculum certainly does, simply because policymakers are relying on stakeholders to implement that new curriculum. It is to a deeper explanation of why consultation and incorporation both matter, in general, but specifically in relation to states in the process of meeting the labour market policy challenges of the early twenty-first century, that I now turn.

How and why consultation and incorporation both matter

Before going on to discuss what the institutions and processes that adequately balance consultation against incorporation look like, consultation and incorporation must be discussed separately as two distinct but equally important features of policymaking. Genuine consultation over the broad aims of policy in a particular area, as well as over the details, is necessary because it can lead to better-informed policy decisions. The state needs to take into account the interests and concerns of key players involved in a specific policy area because stakeholders are often the best experts in the field, even if they sometimes lack the bird's eye view important for linking action in one policy arena to action in related areas, or to the overall shift in development strategies required in a particular historical moment. For example, with respect to the policy areas focused on in this study, we would expect better decisions to be made if the advice of state ministries and agencies were supplemented by the advice and concerns of such groups as the administrative bodies of technical institutes and universities in the case of higher education, trade unions and childcare providers in the case of policies for reconciling family and working life, and migrant rights groups and employers in the case of immigration policy. Furthermore, fundamentally reorienting policy perspectives, under democratic conditions at least, requires the co-operation of what the policymaking literature sometimes refers to as 'street-level bureaucrats', such as teachers or social workers that work for the state, as well as key players in the economy, including unions, workers, employer organizations, and individual firms.

Students of the application of 'discursive' or 'participatory' democracy to policymaking practice would likely agree with this general line of reasoning, since the thrust of their critique is that policy formulation in advanced capitalist democracies has been hijacked by technocrats at the expense of public participation and consultation. This relatively new sub-field of public policy analysis argues for the introduction of practical mechanisms such as 'citizen's juries', not only in order to undercut the role of technocrats or non-elected 'policy experts', but also to reach policy decisions through deliberation and compromise rather than non-deliberative forms of public participation such as referenda (Bohman, 1996; Dryzek, 1990; Mansbridge, 1992). The focus of this literature is very different from that of the developmental state literature, which concentrates on the relationship between the state and generally elite groups such as organized business and individual firms, but also links increased consultation with better policy outcomes.

The main problem with the deliberative approach, however, is that, in its enthusiastic advocacy of increased public participation in policymaking, it is open to criticisms similar to those that have been made of classical pluralist visions of democratic decision-making.[4] Above all, pluralists and proponents of deliberative democracy tend to underestimate the importance of pre-existing power relations within society and between society and the state that are not easily removed despite best efforts to create neutral spaces in which deliberation might take place. In other words, increasing public participation in policymaking through deliberation might be a nice idea, but it is not usually a very good description of how policy is really made, even when efforts have been made to increase consultation with the citizenry. In most cases of consultation between the citizenry and the state, the state inevitably retains a high degree of control over who is permitted into the discussion and under what conditions, and, furthermore, this is exactly what is needed for a major reorientation of national economic and social development strategy. These are highly structured spaces, and not just simply for the purposes of perpetuating social and political power imbalances but because, in the real world, states in the process of reorienting their development strategies around a specific set of goals and values need to incorporate societal groups so that they are loyal to the system as much as they need to genuinely take account of their interests and ideas through consultation.[5]

The incorporative aspects of public policymaking institutions and processes are important because implementing new development strategies often requires acting against the interests of key societal or interest groups. That is where incorporation is most useful. To give an example from the case studies which follow, encouraging the growth of technical education can often be very threatening, in both a real and a perceived way, for universities, which have traditionally enjoyed a favoured status in terms of financing and the legal framework governing them, and thus often a greater degree of academic freedom and autonomy than other types of teaching institution. Diverting resources away from traditional liberal education toward technical training can undercut the favoured status of universities, as can moves to steer the content of teaching programmes in a specific direction.[6] If a policymaking tradition encourages consultation and negotiation, compromise is more likely to be reached over the details of policy without undermining its overall direction. The overall policy direction can still be guided by the state. Where consensus or compromise cannot be reached, the subtle and not so subtle coercive side of incorporative policymaking comes into play. Incorporative policymaking institutions are not only designed to induce co-operation, but are also often accompanied by measures to force co-operation or to constrain interests (Collier and Collier, 1979). At the very least, states can refuse to allow particular groups into the policymaking circle as a form of punishment for lack of moderation or co-operation on their part. This allows the state to control, at the very least, the terms of the discussion and to pursue and in fact gain legitimacy and a measure of consent for its development project. Controlling interests and preventing resistance from them spilling over into open political conflict is not always possible, as Chapter 5's discussion of Greece especially shows, but the more robust a state's consultative and incorporative tradition is, the more likely that it will make use of such strategies.

In the absence of effective incorporative institutions and processes through which trading over policy decisions between players can occur over the long term, states can find the implementation of policy goals against the interests of key interest groups extremely difficult. Without a culture of compromise, the response of such interest groups to required (or desired) policy shifts might be to take to the streets in the case of labour or popular groups or to withdraw investment or political support in the case of elites. Although slightly outside the scope of the policy-level case studies considered here, there is no better example of this occurring than in the field of Greek pension reform. The Greek pension system has been heavily skewed towards the protection of male, full-time, higher-paid and especially public sector workers, often with no coverage at all for workers who have failed to fulfil a requirement of continuous employment within a particular timeframe during the course of their working lives. This requirement particularly affects women, who may have taken time out from the workforce, and thus has significance for the problem of developing the reconciliation of family and working life in Greece. Yet any attempt to reform the pension system, even in a social democratic direction, has been met with fierce resistance from the trade union movement (Matsaganis, 2004, 2005; O'Donnell and Tinios, 2003; Petmesidou, 1991). Over the last two decades, threats on their part have led to no reforms being made at all. Despite attempts to establish ongoing wage pacts in Greece, the fragility and narrow scope of tripartite bargaining mechanisms in this case means that compromise and negotiation over pension reform, among other policies, is impossible.[7]

Students of corporatism, both inside and outside Europe, would likely agree with many of the aspects of the line of reasoning presented above. Neo-corporatist bargaining builds a tradition of compromise and consensus building, often by trading wage restraint on the part of organized labour for other non-wage related policy agreements on the part of the state (often explicit social policy commitments in European cases). This allows the state to pursue specific goals, most obviously gaining control over inflation, the outcome most often emphasized in connection with neo-corporatist wage bargaining. Although the literature on neo-corporatism thus provides an important backdrop to some of the observations made here concerning the importance of incorporating key interest groups, this book moves beyond the pre-existing literature in several different respects. Above all, the neo-corporatist literature has become increasingly narrow in focus, becoming increasingly technical and less interested in the political project of corporatist-like mechanisms than the economic one (Calmfors and Driffill, 1998; Iversen, 1999).[8] The theoretical framework employed here is much more concerned with the broader political role, entailing the reorientation of policy goals around a 'knowledge-based' development strategy, that mediating institutions, whether corporatist in nature or not, play in the national case studies under scrutiny. In addition, and again by moving beyond the wage-setting or even industrial policy arena, a wider range of policy areas are considered in order to test the notion that there are patterns of state–society relations reflected in policymaking institutions and processes that are more or less specific to the particular national context in question.

Foreshadowing the arguments that follow, successful policy reorientation in Ireland, Portugal, and Greece has occurred when policymaking institutions and processes located in the zone of mediation between civil society and the state have a good mix of these two quite different aspects associated with their operation. Genuine consultation and effective incorporation both matter independently, so that a delicate balance must be reached. Unfortunately, if there is what amounts to too much participatory and democratic policy consultation, policy formulation can become an unwieldy mess, with the likely result being either policy stagnation or the government ignoring the debate between interest groups in favour of accepting policy advice from government departments, especially ministries of finance cautioning budget constraint. Yet if the state is too obvious in its control, and especially if the state's strategy is misguided or dominated by specific interests, consultative and incorporative institutions and processes might become regarded by their participants as token, shallow, and no longer having any relevance to the actors involved. There is also the possibility that there are very few institutions and processes established for the purposes of public and/or interest group participation in policymaking at all, let alone any which adequately balance consultative and incorporative functions.

Identifying consultative and incorporative policymaking

What might an institution or policymaking process that effectively balances consultation against incorporation look like? Even though there is no one model, certain institutional forms seem more capable of achieving that balance than others. Determining which are most effective is a matter of surveying the various ways in which states initiate public participation in policymaking. The following discussion divides the main channels for the participation of key interest groups or stakeholders into three main categories: (1) short-term or 'one off' consultative processes, (2) neo-corporatist pact-making and other similar, more permanent, forms of interest group participation, and (3) informal processes and institutions that employ consultative and/or incorporative mechanisms. Short-term or 'one-off' consultative processes are discussed first. This work acknowledges their importance often as first steps toward consultation with either broad-based society or the incorporation of society-based policy 'experts' in certain fields, but also identifies their limitations in that they do not generally have self-enforcing or self-reproducing mechanisms built into them.

Second, longer-lasting forms of policy consultation including both older and newer forms of neo-corporatist pact-making are considered as a special category, since they tend to exhibit certain features which ensure their longer term survival as well as provide mechanisms to ensure that decisions made within their parameters are carried through. Third, a group of informal processes by which societal interests are incorporated into policy formulation is discussed, particularly with respect to the role of political parties and academia as an additional interest group of its own. The main problem here is that, although the influence of interest groups through their subtle incorporation into the political system can lead to some especially interesting results, it does not guarantee consultation with important interest groups when necessary across all policy areas. Inconsistency occurs as a result, and the following discussion will show how relevant that analysis is for the Portuguese case in particular.

A note on interest groups

Before discussing each of these broad categories in detail, it is important to clarify which 'interest groups' or 'policy stakeholders' are important for this analysis. How broad does consultation have to be and which specific interest groups need to be incorporated into policymaking institutions and processes established by the state so that policy is better informed and negotiation and compromise can actually take place? Literature on the role of deliberative democracy in public policymaking seems to suggest that the wider or at least more representative society participation is, the better the outcome. Conversely, the neo-corporatist literature is concerned only with peak labour and business confederations and, in truth, only their leaderships who are involved in negotiating wage-setting agreements. In that, neo-corporatism is an elite game. The explanatory framework adopted here is positioned in the middle of these two visions of the role of interest groups or 'the public' in policy-making. Because this book looks at a wider range of policy areas than is generally considered by students of neo-corporatism, or, for that matter, developmental states who tend to focus mainly on industrial policy, a broader range of interest groups is considered to be important. Yet the analysis is more elitist than proponents of deliberative democracy allow because, as is made clear by the comparative case study discussion that follows, broad-based public consultation is not as important as the incorporation of specific interest groups, since the point here is to improve policy content rather than deepen democracy for its own sake.

While the range of specific interest groups of concern here is broader than that considered by the neo-corporatist literature, organized labour and business are still important players in the stories that follow, especially with respect to immigration policies and the development of policy mechanisms for the reconciliation of family and working life. Their participation in the formulation of higher education policy is not as great, even if some believe it should be greater in order to better coordinate the content of higher education with economic development. In the field of higher education policy, institutions of higher education themselves and the individuals and group interests that dominate various sectors of the higher education system play the greatest role in negotiating policy development. Other groups that might be incorporated into the discussion include students and their student unions, and teachers and their professional organizations. Organized labour and business are most important to the discussion of policies for reconciling work and family life because much of this policy area involves negotiating more flexible working environments, but other groups may include the childcare sector and possibly women's lobby groups, although the latter has proved much less significant in the cases studied here than initially might have been imagined. In the immigration policy arena, migrant and human rights organizations are significant players.

In all cases, however, the importance of interest groups is in their relation to the state and the extent to which they are effectively incorporated into actual policymaking. This sets their role quite apart from the more generalized democracy-supporting role that has been assigned to civil society as a whole by political scientists.[9] Rather, the processes and institutions of interest here populate a relatively neglected space between civil society and the state. We could perhaps refer to this 'zone of mediation' more properly as belonging to *political* rather than *civil* society. Interest groups are important to this analytical framework to the extent that they can be co-opted into political society at the same time as they retain some degree of independence from the state in the way in which they gain membership from civil society and organize themselves internally.

Short-term or 'one-off' consultative processes

Taking what can be described as 'one-off' exercises in policy consultation first, this category covers a number of different sorts of short-lived institution or process. The first of two main sub-types consists of broad-based public consultation exercises. Governments or state agencies engage in such exercises in order to generate initial ideas about what should be done to solve a particular policy problem, or to gauge public opinion on quite specific proposals. In the latter case, much of the detailed policy work has already been done. A second category consists of the more formal establishment of working groups, commissions of enquiry and other similar bodies in which representatives from government and state agencies work closely with interest group representatives but especially policy 'experts' in particular fields. The former may sometimes be related to or be carried out as the result of the work of the latter. For example, a tripartite working group looking at issues of work–life balance might call for the establishment of a public consultation process consisting of several half-day public seminars held in regional centres in order to survey public opinion on key issues in a qualitative manner. Alternatively, a commission of inquiry into immigration policy might call for submissions on a discussion document detailing proposed changes. In all cases, however, the effectiveness and employment of both consultative and incorporative mechanisms depends on the extent to which they are formal, ongoing, and, in general, structured from above.

Those sceptical about the genuine nature of the types of short-term broad-based public consultation processes outlined here tend to argue that they are usually useless exercises in window-dressing; they provide ways for governments to pretend to be interested in what the public thinks without really having to incorporate those interests and concerns into policy content. Undoubtedly this is sometimes true, but, more fundamentally, because short-term and one-off consultation processes often lack structure, although community groups and individuals may use such opportunities to vent anger or frustration at a particular government policy, their views are not shaped into concrete policy proposals that are useful for developing real policy detail. This is particularly true in the case of this first sub-type, consisting of broad-based consultation exercises such as public meetings, seminars, and other fora.

The establishment of government working groups, commissions of inquiry, and other instances where expert opinion from the community is structured into the state's investigation of a particular policy problem or area offers a little more opportunity for interested parties to reshape policy direction. The work of such bodies is generally carried out over a number of years, usually something between one and five, and incorporates individual experts from civil society into working for the state, after which the commission or working group reports back to the government in writing. This has the advantages of being a very formal process and involving individuals with expert knowledge of their field. Opinions are well thought out, extensive research is generally undertaken and depending on the terms of reference of the short-term institution, detailed policy prescriptions as well as general objectives can emerge. Yet there are two main problems associated with this form of interest consultation and incorporation. First, expert opinion may be too elite in these cases, and limited to too narrow a range of interests. In addition, the dynamics of the group may depend on the individuals chosen, whether the chairperson of the committee is any good at his or her job, and so on. Second, governments are generally not required to adopt the recommendations of the committee or working group; they may simply shelve the final reports if they do not like the conclusions.

The use of investigations such as these is especially relevant to the Irish political tradition, inherited from the British who make extensive use of Royal Commissions in particular. Chapter 4 illustrates the advantages and disadvantages of this specific form of one-off consultative and incorporative process rather well. The use of such working groups, committees, and commissions has worked relatively well in the higher education field, beginning as early as the 1960s and leading to early and much needed investment in that area and assisting in the growth of technical and scientific education above all. Similar types of work in the family policy field, however, have been relatively less successful. The Commission on the Family carried out in-depth research and public consultation of its own between 1995 and 1998, but its terms of reference were extremely broad, its recommendations very expensive, and, following a change in government during its existence, it had many of its recommendations dropped. The use of similar types of institution and process is much more alien to the Greek and Portuguese political traditions, where very formal investigation by official groups compromised mainly of experts from the community (not including individuals from the academic community) whose recommendations are made publicly available is not at all common.

To give a further specific and this time comparative example in order to see how some of these issues play out, both Ireland and Greece have used broad-based and generalized short-term public consultation processes in order to gauge public opinion on immigration policy. In Greece, public meetings on the issue have involved clashes of opinion and interest between immigration officials, sometimes the immigration minister himself, and migrant and human rights organizations. Arguably, this has not achieved very much in terms of overhauling an extremely disjointed and ineffectual immigration control system and a minimalist to non-existent migrant integration policy. As Chapter 5 will show in more detail, where improvements in immigration and integration policy have been made, it is usually when individuals with sympathies towards or personal connection with migrant and human rights groups are able to manoeuvre themselves into positions of power within the public administration. In the Irish case, however, public fora of a similar nature are connected to a much more extensive 'consultation process', launched in 2002 and agreed to under a central social partnership agreement. This also involved the formal gathering of written submissions on a government immigration policy discussion paper. The fact that the broad-based consultation process is tied into an ongoing and formal consultative and incorporative institution in the Irish case means that it is more effective.

More permanent forms of consultative and incorporative policymaking

A very basic problem with short-term or one-off policymaking institutions and processes, however, such as those just discussed, is that they are indeed only designed to exist for a very limited period of time. A survey of the various ways in which the state seeks to shape public participation in policymaking reveals that the institutions or processes that are best able to balance genuine consultation against incorporation are those that are ideally self-reproducing but, at the very least, ongoing over a significant period of time. Very short-term exercises in public consultation over specific policies or policy areas generally fail to fulfil incorporative functions because interest groups or individuals representatives of multiple interests are not brought in close enough to the state. They tend to return quickly to civil society or the workplace without having altered their own views and, conversely, they generally have not been able to make state representatives take on board their interests and concerns sufficiently.

Ideally, consultative forms of policymaking would be ongoing so that there is the opportunity for what public policy analysts refer to as 'feedback loops' to be institutionalized. State and non-state actors negotiate over policy detail, the policy framework is implemented, and, crucially, all actors consult over the impact of the policy shift and reformulate it if necessary. This process becomes institutionalized or self-reproducing when the role of interest groups in this cycle is self-consciously established and agreed on. This is one of the major advantages of neo-corporatist type policymaking institutions, which, if effective and capable of reproducing themselves (which they can do unless one of the major players involved defects from the agreement), explicitly outline a timetable for the implementation of the agreement and conditions under which it may be renegotiated.

Neo-corporatist or neo-corporatist-like institutions and processes thus constitute one very specific type of ongoing, peak-level, ideally permanent form of interest group participation in policymaking. The superiority of neo-corporatism is that, as an institutionalized process consisting of the negotiation of formal agreements, it reflects many of the key elements that allow genuine consultation to be adequately balanced against incorporation. Formal social pact-making is self-reproducing and binding in part because it (a) commits 'social partners' to the implementation of very specific policy targets and action, and it (b) tends to induce self-limiting behaviour on the part of the actors involved because the reproduction of the institution relies on compromise, renegotiation, and the co-operation of all actors. Related to that first point, consultative and incorporative mechanisms are more durable when agreements are specific. The more specific an agreement over policy development in a particular area, the more likely it is to be implemented because it is much more difficult for governments to ignore or backtrack on agreements when they commit to specific details. This is also one of the reasons why very generalized and one-off consultative exercises with 'the public' through public meetings and even more focused workshops or seminars do not work very well at all: individuals from civil society whose interaction with state representatives is limited to this might not have a very specific set of demands or interests in mind and, in any case, the whole exercise is aimed at gathering public opinion on general policy goals rather than specific detail.

A second reason for the durability of neo-corporatist-like arrangements is that longer-term, explicit agreements are more likely to have built-in enforcement mechanisms or other guarantees of policy implementation. Unlike short-term formal policymaking through commissions of inquiry or working groups for the investigation of particular policy problems, the binding and public nature of neo-corporatist type systems forces governments to carry through specific commitments. This not only builds confidence in the system, underpinning the continued involvement of key players, but also forges trust between actors, and 'self-limiting' behaviour, otherwise known as an ability to engage in compromise. Having a guarantee that an established agreement over a new policy direction will actually be implemented is very important for building trust between state and non-state actors and among non-state actors who may have conflicting interests, and in the institution or process itself. This eventually strengthens the overall consultative-and-incorporative policymaking tradition in a given national context.

Neo-corporatism, however, as noted much earlier in this chapter, is both a conceptual framework and an actually existing policy-making process that is generally very limited in scope. It usually refers to the specific policy problem of wage setting, and the regulation of the relationship between organized labour, business, and the state that surrounds this problem. Thus it traditionally would have little direct relevance for the selection of policy areas considered here, nor the broader range of groups that are stakeholders in or targets of them. Yet there is good reason to look further at the neo-corporatist model in relation to these case studies. Despite the fact that pressures for labour market flexibilization emanating from economic liberalization supposedly undermine consensus-making wage-setting institutions and instead encourage market-driven wage-setting and eventual wage dispersion, neo-corporatism has made a comeback on the European continent. More surprisingly, it has done so especially in countries that lack long traditions of democratic corporatism, including Ireland, Portugal, and Greece (Pochet and Fajertag, 2000; Royo, 2002).

In Portugal and to an even greater extent Greece, however, what might be referred to as neo-neo-corporatist institutions are still limited to wage setting and occasionally broader labour relations issues. In addition, Greece has also had some problems institutionalizing neo-corporatist wage-setting, with frequent disruptions caused especially by refusal on the part of one of the two major labour union confederations to co-operate (Ioannau, 2000). In Portugal, some negotiation over policies for work–life balance takes place within the confines of neo-corporatist institutions, but it is Ireland where 'social partnership' that extends the neo-corporatist model to cover a much wider range of policy issues has been developed furthest.

While neo-corporatist forms of policymaking that extend beyond the wage setting arena provide the best example of a process that is able to balance genuine consultation against incorporation, other types of institution and process that are also relatively durable should not be overlooked. These often take the form of consultative committees, where invited representatives of interest groups periodically meet with representatives of the state bureaucracy. Such networks are capable of channelling genuine consultation with 'street level bureaucrats' or other policy stakeholders, but the extent to which this consultation is formalized or aimed at agreement on concrete policy detail varies enormously. In addition, there are often no real enforcement mechanisms since these are primarily 'advisory' bodies. A full range of more or less permanent consultative committees and advisory bodies are found in both Ireland and Portugal, but not in Greece. Some prominent examples include the Irish National Consultative Committee on Racism and Interculturalism (NCCRI), a state-initiated but semi-autonomous organization established in 1997, which plays an important role in shaping an approach to migrant integration in Ireland. In Portugal, ACIME (the Alto Comissariado para a Imigração e Minorias Étnicas or High Commission on Immigration and Ethnic Minorities) is responsible for a consultative body similar to Ireland's NCCRI which has much the same role. In Ireland some of the more traditional state bodies emerging out of British-style public administration, such as the Higher Education Authority, for example, also have permanent consultative bodies attached to them, gathering together in this case representatives from university administrations, student and teacher unions, and researchers in the field.

Informal processes and institutions

One objection to the analysis presented so far might be that it places too much emphasis on institutions and processes that are relatively formal in nature. Surely there are many informal mechanisms by which individual interest group leaders seek to influence the state? That problem is that most of these informal institutions and processes are simply not capable of balancing genuine consultation against effective incorporation in the way that formal ones can. Many ways in which the state and civil society clash over policy, such as political protest or civil disobedience, fall outside the scope of this discussion since they do not involve the co-option of interest groups into the space located between civil society and the state. In fact, as this book will later argue with respect to the Greek case, popular protest tends to arise where there is a lack of opportunity for interest group incorporation into formal policymaking channels established by the state. Two specific ways in which individuals, primarily, are incorporated into state institutions are worth mentioning, however, given their relevance for the two Southern European cases in particular.

First, political parties are an obvious means through which individuals are co-opted into high-level politics. Of the three national case studies considered here, Portuguese politics is characterized most by the incorporation of emergent civil society organizations into parliamentary politics, particularly by their leaders being selected as Socialist Party candidates. Several prominent migrant community leaders of African descent during the 1990s, for example, are now members of parliament. This tends to make the Portuguese parliament more representative, but it actually prevents the Portuguese state from maintaining negotiations with interest groups on an independent basis. This book is guided by a strong belief that the reorientation of economic and social development projects requires links between the state and interests that go beyond the interest aggregation mechanisms provided by political parties. This is because much policy detail in advanced capitalist democracies is 'filled in' by state and non-state experts rather than being created through the direct implementation of political party platforms.

Academics constitute a second group of individuals that is frequently incorporated into policymaking institutions and processes, with mixed results. All three of the countries compared here make use of academic expertise in policymaking, but in slightly different ways. In Ireland academics are appointed to commissions of inquiry or become permanent members of consultative committees along with representatives from interest groups, whereas in both Greece and Portugal their influence is often again experienced through their relationships with individual political parties. Given that political appointments to positions in the public administration are much more extensive in Southern Europe than in Ireland's British-inherited system, it is common for academics to move between positions in the university and bureaucracy with changes in government. This is especially the case with the Socialist Party administration in Portugal. While many academics in other countries might envy this influence, it brings some risks when it comes to policymaking. Intellectuals, especially in Southern Europe where until very recently higher education has been reserved for a small elite and who still enjoy a privileged social status, are sometimes too far removed from the lives of ordinary citizens to offer policy advice that best represents their interests. A perfect example here is the disjuncture between the feminist, equality driven motive of policies for reconciling family and working life implemented under the Portuguese Socialist Party during the 1990s, and the fact that most Portuguese women are simply driven into full-time work whether they like it or not due to extremely low wages. That case will be discussed in much more detail in Chapter 6.

Change and continuity in policymaking

In some respects, the preceding discussion, along with the in-depth case study analyses which are to follow in the next three chapters, confirm many of the recent findings on how and why institutions, particularly formal ones, change over time. Until recently, it was common to assume not only that institutions were difficult to change, but that, when they did, it would only be as the result of external shocks. There are varying explanations for why this is the case, with rational choice theorists describing institutions as the result of equilibrium, or in ordinary terms, compromise, being reached between political players, while historical institutionalists point out that institutions shape the behaviour of actors over the long term and produce their own reinforcing mechanisms to ensure their survival.[10] Exogenous shocks do account for some major changes that can be observed across the three national case studies. In Ireland, the development of the social partnership process after 1987 can clearly be traced to the economic crisis that deepened in the several years prior to this date. The shift did not, however, mean the replacement of older forms of policymaking such as select committees or Green and White Paper public submissions, but rather their supplementation and therefore an overall thickening of the layer of consultative and incorporative policymaking found here. In the Portuguese case, it is probably a gross understatement to describe the 1974 revolution as an external shock. The magnitude of the shock, since it occurred along all three levels of the social system – economic, political, and social – surely overshadows the one experienced in Ireland a decade or so later. The revolution, a result in part from a crisis of the Salazarist state, clearly led to a dismantling of many aspects of it in the following decade and this obviously fundamentally changed how policy was made.

More recent institutionalist literature, however, has pointed out that external shocks do not always provide the best explanation for institutional change and continuity (Streeck and Thelen, 2005). There are both instances in which change occurs gradually rather than abruptly and in the absence of any obvious external shocks and instances in which external shocks do not change institutions as much as we might expect. This set of insights is relevant to all three national cases discussed here. First, the development of social partnership in Ireland can be traced to the external shock of an economic crisis that peaked in the late 1980s, but there were also additional long term and underlying pressures for change to the political and policymaking system leading up to this. As argued above, Ireland had a relatively closed policymaking system for most of its existence as an independent state, in which farmers, small business, an ideologically moderate union movement, and the Catholic Church were privileged actors. This arrangement came under pressure in the final decades of the twentieth century because, among other things, of decreasing public acceptance of political corruption as well as cultural changes that undermined the societal grip of the Church.

In addition, the present analysis shows that, even where external shocks are apparently extreme, including a breakdown in the national political regime and specifically democratization in both Portugal and Greece, policymaking traditions do not change as much as we might expect. Surprisingly perhaps, much of Portugal's character as a 'dual society', entailing a sharp disconnect between the worldviews of masses and elites, has survived not only the (initially socialist) revolution but also two decades of European integration. The continued elitism of many bureaucratic actors and academics that is characteristic of such a society can probably be explained by the fact that even revolutionary regimes need to find capable staff for the state to function properly or at all. Inevitably, members of the old regime, or in this case at least the same social class, that staffed the state before the revolution become the 'new' bureaucratic elite.[11] This is reinforced by the highly legalistic nature of the Portuguese administrative system and mode of policy development; those with legal training are highly privileged bureaucratic actors. The second, perhaps less surprising, aspect of the Portuguese policymaking tradition is the survival of an incorporativist tendency, despite the complete obliteration of the Salazar regime.

In Greece, there is also a sharp divide between elite politics and the rest of society, but one that is not moderated by the tradition of incorporation found in Portugal. This can in part be traced to Greece's limited and top-down path to redemocratization after 1974: the state was not dismantled either by the 1968–1974 military junta nor the democratic regime that immediately took its place, so that prior patterns of politics and policymaking survived even more easily than they did in Portugal. Some of these patterns were in fact reinforced, rather than replaced by, the mode of transition from authoritarian rule. If change to the policymaking tradition is to occur in Greece in the future, it is likely to be in an incremental manner and, importantly, stemming from inside the public administration. Chapter 5 points to the case of immigration policy in which most pressures for the government to start consulting migrant organizations have started from within the public administration. Specifically, individuals who occupy some position of power, especially in the recently created Ombudsman's Office and usually educated and socialized in Western Europe or North America, have reached out independently to migrant organizations and tried to push the government towards negotiating with them.

Finally, one of the problems associated with comparing Ireland to Portugal and Greece is that it is all too easy to arrive at a conclusion, whether intentionally or not, that pits Irish 'superiority' as an English-speaking and more politically developed nation against the 'backwardness' of the two Southern European cases. The above discussion has shown that the picture is much more complicated than that. Although Ireland has been advantaged when it comes to the construction of consultative and incorporative policymaking institutions by its more stable political system and inheritance of a British-style parliamentary democracy, there has been a significant change within the Irish policymaking process over the past two decades due to failures of the pre-existing system as much as the result of pressures for wider consultation. Gradually, the system has been opened up so that an increased number of interest groups were able to influence policy at a peak level of interest group aggregation during the 1990s and 2000s, allowing the state, at the same time, to exercise its powers of incorporation and thus retain control over the nature and scope of policy bargaining. To describe Ireland today as a pluralist paradise, however, would still be rather stretching the truth. As the recent banking crisis showed, old clientelist-type relationships between politicians, bankers, and the real estate industry, which continued despite a generally thickened zone of mediation, were at the heart of the Irish economic and political crisis of 2010. While outside the main scope of this analysis, this theme will be returned to briefly in Chapter 7.

Until the early 1970s, Portugal was governed by an authoritarian regime that used both inclusionary and exclusionary tactics in order to stay in power. The legacy of this for policymaking following democracy was that where processes and institutions to bridge the gap between state and society exist, they tend to be more incorporative than consultative and, furthermore, are segmented in fashion, aggregating interests at a very low level of the policymaking system. Greece, on the other hand, has had a long tradition of elite-driven politics and policymaking based on the personal interests of individual government actors that was neither swept away by the short-lived military authoritarian regime that ruled between 1968 and 1974, nor by the somewhat incomplete process of redemocratization that followed. The implications for the content of policy decisions differs between the two Southern European cases as a result: Greece has failed to reorient any of the three policy areas analysed here along the lines suggested in Chapter 2, while Portugal is a little more successful in this regard, even if policy responses are sometimes uncertain and incomplete. The full impact of the three distinctive national policymaking traditions on immigration, higher education policies and on policies for the reconciliation of family and working life are analysed in the following three chapters.

Notes

1 During the fieldwork conducted in the course of this research, nowhere was this strategy more apparent than in Greece, where sometimes it is the only way to get an otherwise unresponsive state to listen. The point will be returned to in Chapter 5. It is less a conscious strategy employed by the EU than one adopted by local lobbyists and policymakers in order to push through progressive social policies in particular.

2 Among the important works here are Johnson (1995) and Woo-Cummings (1999).

3 See Amsden (2001) and Kohli (2004). On the link between economic modernization and authoritarianism in East Asia see Deyo (1989). On how 'developmentalism' when combined with authoritarianism can go terribly wrong see Scott (1998).

4 The critique of pluralism began with Bachrach and Bachrach (1962). The primary target was Dahl (1961). See Hindess (1996) for an extended discussion of the controversy.

5 The utilitarian, rather than idealistic, purposes of consultative policymaking processes are increasingly recognized by national as well as supranational organizations beyond the EU, the OECD being one clear example. See especially OECD (2001).

6 Chapters 4 to 6 show that Irish universities suffered this shift in favouritism as early as the late 1960s, Portugal to some extent from the early 1980s, while the Greek education system still clearly favours universities.

7 Unfortunately perhaps, the most significant changes to the Greek pension system since redemocratization are likely to be induced by the austerity measures forced on the country by the 2010 IMF–EU bailout package. Whether this will actually alter the *distribution* of either wealth or interest group influence remains to be seen, since the austerity measures are simply aimed at cost-cutting only.

8 Arguably the slightly older literature on *state* corporatism keeps this political project much more in focus. See Collier and Collier (1991); Malloy (1977); Schmitter (1974).

9 The literature here is vast. Some of the most important contributions include Cohen and Arato (1992), and, with special relevance for Southern Europe, Pérez Diaz (1993); Robert Fishman (2004); Putnam (1993).

10 Major works here include, on the rational choice side, North (1990), and Weingast (2002). Examples of how historical institutionalists deal with the issue of change and the role of external shocks include Collier and Collier (1991), and Steinmo *et al.* (1992).

11 The de-Ba'athification versus re-Ba'athification debate in the wake of the United States' invasion of Iraq in 2003 speaks exactly to this point. This is a vastly understudied subject in the regime 'transitology' literature. There are very few works on the role of the bureaucracy in democratization and democratic consolidation, and those that do exist tend to view prior patterns of policymaking simply as problems to be overcome, especially in Eastern Europe. See for example Baker (2002).

References

Amsden, Alice, *The Rise of "The Rest": Challenges to the West from Late-Industrializing Economies* (Oxford: Oxford University Press, 2001).

Bachrach, Peter and Morton S. Bachrach, "Two Faces of Power", *American Political Science Review* 56, 4 (1962), 947–52.

Baker, Randall, ed., *Transitions from Authoritarian Rule: The Role of the Bureaucracy* (Westport, CT: Praeger, 2002).

Bohman, James, *Public Deliberation: Pluralism, Complexity, and Democracy* (Cambridge, MA: The MIT Press, 1996).

Buchanan, James E. and Gordon Tullock, *The Calculus of Consent: Logical Foundations of a Constitutional Democracy* (Ann Arbor, MI: University of Michigan Press, 1962).

Calmfors, Lars and John Driffill, "Bargaining Structure, Corporatism and Macroeconomic Performance", *Economic Policy* 6 (1998), 14–61.

Cohen, Jean and Andrew Arato, *Civil Society and Political Theory* (Cambridge, MA: MIT Press, 1992).

Collier, Ruth Berins and David Collier, "Inducements versus Constraints: Disaggregating 'Corporatism'" *American Political Science Review* 43, 4 (1979), 967–86.

Collier, Ruth Berins and David Collier, *Shaping the Political Arena* (Princeton, NJ: Princeton University Press, 1991).

Dahl, Robert, *Who Governs? Democracy and Power in an American City* (New Haven, CT: Yale University Press, 1961).
Deyo, Frederick C., *Beneath the Miracle: Labor Subordination in the New Asian Industrialism* (Berkeley, CA: University of California Press, 1989).
Douglas, Roger, *Unfinished Business* (Auckland: Random House, 1993).
Dryzek, John S., *Discursive Democracy: Politics, Policy, and Political Science* (Cambridge: Cambridge University Press, 1990).
Evans, Peter, *Embedded Autonomy: States and Industrial Transformation* (Princeton, NJ: Princeton University Press, 1995).
Fishman, Robert, *Democracy's Voices: Social Ties and the Quality of Public Life in Spain* (Ithaca, NY and London: Cornell University Press, 2004).
Gorges, Michael J., *Euro-Corporatism? Interest Intermediation in the European Community* (Lanham, MD: University Press of America, 1996).
Hindess, Barry, *Discourses of Power: From Hobbes to Foucault* (Oxford: Blackwell Publishers, 1996).
Ioannau, Christos A., "Social Pacts in Hellenic Industrial Relations: Odysseys or Sisyphus", in Philippe Pochet and Giuseppe Fajertag, eds, *Social Pacts in Europe* (Brussels: European Trade Union Institute, 2000), 219–36.
Iversen, Torben, *Contested Economic Institutions: The Politics of Macroeconomics and Wage Bargaining* (Cambridge: Cambridge University Press, 1999).
Johnson, Chalmers, *Japan: Who Governs? The Rise of the Developmental State* (New York: W.W. Norton and Company, 1995).
Kohli, Atul, *State-Directed Development: Political Power and Industrialization in the Global Periphery* (Cambridge: Cambridge University Press, 2004).
Malloy, James, ed., *Authoritarianism and Corporatism in Latin America* (Pittsburgh: University of Pittsburgh, 1977).
Mansbridge, Jane J., "A Deliberative Theory of Interest Representation", in Mark P. Petracca, ed., *The Politics of Interests: Interest Groups Transformed* (Boulder, CO: Westview Press, 1992), 32–57.
Matsaganis, Manos, "The Limits of Selectivity as a Recipe for Welfare Reform: The Case of Greece", *Journal of Social Policy* 32, 4 (2005), 235–53.
Matsaganis, Manos, "Fighting with the Hands Tied behind the Back: Anti-poverty Policy without a Minimum Income in Greece", in M. Ferrera, ed., *Welfare State Reform in Southern Europe* (London: Routledge, 2004), 33–83.
North, Douglass, *Institutions and Institutional Change and Economic Performance* (New York: Cambridge University Press, 1990).
OECD, *Citizens as Partners: Information, Consultation and Public Participation in Policy-Making* (Paris, Organisation for Economic Co-operation and Development, 2001).
O'Donnell, Owen and Platon Tinios, "The Politics of Pension Reform: Lessons from Public Attitudes in Greece", *Political Studies* 51 (2003), 262–82.
Ó Riain, Séan, *The Politics of High-Tech Growth* (Cambridge: Cambridge University Press, 2004).
Pérez Diaz, Víctor, *The Return of Civil Society: The Emergence of Democratic Spain* (Cambridge, MA: Harvard University Press, 1993).
Petmesidou, Maria, "Statism, Social Policy and the Middle Class in Greece", *Journal of European Social Policy* 1, 1 (1991), 31–48.
Pochet, Philippe and Giuseppe Fajertag ed., *Social Pacts in Europe* (Brussels: European Trade Union Institute, 2000).

Putnam, Robert, *Making Democracy Work: Civic Traditions in Modern Italy* (Princeton, NJ: Princeton University Press, 1993).

Royo, Sebastián, *A New Century of Corporatism? Corporatism in Southern Europe –Spain and Portugal in Comparative Perspective* (Westport, CT: Praeger Publishers, 2002).

Schmitter, Philippe C., "Still the Century of Corporatism?", *Review of Politics* 36, 1 (1974), 85–121.

Scott, James, *Seeing Like a State: How Certain Schemes to Improve the Human Condition Have Failed* (New Haven, CT: Yale University Press, 1998).

Steinmo, Sven, Kathleen Thelen and Frank Longstreth eds, *Structuring Politics: Historical Institutionalism in Comparative Analysis* (Cambridge: Cambridge University Press, 1992).

Streeck, Wolfgang and Kathleen Thelen, eds, *Beyond Continuity: Institutional Change in Advanced Political Economies* (Oxford: Oxford University Press, 2005).

Weingast, Barry, "Rational-choice Institutionalism", in Ira Katznelson and Helen Milner, eds, *Political Science: The State of the Discipline* (New York: Norton, 2002), 693–721.

Woo-Cummings, Meredith, ed., *The Developmental State* (Ithaca, NY and London: Cornell University Press, 1999).

4 Ireland

The previous chapters have outlined the general argument that is further fleshed out below: Irish policymaking since 1987 has gone further towards meeting the labour market challenges of the twenty-first century, in part because of the existence of a comparatively robust 'zone of mediation' consisting of two distinct layers of consultative and incorporative policymaking processes and institutions. On the one hand, the Irish policymaking tradition has been shaped by the prior existence of a consultative tradition that operated at the peak level, was formal in nature, and included non-state policy experts, even if these types of bodies were usually short-term or one-off in nature. On the other, new forms of policymaking were constructed on the foundations of this older tradition but also in response to a long-term economic crisis that had the potential to spill over into a general social and political one. These new processes and institutions were peak level in nature but in some cases provided for the aggregation of and mediation between a much broader set of interests than in the past and, most importantly, were ongoing in nature. This chapter looks further at the relationship between the development of consultative and incorporative policymaking and the evolution of policy responses to new challenges in the fields of higher education, immigration, and the reconciliation of family and working life from the 1990s up to 2008. It begins with a historical overview of the Republic's policymaking tradition. The comparative discussion of the three policy arenas that follows shows how Ireland's policymaking tradition draws on both older and new forms of public consultation and interest group incorporation and that some variation between policy areas could be observed in the 1990s and 2000s in this respect. Consultation between the state and key interest groups in the field of higher or third-level education policy drew most fully on the older consensus-building tradition. Policies for the reconciliation of working and family life, by contrast, have most clearly benefited from some of the newer forms of policy consultation and interest group incorporation, especially the social partnership experiment discussed as one special type of policy process in the previous two chapters. Tracing the course of immigration policy is complicated by the fact that immigration is such a new policy problem for Ireland. Due to the very recent appearance of immigration on the political agenda at all, it is only since around 2000 that consultative processes began to replace a very traditional and outdated policy framework in this area.

From populist corporatism to social partnership in Ireland

Ireland is the national case study with the most developed consultative and incorporative policymaking tradition considered in this book. It might be expected that this is because of the country's at least century-long democratic history, a style of politics that is usually described as consensual and centrist (Mair, 1992) and a stable, ongoing system of public administration. Ireland could thus be considered 'naturally' advantaged in this respect. While true in part, this does not tell the whole story. Ireland's inheritance of a British-style political system, to include policymaking processes that involve formal consultation with policy experts and stakeholders, did mean that the country inherited some bases on which to build a consultative and incorporative tradition. Some of the key features of this more traditional form of interest group consultation and incorporation are discussed below.[1] Yet because of the emergence of a one-party-dominant political system and the creation of a populist coalition through which that party formulated and implemented public policy, policymaking processes actually remained closed to a number of important interest groups in favour of a few privileged and overpowering ones, at least until the late 1980s.

Ireland's post-1987 economic recovery, for reasons discussed shortly, was accompanied by the rise of a new set of consultative and incorporative policymaking processes and institutions that runs alongside and occasionally overlaps with the work of more traditional forms of public consultation, such as select committee hearings or commissions of inquiry. This has increased the number of interest groups incorporated into central decision-making as well as broadened the range of issues formally negotiated. The previous chapter argued that policymaking processes and institutions are more likely to be able to balance incorporative and consultative characteristics where they are formal, ongoing, and include the range of interest groups appropriate to specific policy issues. Because Ireland's 'social partnership' experiment reflects all of these features, it is given special attention here, even though the widening of public consultation in Ireland since the late 1980s is not limited to this particular process and its accompanying institutions. What the remainder of the chapter demonstrates is that the more an issue has made it onto the negotiating agenda of consultative and incorporative policymaking bodies, the more successful the policy responses have been.

Given that Ireland has enjoyed a comparatively stable democratic history for most of the past century, it is easy to overlook the fact that there was nothing inevitable about this outcome (Kissane, 2002). The Irish Free State, later renamed the Republic of Ireland, was formed in 1921 following the 1918 creation of an independent Irish parliament (Dáil Éireann) and the subsequent Anglo-Irish War. This ended when the treaty partitioning the island was signed and was then immediately followed by a particularly violent period of civil war. However, once a truce was reached, normal parliamentary politics soon returned, with a centre–right coalition leading the nation through the first decade of statehood. Thus, despite the upheavals of the early twentieth century, the new state was fortunate in that it inherited a set of political institutions that, by and large, functioned democratically. The colonial regime laid the foundations for post-colonial democracy in the 1920s in the sense that it had a bicameral elected parliament and an established party system, even if these political institutions had been responsible for implementing less than democratic laws in the form of measures designed to exclude indigenous Irish from many aspects of political, economic, and cultural life. This institutional history put the country in a better position to begin a much-needed project of national economic recovery than was possible elsewhere on the European periphery at this time, including in inter-war Portugal and Greece.

In the early 1930s, a new and soon dominant force in Irish politics emerged in the form of Fianna Fáil, headed by charismatic former anti-Treaty faction leader Eamon de Valera. The importance of both de Valera and the new party for the future course of Irish politics is difficult to overstate, with Fianna Fáil adopting a populist style of leadership and aligning itself with key interest groups including organized labour, farmers, who were still mainly small scale and family based,[2] the struggling indigenous manufacturing sector, and the Catholic Church. The seemingly contradictory elements of such a coalition were reconciled through a nationalist ideology that was gradually redefined by the Fianna Fáil leadership. Ensuring loyalty through local networks and clientelist distribution of favours, the party seemed almost impossible to move from power through much of the twentieth century (Allen, 1997; Dunphy, 1995). Early Fianna Fáil ideology combined radical and conservative elements in a distinctive way that has left a strong mark on policy development in many areas. It was radical in the sense that it sought to deepen Irish independence, especially from Britain, by reviving the Irish language and, most importantly in this era, adopting an import substitution industrialization strategy. On the other hand, it was socially and morally conservative, and the close relationship between the party, the state, and the Catholic Church has influenced many areas of social policy in particular (Browne, 1998; Whyte, 1971; Powell, 1992). The implications of this, especially for family law and policy as framed by the constitution, will be returned to shortly.

Ireland's attempt to gain economic independence through protectionism headed into trouble by the early 1950s, suffering many of the same deficiencies as other import substitution industrialization strategies elsewhere in the world.[3] However, unlike nations such as Australia or New Zealand for example, which did not consider abandoning these measures until the late 1970s, Ireland adopted an investment-oriented regime twenty years earlier. This change in direction is usually traced to the 1958 publication of a government report on the status of the Irish economy, generally referred to as the 'Whitaker Report' after its author. Influences on this strategy included the fact that countries in Northern Europe were beginning to benefit from the 'small, open, and corporatist' strategies that have been identified as key to their successes in the post-war period (Katzenstein, 1985). In addition, Ireland was already looking towards closer ties with Europe as early as the 1950s (Mahon, 1986).

The country was finally granted EU membership in 1973. While Irish economic successes in the 1990s have often been credited to European integration, accession clearly took a long time to benefit the country, and it was not until many internal and additional changes had taken place and through which EU Structural Funds could be channelled that membership really took effect. In fact, the period between 1973 and 1987 was an especially difficult one for the country. Referred to by one economist as the 'post-colonial economic vicious circle', the Irish economy had become locked into a continued dependence on Britain despite efforts to the contrary, a reliance on agriculture, high unemployment, mass emigration, and population decline (Mjøset, 1992: 10). By 1981 inflation stood at 21 per cent, the current account deficit ran at 15 per cent of GDP, while government debt reached around 130 per cent by 1986, at which point unemployment had escalated to 16 per cent of the labour force (Honohan and Walsh, 2002: 8). While most OECD countries experienced economic difficulties following the oil shocks of the early 1970s, the problem appeared much worse in Ireland in light of its underlying developmental difficulties and much lower absolute living standards than found elsewhere in Western Europe.

Where opening up to the outside world did appear to take immediate effect was in the realm of cultural politics. From the mid-1970s, the stranglehold over social policy of the Church began to break down, as did, albeit more gradually, that of Fianna Fáil over national politics. By the 1980s, tight governmental control over television and print media had been loosened, and national debates could now take place over sensitive issues such as birth control, divorce, and abortion, even if Ireland's approach to such topics remained, and still remains, conservative by European standards. This general societal opening, combined with Fianna Fáil's failures in the economic arena, caused the party to lose some electoral ground during this period. Fine Gael, more clearly located on the centre–right in terms of economic policy and with a traditional base of support in the small business community, governed in coalition with the increasingly centrist Labour Party between 1982 and 1987 and again with the addition of the centre–left Progressive Democrats from 1994 until 1997. This latter period of coalition government, often referred to as the rule of the 'Rainbow Coalition', is significant because of the attention paid at that time to social policy in particular. Ireland's coalition politics often defy what would be expected on a left-right political spectrum. Fine Gael has at times co-operated with parties to the left of both itself and of Fianna Fáil in order to try to break the dominance of the latter. Another Fine Gael–Labour Coalition came to power in 2010 as the result of Fianna Fáil's crushing defeat in the wake of the Irish banking collapse of that year.

The first attempt to solve the embedded economic crisis that had begun in the early 1970s was carried out by the 1982–1987 Fine Gael–Labour government and mirrored the market-oriented reform packages adopted at approximately the same time in other parts of the English-speaking world. However, the pursuit of such a 'neo-liberal' approach only seemed to plunge Ireland further into crisis, and it was clear by 1987 that things had to change. After 1987 there was a concerted effort to turn the economy around through negotiation with core economic stakeholders and a mixed reform strategy that combined features of a classic structural adjustment programme (focused especially on repaying the national debt and curbing inflation) with less orthodox measures. The recovery eventually became a remarkable one, with phenomenally high rates of growth and employment creation throughout the 1990s, which provides an important backdrop to the analysis of the three main policy areas of interest here. The crisis talks initiated by the state but with active participation on the part of organized business and labour eventually formed the basis of what is referred to as the 'social partnership process' in Ireland, constituting a major site of consultative and incorporative policymaking for the past two decades.

Until the 1990s, state–society relations in Ireland as reflected in interest group politics and policymaking was filtered through two historical legacies. On the one hand, the inheritance of political institutions from the British meant that the bureaucracy took on the form of what is usually termed the 'Whitehall' model of public administration.[4] It was and is a career public service, and the workings of inter-departmental or select committees and commissions of inquiry mark the policymaking process. Such a tradition allows policymakers to consult with and incorporate the interests and opinions of policy stakeholders, such as vice-chancellors of universities in the field of education or doctors' associations in the health policy arena, along with academics or other outside 'experts'. Although such a tradition provides a strong basis for consultative and incorporative policymaking, as discussed earlier, it has its limits. Principally, it is a particularly elitist model. This elitism or 'insider' basis of this form of consultation was reinforced in the Irish case by the almost 'state corporatist'[5] form of interest group mediation administered by the Fianna Fáil party machine. Second, consultation under this system is most often short-term or one-off in nature, and decisions within it tend not be binding on political actors.

Policymaking in Ireland through much of the twentieth century was thus consultative, especially in areas in which technical expertise was particularly important, such as in the case of higher education. Yet policymaking institutions and processes were also in a significant sense closed. Ordinary citizens might have been able to gain some local influence through local clientelist party networks, but, at the national level, some interests were clearly favoured over others. Fianna Fáil's populist coalition included agricultural interests, some local manufacturing participation (although business loyalty has always been divided between Fine Gael and the dominant party), key trade unions, and the Catholic Church. Other interest groups, significantly for this analysis those working on behalf of women but also those representing minority churches or unorganized workers or the Irish Traveller community,[6] for example, were generally excluded from this picture.

This closed system changed significantly from the late 1980s, witnessed not in the rise of new political parties, with no real difference being experienced in the nature of the one-party dominant party system, nor any formal institutional changes, but within the field of interest group consultation and incorporation. More open forms of interest group intermediation developed underneath or in parallel to the old party and parliamentary system (Ó Riain, 2004). The opening

Table 4.1 Summary of provisions of social partnership agreements, 1987–2005

Name of agreement	*Duration*	*Government/Taioseach (Prime Minister)*	*Wage agreement*	*Overall direction of non-wage provisions*
Programme for National Recovery	1988–1990	Fianna Fáil/Charles Haughey	Pay increases not to exceed 2.5% in each of the years 1988, 1989 and 1990	Economic crisis means that agreement is guided by the need to improve the country's macroeconomic health, especially with regard to national debt. Industrial policy measures aim at strengthening industrial and tourism sectors and labour and social policy measures aim to combat high unemployment and poverty rates
Programme for Economic and Social Progress	1991–1993	Fianna Fáil–Progressive Democrats/Charles Haughey	Increases in basic pay of not more than 4.0% in 1991, 3.0% in 1992 and 4.75% in 1993	Cautiously starts to expand scope of policy initiatives beyond wage agreement into tax and social welfare policies, with major focus on reducing unemployment
Programme for Competitive-ness and Work	1994–1996	Fianna Fáil–Labour Coalition/Albert Reynolds	Starting 5 months after expiration of previous agreement, not more than 2% increases in basic pay for first 12 months of new agreement, 2% in second 12 months, 1.5% for next 4 months, 1.5% for next 3 months and 1% for final 6 months	Major focus of policy initiatives is employment growth – written with European Monetary Union in mind
Partnership 2000	1997–1999	"Rainbow Coalition" Fine Gael–Labour–Democratic Left/John Bruton	Not more than 2.5% for first 12 months of agreement; 2.25% for second 12 months; 1.5% for next 9 months; and 1.0% for final 6 months	'Social inclusion' provides the main theme of non wage-related policy initiatives

Programme for Prosperity and Fairness	2000–2002	Fianna Fáil–Progressive Democrat/Bertie Ahern	5.5% for first 12 months; 5.5% second 12 months; 4% for remaining 9 months	An extremely broad range of initiatives is organized into five 'frameworks': (1) the industrial relations-related 'Framework for Living Standards and Workplace Environment', (2) the industrial policy and development-oriented 'Framework for Prosperity and Economic Inclusion', (3) the 'Framework for Social Inclusion and Equality', (4) the educational and training focussed 'Framework for Successful Adaptation to Continuing Change', and (5) the 'Framework for Renewing Partnership', which looks at devolving the partnership approach down to local and enterprise levels
Sustaining Progress	2003–2005	Fianna Fáil–Progressive Democrats/Bertie Ahern	3% for first 9 months; 2% for second 6 months; 2% for final 3 months	Caution in relation to social policy initiatives driven by global economic downturn. Comprehensive policy plan is supplemented by 'ten special initiatives: housing and accommodation; the cost and availability of insurance; migration and interculturalism; long-term unemployment; 'vulnerable' and redundant workers; tackling educational disadvantage; waste management; care of children, people with disabilities and older people; alcohol and drug abuse; including everyone in the information society; and ending child poverty

of peak-level political discussion to previously excluded interest groups was partly forced by the system's own failures to ensure economic and social stability but was also the reflection of the societal liberalization that had occurred since the early 1970s and the need to incorporate new sorts of demands. While similar societal changes were occurring in other mature democracies during this period of time, Irish society was arguably much more deeply conservative than other countries, reinforced by the privileged position of the Catholic Church, especially when it came to policy decision-making. There was thus more to fight against. Moreover, Ireland's essentially democratic and even consensus-making style of politics was marred by a number of corruption scandals, which served to forge a gulf between the citizenry and their political leaders. During the 1990s, the privileged position awarded by the old interest group intermediation system to the Church was further undermined by a series of child (and adult) abuse cases. Taken together, it became clear to political leaders themselves that new alternative channels of political consultation were required beyond the bounds of the electoral system. Although the post-1987 'social partnership' agreements and the processes that built up around them were not the only alternative forms of ensuring greater accountability and government responsiveness to shifting societal interests, social partnership is indeed one of the most widely recognized and researched ones. It also plays a significant role in the case study discussion of Irish family, immigration, and higher education policy detailed in the following chapter, and thus requires further elaboration.

In this context of continuing economic crisis, the Irish government, with formal agreement from both organized business and the union movement, launched its first social partnership agreement, the *Programme for National Recovery 1987–1990*. The content of this agreement had been largely outlined in the National Economic and Social Council's (NESC) *A Strategy for National Development 1986–1990,* and in many respects took the form of a classic wage agreement. The NESC is in itself a tri-partite advisory body. The social partners, 'conscious of the grave state of our national economy' (Government of Ireland, 1987: 5), agreed to modest wage increases of not more than 2.5 per cent each year between 1988 and 1990, in an effort to control inflation and start reducing the national debt. This was significant in the Irish industrial relations environment, which had traditionally operated through free or 'voluntaristic' collective bargaining and which in recent times had become highly conflictual.

Although there is an extensive body of literature on the contribution of this process to creating a stable environment for foreign direct investment in particular (Hardiman, 2004; MacCoille, 2001; Roche, 2000; Rush, 1999; Teague, 1995), for the purposes of this book it is not the wage bargaining itself which is significant but the fact that social partnership gradually became much more than about wages, providing the key platform for interest group mediation. The scope of debate was broadened, as was the range of groups and organizations that were invited by the government to take part in social partnership negotiations. Furthermore, social partnership provided a new form of potentially consultative and incorporative policymaking in this case, layered over pre-existing arrangements for short-term and one-off interest group participation. What made the social partnership agreements different was the fact that they were long term in nature and self-reproducing because they provided mechanisms for their own review and renegotiation. They were also conducted at the peak level and were relatively formal in the sense that interest groups and the state signed off on the commitments made as a result of negotiations, after which agreements were published and widely available to the public. This limited the extent to which governments can ignore or backtrack on commitments made in the agreements.

Following the apparent success of the first agreement, the social pact was renegotiated every three years until 2006. In the process, it was increasingly widened beyond its original aims to cover a wide range of policy issues and incorporated new interest groups into the process of negotiation, some fully as 'social partners' and others as consultative organizations. Before 2000, formal social partnership negotiations took place between the government and three 'pillars': organized labour, highly centralized under the Irish Congress of Trade Unions (ICTU), the comparatively divided business and employer pillar, and the third and separate negotiating pillar reserved for the primary producer sector. In 2000, a fourth pillar was added in order to formalize the participation of the community and voluntary sector. As Table 4.2 illustrates, the number of groups represented became very large. It can be noted that groups were added by invitation from the government, meaning specifically the Prime Minister's Office and his administrative team, and the explanation for why the decision was made to increase the range of groups involved probably lies in the strong commitment to the process that quickly developed on the part of the state. Because the wage agreement and industry policy commitments made in the first social partnership agreement appeared to pay off as early as 1990, political actors believed this provided a model for the negotiation of a much wider range of policy issues. In terms of policy content, wage constraint was traded especially for tax reductions during the early 1990s, while other social policy commitments were layered into the agreements later on.

Social partnership in Ireland as an ongoing process gave rise to several formal bodies. The work of the more academically oriented NESC is scrutinized by the National Economic and Social Forum, on which the 'social partners' have formal representation. In addition, and one of the reasons why the partnership agreements have been considered a success, the implementation of policy commitments made in them is monitored by a Central Review Committee, housed in the Prime Minister's Office but again with representation from the four 'pillars'. Often interacting with the social partnership process, more traditional forms of public consultation have also continued. By 'interaction', it is simply meant that the social partnership agreements frequently initiate and set the framework for other types of public consultation or expert opinion gathering.

Finally, it is important to emphasize that social partnership, just as much as more traditional Irish forms of expert and stakeholder consultation such as commissions of inquiry or calls for public submissions on proposed legislation, is highly structured from above, and thus acts to incorporate as well as consult

Table 4.2 Signatories to Irish social partnership agreements, 1987–2006

Agreement	*The 'Social Partners'*			
	Business	*Labour*	*'Third pillar'/farmer's organizations*	*'Fourth pillar'/voluntary sector*
Programme for National Recovery 1988–1990	Federation of Irish Employers (FIE); Confederation of Irish Industries (CII); Construction Industry Federation (CIF)	Irish Congress of Trade Unions (ICTU)	Irish Farmers' Association (IFA); Macra na Feirme; Irish Co-Operative Society (ICOS)	–
Programme for Economic and Social Progress 1991–1993	FIE, CII, CIF	ICTU	IFA, Macra na Feirme, ICOS	–
Programme for Competitive-ness and Work 1994–1996	Irish Business and Employers' Confederation (IBEC); CIF	ICTU	IFA, Irish Creamery Milk Suppliers' Association (ICMSA), ICOS, Macra na Feirme	–
Partnership 2000 1997–1999	IBEC, Small Firms Association (SFA)*, CIF, Irish Exporters' Association (IEA), Irish Tourist Industry Confederation (ITIC), Chambers of Commerce of Ireland (CCI)	ICTU	IFA, Macra na Feirme, ICOS, ICMSA	Irish National Organisation for the Unemployed (INOU); Congress Centres for the Unemployed; Council of Religious of Ireland (CORI); National Women's Council of Ireland (NWCI); National Youth Council of Ireland (NYCI); St Vincent de Paul; Protest Aid THE COMMUNITY PLATFORM – (Community Workers' Co-operative, INOU, NWCI, Irish Rural Link, Irish Traveller Movement, Focus on Children, Gay and Lesbian Equality Network, One Parent Exchange Network, CORI, Forum of People with Disabilities, Pavee Point, Community Action Network, Irish Commission for Prisoners Overseas, European Anti-Poverty Network Ireland)

Programme for Prosperity and Fairness 2000–2002	IBEC, SFA, CIF, IEA, ITIC, CCI	ICTU	IFA, ICMSA, ICS, Macra na Feirme	INOU, Congress Centres for the Unemployed, CORI, NWCI, NYCI, St Vincent de Paul. Protest Aid. THE COMMUNITY PLATFORM – (Community Action Network, Community Workers Co-operative, CORI, European Anti-Poverty Network Ireland, Focus on Children, Forum of People with Disabilities, Gay and Lesbian Equality Network, Irish Association of Older People, National Adult Literacy Agency, Irish Commission for Prisoners Overseas, INOU, Irish Rural Link, Irish Traveller Movement, National Traveller Women's Council of Ireland, One Parent Exchange Network, Pavee Point, Threshold, Vincentian Partnership for Justice, St. Vincent de Paul, Women's Aid, Voluntary Drug Treatment Agency)
Sustaining Progress 2003–2005	IBEC, SFA, CCI, CIF, IEA, ITIC	ICTU	Macra na Feirme, IFA, ICMSA, ICS	INOU, Congress Centres for the Unemployed, CORI, NYCI, St Vincent de Paul, Protestant Aid
Towards 2016 2006–2016	IBEC, CIF, SFA, IEA, ITIC, CCI	ICTU	IFA, ICMSA, ICOS, Macra na Feirme.	INOU, Congress Centres Network, CORI, Justice Commission, NYCI, National Association of Building Co-Operatives, Irish Council for Social Housing, Society of Saint Vincent de Paul, Age Action Ireland, The Carers Association, The Wheel, The Disability Federation of Ireland, Irish Rural Link, The Irish Senior Citizens' Parliament, The Children's Rights Alliance, Protestant Aid

Notes

* Though listed as a separate party to the partnership process, the Small Firm's Association is in fact a member of IBEC.

** The Community Platform is listed as being a party to the Sustaining Progress negotiations but, along with the National Women's Council, did not endorse the final agreement.

interest groups. When asked about the participation of the Union of Students in Ireland about the group's formal representation on centralized bodies such as the National Qualifications Authority, a student organizer remarked that although such representation is sought after and welcome, 'because these formal institutions are at such a high level, recommendations are almost already pre-approved by the government'.[7] Presumably then, representation has much to do with legitimating decisions on the part of the government and at least feeling part of the inside decision-making on the part of representative organizations. The incorporative aspects of formal consultation are particularly clear in the case of social partnership. While it is outside the scope of this book to consider fully the impact of participation on the organization of interest groups, suffice to say that the Irish government has repeatedly used its powers not only of agenda-setting but also of being able to 'invite' individual interest groups to become part of one of the four pillars in order to moderate the tone of policy debate and exclude specific interests from participating.[8]

Reconciling family and working life

The reconciliation of family and working life as an arena of self-conscious, coordinated state activity and as a topic of national political debate began to emerge in Ireland around 1990. Prior to this, reconciliation issues were framed in terms of women's rights to engage in and be treated equally in paid work. Frequently these rights were pitted against public policies that reflected a traditional belief that women should not be 'forced' to work outside the home. A reorientation of the debate so that it more closely reflected the one taking place elsewhere in Western Europe was facilitated in part by the changing nature of the Irish economy itself. New opportunities opened up by post-1987 employment growth combined with increases in the cost of living that have accompanied the economic recovery encouraged an increasing proportion of Irish women, especially married women, into paid employment. Yet just because objective circumstances change does not mean governments will necessarily respond in a way that better facilitates work–life balance. If the state fails to address the issue, the longer-term consequences of this are likely to be fertility decline as well as increased social and family tensions. Irish policymakers have become increasingly aware of this fact. While changing economic circumstances in the 1990s and 2000s may have helped highlight the problem of work–life balance, actual reconciliation policies were introduced through consultative institutions that gradually incorporated the concerns of trade unions, organized business and, a little less so, women's lobby groups into the policy framework. Two specific policymaking processes responsible for introducing concrete changes after 1990 were a short-term Commission on the Family and the post-1987 social partnership process.

The policy problem

The problem of developing policies for work–life balance in Ireland between 1990 and 2008 consisted of how to cope with the legacies of a family policy, labour law, and social welfare framework that actively discouraged women from participating in paid work in an era when female workforce participation became vital to economic growth. Historically, Ireland represented a classic case of a conservative family policy regime in which a consistently high birth rate was maintained at the expense of female labour force participation. This sets Ireland apart from Portugal, which has experienced a declining birth rate but relatively high female workforce participation, as well as Greece, which has especially low rates of both. The historically low rate of female workforce participation was not only reinforced by the absence of state policy to help achieve a balance between family and working life, as in the case of other 'minimalist and familialist' welfare policies, but in this case actual deliberate efforts to ensure women chose family over work. Such measures included constitutional commitments to encourage women to stay at home as well as specific labour law provisions. The Irish Constitution shares with the Greek, Italian, and Portuguese ones a particularly strong and explicit commitment to supporting specific forms of family life, although the actual family policies of individual governments have remained not only implicit, but also minimalist, in terms of real support given (Hantrais and Letablier, 1996: 27).[9] While historically low levels of state support in terms of services as well as cash benefits have been linked to Ireland's adoption of a laissez-faire economic and social development strategy that shied away from interference in the 'private' sphere, the basic framework determining the context of family policy is better characterized as conservative rather than liberal. What did exist in terms of active family policy was a collection of social welfare benefits aimed at poverty relief, while the apparent policy of non-intervention in the private sphere was justified and reinforced by the strong relationship between the Catholic Church and the state in terms of shaping family policy and social welfare policy in general. Granted both a privileged position in the Constitution and informal access to policymakers from the 1930s, the Church doctrine of subsidiarity meant that state 'interference' in family life was discouraged.[10]

Despite this 'non-interference' stance, the Irish state has actually always intervened in family life by prescribing what a family should look like. The basis of 'non-interference' lies in the Constitution's commitment to preserving the family as 'the natural primary and fundamental unit group of Society', which possesses 'inalienable and imprescriptible rights, antecedent and superior to all positive law'. Yet two, eventually more, controversial clauses specify how families should organize themselves by emphasizing the role of women as mothers (with no corresponding emphasis on the role of fathers). The State not only 'recognises that by her life within the home, woman gives to the State a support without which the common good cannot be achieved', but also that the State shall 'endeavour to ensure that mothers shall not be obliged to engage in labour to the neglect of their duties in the home'.[11] Others have discussed how these constitutional provisions not only evolved out of the social conservatism of the first Fianna Fáil (de Valera) government but how this in turn stemmed from the connection between a gendered and Catholicized form of republicanism that provided the ideological glue for the new Irish Free State (Valiulis, 1995). The Constitution has thus helped to underpin a general and quite distinctively Irish belief that (married) women should not be 'forced' to work outside the home, and for much of the twentieth century a number of legislative measures remained in place that actively discouraged women from doing just this. Chief among these was a marriage bar in the public service, requiring that women working in the public sector must resign after marriage; the 1935 Conditions of Employment Act which allowed women to be excluded from occupations considered 'unsuitable' for them (Pyle, 1990: 89; Richardson, 1995: 130–2); and a tax code based on joint taxation which acted as a strong disincentive towards engaging in paid work on the part of married women. While the principle of joint taxation was legally challenged in the late 1970s, with the Irish Supreme Court ruling against compulsory family-based taxation and after which an alternative form of income-splitting for tax purposes was introduced, conflict over whether full tax individualization would 'force' women into the workforce and undermine the Constitution continued into the twenty-first century (Reid, 2003).

This male breadwinner model might have worked in a closed economy that relied heavily on agriculture (keeping in mind the amount of unpaid female labour the family-farm based sector usually relies upon), and where manufacturing jobs were few and reserved largely for men. But if Ireland was to diversify and modernize its economy and converge towards European living standards by focusing on high-tech, increasingly higher wage, and knowledge-based niche industries, the national attitude toward female workforce participation would also have to change. Over time, it did. The rate of female workforce participation increased sharply during the 1990s, from a rate of 35.9 per cent in 1991 to 54.1 per cent in 2000. There is widespread recognition that women not only benefited from economic growth but also contributed to it, acting as a very important 'reserve army of labour' for investors in the new economic sectors (Fahey *et al.*, 2000). The changing circumstances families found themselves in as a result of this shift helped to increase the amount of public attention and political debate over the tension between family and working life, solutions to which had to be created from scratch in many cases given the pre-existing state policy of 'non-intervention' in family life. Specific policy responses to the problem, however, had to be forged through deliberate efforts on the part of the state as well as specific interest groups. These are discussed in the following section.

The debate over reconciling family and working life in Ireland further intensified after 2000, with the new pressures brought by rapid economic growth often meaning that families required two income-earners in order to survive, especially in the greater Dublin area where much of the growth was centred. In particular, 2004–2005 saw a series of by-elections in the commuter belt areas surrounding Dublin, during which the issue of childcare suddenly became an important and explosive political issue, despite work previously done to meet increased demand. Overall, however, the debate moved away from women's right to work versus the dangers associated with 'forcing' mothers into paid work, towards how to reconcile parental responsibilities and employment in a new environment where 'choice' to work is limited less by discriminatory state practices than by economic necessity. Economic growth had been accompanied by rises in the cost of living, providing a new kind of motivation for women to join the paid workforce. Yet because of belated state action in areas such as the provision of childcare or even equal treatment for women with respect to employment, the Irish state still lagged behind its Northern European neighbours with respect to the reconciliation of family and working life. Overall, however, between 1990 and 2008 not only was the family policy debate increasingly reoriented around new norms and values but this was followed through by increases in funding levels and other forms of concrete policy action as a response to societal demands.

The role of consultation and incorporation in shaping policy responses

Since the conceptualization of measures aimed at the reconciliation of family and working life as a distinct and important arena of state activity is relatively new in Ireland, consultative and incorporative policymaking processes and institutions can be most clearly identified after 1990. Prior to that, however, issues broadly related to this policy area were the subject of a number of peak-level albeit one-off exercises in interest group consultation and incorporation. The most important of these was the (First) Commission on the Status of Women, formed in 1970 and with representatives from state agencies and women's interest groups. The implementation of the Commission's 1973 recommendations included a number of changes to existing labour legislation, to be discussed in the following section. The Commission also gave rise to the formation of a national non-governmental umbrella organization, originally known as the Council for the Status of Women since its initial explicit aim was to monitor the implementation of the Commission's recommendations. Over time, this group, renamed the National Women's Council of Ireland (NWCI), expanded its functions and now has over 150 institutional members. Along with organized labour and business, it consistently gains representation on a wide range of government bodies, including as a formal signatory to the social partnership agreements along with other groups included in the community and voluntary 'pillar' from 1997.

During the 1990s, the two key institutions for translating the long-term concerns of women's groups and the labour movement about the lack of support in Ireland for working families into concrete policy proposals for resolving tensions between work and family life were a Commission on the Family and the social partnership process. While the latter process was more successful over the medium term in directing resources toward specific policies, the Family Commission did help reorient the debate and, at the very least, create the climate for an increasingly explicit national family policy framework. The role and functions

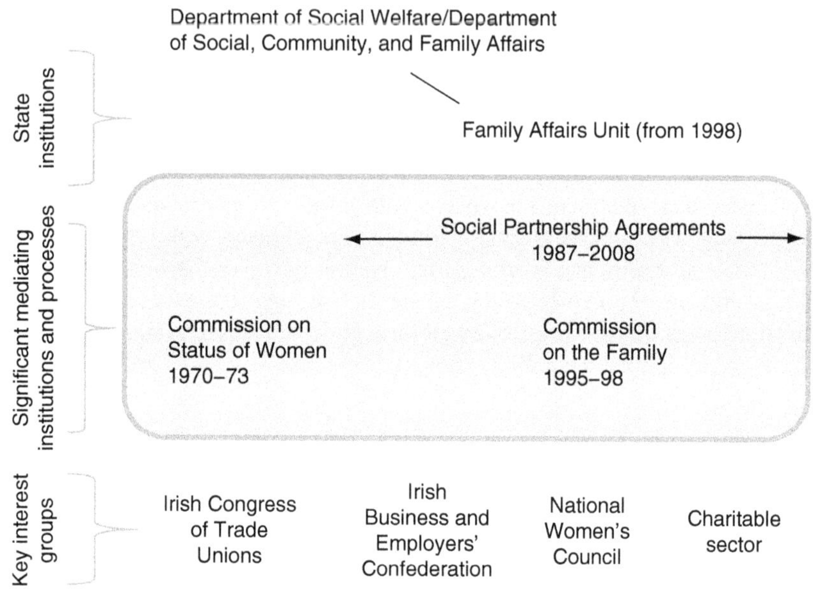

Figure 4.1 The zone of mediation in Irish work–life balance policy.

of these two bodies with respect to the development of policies for work–life balance are worth discussing in detail before moving on to the analysis of the actual policy shifts they were able to facilitate.

The Commission on the Family was established on a temporary basis in 1995 by Pronisias De Rossa, Minister of Social Welfare under the 'Rainbow Coalition' government of 1994–1997. It produced an interim report in 1996 and a final report in 1998, with the latter report being published one year later than intended and after a change in government. De Rossa is a well-known figure on the Irish political left and, as such, brought to the Social Welfare position a strong inclination toward wealth redistribution, particularly a concern to help out the poorest and most marginalized members of Irish society. However, the work of the Commission was also strongly influenced by the recent adoption of Ireland's first divorce law, and the body was charged with investigating ways to keep families together given a public concern that the new legislation would deepen processes of family breakdown. Its mixed and broad goals were thus both radical and conservative in the Irish political environment, and the uneasiness involved in balancing these tendencies was quickly revealed in an early reluctance and difficulty in even defining the notion of 'the family'. At a basic level, the Commission had to retain 'due regard to the provisions on the family in the Constitution intended to support the family unit', which is clearly built around the nuclear family model even if the Commission does not explicitly state this, while also dealing with the more flexible definition of the family 'outlined by the

United Nations' (Commission on the Family, 1998). Thus, the Commission had a broad, complex, and perhaps therefore unenviable task.

Among its chief recommendations with relevance for the policy problem at issue here was the establishment of a Family Affairs Unit to oversee overall family policy development within the Department of Social Welfare, which by 1998 had become the Department of Social, Community, and Family Affairs. This new policy unit would be responsible for co-ordination between government departments, further implement specific policy recommendations, and provide a 'forum for raising awareness about the new and emerging needs of families into the new century'.[12] Much of the Commission's final report also deals with the funding and strengthening of family support agencies, mostly private organizations under contract to central and local government. Extra funding in this area was provided in the government's 1998 budget, in response to a 1997 submission on the part of the Commission. With respect to the issue of the reconciliation of family and working life, many of the Commission's recommendations touch on this theme, even if they are not primarily framed in these terms. The impact of the group's work on some specific policy initiatives in the field will be returned to below.

During the course of this research, several former members of the Commission lamented the limited impact on actual policy development that they believed they were able to make. Although some of these research participants have underestimated the importance of the Commission's work,[13] it is clear that some of the body's recommendations failed to be put into practice. Research participants generally laid out two possible reasons for its perceived failings. First, the change of government preceding the publication of the Commission's final report, and the incoming Fianna Fáil administration's more 'pragmatic' approach to policymaking broke away from the more visionary programme of the Rainbow Coalition. Related to this was a lack of political will when suggested programmes were costed and judged to be too expensive.[14] A second reason offered was bureaucratic disinterest and the fact that, despite the formation of the Family Affairs Unit within it, the Department of Social, Community and Family Affairs, formerly the Department of Social Welfare, has never had a strong policymaking function. It has also been pointed out in an academic article by one of the Commission's members that commissions of inquiry only tend to make a discernible policy impact when their goals are tightly defined. The Family Commission had a broad set of objectives, and thus many of its recommendations were too vague to make any significant impact (Carroll, 1999).

More fundamentally, however, the mixed fortunes of the Family Commission illustrate the problems associated with short-term or one-off consultation processes analysed more comprehensively in Chapter 3, in contrast to mechanisms that are more institutionalized or, at the very least, ongoing. Another reason why the work of the Commission delivered fewer concrete policy results in the field of work–life balance in comparison to the social partnership agreements is found in the membership of the two different bodies. What is notable about the membership of the Commission, in contrast to the social partnership agreements, is that its membership included no representatives from either organized labour or business. This illustrates how family policy in this case was not primarily perceived as an economic issue, if at all. Out of the fourteen members, in addition to the secretariat provided by the Department of Social Welfare, there were four public servants, one economic and social policy researcher, three medical and social work professionals, two representatives from the counselling and family law sector, two charity workers, one local politician, and the former chair of the Irish Countrywomen's Association. It is clear from this that there was a broad scope of expertise involved, but also a bias toward psychiatry, counselling, family law, and action toward combating poverty. This bias was not unreasonable since the terms of reference were directed toward service provision aimed at 'strengthening' families, but it did mean that other issues, important across Irish society, became a little sidelined.

More crucially than anything else, however, policies for work–life balance, as distinct from family policy in general, require the acquiescence if not consent of organized labour, but most of all, employers. One problem in the Portuguese case, the discussion of which follows in Chapter 6, is that no matter how many rights the state in theory guarantees, the take-up of parental leave rights or other workplace-related measures relies on the cooperation of employers. That has been dealt with in Ireland through the partnership agreements in which the negotiation process has ensured that the main business and employers' confederation in particular, the Irish Business and Employers Confederation (IBEC), is accepting of overall policy development in the field. With respect to women's organizations, the NWCI has been a party to the partnership negotiations since 1997 as part of the 'fourth' or community sector pillar of the partnership process. Because this fourth pillar, to include representatives from the Catholic Church, has become wedded to an anti-poverty agenda, measures such as raising benefit rates have provided the main source of focus for these groups.

As discussed in the previous chapter, the social partnership agreements negotiated in Ireland since 1987 became consistently broader in scope. A summary of policy developments made within the context of social partnership related to policies for work–life balance is given in Table 4.3 and some of these are discussed in more detail below. For the social partners, each major commitment made in the initial formal agreements entails sending a representative to sit on a committee or working party that must review and monitor that initiative. The process of negotiating, agreeing on, and monitoring policy is time-consuming, laborious, and ongoing. This, however, is also one of its strengths. Because the same actors remain part of a continuous set of processes, a problem-solving approach can be adopted over a long period of time, without the wheel needing to be reinvented every time an agreement is negotiated. By contrast, commissions and other such one-off, short-term institutions, tend to start from scratch. This point is emphasized not so much to criticize the Commission on the Family, but in order to highlight what makes the social partnership agreements work. In fact, many of the following developments were signalled, overlapped with, or gave effect to the work of the Commission.

Overall, it can be argued, while economic change itself may have helped push the issue of work–life balance more centrally onto the Irish political agenda, consultative and incorporative policymaking has been required to fill in policy detail on the one hand and gain the support of key interest groups on the other. The latter function is filled especially well by the social partnership process because of the fact that, once policy action in this field moves outside the sphere of social policy directly into the workplace, the cooperation of both labour unions and employers' organizations become particularly important. This is not to say either that non-economic groups have been unimportant. Input from childcare associations, the early childhood education sector, charities, and family counselling agencies in particular on policy detail has been incorporated through more traditional forms of policy consultation. The Commission on the Family was one comprehensive attempt to aggregate and filter public opinion, but other short-term bodies designed to investigate specific issues such as childcare or parental leave have also made up part of the thick layer of policy consultation that has surrounded the evolution of policies for work–life balance over the past decade and a half. The contours of this policy evolution are now given in order to outline the impact of consultative and incorporative policymaking in more detail.

The evolution of policies for work–life balance

As highlighted above, until the early 1970s family policy in Ireland was largely implicit and made up of a series of measures aimed at poverty relief or child protection. The state stepped in occasionally when families and Church-based charity failed. One of the first steps, in line with many other OECD countries, was the introduction of a child allowance in 1944, constituting one of the first non means-tested or contributory payments in the country's history (Curry, 1998: 25). General family benefits were limited in the sense that they were at first targeted to families with three or more children, extended to those with two or more children in 1952, and then to all families with children in 1963 (Daly and Clavero, 2002: 20–1). Higher rates were awarded to families with five or more children, disabled family members, and multiple births (Dumon, 1991: 87). Additional child dependent allowances were also paid to families on welfare benefits under most benefit schemes from the 1950s. A third form of family subsidy was the child tax allowance, which co-existed with these other arrangements but varied in generosity over time (Daly and Clavero, 2002: 22). Changes to this basic child allowance system were increasingly oriented toward poverty relief rather than universal coverage with the introduction of a Family Income Supplement (FIS) in 1984, and as a mechanism for encouraging especially single parents into paid work in the 1990s. This shift is returned to below.

Limited welfare state expansion was also reflected in the introduction of the first state maternity benefit in 1911, consisting of a one-off payment based on either a husband or wife's insurance record and covering about 40 per cent of all births during the 1930s and 1940s. A separate means-tested grant was then added

Table 4.3 Expansion of policies for work–life balance under the social partnership agreements, 1988–2005

Name and duration of agreement	*Areas covered in agreement with implications for reconciliation policies*
Programme for National Recovery 1988–1990	Continued review of social welfare payments with a view to raising rates, especially Family Income Supplement. Review of anti-discrimination (pay) legislation signalled.
Programme for Economic and Social Progress 1991–1993	Child Care Bill has already been introduced. Mentions work of the Second Commission on the Status of Women. Amendments to legislation covering part-time work signalled. Childcare – government commits to providing more facilities in the public sector and will carry out research into a variety of additional pilot schemes.
Programme for Competitveness and Work 1994–1996	Increases in both (universal) Child Benefit and (targeted) Family Income Supplement Schemes. New measures to allow lone parent social welfare beneficiaries to keep more of wages when returning to workforce. Further development of employment equality legislation in line with EU guidelines. Childcare initiatives including pilot schemes in disadvantaged areas and provision for parents returning to work and training/education; implementation of recommendations of Working Group on Childcare for Working Parents. Implementation of EU Pregnancy Directive, to be monitored by social partners.
Partnership 2000 1997–1999	Support for families acknowledged as major policy area for work and work of Families Commission noted. Integration of existing separate family and child benefit schemes proposed. New employment equality and equal status legislation is proposed. Continued implementation and monitoring of implementation of Second Commission on the Status of Women recommendations. Action on childcare to include research on employment potential of childcare sector; expansion of pilot programmes to all geographical areas; first consideration of affordability issues. EU Directive on Parental Leave to be implemented.

Programme for Prosperity and Fairness 2000–2002	Commitment to increase childcare provision in both private and community sectors to be funded under 2000–2006 National Development Plan; increase use of school facilities for after-school care. New framework for equality in the workplace stemming from implementation of new Employment Equality Act 1998. National Framework for Family-Friendly policies announced and functions of National Framework Committee are detailed. A number of measures to increase workforce participation, especially women workers. Social Partnership-based review of maternity legislation to begin – establishment of new working group. Review of parental leave legislation to be conducted. Acknowledgement of work of new Family Affairs Unit.
Sustaining Progress 2003–2005	Childcare initiatives include the identification of local needs by County Childcare Committees; existing National Childcare Strategy to be further developed in order to address needs of low income-earners; greater incentives for provision of workplace-based childcare. Implementation of outstanding recommendations from Maternity Protection Review Group. Implementation of adoptive leave protection legislation. Strengthening of Parental Leave Scheme in line with recommendations of review group. Continuation of Work–Life Balance Committee.

in 1953, aiming to cover those not covered by social insurance. From 1952, a maternity allowance, different from a one-off benefit but also based on insurance contributions, paid new mothers six weeks before and six weeks after childbirth at a flat rate equal to the unemployment benefit paid to men and unmarried women at the time (Cousins, 1992). The issue of maternity leave was not addressed until much later, since a long-held assumption was that women cease working after childbirth, if not after marriage. This was also the case with respect to childcare and most other aspects of family policy related to labour market participation, and the minimalist approach was not seriously challenged until the entry of Ireland into the EEC in the early 1970s.

Joining in on European integration created an opportunity for Irish lobby groups, particularly trade unions, women's organizations, and academics, to mobilize around issues of equal pay and gender equality in the workplace. In the case of some specific policy measures, the Irish state did not have a choice about whether to respond to these demands: legal protection for equal pay was in fact a condition of Ireland's entry into the EEC, leading to a series of negotiations between the Irish government and European-level institutions from as early as 1961 (Galligan, 1998: 71). However, concrete legislative changes did not occur until a decade later, when increased internal pressure especially on the part of women's lobby groups and the union movement coincided with the need to conform to the rules of European membership. The 1970–1973 Commission on the Status of Women then played a major part in putting these commitments into practice. The Commission recommended the introduction of a number of provisions aimed at removing active gender discrimination, including the belated removal of the public service marriage bar. European directives on equal pay were finally put into effect with the enactment of the Anti-Discrimination (Pay) Act in 1975, followed by the 1977 Employment Equality Act 1977 and the establishment of the Employment Equality Authority (EEA) as a statutory body in the same year. The EEA was further responsible for stimulating policy debate around these issues and arguing that broader issues of gender equality in Irish society be addressed.[15] In this respect, integration entailed a commitment to putting some of this legislation in place, but internal mobilization made sure that state action was not simply limited to the implementation of formal EU directives.

A number of other changes in the field of the reconciliation of work and family life, even if they were not perceived primarily in these terms, followed as a result of the Commission on the Status of Women's work and its recommendations. In addition to the child benefit schemes already in existence, the FIS was introduced in 1984, aimed at supporting low-income families where the parents were in paid work. As in previous decades, maternity legislation provided another focus of state activity, but rights were somewhat extended from before. The Commission had recommended a minimum entitlement of twelve weeks guaranteed maternity leave, which eventually resulted in the 1981 Maternity (Protection of Employment) Act which gave fourteen weeks protection with an option of an additional four weeks. This was later repealed and re-enacted by the Maternity Protection Act 1994, which had the same provisions but also implemented the European Union Directive 92/85 1992 on protection for pregnant, recently given birth, or breastfeeding workers (Doyle, 1999: 133). The social insurance-based maternity grant was abolished in 1983, by which point it was worth very little in terms of cash value, and the existing pay related scheme was also reduced to 70 per cent of earnings in the following year and eventually abolished in 1988. By 1987, the contributory conditions for the general maternity allowance had been increased, thus covering fewer workers (Cousins, 1992). The general reduction in cash benefits paid by the state reflected the dire financial circumstances Ireland found itself in during the mid- to late-1980s.

However, beyond these adjustments and notwithstanding these very important equality-related changes implemented in the field of labour relations, issues of family law and women's rights outside the scope of the arena of work–life reconciliation took up most of the family policy agenda for the first two decades following Ireland's accession to the EU. Framed very much in terms of 'women's issues', debate over family law and family policy centred around the legalization of contraception, a protracted battle; abortion, which remained illegal until 2013 (and then only under very limited circumstances); and divorce, which was eventually legalized by a 1995 constitutional referendum. Issues such as parental leave, paid or not, flexi-time, and the lack of childcare facilities made minimal impact in the political arena. It was not until the mid-1990s, following initiatives in EU policy such as the Working Time and Parental Leave directives, and a sudden realization that women had largely fuelled as well as benefited from employment growth during the post-1987 boom period, that reconciliation policies seriously began to make their way onto the policy agenda.

The continuation of the state's minimalist and non-interventionist approach with respect to policies aimed directly at reconciling family and working life is reflected in the publications of the European Observatory on Family Policies, which began in 1990 and is an important source for comparing reconciliation policies in member states until about 1995. The Observatory noted the domination of Church–state conflict especially in relation to contraception, abortion, divorce and, increasingly in the late 1980s and early 1990s, connected to the uncovering of child abuse within state and Church-run facilities (Kiely and Richardson, 1996: 69). Otherwise, the Observatory tends to report little or no debate around issues such as paid parental leave or the possibilities of reconciling work and family life through adjustments to the tax and benefit system. Childcare facilities, or rather the lack of them, were a minor exception during this period, with a Working Group on Childcare Facilities for Working Parents formed during the early 1980s with a view to increasing supply. Any serious intensification of efforts to introduce new measures aimed at reconciling work and family life occurred after 1990, even if the minimalist expansion of family policy until this date placed extra limitations on the kind of policies that could immediately be pursued, and especially after reconciliation topics began to be addressed by consultative and incorporative policymaking bodies after 1995. Some of the most important changes during this decade centred on the effects of the tax and benefit system, including the child benefit structure, in order to both reduce poverty and facilitate female workforce participation; increasing the supply of childcare; parental leave legislation; and the development of a framework to encourage the implementation of 'family friendly' policies in the workplace.

Once the Irish economy began to recover after 1987, government attention turned most immediately to poverty relief along with the reduction of income taxes as a means by which to share the benefits of growth. Notably, the first social partnership agreement, the *Programme for Economic Recovery,* made a commitment to reviewing the social welfare system with a view to raising rates, especially with regard to the FIS. By this stage, the FIS was paid to low-income families with children where the parents worked at least twenty hours per week. Through the 1990s, increased attention was given to the ways in which the social welfare and taxation systems interacted, with a view to eliminating disincentives for individuals to engage in paid work. In many countries during the benefit-slashing days of the 1980s and 1990s, 'encouraging' individuals into paid work involved cutting social welfare benefits with little attention to the effect of marginal tax rates on those returning to work. In Ireland, however, the general approach was to allow individuals to both keep social welfare benefits and take up work for a certain period of time in order to ease the transition. Continued review of the family benefit and tax subsidy structure was carried out by, among other bodies and government departments, an Expert Working Group on the Integration of the Tax and Social Welfare Systems and the Commission on the Family. The latter was particularly concerned, as already noted, with issues of child welfare and thus especially the role of the FIS in alleviating poverty.

During the 1990s, some adjustments to the three forms of child support already available were carried out as a result of these investigations. First, the universal, no longer means-tested child benefit, developed since the 1940s, was increased at least eleven times between 1990 and 2001. Traditionally, special attention was paid to larger families with a higher rate paid for the fifth and subsequent children. The broadly shared definition of what constitutes a large family changed in line with contemporary demographic patterns so that a higher rate was awarded to fourth and subsequent children from 1991 and then to the third child in a family from 1995 (Daly and Clavero, 2002: 52–3). Second, Child Dependent Allowances, paid to social welfare recipients with children, received not as much policy attention. Rates were also raised, although not as frequently, and entitlement was extended by including children in full-time education, eventually up to the age of twenty-two. Third, the FIS, paid to low-income workers, was made increasingly generous through changes to the way in which was calculated. In an era of labour market shortages, policy emphasis was increasingly placed on making work pay.[16] In 1997, a One-Parent Family Payment was introduced in order to rationalize several existing different one-parent family support payments and with a view to facilitating the take-up of paid (and especially part-time) work by single parents through higher additional earnings allowances on top of welfare payments.

Turning to the issue of childcare, namely its quality, quantity, and affordability, this area had been an underlying problem in Ireland for the past two or three decades and came to the fore during the 1990s. The issue had been previously looked at in the early 1980s by a Working Group on Childcare Facilities for Working Parents and revisited by a Second Commission on the Status of Women and a new working party a decade later. In 1991, a new Child Care Act, the first major legislation in this area since 1908, was passed. However, the focus of the new legislative framework was on child protection and quality of care rather than addressing the chronic lack of supply and escalating costs of the mostly private care available. In fact, the 1991 Act has been blamed for making child-care even more expensive, since it prescribes, among other things, a very strict caregiver-to-child ratio. Supply and access issues began to be addressed more comprehensively after the passage of the 1991 Act.

Given the surge of women entering or re-entering the workforce, and aided by EU funds aimed specifically at supporting childcare infrastructure, early policy initiatives included a commitment made under the 1991–1993 *Programme for Economic and Social Progress* to open one new facility in the public sector per year and a number of regionally-based pilot schemes to fill gaps in rural supply (Dumon and Neulant, 1994: 50). Significantly, yet another working group was established under the 1997 *Partnership 2000* agreement, with the report of this working group finding a 'crisis' in childcare despite the attention already paid to the issue (Government of Ireland, 1999). The government's intention of meeting the need for increased supply is reflected especially in the *2000–06 National Development Plan*, which is published by the Department of Finance but negotiated with input from the 'social partners' and is the chief mechanism for giving specific funding commitments to many of the policy initiatives agreed to in the partnership agreements. Under the plan, the government dedicated 250 million Irish pounds under the EU supported Regional Operational Programmes for the provision of childcare facilities, thus still aiming primarily at supply issues (Government of Ireland, 2000). The general consensus appeared to be that, while the number of places available improved with government support after 1990, the new and far more neglected issue was that of affordability. Organized labour and business entered negotiations with government departments on this issue, with both groups remaining largely undecided on the precise mechanisms through which the state might subsidize childcare. Tax concessions are one possibility, but the unions in particular were concerned that this method would benefit wealthier parents while failing to meet the needs of low-income earning families. Direct subsidies have also been debated, but it is unclear whether these should be given to parents universally or on a means-tested basis, or directly to private child care providers.

Similarly, developments concerning parental leave legislation were incremental, yet at the same time served to underline the political importance of reducing the work–family trade-off in Ireland as well as going some way towards reducing it. Until the mid-1990s, there was no particular legislation governing parental leave, which was a matter of contract negotiation (Dumon, 1991: 153), with more generous conditions in the public sector. New legislation in 1998 brought Ireland into line with the EU's 1995 Parental Leave Directive, providing for fourteen non-transferable weeks of unpaid leave for each parent, taken as a block, or in parts with employer consent, until a child is five years old. A review of this legislation was agreed to under the 2000–2002 *Programme for Prosperity and Fairness*. The review group comprised the social partners along with representatives from the relevant government departments and the Equality Authority, and, chaired by the Department of Justice, Equality and Law Reform, concluded its review in late 2001. While the working group could not reach consensus on a number of issues, including the introduction of paid parental leave, and the problem of paternity (as opposed to both parental and maternity) leave, it did find that a majority of representatives agreed to an increase in parental leave from fourteen to eighteen weeks, greater protection for being able to take leave in forms other than one continuous block, and the possibility of raising the age of children covered by the legislation from five years (Government of Ireland, 2002: 9–11).

One of the most important policy initiatives, however, in the entire field of policies for achieving work–life balance is the formation of the National Framework for the Development of Family-Friendly Policies (later referred to as the National Framework for Work–Life Balance). This was established initially under the 2000–2002 *Programme for Prosperity and Fairness* in the context of 'a tightening labour market environment and the increased emphasis on human resources as a key competitive element', and was guided by a belief that family-friendly policies 'can serve a dual purpose of contributing to the needs of business as well as meeting the needs of employees with family responsibilities' (Government of Ireland, 2000: 44). A commitment to establishing a National Framework Committee was made under this agreement, to be made up of representatives from the IBEC; the ICTU; the Departments of Enterprise, Trade and Employment, Finance, Justice, Equality and Law Reform, and Social Community and Family Affairs; the Taoiseach (Prime Minister's) Department; and the semi-independent Equality Authority.

The primary objective of the National Framework Committee was to develop and monitor practical measures at the workplace level. Specific activities have included assisting in the establishment of a code of practice for parental leave; the dissemination of information regarding working-time legislation; the launch of an annual Family-Friendly Workplace Day as part of a broader awareness-raising objective; and the development of guidelines establishing best practice for jobs that are difficult to legislate around. The overall approach is thus very different from the one often adopted elsewhere, which centres on forcing enterprises to conform to mandatory requirements. It aims to adopt a bottom-up and consensual rather than a legislative and top-down strategy. The OECD has praised this approach for reducing compliance costs for business and generally promoting flexibility in working arrangements OECD, 2002: 81–7), and it has been accepted by employer and union groups as the main vehicle through which to address such issues of work–life balance in the workplace. In the case of employers in particular, the approach is welcomed as an alternative to mandatory legislation, which 'will always be resisted' by businesses.[17]

The work of the National Framework Committee has seen the issue of family-friendly workplace policies going from receiving no debate whatsoever (Dumon, 1991: 141) to receiving a great deal of public and political attention a decade later. However, some participants in the partnership process are sceptical about the extent to which the debate has translated into real change in the workplace. Despite the change from 'Family-Friendly' to 'Work–Life Balance' in order to describe the work of the Committee, there is still a strong feeling that this policy area is seen as a 'women's issue' and research shows that flexi-time and job sharing arrangements are mostly taken up by female workers in the public sector (Humphreys *et al.*, 2000: 17). The fear here, particularly on the part of female union officials, is that when work–life balance is perceived as a women's issue, there is a lack of interest on the part of the still predominantly male organized workforce in seeing policy initiatives through. Despite this, the sudden turn-around in Ireland's economic fortunes between 1987 and 2008, from a situation of unemployment to an 'era of employee choice' driven by labour shortages (Humphreys *et al.*, 2000: 49), the need for most adults to engage in paid work due to the rising cost of living, combined with the publicity generated by the work of the Committee for Work–Life Balance along with other government departments, meant that these issues made their way onto the public agenda. This is evidenced in the great deal of media attention during this period given to issues such as childcare and the contradiction between labour market trends and the constitutional designation of women's place in the home.

Higher education

The literature on higher education policy in Ireland makes much of the state's commitment to maintaining a 'binary' system, by which is meant an administrative, institutional, and philosophical differentiation between technical and university education. The following discussion is guided by the observation that, while this approach is not unique to Ireland, what makes policy here distinctive is that not only is it especially self-conscious, but there is also a consensus among policymakers and stakeholders around the objectives and implementation of such an approach. Crucially for this analysis, while policy initiatives have been top-down in nature, emanating from within the Department of Education in particular, *intermediary policymaking institutions and processes have played an important role in building that consensus*. In contrast especially to Greece and as the following chapters will show, the Irish binary strategy is guided by concern for the needs of the economy. At the forefront of state planning since at least the late 1960s and consistently reflected in policy documents and discussions developed both inside and outside the country, many of which are reviewed below, the state's strategy has been characterized by an acknowledgement of the importance of the technical education sector to economic development. Although state agencies themselves play an important and independent role in the story about the evolution of Irish higher education policy that follows, consultative and incorporative institutions have been equally important in several different respects. The more traditional short-term nature of consultative and incorporative processes and institutions in this field belies the fact that they have consistently drawn in many of the same interest groups and interest group leaders so that the relationship between state and societal interests here is more ongoing that the one-off nature of commissions and working groups involved in this policy area might suggest. The special relationship between the state and large, important, especially public institutions of higher learning is also a feature of policy development in Portugal and Greece, but the dominance of such groups is moderated in the Irish case since short-term policymaking bodies have tended to draw in a wider selection of interests at earlier stages of policy development. The overall effect is that the Irish state has been consistently better than others at taking on board the interests and concerns of important interest groups in the sector, fulfilling consultative functions, at the same time that a consensus has been built around higher education policy, thus also carrying out incorporative functions.

The policy problem

Ireland began to address the issue of tying higher education participation to labour market needs and concerns much earlier than either Portugal or Greece, beginning heavy investment in the construction of a non-university technical sector in the early 1960s. Similar strategies in Portugal were not pursued until political circumstances allowed it from the late 1970s, while serious attempts to increase participation by expanding the non-university sector began in Greece during the 1980s. Earlier Irish successes meant that the basic problem of increasing participation in higher education had been largely met by the time that the other two countries began to catch up to Western Europe in this respect. More recent challenges have involved the further development of quality control mechanisms that apply across the whole higher education sector and increasing participation and equality of access to higher education, not so much in order to increase the percentage of the labour force with third-level qualifications, but to upskill certain sectors of the population. The latter entails a greater focus on lifelong learning and the needs of mature students. These concerns again relate to labour market ones, specifically, shifting higher education priorities to suit the 'next stage' of economic development that Ireland is expected to go through if it is to return to the pace of growth the country experienced during the 1990s and 2000s. Whereas earlier education policies concentrated on providing a technically trained workforce that would provide an extra attraction for overseas companies considering investing in Ireland, the policymakers in the 2000s turned their attention to the development of indigenous companies, requiring a higher level of scientific and 'entrepreneurial' education.

The role of consultation and incorporation in shaping policy responses

As the following section discusses in much greater detail, the comparative success of Irish higher education policy is tied to an early recognition of the role that education plays in economic development and the pursuit of a consistent and self-conscious 'binary' strategy that sought to put this belief into practice. Many of the individual policy decisions within this overall strategy required the co-operation of institutions, educators and students within the higher education sector. The prevailing forms of interest group consultation and incorporation in the higher education field have been relatively traditional in nature, tending to consist of high commissions, steering committees, and similar sorts of bodies designed to address very specific problems and questions. For the most part, these are short-term, formal, peak-level processes and institutions that involve relatively elite groups, principally the leadership and management of educational institutions, academics, representatives of teaching staff, and, especially in more recent times, student organizations. Higher education, not only in Ireland, is especially conducive to this form of elite-level consultation and incorporation. Even though wider society might benefit from higher education policy, the immediate and direct targets of policies are narrower than in the case of family policy, for example. Higher education policies in the first instance apply only to certain institutions and the groups and individuals associated with them, whereas policies for work–life balance are potentially immediately relevant to all families. Higher education policy is also – at least in Ireland and also in Portugal, but, as Chapter 5 will show, not Greece – often deemed to be a technical rather than political matter and, because of this, on the whole been depoliticized.[18] This means that most of society is happy to turn the making of education policy over to 'the experts'.

The expertise of interest group leaders, especially those who run institutions of higher learning, is important, but so is their co-operation. Because these groups and individuals are also responsible for implementing policy decisions, building a consensus around a new policy direction matters. On the other hand, incorporative mechanisms also work the other way, presenting a subtle threat to such groups that their interests will be ignored if they do not consent to an overall policy shift. Something of this happened between the late 1960s and mid-1980s in Ireland. Priority for investment had been given to the technical education sector during this period, much to the annoyance of some within the university sector. While the universities tried to protect their own privileged position, they were left 'out in the cold' in policy-making terms. Only when they accepted the overall policy shift and in fact joined in by developing scientific and technical training programmes of their own did they regain priority (White, 2001: 184–96).

While higher education is thus especially conducive to high-level elite policy-making in general, including in all three of the national cases analysed in this book, there are some important differences in Ireland. First, there have been greater

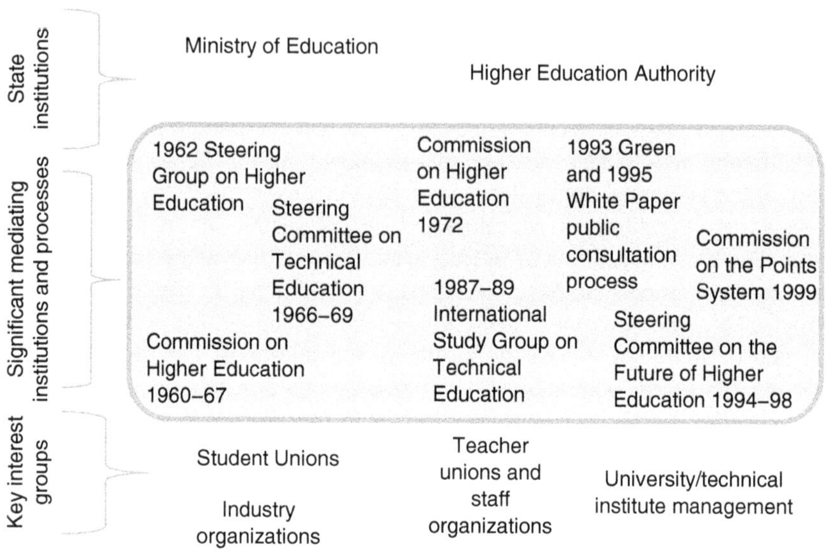

Figure 4.2 The zone of mediation in Irish higher education policy.

efforts to balance representation on committees and working groups across different institutions and to include groups such as student organizations that have not always had the same degree or type of inclusion in other cases. Second, much more policy consultation has occurred in a formal and public manner. Reports of consultative committees and working groups are published and incorporated into legislation in a traceable manner. This is not the case in Portugal, for example, where it is clear that much negotiation occurs between university rectors and government, but much of this happens informally and is thus undocumented. Third, attempts were made in Ireland during the 1990s to expand public participation beyond traditional forms, especially through a multi-layered consultation process surrounding the publication of government White and Green Papers on Education. Those developments are discussed fully below, but what is important to note is that more recent innovations in the policy process both supplemented and built on top of more traditional forms of interest group consultation and incorporation.

The evolution of higher education policy

Until the rapid expansion of third-level education through the establishment of new types of institutions during the 1970s, post-secondary school education and training was provided by universities, a series of schemes administered through local Vocational Education Committees (VECs), and a range of small-scale professional training institutions, especially for teacher training, some of which were aligned to religious establishments. The oldest university in the country (including, at the time, Northern Ireland) was Trinity College Dublin, established in 1591 and with ties to the Protestant Church and thus British colonial power. Later institutions were established in or near Dublin during the late eighteenth centuries including the Royal College of Surgeons in 1784 and St. Patrick's College, Maynooth in 1795, which was chiefly a seminary for much of its existence but later expanded its teaching programmes to become part of the National University of Ireland (NUI) system. Universities were founded at Belfast (Queen's University) in 1845, but it was not until 1908 that the NUI system was established. This, over time, had constituent colleges at Maynooth, Dublin, Galway, and Cork. The universities were permitted a great deal of autonomy from the early stages of their development, which later contrasts with the development of the non-university sector.

Vocational and technical training was administered by local city or county councils through the VECs under legislation dating from 1930. The Vocational Education Act gave these committees the task of providing 'continuation education' to supplement the existing secondary school system by providing alternative vocational second-level schools for young people as well as some degree of adult education through evening classes. The VECs also oversaw apprenticeship programmes until the 1960s, when a new type of industrial training authority was established.[19] Preceding this, however, technical education from the late nineteenth century was provided in Dublin by a series of loosely associated schools. Over time, this loose association developed into the Dublin Institute of Technology (DIT) of which these schools became constituent colleges. Eventually, in 1978, the DIT became unified in a single organization to further coordinate the different training programmes offered (Duff *et al.*, 2000). This early and somewhat more organic development of the DIT is important to highlight, in contrast to the top-down establishment of other regional vocational and technical education providers at a later date. The DIT is also the largest provider of tertiary education in Ireland today.

Higher education policy became a subject of serious political attention in the early 1960s. The abandonment of the protectionist strategies of the de Valera era after 1958 was accompanied by increased state interest and oversight in the field of tertiary education, especially in the technical and vocational or non-university sector. The beginning of this is usually traced to the publication of a government report, *Investment in Education,* in 1965. Written by a steering group that included officials from the Department of Education as well as industry and organized labour, the report was prepared as part of the OECD's Education Investment and Planning Programme. This programme grew out of a 1961 OECD conference on 'Economic Growth and Investment in Education' and consisted of the formation of research teams of experts in at least ten European nations, of which Ireland was one early and enthusiastic member (Ó Buachalla, 1996: 12–14). The research was carried out between 1962 and 1965 and identified a gap between the goals of the new development strategy based on free trade and eventual European integration and what the education system provided in terms of technical education. It was on the basis of this research that the OECD noted, with respect to the government's Second Programme for Economic

Expansion (1964–1970), that an increased orientation toward technical training, science and research and better opportunities for broader participation in higher education was required (OECD, 1969).

The OECD's report was important not because of the external advice it offered to Ireland, but because it involved an investigation team of key domestic players and thus became a means by which to build a consensus over a new technically-oriented policy direction.[20] By the time that this report was published, steps were already being taken in the direction suggested. Two major state bodies, the Steering Committee on Technical Education and the Commission on Higher Education, were responsible for turning this general desire to increase the number of science and technology, business, and engineering graduates into concrete policy proposals during the 1960s. The Steering Committee on Technical Education met between 1966 and 1969, reported in 1967 and 1969, and followed through on a 1964 government announcement of its intention to create a series of Regional Technical Colleges (RTCs). These were originally intended to provide education mostly at the secondary level in technical subjects, but by the end of the decade it was clear that they would also offer awards and qualifications at the tertiary level. The most immediate concern was to provide courses 'aimed at filling gaps in the industrial manpower structure, particularly in the technician area' (Steering Committee on Technical Education, 1967: 11). Because the type of training was important for the economy, but there was little actual public demand for such skills, this demand 'must be stimulated artificially', with the RTCs providing one of the main mechanisms for achieving this (Steering Committee on Technical Education, 1967: 7). The network of institutions was not only supposed to provide technical education for an expanding economy, but their regional basis was intended to assist in ensuring access to education for students living in areas outside the main urban centres, in the process ensuring even economic development across the country.

The Commission on Higher Education investigated a range of issues in the policy field beginning in 1960 and eventually completing its final report in 1967. Its most important recommendations for the long term included the establishment of 'New Colleges' to provide both degree-level and shorter courses in a wide range of technical and non-technical subjects to increase participation in third-level education. It recommended that these be established one each in Dublin and Limerick, the two institutions later becoming known as the National Institutes of Higher Education (NIHE) and being founded in 1964 and 1969 respectively. Funding was to be based, not simply on student numbers, but also with a view to the 'range of activities' offered by the institutions (Commission on Higher Education, 1967: 93).

Another important issue that the Commission attempted to deal with was the question of university autonomy. The newly developing non-university sector was to be more or less directly controlled by the Department of Education. This established a potential for tensions in the sector to rise, however, since while the non-university institutions were to be funded directly and did not have their own power to confer degrees and other awards, universities were treated differently.

This lack of autonomy in the non-university sector contrasting with a high degree of independence for the universities is a hallmark of Ireland's 'binary' approach to tertiary education and has remained in place since its inception. While the independence of universities could not really be questioned, policymakers noted the difficulty of 'reconciling University autonomy with state coordination' (OECD, 1969: 80). It has also been noted that the university sector was not given priority for investment and development during this era, and even that it 'in some quarters came to be regarded as a brake on economic development' (White, 2001: 96). This may have reflected what was described to this author as a traditional Department of Education view that universities are 'self-indulgent and arrogant and not contributing to Irish life.'[21] It was not until the 1980s that the universities too could play an important role in science, research and development, but their traditional and non-technical role was emphasized up to that point.

A partial answer to the question of the tension between autonomy and policy coherence was found in the Higher Education Authority (HEA), established on an ad hoc basis in 1968 before becoming a statutory body in 1972. The HEA was to have a dual function, on the one hand as a semi-independent body for the provision of policy advice and review for the tertiary education sector as a whole, and on the other as a funding agency for the university sector only. This clear distinction between the university and non-university sectors, often referred to in later policy documentation and literature as the HEA and non-HEA sectors, is further underlined by the formation of the National Council for Educational Awards (NCEA) in the early 1970s, although the legislation governing the Council was not enacted until 1979. The National Council for Educational Awards Act gave the NCEA statutory powers to provide for awards to be made at degree, diploma and certificate level in non-university institutions, as opposed to universities which award their own degrees.

In 1974, a new government announced a set of proposals that would have seen a move away from the 'binary' system that was so clearly established by this time. However, most of this was abandoned, especially since it included proposals that appeared to undercut university autonomy and thus attracted a great deal of opposition from that sector.[22] Rather, the following years saw more consolidation than change, with the policy focus shifting to ensuring greater access to higher education as the economy struggled to develop and the population of young Irish boomed. During the 1970s, enrolments in primary and secondary schools increased dramatically, so that much research and effort during the latter half of that decade and the next focused on meeting increased demand in the higher education sector. In addition, it was noted in one study, for example, that around two-thirds of students that enrolled in first-year tertiary education came from the highest socio-economic groups (Clancy and Benson, 1979: 30). Concerns over equality of access became the flip side of the debate over the role of education in developing the economy, with policy analysts urging that both goals could be met at once.

One of the obstacles to fully addressing issues of access in Ireland has been the adoption of a highly centralized and inflexible 'points system' for entrance into courses with limited numbers of places available. The points system was adopted by the NUI in 1970 for certain subjects where the number of applications outstripped supply and was expanded to the other universities by the late 1970s and eventually adopted by the non-university sector in the early 1990s. The system works by totalling the number of points gained in the Leaving Certificate Examinations at secondary level. Students take six subjects, including English, Irish and one other language. The ranking and assigning of students to courses is carried out by the Central Applications Office, a limited and private company used by the universities since 1976. Unlike other countries in which interviews, writing samples, socio-economic background, quotas for specific ethnic groups, or disability might be taken into account, this is not possible given Ireland's highly centralized admissions tradition. In addition, the particular subjects taken for the Leaving Certificate are not normally taken into account; there are usually no pre-requisites for university courses. This later drew complaints that it biases secondary school students toward 'easy' subjects, to the detriment of particularly science subjects taken up at this level, and that this may then filter through to the tertiary system. While alternatives to the points system were considered during the 1970s and again by the Commission on the Points System in 1999, it remained largely unchanged.

However, this did not prevent actual student numbers from increasing during the 1980s, and, while the basic structure of the binary system was not altered, there was some reassessment of the role of specific institutions within it. It has been noted, in particular, that the university sector, which had been somewhat sidelined since the 1960s, was reassessed by policymakers in light of the global turn towards engineering and computer science in the 1980s (White, 2001: 187). The idea was that the universities would be able to provide higher-level research in these fields than could be offered by the largely teaching-oriented non-university sector. During the first half of the 1980s, the NUI was dissolved to allow each of its formerly constituent colleges (University College Dublin, NUI Galway, NUI Maynooth, and NUI Cork) to become fully independent universities. In addition, an International Study Group on Technological Education in 1987 found that academic standards at the two NIHEs were equal to that of the universities and that they should be permitted greater autonomy and their own degree awarding powers. That resulted in the passing of the twin University of Limerick and Dublin City University Acts in 1989. Apparently, this transfer 'was achieved with remarkably little public discussion or worry about academic drift or the effect of the transfer on the rest of the technological sector' (Duff *et al.*, 2000: 61).

By 1990, participation in third-level education in Ireland had expanded to the point where it was placing a great deal of pressure on existing institutions. The number of full-time students increased more than four-fold from a total of 18,693 in the 1965–1966 academic year, to 88,193 in 1993–1994, with additional students in part-time education and training (Walshe, 1999: 117). Much of this expansion occurred during the cash-strapped decade of the 1980s, and the non-HEA sector in particular suffered from a severe lack of investment in basic infrastructure, most of which had not been updated since the formation of the RTCs in the 1970s. In 1991, a new OECD review of Irish education policy was published, which set the course of policy reform for the next decade. The OECD routinely surveys the higher education systems of its members, but these surveys consistently seem to have made a greater impact on Irish policies than in either the Portuguese or Greek cases. While much of this report focused on primary and secondary education, the general view was that while the overall system was well targeted toward the provision of technical education, it lacked coordination and suffered from a shortage of resources (OECD, 1991). In the context of economic recovery after 1987, education in general became a major area of policy development during the 1990s aimed at increasing quality and updating the relationship between higher education and economic needs, even if the basic parameters of the higher education system remained unchanged.

Many of the legislative changes influencing higher education during the 1990s stemmed from government initiatives signalled in a June 1992 Green or discussion paper entitled *Education for a Changing World*, followed by a 1995 White Paper, *Charting our Education Future*. While these two documents were issued by the Department of Education and involved much initiative from individual education ministers, they were also influenced by a series of consultation measures aimed at gaining consensus around key proposals, especially in the three year period between the publication of the Green and White Papers. These included the calling for public submissions, 'innumerable seminars and conferences, some private, the others public, up and down the country' (Walshe, 1999: 31), and the convening of the National Education Convention in October 1993, bringing together stakeholders from across the education sector. The success of the National Education Convention and its subsequent influence on government policy has been described as 'unprecedented' by Irish observers.[23] As outlined above, these developments expanded and built on the pre-existing tradition of peak-level negotiation between the state and elite interest groups. In addition, a Steering Committee on the Future Development of Higher Education, comprising representatives of government, higher education institutions, and other sector groups, conducted significant research during the mid-1990s that fed into some of the decisions made in the 1995 White Paper.

One objective of all this state activity during the 1990s was to give coherence to the entire education system, so that much of the policy consultation and subsequent government action related to education at the primary and secondary levels. That does not concern us here, but it may be noted that much discussion related to ongoing consideration of the role of the Catholic Church in administering the school system. In addition, as the original Green Paper spells out, the new approach toward the education system to include the tertiary sector was aimed at educating students to participate 'in an enterprise culture', preparing students for the changing world of work, as well as improving access for disadvantaged groups (Department of Education, 1992: 3). The seemingly increased emphasis on science and technology gained criticism from some quarters that the Irish approach to education was becoming increasingly utilitarian and failed to recognize the broader role of education in producing well-rounded citizens. However, the underlining of the economic role of education, accompanied by a concern for access issues which were taking on a new dimension in the new age of labour shortages, was nothing especially new in the Irish context, as the previous discussion shows. This continuation of the basic policy direction is further reflected in the differential treatment of the university and non-university sectors during the decade. What was new was an intensified concern with quality and quality control across both sectors, rather than simply increasing the numbers of students in higher and especially technical higher education, which was arguably the focus in previous decades.

Substantial changes to the status of the RTCs occurred during this decade. In 1992 a new Regional Technical Colleges Act and parallel Dublin Institute of Technology Act were passed. The unique role of the DIT was recognized, with the institution now permitted to confer its own awards, an opportunity not opened up to the RTCs. Amendments to these two pieces of legislation in 1994 permitted a greater degree of institutional autonomy by removing them from the direct control of the local VECs. In 1998, the RTCs were renamed Regional Institutes of Technology (RITs), reflecting in particular some very sophisticated research and high-level teaching programmes developed in the non-university sector up until this time. By far the most important change, however, appears to be in the increased levels of funding allocated to the regional institutes during this decade. Paul Hannigan of Letterkenny Institute of Technology described the contrast in these terms: running an RTC in the 1980s was 'a firefighting experience, battling with continuing incoming numbers' with very few resources, while the 1990s saw significant upgrades especially in infrastructure.[24] Clearly the economic recovery during this era allowed greater resources to be devoted to the RITs without taking anything away from the university sector.

Despite the upgrading of these institutions and the transfer of the two National Institutes of Higher Learning in Dublin and Limerick to university status in 1989, the state remained committed to 'system differentiation' during the 1990s, with the 1995 White Paper stating that: 'The diversity of institutions and the separate missions of the two broad sectors will be maintained to ensure maximum flexibility and responsiveness to the needs of students and to the wide variety of social and economic requirements' (Department of Education, 1995). This enduring belief in the benefits of a self-conscious binary strategy for higher education seems to have affected the decision to decline the DIT's application for university status in 1997. An international review group considering the issue voiced concern that DIT might 'drift away from the teaching of practical subjects' at various levels, 'which are of such inestimable value to industry and commerce, and to local communities' (Higher Education Authority, 1998). While some at DIT were initially very disappointed by this outcome (Duff *et al.*, 2000: 64–71), the institution has more recently chosen not to reapply for university status. This seems to stem from a realization that DIT, with its own power to confer awards and considerable freedom to design its own teaching and research programmes, can achieve good things within the existing system.[25]

While the upgrading of the technical institutes and their changing status in the law was mostly welcomed by the non-university sector, proposed changes to the governing structures and funding of universities met with more opposition. Three specific areas of tension were: government proposals that were viewed by the universities as undercutting their traditionally autonomous status, including changes to the way in which universities are governed and proposals to increase the role of the HEA in ensuring quality in teaching; proposals surrounding the dissolution of the NUI into separate and independent universities; and funding, especially the removal of student fees paid directly to universities. The first and second sets of issues became major points of conflict between the state (involving not only the government of the day, but also the independent state body, the HEA), and the individual universities, and many of the most contentious proposals were dropped or watered down between the publication of the 1995 White Paper and the enactment of a new Universities Act (Walshe, 1999). This 1997 Act laid out the responsibilities of universities, paying greater attention to quality assurance than in the past, and also dealt with the reconstitution of the NUI system.

The new emphasis on quality was also reflected in the restructuring of the awards and qualifications system under the Qualifications (Education and Training) Act 1999, which replaced the existing NCEA with a National Qualifications Authority, responsible for overall policy and general oversight, and two further separate bodies, the Further Education and Training and the Higher Education and Training Awards Councils (White, 2001: 236–7). Changes to the qualifications framework are important for the story told here because they are the principal means by which states can influence the content and quality of courses.

The abolition of tuition fees for undergraduate students in 1996 was understandably popular with students, but has been criticized as a regressive step that advantages already privileged students and their families by academics and some social action groups, and as a move that endangered the financial health and thus quality of teaching programmes by the universities.[26] While state officials in the education field believe that the universities well overstated their case,[27] the issue of how best to ensure equity in terms of access to higher education remains. Universities are still funded almost entirely and directly by the state through a combination of block grants and 'fees' paid per and on behalf of students from the state budget. In the period 1995–2000, this saw the contribution of the state to funding higher education, including both the university and non-university sectors, remain stable at around 1.3 per cent of GDP, which is also about the OECD average (OECD, 2004: 14).

Two recent and important reports are both representative of some of the contemporary issues facing higher education in Ireland and proving influential on the public debate. The OECD's 2004 report on Irish higher education policy pointed especially to the need to better coordinate different elements of the existing system, as well as presenting a series of suggestions as to how to move away from the reliance on direct state funding in order to improve the quality of teaching and research programmes and move into new fields. *The University*

Challenged (2001), commissioned by the HEA and referred to as the Skilbeck report, pointed to similar issues involved in adapting to globalization, Europeanization, and the resulting new research and teaching environment. Access and equity issues also tend to be framed in these terms, with policies aimed at expanding life-long learning tied into the labour market challenges posed by the workings of the new economy.

The 2004 OECD report underlined how well Ireland's 'binary' higher education system had served the country, emphasizing the 'extent to which the [technical] institutes see themselves as different from the universities' and the special role they play in local economic development, promoting wider participation in education through their regional focus and through 'provision of ladders of opportunity through different educational levels', and their support for apprenticeship, applied knowledge, and skills-based training (OECD, 2004: 20). However, the differential treatment of the university and non-university sectors, with the former awarded greater autonomy and overseen by the HEA and the latter administered directly by the Department of Education and Science, as it is now known, is seen by many as hampering co-ordination within the sector as a whole and a barrier to research collaboration between institutions. The report suggests that the basic 'binary' structure be maintained, but that a new buffer organization be formed in order to oversee the entire sector and to replace the HEA, possibly to be named the Tertiary Education Authority. Little objection was raised to such an institutional reconfiguration.

The focus on collaboration and moreover the need for institutional specialization, forced not only by the realization that 'in a small country, no single institution can excel at everything' (O'Hare, 2005: 14)[28] but also by the pressures of needing to engage in increasingly technology-intensive research, is also extensively discussed in the Skilbeck report (Skilbeck, 2001). This has fuelled increased policy focus on strategic planning, research evaluation, the attraction of private sources of funding, and quality assurance in teaching programmes. Much of this current debate is also coloured by overall state and sector group concern over the 'next stage' of Ireland's economic growth. Whereas the post-1987 recovery was largely fuelled by overseas investment, especially in the computing and pharmaceutical industries, the concern was now to create indigenous industries that will survive any shift in overseas investment to new regions competing on the basis of low labour costs.[29]

Ireland's economic transformation, and especially the tightening labour market during the 1990s and 2000s, also gave new life to the traditional concern with ensuring equality of access to higher education. While this was previously seen in terms of encouraging students from lower socio-economic backgrounds into education, and this concern remains, there is also a shift to a focus on adults or 'second-chance' students, and those disadvantaged by disability or ethnic background. The Commission on the Points System, reporting in 1999, was charged with looking at the impact of the existing centralized system for entry to higher education on these groups, and noted especially that only two per cent of university students were adults in 1997 (Commission on the Points System,

1999: 12). While the Commission recommended that the points system be retained, it also suggested that additional programmes at the level of each institution be introduced in order to increase adult participation and retraining. A target was set at 15 per cent of places for students over the age of 23 to be made available by 2005, to be increased to around 25 per cent by 2015, 'a proportion which would bring Ireland closer to the average participation rate for mature students in OECD countries as a whole' (Commission on the Points System, 1999: 105). Increasing broader access, however, has always been a main focus of the RITs and the DIT, many of which have extensive programmes for encouraging this (Dublin Institute of Technology, 2005).

Immigration

The history of immigration policy in Ireland is a short one, and is clearly overshadowed by the country's history as a nation of migration. Net immigration did not become a fact, let alone a policy issue, until well after the post-1987 economic recovery had begun. Policy responses, therefore, are both delayed and rather underdeveloped, especially in comparison to the fields of family and higher education policy discussed above. Although state action in this area was stepped up during the early 1990s, much of the new migratory flow was left to the market to regulate, with mixed results. Part of the explanation for the neglect of immigration policy until very recently lies in the simple fact that it is only very recently that failures in this 'market-led' approach to immigration policy have become visible. This is even in comparison to the other EU members that are considered new countries of migration, including Portugal and Greece. The remaining part of the explanation lies in the fact that it was left off the agenda of, importantly, the social partnership agreements and outside the scope of other consultative policymaking processes during the 1990s. It was not until the second half of the following decade that moves towards state regulation of economic migratory flows began in earnest.

The policy problem

The history of Irish immigration policy until the mid-1990s is extremely limited and thus easily summarized. The basis of all legal immigration was laid out by the Aliens Act of 1935, which was later supplemented and amended through various orders, the most important being the Aliens Order of 1946. This legislative framework laid out the rules and regulations governing border control in Ireland, placing responsibility for overseeing this arena with the Ministry of Justice. In particular, it gave broad powers to the Minister of Justice to expel migrants deemed to be illegal, a provision that formed the basis of much legal dispute during the 1990s. In reality, however, there was very little inward migration, with the exception of the acceptance of small groups of European refugees during the period surrounding the Second World War (Tracy, 2000). This made Ireland a particularly culturally homogenous society, a fact that was not altered until very recently. As in the other two national case studies discussed in the following chapters, immigration was overshadowed and its impact undermined by the deep-seated tradition of migration that developed in Ireland following independence. Between 1946 and 1966, a net total (which takes into account the numbers arriving as well as those leaving) of almost eight hundred thousand Irish left the country, giving rise to a concern that the Irish population would go into permanent decline.[30]

Net migration continued to drop during the 1980s and into the 1990s, and it was not until 1996 that migration data reveals that the numbers of migrants entering the country began to outweigh the numbers of Irish residents departing. In 1991, an inward flow of around 33,000 migrants was still outnumbered by the 35,000 who departed. By 1996, however, around 7,000 more migrants entered the country than departed. This pattern intensified over the next decade, with net migration of almost 30,000 individuals during the year 2000, jumping to over 40,000 during 2004. This was despite the slowdown in economic growth that occurred after late 2001.[31] During the earlier part of this decade of migration, the vast majority of migrants were Irish citizens returning from the United Kingdom, supplemented by a boom in the arrival of asylum seekers. Labour migration, initially from other EU member states to include Eastern Europe after 2004 due to Ireland's notably generous policies toward new accession countries, but increasingly from elsewhere in the world, began a little later. The trend continued until 2008, after which the migration flow began to slow, then reverse. This was in part in response to a tightened regulatory framework, discussed below, but also in response to the global economic crisis, which led to, once again, mass emigration, as well as a halt to new arrivals from elsewhere in the world. The focus of this discussion, and this book, however, is on the period preceding the economic crisis. Note then, that the problem of how to develop an adequate legal framework to cope with the changing migration reality was thus a very new one in Ireland during the 1990s and 2000s, even in comparison with Portugal and Greece which started to receive significant numbers of migrants as early as the 1970s, even if large numbers of these were at first return migrants from Portuguese-speaking Africa in the former case, and Europe and North America in the latter. As in the two Southern European cases, the bulk of new migrants to Ireland initially filled gaps in unskilled or low skilled segments of the labour market, but more attention and interest was paid during the period after 2005 to the recruitment of skilled workers and entrepreneurs.

The role of consultation and incorporation in shaping policy responses

As the following section further details, the Irish immigration regime began adjusting to the rapidly changed migration reality rather belatedly. At the time of writing, a comprehensive legal framework is yet to be implemented. Until the late 1990s, there were few interest groups actively lobbying on the subject, including migrant and human rights organizations but also organized labour and business. In addition, and perhaps partly because of the lack of interest on the part of the latter organizations, labour migration especially was one of the few major policy issues that was neither the subject of the social partnership negotiations nor of alternative forms of policy consultation until quite recently. During the course of this research, an ICTU representative acknowledged the 'failure' of the social partnership process to conceptualize and deal with the challenges posed by this issue during the 1990s and 2000s. Referring to the social partnership process as a 'problem solving rather than advocacy' approach for interest groups, she argued that the system works well when agreement can be reached over what the policy problem in question actually is and when the partnership agreements are very specific about what agreement has been reached. In the case of immigration, there was 'no consensus yet' on the problem that immigration poses, delaying policy development during the 2000s.[32]

It is true that the immigration issue has been paid far less attention at this level than have other policy problems, but, on the other hand, its prominence on the social partnership negotiating agenda did rise after 2000. The first steps towards incorporating a review of immigration policy into the social partnership process were made under the *Programme for Prosperity and Progress,* in effect between 2000 and 2002. This agreement mentioned the need for a consultative approach to immigration policy for the first time, as well the need for policy to be developed in order 'to address the needs of the labour market'. This short statement was particularly vague, but it did signal the launch of a public consultation process that took place during 2001 and 2002 and which helped lay the ground for developments in the immigration policy field between 2005 and 2008 (Government of Ireland, 2000: 118). This increased concern gave rise to a

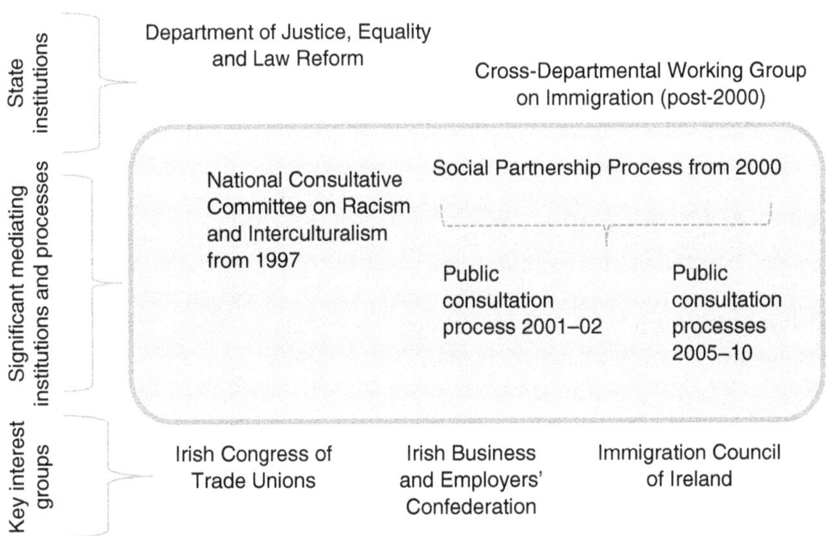

Figure 4.3 The zone of mediation in Irish immigration policy.

broader set of consultative exercises, mostly fitting into the one-off or short-term category outlined in Chapter 3, but at a peak governmental level.

Four actions were taken under the watch of the Fianna Fáil–Progressive Democrat Coalition Government after 2000 following on from the announcement made in the *Programme for Prosperity and Progress.* First, a comparative study outlining some of the alternative labour immigration frameworks available to Ireland was commissioned and carried out by the International Migration Organization. Second was an internal review of processes and procedures in place at the Immigration and Citizenship Division of the Department of Justice, Equality and Law Reform; third was the establishment of a Cross-Departmental Working Group on Immigration to coordinate policy development and delivery. Fourth, and most important for the purposes of this book, a public consultation process was launched in 2001 and reported back on in 2002. This consultation exercise involved the presentation and analysis of sixty-six submissions, some from individuals but most significantly from non-government organizations, organized labour and business, and migrant and human rights lobby groups (Department of Justice, Equality and Law Reform, 2002). With labour migration as a key focus, this consultation process then went on to inform the publication of a 2005 public discussion paper on immigration policy. That consultation exercise led to a proposed Immigration and Residency Bill, which failed to be enacted in both 2008 and 2010.

Post-2000 exercises in public consultation, both within and outside the social partnership process, also helped channel the efforts of human and migrant rights organizations. Increased activism in these quarters came in response to a wave of anti-migrant and especially anti-asylum seeker sentiment that erupted in the mid-1990s. The most notable of these was the 2001 formation of the Immigration Council of Ireland, a non-governmental but comparatively well-resourced umbrella group that has become one of the major lobbying forces in the immigration policy arena. The gradual incorporation of interest groups into the policymaking process has also taken place, albeit in an arena somewhat peripheral to immigration policy and especially labour migration policy, on issues of migrant integration and anti-racism. One of the most important of these developments is the NCCRI. This semi-autonomous body was established in 1997 by the Department of Justice, Equality and Law Reform, and is responsible for 'equality proofing' government policy, allocating resources to organizations that work on behalf of ethnic minorities, and overseeing the Advisory Committee on Racism and Interculturalism. The Advisory Committee is described as a 'partnership body' in the sense that it draws together state agencies and community representatives into a permanent consultative institution. The work of this organization overlaps with the National Action Plan Against Racism, which is surrounded by a participatory policymaking process launched in 2001. Such developments do seem to have gone some way toward undercutting the xenophobic currents that emerged with the appearance of the 'refugee problem' during the 1990s.

The evolution of immigration policy

In fact, coping with the 'refugee problem' in the 1990s provided the first point of departure from the immigration code established by the Aliens Act as far back as 1935. The development of a policy framework governing labour migration to Ireland will be discussed shortly, but, before that, some analysis of policies related to refugees and asylum seekers is required. It was argued earlier that refugee policy is of relevance to this book only insofar as it overlaps with and is integrated into a national strategy for labour migration. There are several additional reasons why it is important to discuss Irish policies toward refugees and asylum seekers during the 1990s in relation to the country's general immigration policy. First, the arrival of new groups of asylum seekers in the early 1990s is obviously related to the Irish economic boom that began around this time. Asylum seekers are clearly not stupid; they may have legitimate reasons for fleeing their own countries, but it is reasonable and rational to flee to a new country that is capable of offering not only protection for basic human rights but also economic opportunities that might underpin a new life. Second, as the first new types of groups to arrive were very different from the groups of return migrants that had dominated until this time, asylum seekers did present a major challenge to the existing legal framework governing immigration, and thus helped set the tone of the political debate. This was not always in a positive direction, since Irish policy discourse over the past decade has at times been injected with heavy doses of xenophobia and racism, especially on the part of the mainstream media and certain political elites. Third, and perhaps related, the refugee 'problem' in Ireland has parallels in both Portugal and Greece, where illegal migration rather than the arrival of asylum seekers has provided the greatest challenge to forging a comprehensive immigration strategy.

It has been noted that the initial arrival of asylum seekers in the 1990s, alongside what until then was largely return migration by Irish citizens, was so significant that '[t]he term "refugee" therefore entered popular parlance as synonymous with the first wave of non-Irish immigrants who arrived of their own accord'. Put more bluntly, 'for the first time, a group of non-white people became visible' (Allen, 1999: 99). This phenomenon has even influenced both primary and secondary research available on immigration policy overall, with the research focusing overwhelmingly on refugees and asylum seekers (Hughes and Quinn, 2004: 37). To give an idea of the scale of Ireland's rapid transformation into a reception country for asylum seekers, while there were only thirty-nine officially recognized asylum seekers in the country in 1992, there were as many as 10,325 by 2001 (International Organization for Migration/Department of Justice, Equality and Law Reform, 2002: 11). This is despite a number of measures designed to 'toughen up' against possibly illegitimate claimants over these nine years.

The first major piece of legislation related to this area was the Refugee Act of 1996, which was influenced not only by events occurring in Ireland, but also by European-level moves to coordinate policies related to asylum seekers.

Specifically, Ireland was involved, along with other European Union members, in the negotiations leading up to the signing of the Dublin Convention. This agreement came into force in 1997, and aimed to prevent individuals from applying for refugee status across a number of European countries by only allowing applicants to process their claims in the original country in which they entered the European Union. The 1996 Irish legislation thus enacted the 1951 Geneva Convention on the Status of Refugees and the 1967 Protocol related to the Status of Refugees at the same time that it outlined the process for applying for refugee status. The Refugee Act was then amended by the Immigration Act 1999 and the Illegal Immigrants (Trafficking) Act 2000, with the new Immigration Act related to the regulation of immigration in general but clearly relevant and possibly most relevant to asylum seekers. Earlier that year, a High Court decision had struck down provisions of the 1935 Aliens Act which allocated extraordinary responsibilities for expelling illegal aliens to the Minister of Justice on the basis that the Act did not set down any policies and principles by which such decisions would be made, thus violating the country's Constitution. The government's response was to attempt to re-enact these powers through the 1999 Immigration Act. A later iteration of this dispute between legislature and judiciary played out in 2004 along practically exactly the same lines, leading to the introduction of a new Immigration Bill later that year.

During 2000, provided for under Social Welfare legislation, a system of direct provision for asylum seekers was established, institutionally delegated to the new Reception and Integration Agency. Instead of providing asylum seekers with social welfare benefits or allowing them to work, they would now be housed together in dedicated centres, provided food directly, and allocated a very small living allowance. While governments argue that this policy is designed to benefit asylum seekers by making sure their needs are met, advocacy groups tend to see it as a cynical attempt to reduce the number of application for refugee status, since the services provided are very basic and personal freedoms are somewhat circumscribed. It should be noted, however, that the direct provision does not go as far as some countries seeking to reduce asylum seeking have done, such as the establishment of permanent and secure 'detention' centres.

Further legislative action aimed at regulating and curbing the influx of asylum seekers occurred after 2000.[33] The Immigration Act 2003 further amended the 1996 legislation related to refugees and asylum seekers, including a controversial clause to make carriers such as airlines or passenger ferries responsible for checking that passengers are carrying the correct travel documentation and imposing fines if they do not (a move that has the potential to conflict with United Nations' conventions on the ability of refugees to travel without documentation). The Act also aimed to streamline and speed up the asylum seeking process in order to reduce the numbers waiting to have their refugee status determined. Also in 2003, moves were made to prevent children in Ireland from being guaranteed automatic citizenship and to prevent parents of Irish-born children automatically being guaranteed residency rights (*jus soli*). More significantly on this theme, a national referendum was held in 2004 on whether to alter the Irish

Constitution to allow the legislature to determine citizenship requirements, something that had been blocked in the past, and whether to extend automatic citizenship only to children with at least one parent who is or who is entitled to be an Irish citizen. The constitutional amendment was passed by an overwhelming majority of citizens, and the new powers were exercised in the passage of the Irish Citizenship (Amendment) Act 2004.

This analysis shows that the issue of refugee and asylum seekers received considerable legislative action and attention in the period after 1990. The policy debate surrounding these developments reads like a tug-of-war between refugee advocacy groups and a series of governments determined to decelerate the inflow of asylum seekers that accompanied the Irish economic recovery. Two unfortunate consequences stem from this. On the one hand, government rhetoric during this period often sought to tap into xenophobic undercurrents that are undeniably present in Irish mass political culture and only different from similar happenings occurring elsewhere in Europe in the very recent emergence of immigration as a national issue. This was fed by alarmist media reports that tended to overstate the impact of the 'refugee problem' on the economy. It can also be noted, however, that public anti-refugee sentiment actually appeared to wane over time, so that, by around 2003, public opinion appeared to have swung further in favour of asylum seekers, measured in public support for asylum seekers in several high-profile cases in which young people in particular were under threat of expulsion from the country. It seems the case that the depth of racism and intolerance was not as deep as a number of politicians seemed to think, and the crackdown on asylum seekers and possible illegal migration as a means of gaining popular support had been somewhat miscalculated. A worker for a non-governmental organization in the immigration field put it this way: many of the mechanisms put in place, such as restrictions placed on health and education services to undocumented migrants, are circumvented 'in a very Irish way', in that such services are extended anyway despite any restrictions outlined by law.[34] As the following section on integration issues shows, government agencies themselves are in fact in part responsible for undermining the racist rhetoric of some individual politicians, despite the ongoing temptation to resort to this strategy.

On the other hand, and perhaps more importantly for the purposes of this book, the dominance of the political debate by the 'refugee problem' diverted attention from the need for the country to review and reformulate its labour migration scheme. As noted above in the discussion on family policy, Ireland faced a labour shortage by the late 1990s. It would have to look at importing labour once indigenous sources, such as women who had previously opted out of the paid workforce, had been exhausted. Furthermore, as the discussion on higher education revealed, although Ireland has done well in terms of skills development in the general population over the past several decades, the need to further attract skilled labour in new industries such as information technology had been recognized by both government officials and interest group leaders, especially from organized labour and business in this case. In this context, a fully comprehensive labour migration scheme was extremely slow to get off the ground, but analysis of the current debate as well as past developments is necessary to illustrate how policy is gradually being reoriented toward these goals and how the 'social partners' are playing a role in this reorientation.

During the first decade or so following Ireland's post-1987 economic boom, most of the need for skilled workers in particular was filled from local sources, including Irish citizens returning from overseas. Although accompanied by a steady increase in the number of asylum seekers, data shows that both return migrants and the small numbers arriving from non-EU states were much better educated than the average Irish worker, and thus filled a major skills gap in the labour market (Barrett and Trace, 1998). This began to change, however, as the decrease in the proportion of return migrants as a percentage of overall immigrants declined. One estimate puts this at peaking at 55 per cent in 1999, declining to at least 40 per cent by 2003, and falling further after that (Immigrant Council of Ireland, 2003: 5). A shift in migration patterns toward unskilled or low-skilled workers was clearly taking place, which could be measured in several ways. While the earnings of non-EU migrants in the mid-1990s were on average higher than Irish workers, reflecting higher skills levels, a decade later migrants are less skilled and earn much less (Hughes and Quinn, 2004: 2). Furthermore, analysis of the country of origin of migrants shows that the proportion of non-EU migrants from OECD countries was declining, with the share of those from EU accession and EU applicant countries and elsewhere in the developing world, notably South-East Asian migrants taking up positions in the service sector, increasing. With that, migrants were increasingly concentrated in the service industry, especially the hotel and restaurant sector (Ruhs, 2003: 21).

All this occurred, for better and for worse, under a labour migration system that had not undergone major change since it had been established well before the 1990s. Ireland's labour migration system is 'employer-driven' in that only employers may recruit and hold permits for overseas workers. In this system, foreigners from outside the EU wishing to work in Ireland are granted one out of four types of permit, namely short term 'work permits', 'work visas' or 'authorizations' for longer term stays, intra-company transfer permits, and permits for trainees. However, by far the majority of foreign workers take advantage of the work permit system, and thus it is the main source of debate over labour migration in Ireland. In order to employ a foreign worker, employers must first prove that they have been unable to fill a vacant position from either within Ireland or within the EU, then apply to bring a particular foreign citizen to the country in order to fill that job. Work permits are then valid for up to one year, which the employer may apply to have renewed. There are a number of problems with the work permit system, some of which inform the current attempt to negotiate a more comprehensive labour migration strategy that is discussed below. The most common accusation, not limited to Ireland but found wherever such systems exist, is of employer abuse of the system and the resulting exploitation of foreign nationals that can result. Because it is the employer who holds the work permit, workers may be promised work conditions and levels of pay that differ from what they are actually given, and because workers are permitted to work with that employer only, they are unable to compete freely on the labour market for a better job (Immigrant Council of Ireland, 2003: 32).

The 'labour market test', which requires employers to make an attempt to recruit workers from EU and Irish sources first, has been in place since 2000, and was strengthened in 2003 and further reformed in both 2004 and 2006. In addition to a reinforcement of the requirement that employers gain a letter of clearance from FÁS, the state's employment agency, certifying that the job vacancy has been advertised for a certain length of time before applying to the Department of Enterprise, Trade and Employment for a work permit, new procedures were introduced under the Employment Permits Act 2003 that barred employers in some sectors of the economy from applying. This latter measure is based on a quarterly labour market survey conducted by the Department of Enterprise, Trade and Employment designed to identify labour market gaps. The Employment Permits Act 2004 brought in tougher penalties for illegal employment and put in place procedures for facilitating the issue of work permits in sectors of the economy identified as having high need (Quinn and Hughes, 2005: 28). In addition, a separate system of work visas and authorizations was introduced in 2000 to enable the entry of skilled workers in specific areas of high need, especially information technology, engineering and town planning, and health and social welfare. This type of visa is issued directly to workers through overseas Irish consulates and thus bypasses the work permit system (Immigrant Council of Ireland, 2003: 37). However, this alternative system attracted far fewer workers than the traditional work permit system, perhaps simply because it was so new and was thus not yet well understood by potential migrant communities. The 2006 reform further attempted to address the vulnerabilities of workers in an employer-driven system.

A reflection of the shift from return migration accompanied by an influx of asylum seekers towards large-scale labour migration is that, during the period 1997 to 1999, the number of applications for asylum exceeded the number of new work permits issued, but, since 2000, the number of work permits has grown much more rapidly than asylum applications so that, during the period 2000 to 2002, work permits accounted for 67.6 per cent of applications for work permits and asylum taken together. The total number of work permits issued to non-EU nationals increased from 5,750 in 1999 to 40,504 in 2002 (Ruhs, 2003: 4–10). A sign that policy might have been out of step with real trends here is that in 2001 the government predicted that 12,600 immigrant workers would be needed each year for the next six years to fill labour demand, and yet between January and July 2002 as many as 20,000 new work permits were issued (Watt, 2002: 7).

The Irish state's attempt to keep control over the scope of non-EU labour migration through the work permit system was matched by a deliberate policy of filling labour market gaps primarily from within the EU, to include the 2004 EU accession countries of Central and Eastern Europe. As the next two chapters show, much of the immigration policy action in other EU member states connected to European integration during the 1990s related to meeting the requirements of the Schengen Agreement, which commits signatories to allow free movement of individuals within the Schengen area. Ireland, along with the UK, is not part of this agreement, but the two countries already share a Common Travel Area Agreement that does affect some policy decisions. Irish consideration of EU developments is reflected more readily in the debate over how to treat new member states when it comes to labour market issues. The EU's policy toward the 2004 accession countries allowed existing member states to place a bar on workers from the new member nations for up to seven years. Other European countries, especially Germany, which has consistently suffered high unemployment, feared a sudden influx of workers from the East. Ireland's decision not to place such a bar has been described as 'possibly the most significant labour immigration policy decision taken by the Irish government in recent years' (Ruhs, 2003: 2) and witnessed a flood of arrivals from Eastern Europe. Irish exceptionalism here can probably be explained by the fact that labour shortages were being experienced when this decision was made. Yet, despite government attempts to limit the number of non-EU migrants arriving to work in Ireland, it is clear that up until the 2008 financial crisis at least, the trend was for increased inward migration from both within and outside the EU.

Irish responses to new immigration challenges reflect a balancing act that many OECD countries face with respect to labour market issues. On the one hand, unskilled migrant labour is useful and, in times of growth, the economy needs it. Migrants often perform tasks and accept a lower material threshold of living than Irish workers. Yet this has to be carefully managed. Very liberal immigration policies, like that extended to the EU accession countries in 2004, can create their own problems. During the period in which the research for this book took place, a sudden arrival of especially Polish workers had created a welfare crisis in central Dublin. Even if many of these workers arrived with a number of skills, especially in construction and related trades, and gaps in the labour market here would suggest they would find jobs, language barriers for one thing provided obstacles to their immediate employment. Catholic charities were left to pick up the pieces. In addition, despite Ireland's investment in technical and scientific training over past decades, it is argued that the country would also benefit from increased skill-based migration. Like most other OECD countries, there are gaps in the health care professions in particular, although Irish policymakers have stressed the need to attract scientific researchers and entrepreneurs or self-employed migrants (Department of Justice, Equality and Law Reform, 2005: 59–65).

The negotiated approach to immigration policy that developed after 2000 culminated in a 2005 discussion document on proposals for a new comprehensive immigration framework. The discussion document argued that existing Irish immigration law 'is not suitable for the needs of the modern Ireland, now a country of net inward migration'. Although legislative reforms have been carried out over the past decade, these have been 'stop-gap measures generally brought forward to address specific aspects of immigration that needed an urgent legislative response'. Proposed changes presented in the discussion document would constitute a 'root-and-branch replacement of the present law' which can be 'modified as needs will require and that will provide a fair and transparent set of procedures for the day-to-day implementation of these policies' (Department of Justice, Equality and Law Reform, 2005: 21). While the proposed Immigration Bill clearly focused on labour migration, it was also informed by a new post 11 September emphasis on border security. The increasing importance of economic migration, including on a short-term basis, must be coordinated with a new system of permanent or long-term migration. Up until this point, Ireland rather strangely had no system of residence permits. This would be reviewed in order to 'select people as potential future citizens, not just workers' (Department of Justice, Equality and Law Reform, 2005: 15). Additional schemes are required in order to attract entrepreneurs, researchers, and, something that was mentioned in the 2004 OECD review of Irish higher education policy, international fee-paying students. There is no signal, however, that the system of employer-based work permits is likely to be abandoned.

The debate in the latter half of the 2000s, then, was informed by the presumed failures of the market-led approach to immigration that prevailed during the 1990s. In particular, Irish advocates for migrants and their communities are generally extremely critical of national immigration policy, generally reflecting a view that:

> There is no coherent legislation or social policy on immigration, and any provisions have been ad hoc, piecemeal and designed, to a large extent, (a) to control immigration and present it as a 'security matter' rather than to promote the rights of immigrants, and (b) to exclude rather than provide a clear route of access for immigrants to Ireland. The emphasis in our system is on meeting the demands of the economy for labour rather than on upholding the rights and meeting the needs of immigrants and their families. The result of this employer-led and market-driven policy is that immigrants to our country are insecure and vulnerable to exploitation.
>
> (Immigrant Council of Ireland, 2003: vii)

Furthermore, policy fragmentation is evident in the way that labour migration is institutionally differentiated and differently overseen from other aspects of immigration policy. Labour migration and more specifically the work permit scheme is administered by the Department of Enterprise, Trade and Employment, and yet all other aspects of immigration policy and migrant integration are handled by the Department of Justice, Equality and Law Reform. That need for a comprehensive system of working and residency permits has been recognized by the state and does appear to be in the process of being incorporated into government legislation. Into this overall framework, there are a myriad of seemingly small and technical issues to be resolved. One of the ones often mentioned by migrant advocacy groups is changing legislation to allow those on student or other short-term visitors visas to apply for work permits and longer-term stays once already in the country. In addition, there has so far been little attention to the absence in law for a right to family reunification and this constitutes a current 'big issue' for non-governmental organizations in the field.[35]

During the time in which the field research for this analysis was being carried out, however, Ireland's relationship with the rest of the EU with respect to immigration policy appeared to dominate the political agenda. Following the opening up of the Irish economy to the new accession countries in 2004, large numbers of migrants most notably from Poland arrived ready for work. Despite labour market gaps across some sectors of the economy, many of these new migrants were unable to find jobs immediately, in many cases because of a lack of English language skills. Because such workers are not immediately entitled to the benefits of the social welfare system, this began to put pressure on private charities, especially church-based ones, whose resources are extremely limited. A related problem, mentioned by both organized labour and business during the course of this research, is the existence of barriers to the recognition of the qualifications of EU migrants. While in theory they have free access to the Irish labour market to work in the skilled jobs that they may be trained for, either a lack of recognition processes or resistance from local professional organizations can result in these workers being forced into unskilled and low-paid jobs.[36]

Summary

Taken together, the development of policies for the reconciliation of family and working life, higher education and immigration demonstrate the multiple layers of Irish consultative and incorporative policymaking at work. Traditional peak-level and formal but one-off or short-term consultation with experts and stakeholders, represented by such arrangements as commissions of inquiry, have been consistently used to build consensus around policy shifts in the higher education field. Older forms of consultative policymaking also shaped early developments associated with the formulation of policies for work–life balance, to include the 1970–1973 Commission on the Status of Women and the Commission on the Family two decades later. However, it is newer forms of consultative and incorporative policymaking, represented by the social partnership process, that have been primarily responsible for forging consensus around specific policy measures in that field. In the case of immigration policy, a lack of central consultation between the state and interest groups delayed the evolution of an adequate response to the new migration reality in the 1990s. Since 2000, however, the take-up of immigration as a topic of negotiation within the context of social partnership broadened policy consultation in this arena as well.

Notes

1 For an overview of these traditional forms of interest group incorporation, common to Westminster-style political systems, see Murphy (2004).
2 The small-scale and associated inefficiency of Irish farming, especially in the West (see Campbell, 2005: 8–41), can be traced to the forced break-up of land into small plots under early colonial rule. The inclusion of agricultural interests in this populist

coalition sets it apart from others of its type, especially in South America in the three decades before 1960. This only further highlights the primacy of nationalism over class-based interests and ideologies in twentieth century Ireland.

3 The failure of the import-substitution-industrialization also caused some Irish academics to liken Irish fortunes to those of Latin America, thus entering the *dependista* versus modernization theory debate. See in particular O'Hearn (1989) and also Jacobsen (1994).

4 On the features of the model and how it has changed over time in the British case see Marsh and Smith (2001).

5 In the sense used by Schmitter (1974).

6 A distinct indigenous ethnic minority. Until very recently, society in the Republic of Ireland was overwhelmingly ethnically (and religiously) homogeneous, with this exception.

7 Interview with leadership of Union of Students in Ireland, Dublin, 28 April 2005.

8 The two most important examples here are the exclusion Irish Small and Medium Enterprises Association since it frequently clashes with Ireland's main peak business and employers' representative, the IBEC, and the battle fought between the government and the umbrella organization, the Community Platform, which was eventually expelled from the partnership process permanently after it refused to sign the 2002 *Sustaining Progress* agreement.

9 In Spain, which otherwise shares many features of the 'Southern European' model of social policy, there has been a resistance to making such constitutional commitments since explicit state 'intervention' and moulding of family life is so closely associated with the Francoist regime.

10 On the failure of the Mother and Child Scheme and its importance for establishing a pattern of Church–State relations, see Noel Browne (1998): 41–50; Curry, 1998: 10; Powell, 1992: 233.

11 Article 41 of the *Constitution of Ireland* (1999 [1937]): 158–160. On the debate surrounding Article 41, see Doley, 'Gendered Citizenship in the Irish Constitution', Murphy and Twomey (1998): 121–33.

12 Commission on the Family, *Strengthening Families for Life* (1998): 8.

13 Daly and Clavero (2002) places a considerable amount of weight on it.

14 Interviews with community representatives on the Commission on the Family from the family counselling and charitable sector conducted in Dublin 26 April 2005 and 5 May 2005 made essentially the same point.

15 See for example Employment Equality Agency (1978).

16 See especially the summary statement of the Government of Ireland *Report of the Expert Working Group on the Integration of the Tax and Social Welfare Systems,* (1996): IV.

17 Interview with Maria Cronin, Policy Officer for the IBEC, Dublin, 17 June 2005.

18 The same cannot necessarily be said for primary and secondary school education in Ireland, because this has been a site of struggle over Church–state relations in a way that higher education has not. Primary and secondary schools in Ireland are funded by the state but are almost exclusively run by the Catholic Church.

19 For more detailed summaries of the developing role of the VECs, see Conlon (1995), and O'Reilly (1989): 152–69.

20 For an in-depth look at the relationship between the OECD and local elites here see Walshe (2011).

21 Interview with Dr Don Thornhill, former Secretary of Education and member of HEA, Dublin, 1 June 2005.

22 More extended discussion of the 'Burke' proposals can be found in Duff *et al.* (2000): 56, and White, 2000: 118–30.

23 Professor Áine Hyland, quoted in Walshe (1999): 43.

24 Interview with author, 15 June 2005.

25 Interview Brian Nolan, DIT President, 24 May 2005. See also Dublin Institute of Technology (2005).
26 Patrick Clancy, University College Dublin (2005), 107.
27 Interview with Dr Don Thornhill, former Secretary of Education and member of HEA, Dublin, 1 June 2005.
28 O'Hare is a former president of the Dublin City University, formerly the National Institute of Higher Learning at Dublin.
29 See especially the report by the HEA/Forfás (2002). See also Steering Committee Report: 8.
30 Data calculated from Allen (1999): 94, from Central Statistics Office data.
31 This discussion is based on Central Statistics Office data in Hughes and Quinn (2004): 7.
32 Interview with Esther Lynch, Policy Officer, ICTU, 6 May 2005.
33 There is an extensive discussion of these developments in Quinn and Hughes (2005).
34 Interview with Denise Charlton, CEO, Irish Immigrant Council, 20 May 2005.
35 Interview with Denise Charlton, Immigrant Council of Ireland, 20 May 2005.
36 For an extended discussion on the fortunes of accession country workers during the first two years following EU enlargement, see Boyle *et al.* (2006).

References

Allen, Kieran, *Fianna Fáil and Irish Labour: 1926 to the Present* (London: Pluto Press, 1997).

Allen, Kieran, "Immigration and the Celtic Tiger: a Land of a Thousand Welcomes?", in Gareth Dale and Mike Cole, eds, *The European Union and Migrant Labour* (Oxford and New York: Berg, 1999), 91–111.

Barrett, Alan and Fergal Trace, "Who is Coming Back? The Educational Profile of Returning Migrants in the 1990s", *Irish Banking Review* (1998), 38–51.

Boyle, Nicola, Gerard Hughes, and Eskil Wadensjo, "Freedom of Movement of Workers from Central and Eastern Europe: Experiences in Ireland and Sweden", Working Paper 5 (Swedish Institute for European Policy Studies, 2006).

Browne, Noel, "Church and State in Modern Ireland", in Tim Murphy and Patrick Twomey, eds, *Ireland's Evolving Constitution, 1937–97: Collected Essays* (Oxford: Hart Publishing, 1998), 41–50.

Campbell, Fergus, *Land and Revolution: Nationalist Politics in the West of Ireland 1891–1921* (Oxford: Oxford University Press, 2005).

Carroll, Dierdre, "Cross-Cutting Initiatives in Public Policy: Some Irish Examples", in Gabriel Kiely, Anne O'Donnell, Patricia Kennedy, and Suzanne Quin, *Irish Social Policy in Context* (Dublin: University College Dublin Press, 1999), 311–15.

Clancy, Patrick, "Education Policy" in Suzanne Quin, Patricia Kennedy, Anne Matthews, and Gabriel Kiely, eds, *Contemporary Irish Social Policy* (Dublin: University College Dublin, 2005), 80–104.

Clancy, Patrick and Ciaran Benson, *Higher Education in Dublin: A Study of Some Emerging Needs* (Dublin: Higher Education Authority, 1979).

Commission on the Family, *Strengthening Families for Life: Final Report to the Minister for Social, Community and Family Affairs* (Dublin: Stationery Office, July 1998).

Commission on Higher Education 1960–1967, *Presentation and Summary of Report* (Dublin: Stationery Office, 1967).

Commission on the Points System, *Final Report and Recommendations* (Dublin: Stationery Office, 1999).

Conlon, Sean, "Adult Education with the Vocational Education Sector", in Marie Morrissey and Hannele Rossi eds, *Issues of Adult and Occupational Education in Ireland and Finland* (Helsinki: National Board of Education [Finland], 1995).

Cousins, Mel, "Pregnancy and Maternity Benefits: A Case Study of Irish Social Welfare Provision", *Administration* 40, 3 (1992), 220–33.

Curry, John, *Irish Social Services.* 3rd ed. (Dublin: Institute of Public Administration, 1998).

Daly, Mary and Sara Clavero, *Contemporary Family Policy: A Comparative Review of Ireland, France, Germany, Sweden and the UK* (Dublin: Institute of Public Administration/Department of Social and Family Affairs, 2002).

Department of Education [Ireland], *Education for a Changing World: Green Paper on Education* (Dublin, June 1992), 3.

Department of Education [Ireland], *Charting Our Education Future: White Paper on Education* (Dublin, 1995).

Department of Justice, Equality and Law Reform [Ireland], *Review of Submissions on the Public Consultation on Immigration Policy* (Dublin: Stationery Office, July 2002).

Department of Justice, Equality and Law Reform [Ireland], *Immigration and Residency in Ireland: Outline Policy Proposals for an Immigration and Residency Bill* (Dublin: Stationery Office, 2005).

Doley, Dolores, "Gendered Citizenship in the Irish Constitution", in Tim Murphy and Patrick Twomey, eds, *Ireland's Evolving Constitution, 1937–97: Collected Essays* (Oxford: Hart Publishing, 1998), 121–33.

Doyle, Anne, "Employment Equality Since Accession to the European Union", in Gabriel Kiely, Anne O'Donnell, Patricia Kennedy, and Suzanne Quin, eds, *Irish Social Policy in Context* (Dublin: University College Dublin Press, 1999), 128–45.

Dublin Institute of Technology, *Access Initiatives in DIT* (Dublin: DIT, 2005).

Duff, Thomas, Joseph Hegarty, and Matthew Hussey, *The Story of the Dublin Institute of Technology* (Dublin: Blackhall Publishing, 2000).

Dumon, Wilfried, ed., *National Family Policies in EC Countries in 1990* (Luxembourg: European Observatory on National Family Policies/European Commission, 1991).

Dumon, W. and T. Nuelant, *European Observatory on National Family Policies: Trends and Developments in 1992 Technical Annex* (Leuven, Belgium: European Observatory on Family Policies, 1994).

Dunphy, Richard, *The Making of Fianna Fáil Power in Ireland 1923–1948* (Oxford: Clarendon Press, 1995).

Employment Equality Agency, *Women's Place in the Irish Economy: Present and Future*, Report of the Seminar at Trinity College (Dublin, 25 November 1978).

Fahey, Tony, Helen Russell, and Emer Smyth, "Gender Equality, Fertility Decline and Labour Market: Patterns Among Women in Ireland", in Brian Nolan, Philip J. O'Connell, and Christopher T. Whelan, eds, *Bust to Boom? The Irish Experience of Growth and Inequality* (Dublin: Institute of Public Administration, 2000), 244–67.

Galligan, Yvonne, *Women and Politics in Contemporary Ireland: From the Margins to the Mainstream* (London and Washington: Pinter, 1998).

Government of Ireland, *Programme for National Recovery* (Dublin: Stationery Office, 1987).

Government of Ireland, *Constitution of Ireland* (Dublin: Stationery Office, 1999 [1937]).

Government of Ireland, *National Childcare Strategy*, Report of the Partnership 2000 Expert Working Group on Childcare (Dublin: Stationery Office, January 1999).

Government of Ireland, *Programme for Prosperity and Fairness* (Dublin: Stationery Office, 2000).

Government of Ireland, *Programme for Prosperity and Fairness: Report of the Working Group on the Review of the Parental Leave Act 1998* (Dublin: Stationery Office, April 2002).

Hantrais, Linda and Marie-Thérèse Letablier, *Families and Family Policies in Europe* (London and New York: Longman, 1996).

Hardiman, Niamh, "From Conflict to Coordination: Economic Governance and Political Innovation in Ireland", *West European Politics* 25, 4 (2004), 1–25.

Higher Education Authority, *Report of the application by the Dublin Institute of Technology for establishment as a University under Section 9 of the Universities Act 1997: Report of the International Review Group to the Higher Education Authority* (Dublin, November 1998).

Honohan, Patrick and Brendan Walsh, "Catching Up with the Leaders: The Irish Hare", *Brookings Papers on Economic Activity* 1 (2002).

Hughes, Gerard and Emma Quinn, *The Impact of Immigration on Europe's Societies: Ireland* (Dublin: ESRI/European Migration Network, 2004).

Humphreys, Peter, Síle Fleming, and Orla O'Donnell, *Balancing Work and Family Life: The Role of Flexible Working Arrangements* (Dublin: Department of Social, Community, and Family Affairs/Institute of Public Administration, 2000).

Immigrant Council of Ireland, *Labour Migration into Ireland* (Dublin: Immigrant Council of Ireland, 2003).

International Organization for Migration, *International Comparative Study of Migration Legislation and Practice* (Dublin: International Organization for Migration/Department of Justice, Equality and Law Reform, 2002).

Jacobsen, John Kurt, *Chasing Progress in the Irish Republic* (Cambridge: Cambridge University Press, 1994).

Katzenstein, Peter J., *Small States in World Markets* (Ithaca, NY and London: Cornell University Press, 1985).

Kissane, Bill, *Explaining Irish Democracy* (Dublin: University College Dublin Press, 2002).

Kiely, Gabriel and Valerie Richardson, "Ireland", in John Ditch, Helen Barnes, and Jonathan Bradshaw, eds, *Developments in National Family Policies in 1995* (University of York: European Observatory on Family Policies/Commission of the European Communities, 1996).

MacCoille, Conall, "Smoothing Adjustment Through Modified Wage Bargaining", *Irish Banking Review* (2001), 15–26.

Mahon, Denis T., *The Tortuous Path: The Course of Ireland's Entry into the EEC, 1948–73* (Dublin: Institute of Public Administration, 1986).

Mair, Peter, "Explaining the Absence of Class Politics in Ireland", *Proceedings of the British Academy* 79 (1992), 383–410.

Marsh, David, David Richards, and Martin J. Smith, *Changing Patterns of Governance in the United Kingdom: Reinventing Whitehall?* (New York: Palgrave, 2001).

Mjøset, Lars, *The Irish Economy in a Comparative Institutional Perspective* (Dublin: National Economic and Social Council, 1992).

Murphy, Gary, "Interest Groups in the Policy-making Process", in John Coakley and Michael Gallagher, eds, *Politics in the Republic of Ireland* 4th edition (New York and London: Routledge, 2004), 352–83.

OECD, *Reviews of National Policies for Education: Ireland* (Paris: Organisation for Economic Cooperation and Development, 1969).

OECD, *Reviews of National Policies for Education: Ireland* (Paris: Organisation for Economic Cooperation and Development, 1991).

OECD, *Babies and Bosses: Reconciling Work and Family Life, Vol. 2: Austria, Ireland and Japan* (Paris: Organisation for Economic Co-operation and Development, 2002).

OECD, *Review of National Policies for Education: Review of Higher Education in Ireland. Examiner's Report* (Paris: Organisation for Economic Co-operation and Development, 2004).

O'Hare, Danny, "Wanted: Integrated Planning for Third Level", *The Irish Times* (31 May 2005), 14.

O'Hearn, Denis, "The Irish Case of Dependency: An Exception to the Exceptions?", *American Sociological Review* 54 (1989), 578–96.

O'Reilly, Barney, "Issues in the Development of Vocational Education", *Administration* 37, 2 (1989), 152–69.

Ó Buachalla, Séamus, "Investment in Education: Context, Content and Impact", *Administration* 44, 3 (1996), 10–20.

Ó Riain, Séan, *The Politics of High-Tech Growth* (Cambridge: Cambridge University Press, 2004).

Powell, Frederick, *The Politics of Irish Social Policy 1600–1990* (Lewiston, NY: Edwin Mellen Press, 1992).

Pyle, Jean Larson, *The State and Women in the Economy: Lessons from Sex Discrimination in the Republic of Ireland* (Albany, NY: SUNY Press, 1990).

Quinn, Emma and Gerard Hughes, *Policy Analysis Report on Asylum and Migration: Ireland 2003 to Mid-2004* (Dublin: ESRI/European Migration Network, 2005).

Reid, Liam, "Study finds Fears Unfounded over Tax Individualisation", *The Irish Times* (6 October 2003).

Richardson, Valerie, "Reconciliation of Working and Family Life" in Imelda Colgan McCarthy, ed., *Irish Family Studies: Selected Papers* (Dublin: Family Studies Centre, 1995).

Roche, W. K., "'Collaborative Production' and the Irish Boom: Work Organisation, Partnership and Direct Involvement in Irish Workplaces", *Economic and Social Review* 31, 1 (2000), 1–36.

Ruhs, Martin, "Emerging Trends and Patterns in the Immigration and Employment of Non-EU Nationals in Ireland: What the Data Reveal", Working Paper No. 6, (Dublin: The Policy Institute, Trinity College Dublin, 2003).

Rush, Michael, "Social Partnership in Ireland", in Gabriel Kiely, Anne O'Donnell, Patricia Kennedy, and Suzanne Quin, eds, *Irish Social Policy in Context* (Dublin: University College Dublin Press, 1999), 155–77.

Schmitter, Philippe C., "Still the Century of Corporatism?", *The Review of Politics* 36, 1 (1974), 85–131.

Skilbeck, Malcolm, *The University Challenged: A Review of International Trends and Issues with Particular Reference to Ireland* (Dublin: Higher Education Authority/Conference of Heads of Irish Universities, 2001).

Steering Committee on Technical Education, *Report to the Minister of Education on Regional Technical Colleges* (Dublin: Stationery Office, 1967).

Teague, Paul, "Pay Determination in the Republic of Ireland: Toward Social Corporatism?", *British Journal of Industrial Relations* 33, 2, (1995), 253–73.

Tracy, Marshall, *Racism and Integration: A Comparative Analysis* (Dublin: Trinity College, Department of Sociology, 2000).

Valiulis, Maryann Gialanella, "Power, Gender, and Identity in the Irish Free State", *Journal of Women's History* 6, 4 (1995), 117–35.

Walshe, John, *A New Partnership in Education: From Consultation to Legislation in the Nineties* (Dublin, Institute of Public Administration, 1999).

Walshe, John, "A Quiet Revolution – International Influence, Domestic Elites and the Transformation of Higher Technical Education in Ireland 1959–72", *Irish Educational Studies* 30, 3 (2011), 365–81.

Watt, Philip, "Introduction and Overview", in National Consultative Committee on Racism and Interculturalism, *Migration Policy: Reform and Harmonisation* (Advocacy Paper One, Dublin, December 2002).

White, Tony, *Investing in People: Higher Education in Ireland from 1960 to 2000* (Dublin: Institute of Public Administration, 2001).

Whyte, J. H., *Church and State in Modern Ireland, 1923–1970* (Dublin: Gill and Macmillan, 1971).

5 Greece

This chapter makes two main arguments. The first is that Greece is the country in this sample that has reoriented its policy goals and strategies around the requirements of twenty-first century development needs the least. In the European context, it is undoubtedly the EU member state that has lagged furthest behind *all* those states that joined in on the regional integration project before 2004. The failure of Greece to 'converge' toward Western European living standards is frequently discussed in the wider economic and social science literature, but the focus here is on the wide gap that still often exists between the way that both government officials and interest groups conceptualize major policy problems, the extent to which they implement solutions to them, and the construction of a labour market support structure based on the requirements of a knowledge-based development strategy. This analysis holds true across all three specific labour-market related challenges discussed in this chapter. Policies for the reconciliation of family and working life remain wedded to a 'population policy' framework that has failed either to significantly lift fertility rates or to encourage greater female formal workforce participation. Higher education policy has been reformed several times since 1974, but measures to enhance quality assurance, in particular, lag behind those of most developed countries. Meanwhile, the serious long-term problem of illegal immigration has not been solved by the ad-hoc regularization schemes favoured by Greek policymakers.

The second argument this chapter makes is that at least part of the explanation for these failures lies in the way that politics occurs in Greece, focusing especially on the relationship between state and society as reflected in the construction of intermediary policy institutions and processes, or rather the lack of them in this case. In the absence of a zone of mediation constituted by strong, formal links between key interest groups and the state, policy can become not much more than a reflection of inter- and intra-political party conflict. This is demonstrated by several cases in which changes in government simply result in the reversal of recent legislation, with no ongoing commitment to a specific set of policy goals. Policy evolution tends not to benefit from the expertise that could be provided by important societal interest groups. Parties in Greece not only dominate the state, but they also maintain clientelistic relationships with specific interest groups. This often gives these particular groups undue influence over certain policy areas at the expense of broader participation in policymaking.

In addition and connected to this last point, past policies in some of the areas under discussion have tended to consist of special privileges awarded to specific client or otherwise favoured groups. This is clearly the case in the fields of family and higher education policy analysed here, with policy consisting of privileges to large family organizations in the former and students and teacher unions in the latter case. Policy based on awarding special privileges to certain groups tends to be inefficient at addressing labour market challenges on the one hand and extremely difficult to overturn on the other. Naturally, such groups fight hard to retain their special benefits and services, and they are organized precisely to perform this function. In other national settings, overriding these privileges can be achieved through a process of negotiation with interest groups and, as Chapter 3 argued in detail, this is where the incorporative properties of consultative policymaking matters most. In Greece, the absence of such linkages between society and the state, as opposed to the clientelist relationships between political parties and interest groups that do exist, generally makes this kind of negotiation impossible. After a discussion of the historical forces that have shaped state–society relations in Greece, and policymaking traditions in particular, this chapter further analyses the influence of a missing 'zone of mediation' on specific outcomes in the family, higher education, and immigration policy fields.

Greece's missing zone of mediation

Greece is the country in this sample with the weakest consultative and incorporative policymaking tradition. Arguably, this can be traced to a pattern of state formation in which a modern nation state was imposed through foreign intervention with little organic relationship between state and society. To this end, much is often made of the fact that modern Greece is the result of foreign intervention and that there is something manufactured about the Greek nation-state. A mid-twentieth century observer noted that: 'Continued foreign interference in the internal affairs of Greece has had dire repercussions. Perennial economic and political crises have been to no small degree a result of foreign meddling' (Vucinich, 1949: 266). Like Ireland, the modern Greek state was born out of violence. The country was initially established as a West European-inspired buffer against the Ottoman Empire, the remnants of which Greece engages in border disputes right up to the present day. The Greek War of Independence (1821–1829) could not have been waged, let alone won, without foreign aid and inspiration, and the creation of the new Greek nation was justified and sold to local elites on the basis that ethnic Greeks were the rightful inheritors of the classical Greek tradition based on art, literature, and political democracy. That classical tradition, which most Greeks at that point were completely alienated from and unfamiliar with, was conceptualized as European and progressive and pitted against the supposed backwardness and 'darkness' of the Oriental East. This left Greeks to grapple for at least the century and a half following independence with the contradictions between their new identification with Western Europe and the many aspects of their culture inherited from their status as subjects of the Ottoman Empire.

After the struggle for independence was won, a constitutional monarchy was established by foreign powers and remained in place until the early twentieth century. Instability in a system with an already very thin veil of political legitimacy intensified during the late nineteenth century, leading eventually to the Greek version of a republican revolution that resulted in the instalment of Eleftherios Venizelos as Prime Minister in 1911. Although Venizelos was later celebrated as a key modernizing figure in modern Greek history, his initial period of rule actually ushered in yet more instability for the country.[1] The First World War was surrounded by conflict between republican and monarchist forces, and an eventual war with Turkey between 1919 and 1922. The dislocation of peoples during the period immediately following the First World War and in the wake of the collapse of the Ottoman Empire is difficult to overstate, resulting in the arrival of hundreds of thousands of ethnically Greek refugees from Asia Minor. The period of instability that marked the 1920s was eventually turned around by the return of Venizelos as Prime Minister, who oversaw a significant number of national development projects between 1928 and 1932. Yet the promise of success revolving around these actions was soon dashed by the onset of the Great Depression, leading to a series of coups and counter-coups in Greece. With war brewing in Europe, formal dictatorship was established in 1936 under the guidance of General Ioannis Metaxas.

Political change during the Metaxas period echoed that being experienced elsewhere in Europe, and especially Southern Europe, at approximately the same time. As in Portugal, fascism was never fully embraced even if the regime displayed fascist tendencies. The Metaxas regime (1936–1940) stressed conservative and collective values but also exhibited a developmentalist streak, notably establishing the nation's first social insurance scheme. Greece, however, refused to co-operate with the Axis powers as war broke out in Europe, with Metaxas famously refusing to allow Mussolini to cross onto Greek land near the beginning of the war. Tragically for Greece, this resulted in the country being invaded shortly afterwards and remaining under occupation until Italian and German forces evacuated in 1944. Immediately following occupation and stemming from the internal social and political conflict that sharpened during it, civil war between communist and anti-communist forces raged. The 1946–1950 civil war had long-term significance not only because it seriously damaged the economy even more than it had already been destroyed under foreign occupation and ensured a decade of social misery to follow as a result but because of the conflict's impact on national political culture and institutions. The Greek right emerged from the conflict in a clearly dominant political position and was thus able to implement a series of anti-communist (and generally anti-leftist) legislative measures that barred such forces from gaining political and intellectual power, even though the country became ostensibly democratic. The two main political groupings reflected early twentieth century ones more than anything else, with the regrouping of monarchist and anti-monarchist factions into political parties that were now at least united by their hatred of communists (Close, 1995).

During the 1950s and 1960s, Greece was thus officially democratic but took on the form of a 'hard' democracy where overt political repression was used widely in conjunction with somewhat more subtle forms of institutional bias. Although civil rights were in theory guaranteed by a new democratic constitution, 'these were rendered useless by a variety of emergency measures, some dating from the Metaxas period, others from the civil war' (Legg and Roberts, 1997: 47). The cultural and institutional legacies of such a constrained and elitist democracy were reflected not only in formal politics but in a variety of other social and economic institutions as well. Notably, left-leaning academics were systematically removed from universities and other places of learning (Papstratis, 2000). Since twentieth century Greek political history, aside from the civil war period, was marked by unstable democracy biased in favour of elite social groups and the political right, interrupted occasionally by military coups, the breakdown of 'democracy' in 1967 and the establishment of a short-lived military regime afterwards is not all that surprising. Given that history and the fact that the Greek colonels' regime did not significantly alter the state apparatuses from how they had previously operated, it is not particularly surprising that, when democracy returned in 1974, the political system retained many of its elitist tendencies.

Especially in light of the literature on 'bureaucratic authoritarianism' in Latin America and elsewhere, which observed that militaries increasingly installed themselves as technocratic managers of the state during the 1960s and 1970s and that this represented a new form of authoritarian rule, students of Greek politics have found the 1967–1974 military regime difficult to categorize. In some senses the Greek colonels' regime resembled bureaucratic authoritarianism in that it intervened in order to secure political order in the context of social mobilization and political polarization, but when in power the regime did not really attempt to implement a structural adjustment programme, instead opting for a state-led development strategy.[2] More importantly for the purposes of this research, however, the military intervention represented a continuation of personalist and factionalist politics rather than a long-term attempt to gain control over the state bureaucracy by the military as an institution. The coup, led by George Papadopoulos, was backed by only one sector of the army, and had too narrow a support base in broader society. What is more, the regime spent much of the time attempting to consolidate its control, both horizontally, with resistance from non-military political elites along with other military factions especially in the air force and navy, as well as vertically. Social mobilization had led to the coup occurring in the first place but carried on through the junta's duration, culminating in the long drawn-out Athens' Polytechnic student protest in 1973 that became a major catalyst for the regime's downfall.[3]

As is well known, the Greek colonels did themselves no favours at all by intervening in Cypriot politics in 1974 and thus choosing to embark on another military confrontation with Turkey over a territorial issue. That led to a realization on the part of those elements of the military hierarchy that still actually supported the colonels' regime that holding direct power over the state was not really beneficial to itself in any case. This indicated a break by the military-as-institution from the military-in-politics in Greece, and a comparatively rapid transition to democracy, with the military practically handing power immediately back to the civilian political elite, followed that year.[4] While democrats might celebrate the fact that Greece's last authoritarian regime was a short-lived one and that it did not fundamentally alter state–society relations as the result of both this fact and because its penetration of the state apparatuses was comparatively shallow, the problem is that this allowed prior patterns of elite politics and state–society relations to be more or less resurrected during the democratization period. This has proved a problem for the quality of democracy in Greece and, specifically for the purposes of this research, the construction of consultative and incorporative policymaking institutions since these were completely alien to the *pre*-authoritarian Greek political tradition.

Twentieth century Greek politics had been elitist, personalist, and biased in favour of the political right, even resulting in the domination of politics by successive generations of the same family. This pattern was not exactly broken by the breakdown of authoritarian rule, with power under the new democracy alternating between the Papandreou and Karamanlis families, the involvement of both of which actually precedes the military coup. The innovation of the democratization period was that political parties took centre stage, primarily as support bases for powerful party leaders. Government since 1974 has been dominated by Andreas Papandreou's Pan-Hellenic Socialist Party (PASOK), with Papandreou as prime minister between 1981 and 1989 and again between 1993 and 1996. Andreas Papandreou's father, George, led the liberal Centre Union Party in the 1960s, and his grandson, also named George Papandreou, was elected as PASOK's leader in 2004. While PASOK self-identifies as a socialist party, it is more accurately described as a populist one and is not always easy to place on the centre-left, not only in policy terms, but also because of its internal organization and use of patronage networks. New Democracy, led by Constantine Karamanlis, is accurately described as a conservative party of the right, and provided the alternative power base.

The domination of Greek politics by these two main political parties headed by strong leaders has proved overwhelming, including manipulation of the constitution to generate specific political outcomes, extreme politicization of the public service, and public policy content coming second to internal party struggles (Diamandouros, 1998; Mavrogordatos, 1993; Rigos, 1999; Sotiropoulos, 1996, 2000). Although much of this is blamed on PASOK's failure to modernize and democratize public administration during its time in office, it is not readily apparent that New Democracy has behaved very differently when in power (Pappas, 1998). In this context, party competition is intense and policy goals are often clearly subordinated to strictly political ones. Politicization of this kind, including repeated policy reversals, often extends well beyond the parliamentary and bureaucratic spheres: university politics and governance, for instance, has been strictly organized along party political lines. As will be discussed later, this has often been to the detriment of the tertiary education system.

Greece's political culture, then, is profoundly marked by a number of 'authoritarian legacies' inherited from the pre-democratic era. However, it must also be noted that the particular path taken toward democracy has also had an observable impact on Greek political culture up until the present day. Some of these 'transitional' legacies, ironically perhaps, further reinforce rather than break pattern with prior authoritarian legacies. First of all, the mobilizational aspects of the dictatorship's downfall reinforced the view of political competition as a zero-sum game. Politics – and policy formulation – is not about compromise, but about stating and pursuing objectives in absolute terms. Not only is this reflected in the nature of Greek party politics, discussed above, but at the level of political culture, this underscores a peculiarly Greek notion of democracy. Democracy tends to be viewed by ordinary Greeks as being about the unrestrained pursuit of individual 'rights', rather than about accommodation between individual and collective interests. In the words of one Greek historian, many Greeks are 'willing to expand their own freedoms at the expense of others'.[5] Second, the Athens Polytechnic protests of 1974 gave birth to a new cadre of political activists, many of whom eventually entered formal politics especially as members of parliament representing PASOK or other left of centre parties. Many of these politicians later lost their connection to any particular progressive political programme, but remained in positions of political (and economic) power long afterwards, difficult to remove from these positions given their status as 'heroes' of the Polytechnic protests. In a sense, this trend has reinforced rather than undermined the elitist nature of Greek politics.

The combination of the colonization by the state of the party-based patronage system with the continuation of personalist politics has profound consequences for the policymaking process, and therefore policy decisions, in Greece. In short, there are very few institutions and processes that are available to bridge the gap between policymakers and policy stakeholders. Those that exist are extremely limited in the range of policy issues addressed and the number of players involved. Historians and social scientists often argue that many of the problems involving the colonization of the state by political parties relate to the broader observation that Greece suffers from a strong, overbearing state and a weak, undeveloped civil society. That is an argument often made about Southern Europe as a whole and Greece especially, but does not really describe the reality. Greece has a mobilizational aspect to its political culture, demonstrated by everything from Greenpeace posters plastered across the centre of Athens to noisy and occasionally violent street protests particularly during the annual anti-authoritarian 17 November celebrations to the numbers of bricks thrown through French-owned shop windows or the United States embassy, depending on which foreign power is least popular at the time. To outside observers, Greek citizens seem more politically active than Portuguese or Irish ones, and society actually appears particularly mobilized. The problem is that social movement activity is not the same as having a 'civil society' of the type that current thinking in political science presumes to underpin stable democracy (Putnam, 1993). In fact, elements of Greek social movement-ism are decidedly uncivil, if by that is meant destabilizing the political system.

The problem is not that there is no foundation for civil society but rather that the Greek political system makes few attempts to reach out to important interest groups and the citizenry at large in order to help create a stabilizing civil society. When there are clashes between state and society over policy issues, these can be highly charged, but there are few established channels for mediating between social groups and between social groups and the state in such a way that can inform actual policy decision-making. This image of the Greek state as weak in the face of a mobilized society, which is actually only enhanced by colonization of the state by political parties and their associated interest groups – labour unions in the case of PASOK and the Orthodox Church in the case of New Democracy for example – had led others to describe the state as a 'colossus with feet of clay'.[6] It appears overbearing but is actually rather weak, especially when it comes to actual public administration rather than the legislative branch of government.

The best example here is the relationship between successive governments, especially PASOK ones, and the labour movement, which surely amounts to a 'capture' of government policy by a minority interest group if ever there was one. The majority of Greeks do not belong to labour unions: in 1995 overall union density was reported at 27 per cent of the workforce, but levels in the public sector can reach up to between 75 and 90 per cent (Seferiades, 1999: 15). Yet the labour movement provides fierce resistance to policies that threaten its members. Although that is generally the purpose of labour movements, the Greek one is especially well known for putting particular interests ahead of collective ones and being able to block reforms aimed at spreading social benefits more evenly across society. The problem is exacerbated by the concentration of the labour movement in the public sector, reinforcing the clientelist relationship between unions, political parties, and the state. The stranglehold over policy sometimes exhibited by the unions is facilitated by the fact that there are so few alternative channels for other interest groups to influence policy decisions. In addition, while Greece has an established tri-partite wage-setting system, issues such as immigration, higher education and family policy reform generally do not fall within the parameters of negotiations carried out within it. The collective bargaining system, in this instance, reinforces a rather unhealthy relationship.

In the vacuum left by the absence of mediating policymaking processes and institutions capable of balancing consultation with incorporation, policy issues often become a battleground for waging power struggles within governing parties. Greeks are particularly cynical about this, and the present chapter details specific instances where policy stakeholders interviewed during the course of this research believe this to be the case. Attempts at administrative reform that could potentially alter the pattern established by the combination of patronage running through the public administration and personalist politics at a governmental level have also been manipulated for political reasons. One Greek analyst describes a process of repeated attempts at administrative reform that, while ostensibly aiming to curb clientelism in the Greek bureaucracy, usually serve to reinforce party patronage given that they have been initiated and shaped by either PASOK or New Democracy (Spanou, 1996).

On the positive side, there are a few identifiable changes relevant to the policy areas under consideration here that deserve mention. In particular, migrant rights organizations have long been interested in establishing genuine consultation processes with successive governments. While the decision was later undermined by the post-2008 debt crisis and political fallout, state representatives agreed to enter dialogue with such organizations in 2005. Some of the impetus for this change has come from the interest that the Greek Ombudsman's Office has had in the immigration issue. This Office was established in the late 1990s in order to provide checks on other government agencies on behalf of the public and has proved capable of retaining an independence not generally found in Greek public administration. It has more recently broadened its functions to include greater responsibilities for ensuring equality in the state's treatment of citizens (Greek Ombudsman, 2006). Whether the consultation process has any real impact on national-level immigration and migrant integration policy, however, remains to be seen. It is to the specific stories of family, immigration, and higher education policies that we now turn.

Reconciling working and family life

The formulation of policies capable of assisting in the reconciliation of work and family responsibilities is mostly a neglected issue in Greece. The debate surrounding this policy area diverges from that occurring elsewhere in the OECD because it is framed in terms of 'population policy' rather than 'work–life balance'. The reasons for this are discussed further below but are clearly connected to the prevalence of conservative social forces in politics, including the nominally socialist party, PASOK. Greek policymakers have at times been concerned with the problems associated with an aging population but believe the solution to these problems lies in providing incentives to increase the national fertility rate rather than introducing measures to increase the number of women in paid work. Why they have done so, however, is a bit of a mystery, since such policies have done nothing to turn around a particularly low fertility rate, but clearly beliefs about the need to preserve Greek ethnicity are involved. This is a subject discussed in the following pages. This has meant that 'family' policy has been mainly limited to a series of benefits and subsidies provided to large families, usually defined as families with three or more children. These policies have not appeared to be effective in driving up the fertility rate, which continues to fall, but have skewed resources away from families in general and towards a specific group of families instead. These policies have since proved extremely difficult to repeal. The following discussion connects this difficulty to the much broader issue of welfare reform in Greece since it is innately connected to it.

The policy problem

It can be argued that Greece, not only among the three countries studied here but also within the OECD as a whole, has represented one of the biggest failures in terms of recognizing and responding to the problem of formulating policies to, on the one hand, encourage female workforce participation and, on the other, combat a declining fertility rate. By the late 1990s, Greece not only had one of the lowest birthrates in Europe, 1.32 in 1995 compared to a EU average of 1.42, but it continued to have the third lowest female economic participation rate, ranked just above Italy and Spain.[7] The percentage of children in Greece, measured as a percentage of the population aged under fourteen, decreased quickly from 23.7 per cent in 1991 to 15.6 per cent in 1998 (Charalambis *et al.*, 2004: 26). While the issue of abortion lies slightly outside the scope of this research, it is worth mentioning for the debate it has sparked in Greece in relationship to these demographic trends: the abortion rate is especially high and ethnographic research suggests that this often reflects a rational choice, often on the part of well-educated and married women, based on the financial circumstances of the family rather than an actual desire on the part of women not to have children at some point in the future (Georges, 1996; Paxson, 2004). Although this shows that the problem of the work–family tradeoff is arguably as problematic in Italy and Spain as it is in Greece, barriers to the formulation of policy capable of addressing issues of work–life balance seem particularly high and especially strong in the case of Greece. Policy responses have been minimalist and, where they do exist, aimed mostly at 'large families' with three or more children and thus almost completely ineffective for easing the tension between work and family life experienced by most families.

It will shortly be argued that part of the explanation for such policy failures lies in the nature of state–society relations in Greece and, more specifically, the missing zone of mediation that characterizes the political system. Before that, however, the challenge of reforming the Greek welfare state in general needs to be discussed. The analysis of family policies per se cannot be separated from this more general analysis, for at least three reasons. First, the tax and benefit system has been the main mechanism for policies aimed if not at reconciling family and working life and encouraging greater female workforce participation, then at least at achieving a higher fertility rate. While changes have been made to maternity and parental leave rights in recent times, successive governments have not paid nearly as much attention to these, nor to childcare issues or workplace based 'family friendly' measures as in Ireland or Portugal. Second, the debate over welfare reform and the struggles over the future of Greece's pension system specifically dominated all fields of social policy discussion between 1990 and 2008. It occupied the attention of all major interest groups in Greece, including the state as well as outside academics, to the point where other pressing social policy issues have been further neglected. Third, even if this is not fully recognized in Greece, the question of family policy and especially female workforce participation, as Chapter 2 outlined, is intimately connected to the problem of pension reform and sustainability in OECD countries. Providing for an aging population, including maintaining pension systems, requires expansion of the tax base.

In many respects, the Greek welfare state is the most typical of what has been referred to as the 'Southern European' model, core features of which include the adoption of social insurance or contributory rather than universal coverage funded from general taxation, except when it comes to health care; a lack of generosity; and the fragmentation of delivery and inequality in benefit levels along occupational lines. The Greek system had its true beginnings during the Metaxas dictatorship of the 1930s, including the creation of the IKA, the country's largest social insurance agency, in 1934 (Katrougalos, 1996: 47–8). The problem has historically been the fact that different sectors of the workforce are covered by different insurance schemes, to the point where at times large groups of workers have not been provided for at all. Public sector workers and professions such as banking have always been more favourably treated. Such a system is not only inefficient and costly to deliver, but it is also inherently unequal.

Compounding the problem of fragmentation in delivery and thus patchiness when it comes to coverage is the fact that spending is heavily skewed toward pensions and away from social risks such as poverty or unemployment that cannot be insured against. While overall spending on welfare has traditionally been low in European terms, at 21.6 per cent of GDP in 1991 compared to an EU-15 average of 26.4, it has caught up in recent years, climbing to 26.4 per cent of GDP in 2000 compared to an EU average of 27.3 per cent. Yet at least 90 per cent of this spending goes into pensions, leaving other aspects of social policy underfunded (Matsaganis, 2005a: 236–7). Added to that is the fact that the pension system treats some occupational groups much better than others, leading many analysts to describe the Greek welfare state in harsh terms. According to these analysts, the pension system is not only 'bloated and grossly inequitable' (Matsaganis, 2005a: 236) but is also often presented as a prime example of interest group capture of the state by the middle classes in a clientelist political system (Petmedisou, 1991). It should also be noted, with direct relevance for female workforce participation, that the traditionally high threshold of contributions for many pension schemes, twelve continuous years of full-time service for example, can act as a disincentive for women especially to take up paid and particularly part-time work or in fact take time out from the workforce to have children. It can also act as a force pushing women out of work once their minimum period of service is finished, since many schemes do not provide much better pension rates once minimum requirements are filled (Burtless, 2001: 482).

The issue of pension reform has remained firmly on the Greek political agenda at least since 1995, yet reforms of the system aimed at reducing costs and ensuring a more equitable and efficient distribution of resources have been minimal and some of those which were passed were quickly reversed. The most sustained effort was undertaken by the 'modernizing' Simitis government that came to power in 1996 following the replacement of Papandreou by Simitis as the leader of PASOK. Several attempts to overhaul the pension scheme and target overall social policy to the poorest members of society, many of whom remained uninsured, were made during this period, but failed due to pressure and protest on the behalf of interest groups, especially unions whose members benefit from inequalities in the system. Several authors have argued that the state revealed itself to be weak in the face of such opposition, belying traditional descriptions of the Greek state as overbearing and civil society as weak (Featherstone, 2003; Matsaganis, 2005a). This, as the remainder of this discussion illustrates, has a parallel in family policy itself, in which special benefits targeted toward large families have been fiercely defended by organizations representing those families, even if those policies are wholly ineffective for resolving work and family life across Greek society as a whole.

The challenge of developing policies for the reconciliation of working and family life is thus both similar and quite different from that experienced by policymakers in the Irish and Portuguese cases. All three countries have had to build policies to help families resolve tensions between working and family life on minimalist and, especially in the Southern European cases, 'familialist' social welfare foundations. Yet the problem itself is actually much worse in the Greek case because the country has both lower fertility rates and lower rates of female workforce participation than found in either Ireland or Portugal. This is then compounded by the ongoing failure to shift away from a social policy framework based on special privileges towards one based on either universal entitlements or effective targeting. This failure is reflected in failed attempts to reform Greece's welfare state in general but also specifically in the family policy arena.

The role of consultation and incorporation in shaping policy responses

There is very little evidence to suggest that family policy in Greece has been or is the product of careful mediation between interest groups on the part of the state, or of negotiation between the state and such interest groups. There are no major intermediary institutions or processes responsible for formulating policy in this area. The state agency with the closest possible relevance for channelling interests would very likely be the General Secretariat for Gender Equality, but the role of this organization is mostly confined to enforcing existing policies and overseeing research conducted by the semi-autonomous Research Centre on Gender Equality (KETHI). The Secretariat has at times listed work–life balance as one of its areas of interest but it has no formal consultative processes attached to it. Furthermore, according to the General Secretary of the organization, who took up the newly-created position as head of the General Secretariat at the end of 2009, work–life balance during the 1990s and 2000s was a policy priority pushed by the EU, rather than something that organically emerged at the top of the Greek gender-equality agenda: there is 'no real pressure' to change aspects of policies for work–life balance such as parental leave legislation. More urgent policy priorities include family violence and other aspects of family law.[8]

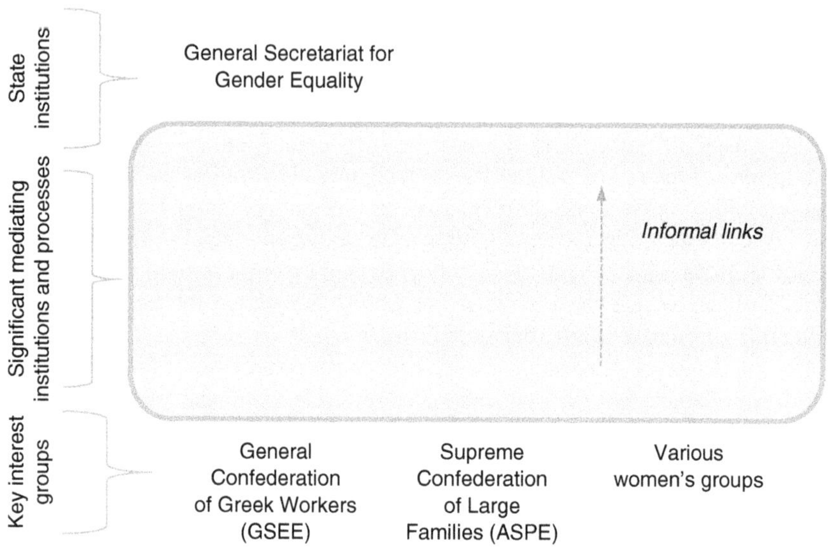

Figure 5.1 The zone of mediation in Greek work–life balance policy.

The absence of formal or relatively formal consultative and incorporative processes and institutions does not mean, however, that interest groups have not played some role in shaping family policy outcomes in Greece. Rather, it is that the involvement of these interest groups in formal policymaking is limited, and that activity outside formal policymaking channels has not always been helpful for the purposes of modernizing policy responses. Two major interest groups of relevance here are trade unions and organizations representing large families. Organized labour, which can often act as a progressive force in the formulation of policies for work–life balance, appears to have confined itself in this case to what it considers strictly industrial relations issues with little room for taking on a broader social activist role in this policy area. This means that during the post-authoritarian period under discussion here, the trade union movement has played some role in negotiating extended maternity and parental leave provisions for its members, for example. Yet it should be noted that the labour movement in Greece, especially as represented by the General Confederation of Greek Workers (GSEE), is dominated by unions representing professional and public sector workers. The most vulnerable workers, who do not enjoy anything like the floor of rights and benefits awarded to public sector and professional workers – women in the service sector, for instance – are mostly unorganized and unrepresented. That both explains and reinforces the fragmented and occupationally differentiated basis of labour rights and social welfare policies in Greece, including a pension system that actually provides a disincentive to female workforce participation in many instances. The relationship between the union movement and the state arguably represents a case of 'inegalitarian corporatism',[9] where the close relationship between the state and a labour movement that represents some sectors of the workforce much better than others serves to defend rather than reduce social inequalities.

The other group that appears to have an influence on Greek family policy well out of proportion to its size is the Supreme Confederation of Large Families (ASPE). The previous section pointed out that attempts to retarget the series of 'many children' benefits during the late 1990s were defeated mostly through resistance on behalf of this organization with support from other conservative forces. For foreign as well as some local researchers, the apparent weight of this organization in determining family policy outcomes is baffling. Why should a group that represents a minority of families in Greece, those with at least three or more children, have any influence at all? According to one local researcher and former advisor to the Simitis government, the ASPE has been 'a real problem' in relation to family policy, made up mostly of fathers 'which must be because their wives are at home with all those children', and 'very, very reactionary, like something out of the Middle Ages'. He also argued that the source of its political leverage lies in a Greek myth about racial purity that still has widespread support among policymakers in Greece.[10] The group is also aligned with the Orthodox Church. Although, compared to the Catholic Church in Ireland, the Orthodox Church has traditionally been comparatively hands-off in policy terms, there has been a recent politicization of its discourse (Stavrakakis, 2002). The myth of preserving racial purity influences not only the way that family policy is conceptualized but also general attitudes toward immigration, as discussed below.

The commitment the Greek Constitution makes to protecting 'large families' specifically, outlined in detail below, adds greater justification to the claims of organizations such as the ASPE. A more general conclusion in relation to that fact is that, once special benefits aimed at particular groups become entrenched, they are very difficult to withdraw even when such benefits do not solve the problem they are supposed to address and even where resources could be much better spent elsewhere. One way in which states in mature democracies might cope with this problem is to 'activate' other interests and build alternative bases of support to dilute the influence of organizations such as the ASPE. This is one of the reasons why dialogue with a broader range of interest groups is so important, rather than allowing one particular group or organization to dominate. Suggestions here include childcare workers, feminist elements of the union movement, or progressive family organizations. One problem in Greece is that either such groups do not exist or else they lack centralization, and thus the ability to present a united voice.[11] The fragmentation of interests, however, does not let the state off the hook. As the literature on interest groups, and corporatism in particular, shows, state policies and actions play no small role in the centralization and strengthening of interest groups. Dialogue between interest groups and the state requires some centralization if not 'monopolization' of interests so that consultation and incorporation can take place in some coherent way. The lack of such efforts in Greece can certainly be observed in the family policy arena.

The evolution of policies for work–life balance

Greece is presented in the comparative literature as yet a third national case, like Ireland and Portugal in this respect, in which constitutional commitments to protecting the family are contradicted by the low levels of actual support given (Dumon, 1991: 25; Hantrais and Letablier, 1996: 45–50). The official commitment to the family is not matched by an explicit policy framework that is capable of adequately supporting families and, importantly, reconciling tensions between work and family life. Greece's constitutional commitments and family policy outcomes, however, are not as contradictory as many analysts assume. Rather, the constitution explicitly identifies special types of family that deserve differential treatment. Declaring that the family is 'the foundation stone for the preservation and the advancement of the Nation', the 1975 Constitution then commits the Greek state to the protection of motherhood, the encouragement of home ownership, and the protection of large families and families with certain members, such as those serving in the military, the disabled, the old and the sick (Loukia, 1994: 87–8). The singling out of specific groups for preferential treatment is entirely consistent with Greece's fragmented welfare state in general and is reflected in the development of family policy in particular. Nowhere has this had more of an impact than in the evolution of the targeting of family benefits to 'large families', a theme that has already been introduced above and which will be detailed below.

Another feature of the way in which this policy issue has been and continues to be framed in Greece is the predominance of 'population' over 'family' or economic concerns. When national debates over this issue do take place, it is usually within the context of the 'demographic crisis' rather than anything to do with promoting work–life balance. Whereas social scientists and policymakers in Western Europe are concerned with formulating policies to encourage both increased fertility and female workforce participation rates as solutions to the problem of an aging population, the focus in Greece has been almost entirely on the fertility part of the equation. The issue of work–life balance is confined to academic circles, with perhaps some additional support from some trade unions representing a limited number of workers. This puts the political debate in Greece much further away from that which has occurred at the EU level and on the part of international institutions such as the OECD than is the case in either Ireland or Portugal. In part, this is because family policy is perceived primarily as population policy, which in turn is coloured by concerns about racial 'purity.'

The Greek concern over population decline began in the context of mass outward migration in the 1960s but has reoccurred periodically since. Interview-based research shows that population concerns are shared not only by conservative and frankly xenophobic elements on the Greek right, represented by right-wing political parties and conservative family associations including the ASPE, but even by the supposed centre-left, represented in particular by PASOK parliamentary representatives. Population concerns take on a racial dimension, since many of these forces frequently express concerns about the declining fertility rate in Greece in comparison to its arch-rival, Turkey, and the 'diluting' of Greekness through the immigration of non-Greeks from the Balkans. The focus on solving the 'demographic crisis' through encouraging increased fertility further reinforces the preference for family policies targeted on large families. The problem is that such strategies simply do not work, despite their enthusiastic following. Greece does not actually have a large number of large families, and is arguably one of the European countries that have carried on the nuclear family pattern the longest. Many people choose not to marry and have children, but in 1998 Greece had the highest incidence of two-parent, two-child families in the EU.[12] One reason why such policies continue to be pursued despite being so out of touch with current realities is found in the relationship between a limited number of lobby groups and the state.

During the 1980s, PASOK's reformist agenda in the family policy arena did not extend much beyond the removal of some forms of gender discrimination from the legal code. Family law until 1983 dated from 1946 and 'expressed the social values of a former age' (Symeonidou, 1997: 76). That is putting it mildly. For a country that had just joined the EU, the laws governing family relationships appeared decidedly anti-modern. PASOK's reform package included the secularization of marriage and the outlawing of the widespread practice of the dowry, the removal of the legal distinction between legitimate and illegitimate children, and a formal guarantee of gender equality. In the realm of employment law, it was not until 1984 that a ban on the firing of pregnant workers was introduced (Symeonidou, 1990: 134). Beyond that, family policy largely consisted of the maintenance of a small range of family benefits and maternity leave provisions. After 1990, having witnessed an increase in the number of women entering the paid workforce but more significantly the re-emergence of the 'demographic crisis', some increased attention to family policy can be observed.

Family or child benefits were first introduced in the late 1950s, a little later than most of Western Europe including both Ireland and Portugal and with little change to their structure until the early 1990s. The overall level of provision remained low and, since it was tied into the social insurance-based welfare

Table 5.1 Major developments in Greek family policy

Year	*Policy development*
1958	First family allowance scheme, gradually supplemented and overlapped with additional employment-based benefits
1975	Expansion of maternity leave in public sector
1984	Family law reform package introduced
1984	Expansion of maternity leave in public sector, introduction of limited unpaid parental leave rights
1990–1992	Introduction of three separate "many children" allowances and benefits
1992	Expansion of parental/maternity leave in public sector
1997	Income tests introduced for many children allowances
1999	Introduction of paid maternity leave in public sector
2002	Income test on many children allowances revoked

system, consisted of a series of fragmented, complicated, and sometimes overlapping schemes. For most of this period at least four different types of mostly contributory child benefit schemes were in existence, with much more generous provision available to public sector workers. Fragmentation across occupational lines resulted in some children being covered by more than one benefit scheme while others received nothing (Symeonidou, 1990: 141–2). Higher rates or additional benefits were generally awarded for third, fourth, or subsequent children, but the large family focus of the child benefit system did not become fully entrenched until the 1990s, when the concern over population decline peaked. In addition, there are a number of child-related exemptions built into the tax code.

During the 1990 election campaign, after which a decade of government under PASOK was followed by a very brief period of rule by the centre-right under New Democracy, Greece's demographic problems became a topic of national debate. In the context of prolonged economic misfortunes and failings, all major political parties made the perceived special needs of large families central to their welfare policy proposals. While New Democracy proposed additional tax allowances for large families and increased child allowances, populist PASOK's proposals included preferential access to employment in the public sector for heads of large families, marriage bonuses for public servants, and preferential rates for public services for those families with three or more children (Dumon, 1991: 26–8). These latter suggestions may appear unusual by international comparison, but not so in the Greek national setting, where public service employment still shows strong signs of patronage politics.

A series of 'many children' benefits were thus introduced from 1992, with some modifications and reversals of these modifications since. The crucial legislation here is New Democracy's Law 1892 of 1990, concerned directly with the issue of fertility decline (Sarikaki, 2001: 8). The most important of these were the third child benefit, a large family benefit, and a lifetime pension for mothers of large families. All of these were to be paid out of general taxation and were thus non-contributory but delivered through the state's Agricultural Insurance Organization. The 'third child' benefit was originally awarded to families on the birth of the third child until the point when this child reached three years of age. Rates were raised in 1997 and the age of the child increased to six years. 'Large family' benefits were targeted at families with four or more children aged under 23, with the level of payment varying according to number of children. The lifetime pension, probably the strangest measure to consider with the respect to the issue of work–life balance but supposedly designed to create an incentive for women to have many children and help out with the demographic problem, was to be provided to mothers of four or more children who no longer qualified for the large family benefit since their children had now grown up.[13]

The attempt to 'modernize' the welfare state under Prime Minister Simitis during the late 1990s included measures to cut back expenditure on many-children allowances by targeting them towards poorer families. The debate that surrounded the introduction of such proposals in 1996 was described at the time at a 'heated' one (Ditch *et al.*, 1998: 65) and included fierce resistance on the part of lobby groups working on behalf of the beneficiaries of existing policies. Chief among these was the ASPE.[14] Rather than entering a process of negotiation with the government, however, resistance took the form that it often does in Greece: oppositional street protests. The welfare modernizers did manage to impose an income test on the many-family benefits in 1997, but most of these reforms were overturned in 2002 in the legislature. Furthermore, elsewhere in the OECD, child benefits have become increasingly targeted towards poor families and especially single-parent families that often fall into this category. There has been little or no attention to this latter issue in Greece. One explanation for this is that not only is the proportion of children born out of wedlock still relatively small, but having children out of wedlock is still 'socially unacceptable' in a way that is no longer true in most developed countries (Sarikaki, 2001: 10). Lone parenthood has thus 'not been considered a social problem requiring greater state intervention' (Carlos and Maratou-Alipranti, 2000: 43).

The support of families with many children is thus the primary mechanism for addressing issues of fertility decline, if not work–life balance, in Greece. Other possible measures that more directly address issues of work–life balance deserve some attention, however, since, although Greece has a comparatively low level of female workforce participation, almost half of women do work outside the home. Taking maternity leave and benefits first, like much else in Greece, rights in this area vary according to occupational status. In particular, there has always been differential treatment of public and private sector workers with respect to leave entitlements, with maternity benefits varying according to levels and type of social insurance contribution. In a monitoring report for the EU, Christos Bagavos (2004: 13) describes a 'typical' set of maternity leave entitlements as seventeen weeks in the private sector and up to five months in the public sector. Although this brings Greece into line with the other more minimalist maternity leave regimes in Europe, compensation in the form of pay and additional benefits has reportedly been the lowest in the EU (Papadopoulos, 1998: 50). Paid maternity leave was introduced in the public sector only in 1999.

EU activity in the arena of parental leave has had impact on countries with previously minimalist or non-existent schemes, such as Ireland and Portugal. The 1996 EU Parental Leave Directive, however, did not specify a particular set of entitlements that each member state must adopt nor did it state that parental leave would necessarily have to be paid leave. It was up to individual states how they would respond to the objectives stated in the Directive, the result being that some countries are still far more generous than others. It thus constituted an 'indirect' influence on national policy as much as a direct one. Greece still guarantees one of the least generous sets of leave entitlements, and, what is more, legislation did not change much in response to EU developments in this field. A set of parental leave provisions was introduced into the legal code in 1984, establishing that parents in workplaces with more than 100 employees are entitled to unpaid childcare leave of up to three months until the child reached two and a half years. Because this only applied to larger workplaces, this covered approximately 41 per cent of men and 38 per cent of women at the time it was introduced (Symeonidou, 1990: 135). Working parents are also entitled to six unpaid days per year to take care of sick children. Under the 1993 national collective bargaining agreement, the upper age limit for children to which the main parental leave provision applied was raised to three and a half years (European Union Industrial Relations Observatory Online, 1998). Law 2085/92 also extended parental leave to up to two years in the public sector, although this would affect pension rights for women who took the option up (Dumon and Nuelant, 1994: 43). Overall, however, because parental leave is generally unpaid, it understandably suffers a low take-up rate and in any case is considered mainly a 'women's thing' (Bagavos, 2004: 13). It has also been suggested that men who do take up parental leave options in Greece frequently use this time for activities other than caring for children.[15]

Flexi-time, job sharing, and part-time work are often posited in the industrial relations literature as among the best ways for parents to reconcile family and working life, not least because they can provide the basis for employment contract negotiations and thus gain support from employers as well as employees. Unsurprisingly perhaps, given the importance of Greece's pension system in determining labour market structure, part-time work has generally been discouraged. In fact, it was not until 1990 that most of the basic rights enshrined in labour law were extended to part-time workers, and part-time work tends to be of low pay and confined to the retail sector, thus not designed around family needs as the Nordic vision of high-quality part-time work envisages (Kyriazis, 1999: 50). The lack of formal legal provisions and the absence of flexi-time arrangements in patterns of collective bargaining, however, belie the fact that much informal working time flexibility occurs as a result of the fact that Greece has such a high proportion of very small, often family-run businesses, in which flexibility is fundamental (Papalexandris and Kramer, 1997).

Research tends to show that childcare, or rather the lack of it, is probably the greatest obstacle parents face when entering or re-entering the workforce. Greece is no exception here, with low levels of formal provision especially with respect to children aged under three.[16] Some serious attention was given to expanding provision for those aged between three and six during the 1990s, with a new network of public nursery schools created in 1997. These would stay open until four o'clock in the afternoon, much later than in the past, and, although these were envisaged by the government as having more of an education purpose than anything else, survey data shows that parents are increasingly relying on these services for the purpose of work–life balance (Bagavos, 2004: 13). State-led development in this area has, however, increased relatively recently from a low base and in the context of an era of fiscal discipline meaning that the pool of resources available has been limited (Sarikaki, 2001: 12).

In sum, Greek policies for the reconciliation of family and working life are the least developed of all three national cases analyzed in this book. Policies consist of limited labour legislation on the one hand and mainly large family-oriented benefits on the other, with little connection made between the two. At least part of the explanation for why this is the case lies in the inability of Greek policymakers to build a consensus around the required policy shift. When attempts have been made to redirect resources in such a way that more families are assisted through the tax and benefit system, fierce protest on the part of lobby groups, especially the ASPE on behalf of large families, has prevented a permanent shift from taking place. The ability of such a minority organization to block attempts at reform is explained in part by the absence of a consultative and incorporative tradition that is capable of cultivating relationships between the state and a wider range of interest groups. That in turn might be explained by a lack of interest on the part of political party leaders in creating such a tradition. Greek family policy has not benefited from the type of 'enlightened leadership' experienced in Portugal. Part of the reason why a group such as the ASPE is able to have any leverage at all is because of broadly shared ideas concerning racial purity and population policy amongst the political elite. It could be speculated that politicians aligned with the two main political parties (although not the smaller leftist parties) also wish to avoid further confrontations with the Orthodox Church, to which the ASPE in particular is aligned. Conflict in recent years has centred on the removal of religious status on national identity cards, something the Church has opposed. A full analysis of why political leaders in Greece align themselves with such conservative ideologies, and not with gender equality objectives as mainstream political actors do in the Portuguese case, is well beyond the scope of this book, but the gulf between Greek policy goals and values and the policy requirements of a development strategy for the twenty-first century is clear in this case.

Higher education

Greece's greatest challenge in the field of higher education policy has been how to reorient a system designed primarily for the teaching of classical, elite subjects around the needs of the modern economy in which the content of higher education must be increasingly work related and participation much more broad based. Reforms of the past three decades have gone some way towards increasing participation and expanding the range of courses offered by institutions of higher learning, but Greece still has much further to go in the implementation of quality control mechanisms and in increasing the relevance of higher education and training to the needs of a high-wage, high-skill, post-industrial economy. More recent attempts to address these concerns were met with and stalled by fierce resistance, especially on the part of teachers' unions and the student movement. The lack of a strong consultative and incorporative tradition only adds to this impasse since it leaves few channels open for forging compromise over the future direction of policy content.

The policy problem

As the next chapter will detail, Portugal's problem in the field of higher education has been to expand participation while keeping control over quality.

Greece's problem has been a little different. It too has been concerned with increasing participation but from a higher starting point. Despite the dispersion of a good proportion of the country's population across islands and isolated mountain areas in the north of the country, educational participation rates in the late 1960s were much higher in Greece than in Portugal. An estimated 48.7 per cent of young people aged between fourteen and seventeen were enrolled at school in Greece in 1969, compared to 21.8 in Portugal. For those aged between eighteen and twenty-two, covering at least the initial years of higher education, the participation rate was 15.4 per cent in Greece compared to 9.8 per cent in Portugal (OECD, 1974: 30). Broadening participation in higher levels of the education system over time, however, has still been a challenge given that a lack of resources has continuously placed restrictions on the number of places available, especially in the preferred university sector. Yet arguably Greece's greatest problem in the higher education field has been the fact that the system has tended to supply the *wrong kind* of education and training, especially with respect to labour market needs. The Greeks are very proud of their classical heritage, and, until relatively recently, the curricula of upper secondary and third-level education institutions have been biased heavily towards classical studies. Somewhat bizarrely, most classes at upper secondary and the third level were not taught in the modern language that most Greeks actually speak, referred to as *demotiki,* until the return of democracy in 1974. The alternative, *katharevousa,* is a nineteenth century invention, a modern interpretation of ancient Greek used for official purposes.[17]

The 'language debate' over which version should be used in schools and universities became symbolic of a much broader clash between modernizers and conservatives with respect to the Greek education system, but one that also had real-world consequences in terms of the underdevelopment of technical and labour-market relevant higher education in Greece. This is not to say that the development of technical higher education has been neglected altogether, and these efforts are discussed in detail below, but rather that this form of education has most clearly been regarded as an inferior form of education in Greece. This reflects the great difficulty Greece has had in breaking with the country's attachment to the classical tradition. The result of a lag in efforts to tie the education system firmly to labour market needs is reflected in the unusually high number of unemployed graduates in Greece. There is an assumption in the literature and in general common sense that a higher level of educational attainment guarantees an individual a better chance of securing a good job. The Greek experience shows this is not always the case. Young Greeks with a third-level education qualification are up to 75 per cent more likely to be unemployed than those with no upper secondary school qualification (Liagouras *et al.*, 2003: 14).[18] One half of the solution to this problem lies a little outside the scope of this research: the lack of employment opportunities for the highly qualified, especially outside the public sector, suggests that an industrial policy aimed at promoting job growth in highly skilled areas is required. The other half of the solution, however, lies firmly within the frame of analysis employed here: the higher education system needs to provide better training in the skills required for the contemporary labour market. While labour shortages in technology-intensive industries may not be apparent yet, Greece will never be able to develop these types of industries without a differently educated labour force.

Another factor contributing to the high level of unemployed, seemingly over-educated young people in Greece is that many families send their children overseas to be educated. Large numbers of degrees have been awarded to Greek students in North America and Europe over the past half century. In 2001 there were up to 57,000 students studying abroad, representing about 30 per cent of those in Greek institutions of higher education (Lianos *et al.*, 2004: 151). Some of these foreign-trained graduates do not return, leading to concerns over a national 'brain drain', but others do, adding to the pool of Greek-trained students. If they have been trained in Western Europe, they are often better qualified than their Greek-trained counterparts.

One of the principal reasons behind this tradition is that the Greek higher education system has never been able to provide anything like enough places to meet demand. Higher education in Greece is constitutionally guaranteed free, including textbooks and meals for students. This sounds very generous, but the generosity is undercut by the fact that, although there is hardly any private funding for education and research in Greece, the level of public spending is no higher than in most other developed countries. In 2003 the state spent 1.5 per cent of GDP on higher education, compared to an OECD average of 1.3 per cent. More significantly, perhaps, this only translated into total spending, including all books and other generosities from the state, of US$4,924 per student against an OECD average of $11,254 (OECD, 2006). The result is that the numbers of students permitted into public institutions, and all institutions are public in this case, are restricted, some sectors of the system are severely underfunded, and quality suffers as a result. The literature on higher education often reflects very serious doubts about the level of quality across the university and non-university sectors. That issue will be returned to at length shortly. The commitment to free education also actually reproduces social inequality since it tends to be students from wealthier families that gain access to free public, and especially university, education in the first place.[19]

Despite efforts over the past three decades to expand participation in higher education and increase the variety of programmes offered through the non-university technical sector, Greece stills suffers from a basic set of problems in this field. First, the high number of unemployed graduates suggests either that education is not tied in closely to labour market needs or that economic development strategies themselves are not tied in closely enough to what the education system can offer in terms of labour power. Second, the free education system costs the state enough in monetary terms, yet it means that it cannot guarantee access to higher education for large numbers of young people. Demand outstrips supply and potential solutions to the problem such as permitting the development of private institutions, introducing fees, or forcing the universities to accept more students, have been fiercely resisted by key interest groups. That clash of interests and the inability to create policymaking processes capable of bringing those on board so that they can play a constructive role in policymaking is discussed next.

The role of consultation and incorporation in shaping policy responses

The discussion of the evolution of the Irish higher education system contained in the previous chapter showed that the construction of a range of state institutions and organizations in which interest groups are formally represented is highly likely to happen in this particular policy area. The seemingly technical nature of some policy decisions and the fact that the most important interest groups are already part of the social elite increases this likelihood. Consultative processes in the field of higher education can be identified in Greece, but the range of groups represented in them is narrower than in Ireland, or, for that matter, Portugal, and, from the evidence that exists, not particularly robust. In the absence of institutions and processes designed to incorporate interest group opinion, proposed changes are often stridently resisted by interest groups in an unconstructive manner.

Most importantly, however, a National Council for Education (ESYP) was established in 1995 and charged with building an education policy consensus. In theory, the ESYP represents the interests of a range of groups across the entire education system, including government ministries, political parties, university rectors, presidents of technical institutes, the Orthodox Church, teaching staff in higher education, the Confederation of Parents, Confederations of Primary and

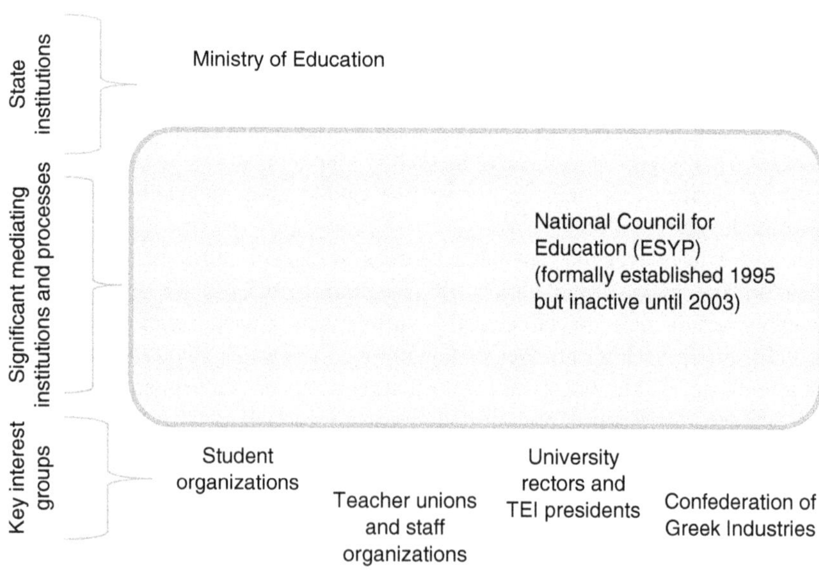

Figure 5.2 The zone of mediation in Greek higher education policy.

Secondary School Teachers, the National Students' Union, and the Confederation of Greek Industries (OECD, 1997: 23). Forging a consensus, however, in the absence of a strong consultative and incorporative tradition was not easy. Major reforms in relation to higher education policy were attempted in the mid-2000s, yet these were only partially successful. More importantly for this analysis, proposed reforms were met with fierce resistance on the part of the teachers' unions and student organizations, spilling outside formal established channels and onto the street, causing major disruptions to the education system. The details of these clashes are discussed further below.

The evolution of higher education policy

Until the late 1950s, the Greek education system consisted of six years of compulsory primary education followed by six years of secondary school. The latter was heavily skewed toward the study of the humanities, the Greek classics in particular, and this carried through into higher education. Third-level studies were generally limited to university and university-level institutions, with the addition of several independent schools for the purposes of teacher training in particular. Economic development concerns led to a series of reforms towards

Table 5.2 Major developments in Greek higher education policy

Year	*Policy development*
1964–1966	Introduction of free third-level education, *demotiki* introduced as language of instruction (Papandreou reforms). University of Patras opened
1967	Repeal of Papandreou reforms to higher education
1967–1974	First KATEEs or third-level technical institutions established
1970–1984	Opening of seven new universities
1974	All levels of education declared free under new constitution; *demotiki* reintroduced as language of instruction
1978	Legislative strengthening of university autonomy; introduction of national entrance exams
1982	Law 1268 outlines major changes to university governance ('departmentalization'); gives additional subsidies and benefits to students; regulates postgraduate study
1983	KATEEs become Technical Education Institutes (TEIs)
1992	Law 2083 outlines changes to university governance; removal of student privileges and benefits; strengthening of postgraduate requirements; establishment of Committee for the Evaluation of Higher Education
1997	PASOK reform package revokes 1992 changes to student privileges and university governance. Education 2000 Act introduces 'open' access to higher education
2001	Law 2916 gives TEIs equal status to universities
2005	National programme for evaluating institutions introduced but not yet fully implemented
2006–2007	Introduction of major reform proposals to remove state monopoly on higher education, increase university/TEI autonomy and remove a number of student privileges

the end of that decade, mainly at the secondary level. Secondary school was divided into two stages of three years each, the first being very general before dividing into vocational training, which effectively prevented these students from entering higher education since they would not be eligible for university entrance, and a traditional stream. The latter retained its classical focus and thus 'stifled any significant growth in scientific, technical or vocational education' (OECD, 1980: 11). At the third level, two new engineering schools were established in Athens and Thessaloniki around this time.

Secondary school reform continued to be the main source of focus for the first Papandreou government between 1964 and 1966, surrounded by much rhetoric about the need to democratize education (OECD, 1980: 13). The school leaving age was raised to fifteen, adding three years of compulsory education, *demotiki* was introduced into the classroom with a new requirement that the Greek classics be taught in the modern translation, and the guarantee of free education was extended to the third level. Some of these reforms never had a chance to take full effect, since they were repealed by the military regime after 1967. Yet the junta also carried through more of the practical measures in the field of higher education that had been debated during the 1960s, including the establishment of new universities and the creation of a technically oriented higher education sector. This saw a near doubling in the number of students in higher education from 54,261 in 1965 to 92,920 in 1974 (Fakiolas, 1979: 54).

Until 1964 when the University of Patras was established, there had been only three universities and six university-level schools in Greece, all located in the two major cities of Athens and Thessaloniki. Seven more universities were established in response to increasing demand, especially in the regions, both during and after military rule: the University of Ioannina in 1970, the University of Thrace in 1973, the University of Crete in 1973, the Technical University of Crete in 1977, the University of the Aegean in 1984, and the Ionian University and the University of Thessaly in 1984 (Saitis, 1988: 249). Perhaps the more significant development that occurred under military rule, however, was the move to establish a series of non-university technical schools. These centres are referred to in the literature by their Greek acronym, KATEE. Five KATEEs were in operation by 1974, including the two engineering schools that had been opened in 1958, with significant funding from the World Bank (OECD, 1982: 35).

After 1974, the national democratic constitution again guaranteed Greek citizens a right to a free education, including higher education. Article 16, importantly and recently contentiously, also bans private higher education. Under the centre-right Karamanlis government that steered public policy until PASOK was elected in 1981, a number of educational reforms were introduced, initially mainly at the primary and secondary level. *Katharevousa* was again replaced with *demotiki* as the official language in all aspects of public life to include schools, so that the teaching of Greek classics would now be in translation; compulsory schooling was again raised to nine years; a reorganization of secondary teacher training took place; and further attention was paid to technical and vocational training at the secondary level (Panourgia, 1990: 74).

In the field of higher education proper, the return to democracy cemented a commitment to a binary structure. Greece therefore had the same structure as Ireland and Portugal, but with a qualitative difference. Whereas successive governments in the other two countries have made efforts, especially in the Irish case, to avoid creating a hierarchy between the university and non-university sectors by elevating the status of scientific and technical education provided by the non-university sector, the Greek state sanctioned and reinforced this hierarchy. Legislation governing higher education in Greece, at least until 2001, referred to the two different sectors as 'higher' and 'highest' education. 'Higher' education included all non-university post-secondary schools and centres, including the KATEEs, which operated in the immediate post-authoritarian period. 'Highest' education referred to those institutions with university status and are referred to by their Greek acronym (AEI) (OECD, 1980: 32–3).

The problem is that this elevated the status of university at the expense of non-university education. Students still showed a clear preference for gaining access to the (public) universities first, something that is also the case in Portugal. In the initial stages of the development of technical higher education, this lack of prestige had a serious impact on the operation of the KATEEs and is posited as a major source of their demise by 1982. Other reasons included a shortage of full-time staff, infrastructure and equipment; their association with the military regime since their development had begun under it; and that they served less as a good in themselves than as a way to satisfy demands for higher education that could not be met by the university system (Kalamatianou *et al.*, 1988: 273; OECD, 1982: 36). The end result of these failures was the replacement of the KATEEs with a new system of technical higher education in 1983, referred to as the Technical Education Institutes (TEIs). While attempts have been made to elevate their status, they are still considered by the general public as an inferior form of higher education.

There is an internationally recognized distinction, adopted by both the EU and the OECD, between technical and vocational training that operates at the 'second level' of the education system and that which operates at the 'third level.' Third level technical training is more advanced, often carried out by polytechnic-type institutions, and offers diploma and degree courses. Second-level training offers qualifications equivalent to high school level. Much of the development of technical education after the reconstitution of the KATEEs as TEIs occurred at the post-secondary level but did not form part of the third-level system as such, the discussion of which lies outside the scope of this research. Suffice it to note that a considerable effort was made to develop vocational and apprenticeship training under the direction of Greece's Manpower Agency (OEEK), during the 1980s and 1990s.[20] Much of the development of the technical and vocational training was initiated by the government of the time but with significant backing and encouragement of international organizations, particularly the OECD and the EU.

As for the TEI's themselves, no major change occurred to their operation until 2001 when a very significant attempt was made to elevate their status and allow them to conduct higher level research and teaching than they had been permitted in the past. Law 2916/2001 designated TEIs as forming the 'Technological Sector of Higher Education' and they were given the same constitutional status and accompanying degree of independence as universities. This means that they could, for example, grant postgraduate degrees (Eurydice, 2005).

Turning now to the development of the university sector in the immediate post-authoritarian period, a minor set of reforms to the university or AEI system was made in 1978 involving the introduction of national entrance exams and the reestablishment of university autonomy, which had suffered considerably under military rule, and the role of state oversight (OECD, 1980: 9). Major reforms, however, did not occur until the early 1980s and, even then, did not seem to solve some of the very serious problems associated with the operation of 'highest' education in Greece. Descriptions of Greek universities in the late 1970s and early 1980s are extremely unflattering. One contemporary commentator pointed out that very little research was carried out at Greek universities, with 98 per cent or so of budgets dedicated to teaching, and mostly undergraduate teaching at that. This lack of research reflects the 'unreasonably high prestige university teaching has both within the university community and socially, and it is reasonable to assume that the authoritarian teaching methods and the harshness of the examination system become an academic alibi for the absence of research' (Gavrogly, 1981: 97). Presumably the author means here that attempts to appear 'strict' can be used as a way to look as if high standards were being enforced even when they were in fact not.

The rigidity and overly bureaucratized nature of Greek universities during this period was a constant complaint, as was the quality of teaching. Also, official guidelines for the way in which universities were supposed to operate often bore no relation to their actual operation, and many of these problems were not entirely solved during the 1980s. Another contemporary observer noted that,, apart from a few cases in which lecture attendance was obligatory, few Greek university students ever attended classes. 'Usually students attend a few lectures at the beginning of the academic year and then drift away to private tutorial colleges' in which they 'attend the same lectures delivered by the university teachers'. One reason given for why 'some students have never attended a lecture at the institution from which they graduated' is that they could not find a place in the classroom given the problem of very low staff to student ratios. 'Lectures may be delivered to a maximum of 1,000 students, many of whom may be standing. In addition, the ability to impart knowledge skilfully has been used very rarely as a criterion for the appointment of teachers' (Fakiolas, 1979: 59). Added to this set of problems was, and still is, the extremely tough competition that exists for getting into higher education in the first place. In 1980, up to 100,000 students competed for 22,000 places available across the entire higher education system, with fewer than 15,000 of these places in universities (OECD, 1982: 34).

Shortly after coming to power in 1981, PASOK introduced a reform package aimed at fundamentally changing the way in which universities operated. Part of the reason for the overly hierarchical and bureaucratic nature of Greek universities, at least until the early 1980s, was located in the 'chair' system that had operated since their establishment. This awarded individual chairs within faculties or schools, and not departments, which at this point did not really exist, near absolute authority over a particular area of teaching within a larger faculty. Policymakers had recognized this as a problem since at least the 1960s, but earlier efforts to undercut the power of the chairs had been stalled by fierce resistance from the universities themselves. The most recent attempt, under the Karamanlis government in 1978, had resulted in the construction of an alliance between chairs, their 'assistants' meaning other professors, and students, culminating in a 100 day strike in that year (Grant, 1986: 22).

PASOK's reform package, codified in Law 1268/82, was more successful, in part because it was couched in the language of 'democratization' and included provisions to guarantee student representation equal to that of the teaching staff in electoral bodies responsible for selecting university administrative and academic staff. Up to this point students had received no formal representation on such bodies, and this is one of the reasons why PASOK's 1982 legislation is often described as 'radical'. The new framework also mandated that old faculties would be divided into departments and that each department would be governed by an accountable collective rather than an individual chair; established a formal system for the award of postgraduate degrees, including new masters' programmes; introduced a new ranking and tenure system for academic staff; and extended a number of benefits to university students, including not only free meals and textbooks but also transportation subsidies, interest-free loans, and a number of other benefits.[21]

'Access' issues in the field of education are rarely discussed in relation to achieving equality of access across socio-economic, gender, age, and ethnic lines in Greece, whereas it is common to do so in Ireland and is at least a frequent source of academic discussion in Portugal. Instead, access issues have centred on the very basic problem of expanding the number of places available. The number of university places available to secondary school graduates remained low in comparison to applications until 1981 at around 12,000 places per year. This was doubled to 23,000 by 1985. Expansion of participation in the non-university higher education sector was also encouraged, increasing from 9,300 in 1981 to 21,200 in 1986. This still left an imbalance between supply and demand, however, since 150,000 students sat national entrance examinations in 1987, meaning at least two-thirds of students missed out on a place in either kind of institution (Karmas *et al.*, 1988). Increasing numbers of students sought degrees abroad during the 1990s. The gradual expansion of access was met in part by the construction of a new series of institutions; the number of universities operating had increased to seventeen by the late 1980s. Looking ahead, the annual acceptance of students to higher education across both university and non-university sectors was not significantly altered until 2000, when a new near open access policy placed new resource pressures on public institutions.

Since PASOK's reforms of the 1980s, most significantly in relation to the university rather than the technical education system, there have been several pieces of legislation passed that modify or change PASOK's original framework. However, for the most part no major set of reforms has survived governmental change since 1982. This is despite the fact that the Greek higher education system still suffers some serious defects, especially in the area of quality control. At the time of researching and writing this book, a major new framework to govern higher education was about to be passed by the centre-right New Democracy government, proposals for which were met by enormous resistance from the sector. The fact that this resistance turned into a clash of interests that brought the university system to a standstill, rather than a process of negotiation, is highly significant for the analysis of the way in which policy is formulated in Greece. The contours of the contemporary controversy will be returned to below, but it is first important to outline New Democracy's earlier attempts to modify PASOK's reforms of the 1980s, and the reversal of most of these attempts shortly afterwards.

Major alterations to the 1982 reform package were introduced in 1992 under Law 2083/92. As in the reforms of a decade earlier, much of this related to university governance: the representation of students on university governing bodies was reduced to 50 per cent of faculty and new systems were introduced for the election of university officials. Several other reforms undercut the privileges previously awarded to university students, including the limiting of the free text programme to low-income students, and a time limit placed on the number of years a student had to complete a programme and thus receive financial aid. The system of postgraduate study that had gradually been evolving since the 1980s was formalized, and broadening access to higher education was given some attention through the creation of an Open University for distance learning as well as a new Centre for the Greek Language. A Committee for the Evaluation of Higher Education was established in order to explore possibilities of introducing quality control mechanisms. At the time of writing, a national system for the review of higher education institutions had only just been introduced under Law 3374 of 2005, meaning it is too early to assess its effects.

On returning to power in 1994, PASOK modified or reversed all of these changes except those related to the structure of postgraduate degree programmes and the establishment of the Open University, the Greek Language Centre, and the Committee for the Evaluation of Higher Education. More significantly, however, PASOK replaced the 1982 comprehensive law on higher education with a new framework law in 1997, referred to as the Education 2000 Act (2525/97). This legislation committed the government to providing a better environment for research and postgraduate study and eventual national quality control mechanisms. Most significantly for the purposes of this discussion, however, the Act abolished the national entrance exam system that had regulated and limited the number of students able to access post-secondary education and training since the beginning of the expansion of higher education (Eurydice, 2000: 268–9). Providing 'open' access is obviously a significant departure in the Greek context, and was brought into effect in 2000. By 'open access' it is meant that students have a right to enter higher education so long as they achieve a certain minimum pass mark in the reformulated national exam. Minimum pass marks for certain types of courses are determined by the state and caps on numbers are placed on some institutions.

The potential problems caused by the sudden introduction of open access to higher education should perhaps be obvious, especially given the budgetary constraints on a system that is funded almost entirely by the state. As the Portuguese case also clearly shows, a sudden explosion in the number of students entering institutions of higher learning can have a detrimental effect on quality, not only because many students might not be prepared well for higher education, but, in the Greek case, mainly because it overburdened what were already underfunded institutions. Since the system has always permitted the government to set the number of students an institution must take on an annual basis, the rapid expansion has become a major point of contention between individual institutions and the state. It is just one source of tension that surrounds the contemporary battle over higher education in Greece, an issue that will be returned to in a moment.

In addition, while the introduction of 'open' access was supposed to be accompanied by similarly radical efforts in the area of quality control, these have been much slower to reach implementation stage. Closely connected to the quality control issue is the inability to address one of the long-standing problems associated with higher education in Greece that was discussed above: the disconnect between higher education and the operation of the Greek labour market reflected in the high number of unemployed graduates. The quality issue has been further underlined by the increased number of foreign students enrolled in Greek universities, especially as part of EU-based exchange programmes. Constant complaints from European and other foreign students centre on continued problems of inefficiency, hierarchy, and over-bureaucratization in Greek universities (Giannarou and Karanatsi, 2007), which, as the preceding discussion details, have been considered serious problems in the country for the past three decades. One simple issue illustrates the gulf that still exists between the way that higher education courses are conducted in Greece and elsewhere in the developed world: the fact that the 'textbook' issue is not only a subject of political debate but also considered an appropriate area of state oversight. University professors still retained a tradition of prescribing one textbook (often their own), which, as we have seen, is provided to students by the state. Most institutions do not have proper libraries attached, and the reform package proposed in 2007 proposed drawing up a centralized university book list on the basis of advice of institutions but with Ministry of Education approval.

The decision to introduce 'open' access, even if in reality numbers are still limited by the various entry criteria pertinent to different courses, institutions and sectors, before issues of quality control and better tying course content in Greece to developing labour market needs have been addressed, gave the New Democracy government elected in 2004 the unenviable task of the further reform of higher education. A reform bill for higher education was introduced in 2006 and debated over the following months, guided by the work of the National Council for Education's Committee for Tertiary Education (2004–2007). Among the points of contention between university administration, student groups, teacher unions and the state were proposals to alter Article 16 of the Constitution to allow the development of private institutions of higher learning, something that had been banned until this point. This direction of the reforms was opposed especially by the Panhellenic Federation of University Teachers' Associations (POSDEP), in alliance with student organizations, guided by the belief that it would undermine the status of the public system. A second major thrust of the proposals aimed at increasing institutional autonomy in various ways, to include changes in the way that universities are financed and administered. Despite past reforms aimed at decentralization, there was an international consensus, shared by many Greek policymakers, that the administration of higher education in Greece was overly centralized with too much interference from the Ministry of Education.[22] Although it might be assumed that institutions would want greater autonomy, this exploded into an argument between university rectors and the government over to what extent student numbers should be capped.

A third set of proposals threatened to undercut some of the privileges awarded to students. One of these was aimed at preventing the possibility of becoming a 'perpetual student', an expensive phenomenon given the additional benefits awarded to students on the part of the state. It was eventually agreed, despite resistance, that full-time students would be required to complete their degrees in double the minimum amount of time usually required to complete. A standard four-year degree would thus have to be completed in eight years. A second point of controversy, which no doubt appears rather obscure outside the specific Greek context, involved the lifting of the 'sanctuary' law that was applied to university grounds after 1974. One of the precipitating events of the downfall of the military regime in 1974 was a student sit-in at the Athens Polytechnic late the year before, ending in the deaths of at least twenty students after tanks crashed through the campus gates. As a symbolic gesture, no branches of the state repressive apparatuses, including the regular police, have been permitted to enter university and polytechnic campuses during the democratic period. The accusation is that this had led to a crime-wave, the proliferation of illegal drugs and the like, on campuses across the country.

Taken together, the proposals to alter Article 16 to allow private institutions to operate and the removal of certain student privileges have sparked widespread resistance and outrage on the part of the teachers' unions and the student movement in particular. The introduction of the proposals in mid-2006 was accompanied by a wave of protests, especially in Athens and Thessaloniki, at the beginning of the Autumn Semester of that year. This resistance only escalated during the winter and spring of 2007, leading eventually to the launching of an indefinite strike called by the POSDEP in February of that year and the cancellation of most winter exams and classes in a number of the larger institutions. Accompanying industrial action on the part of teachers was a series of violent clashes between students and police in Greece's two main cities. The use of tear gas, water cannons and Molotov cocktails as tools in the 'negotiation' over the future direction of higher education policy in Greece should make it very clear that policymaking is not primarily channelled through incorporative and consultative mechanisms in this case. The problem is increased because the struggle appears to be less over ideals, even if POSDEP in particular might have good ideological reasons for defending the current public education system, than over interests. This is particularly the case for students, who clearly benefit from the array of special benefits accorded to them even if this prevents a more efficient and equitable distribution of resources from taking place.

Where the reform package was most successful, according to one of its key architects, was in depoliticizing higher education in order to assist governments facing the challenge of reforming higher education in the future. In particular, party politics had up until this point played a strong role in higher education administration, where only students with political party affiliations were able to vote in university-wide elections. The Committee for Tertiary Education successfully introduced a measure to allow all students to vote, dealing the party system at university level 'a very important blow'.[23] What this illustrates is that while Greece has a particularly weak consultative and incorporative policymaking tradition, even in the field of higher education in which tendencies toward the participation of interest groups in peak-level policymaking is strong in other national cases, reforms were introduced during the 2000s under the umbrella of the ESYP once a group to look at higher education policy was formed. Yet because of the weakness of the consultative–incorporative tradition, 'unincorporated' teacher and student unions were still able to bring the education system to a standstill and limit the overall scope of reform.

Immigration

The formulation of policy to deal with the challenges posed by immigration is a relatively new problem for Greece, although it is one that has been building for some time. Intensifying after 1989, mass illegal migration especially from the former communist states with which the country shares borders, especially but not only Albania, has meant that the issue of combating illegality has dominated the immigration policy agenda. Yet this has not been effectively dealt with. Government responses have ranged from mass deportations of illegal migrants and denials that Greece is now a country in which a significant proportion of the population is foreign born, to several major regularization programmes. These regularization schemes have helped to push immigration more firmly onto the political agenda, but have not necessarily assisted in altering the precarious legal position that most migrants live in. In addition, two other strands of migration policy were largely neglected from 1990 to 2008: better tying immigration into a national economic development plan, and measures to facilitate the social integration of migrants. Throughout, what has been clearly absent is the participation of migrant and human rights' groups in government decision-making, with policy being driven instead by inter- and intra-political party rivalries.

The policy problem

During the 1990s and 2000s, Greece found itself grappling with its new identity as a destination of choice for economic migrants, especially those arriving from north and east of the country's borders. Over the course of the past quarter century, a pattern of mass outward migration has been replaced with one of large-scale inward migration. While Greece shares much with Ireland and Portugal in this respect, it differs from them in several important elements. First, the scale of immigration is immense and has proved almost overwhelming at times; second, the majority of migrants to Greece come from just one country, namely Albania; and third, immigration is by and large illegal, with recent attempts to combat the problem of illegality faltering and incomplete.

While large numbers of Greek citizens had chosen to look for better economic opportunities overseas since at least the late nineteenth century, outward migration peaked during the 1960s. Official figures reveal that about 1.24 million people, or 13 per cent of the population, departed Greece more or less permanently between 1955 and 1977 for North America, Australia, and Europe, most especially Germany (Lianos, 1993: 249). Others still, often in this case political refugees fleeing the anti-communist crackdown that followed the civil war, settled in Eastern Europe and North Africa. Yet the widespread phenomenon of return migration also ensured that Greece actually became a country of net immigration as early as 1973. Although most 'migrants' during the 1970s and early 1980s were Greeks returning from abroad, a steady trickle of foreign workers also began to arrive in the country. Concern about labour shortages, despite the fact that so much of the indigenous population had left in search of employment, led to the formal recruitment of around 20,000 foreign workers, many of whom came from Asia and North Africa, with Pakistanis and Egyptians showing particularly strongly in early immigration data (Kiprianos *et al.*, 2003: 151–2). That recruitment was based on a legal framework that had been in place since 1929 and last revised in 1948 governing foreigners residing in Greece, which provided for work permits to be issued but only in the country of a migrant's origin. The restrictive and limited nature of Greek immigration law, however, meant that, in addition to those formally recruited, the vast majority of foreign workers arrived illegally, setting in motion a tradition of irregular migration. Although official data suggests that the number of legal foreign workers residing in Greece was 28,422 in 1990 and 33,912 in 1992, it is estimated that by the year 2000, around one million migrants actually resided in Greece, making up around ten per cent of the population.[24]

That steady trickle of (mostly illegal) migrants that carried through the 1980s became a river after 1989. While the end of communism in Central and Eastern Europe also gradually had an impact in both Ireland and Portugal, the effect of the collapse of the Berlin Wall was greater and more immediate in Greece, in part because it sits in close proximity to several former communist states but also because of the apparently porous nature of the country's borders. The new migratory flow included not only returning political refugees but also groups of ethnic Greeks whose ancestors had settled in the neighbouring Balkans or further afield in the former USSR and who are treated preferentially under Greek law.[25] Yet such cases were in fact a minority and, in any case, being 'ethnically' Greek does not guarantee successful integration into Greek society, given the language barriers and intolerance toward migrants that still exist (Diamanti-Karanou, 2003; Halkos and Salamouris, 2003).

Because of the fact that most of Greece's migrant population arrived through irregular means, the number of foreign workers and residents along with their nation of origin is often difficult to determine. Most studies rely on the data collected during Greece's first two regularization processes that took place in 1998 and 2001, yet this can only be considered a sample since only part of the migrant population became legal under these schemes. While the details and variable success of these legalization programmes will be discussed in the following section, data collected as a result of them is able to give some picture of the character of the migrant population, even if incomplete and likely to be underestimating the total number of migrants. Above all, the data illustrates that around 86 per cent of migrants who arrived illegally during the late 1980s but especially into the 1990s came from former communist countries in Eastern Europe, and this figure does not even count others from Central European countries such as Poland. Most importantly, 65 per cent of migrants overall were from one single country source, Albania, followed by the next highest single contributors, Bulgaria and Romania.[26] This only confirmed what had already been a source of tension in Greek society – the sense that Greece was being 'invaded' by its neighbours and the perception held by many Greeks that Albanians in particular were responsible for the country's escalating crime rate.

The tendency of anti-Albanian prejudices to inflame political debate over immigration made the formulation of policy designed to address the problem of illegality only the more difficult in Greece. This point will be returned to shortly, but for now it is important to note that the image of Albanians as being responsible for ruining Greece through crime and other exercises in social deviance does not entirely match the reality that most migrants, illegal or not and Albanian or not, arrived in Greece to work. Migrants, as in both Ireland but more especially Portugal, are inserted into the labour market largely as unskilled workers, heavily concentrated in the construction and service sectors in urban areas. What appears to be a uniquely Greek feature, however, is the high concentration of migrants in rural regions, performing seasonal work but providing a year-round source of wage labour as well. More migrants live and work in rural areas than do Greek citizens (Kasimis and Papdopoulos, 2005: 101). Given the fact that many workers remain in Greece illegally despite government regularization programmes, there are also a large number of migrants working in the informal economy. However, many *Greeks* also work in the underground economy, with perhaps 30 per cent of Greece's total economic activity generated informally and 20 per cent of workers remaining unregistered and not paying taxes (Fakiolas, 2000: 61). The following section details haphazard attempts to combat illegal migration as they have evolved since 1991, with particular emphasis on the promises and problems associated with Greece's regularization programmes.

The role of consultation and incorporation in the shaping of policy responses

Although both Irish and Portuguese immigration policies are far from perfect, Greece has had even more difficulty adapting to its new role as a labour importer than the other two countries. Not only has it restricted policy innovation largely to regularization schemes that have not solved the problem of widespread illegality, but it also lags behind in terms of migrant integration policy.[27] Some pressures to address integration issues have mounted in the past few years, but these have been outweighed by anti-immigrant stirrings from political leaders. But for now, the question remains as to *why* Greek immigration policy has been so fragmented and has generally failed to achieve its goals. One possible explanation is that the problem is so much worse in Greece, since this is the country that has been affected most significantly by the outpouring of economic refugees from Eastern Europe. Yet that should have urged Greek policymakers into formulating a more comprehensive response, rather than a less comprehensive one.

In some countries, politicians in particular are wary of addressing the issue of immigration because of the contentious politics that often surround this policy area. When politicians invoke the issue, it is quite often to stir up populist sentiment to draw on the xenophobic elements that appear to exist in all societies, with Greece proving no exception. During the course of this book research, the Greek migration policy activists interviewed were reluctant to paint a picture of Greeks as being any more anti-immigrant than anyone else, but it is clear that an anti-Albanian backlash has shaped public opinion on the issue. Asked why negative attitudes toward Albanians were apparently so prevalent, one human rights campaigner gave the opinion that it had to do with the fact that Greek society is still highly clientelistic. The country has 'a lot of rapid social mobility based on personal connections'. New migrants are not part of that structure, yet enjoy success based on hard work and saving money. The backlash is thus a form of jealousy, revealed in a highly publicized controversy over Albanian children being permitted to 'carry the flag' on parade day (a well-entrenched tradition that involves the highest achieving child in the school acting as flag-bearer on Greece's main national holiday, 28 October, which celebrates the country's refusal to enter the Second World War on the side of the Axis powers).[28] Albanians 'cause' this problem because they aim to settle permanently in Greece, whereas new migrants such as 'Asians and Indians' tend to avoid this problem by making their residency in the country temporary, carrying on a tradition of young men working overseas for several years and sending their money home.[29]

Yet if negative attitudes toward migrants, those from the Balkans in particular, provided an explanation in itself for Greek failures in the immigration policy field, Greek politicians would be known for being particularly responsive to public opinion. But they are not. In addition, evidence from the other case studies shows that government activity can have a strong impact on public attitudes toward migrants, especially in Portugal through the work of ACIME in promoting tolerance. Part of the explanation, consistent with the overall premise of this book, lies in the fact that successive governments have made little or no effort to consult interest groups in this case. This analysis is backed up by one participant in efforts by NGOs to influence policy decisions in this field, and is worth quoting at length for the story it tells about immigration policy failures. Despite the important impact that immigration has had in Greece over the past fifteen years, recent efforts to grapple with the issue:

> have not, however, led to the development of a 'large scale' mainstream immigration policy. Instead, the low-scale and inefficient legislative framework has brought about a situation in which immigrants become integrated into the deregulated, informal economy, in an atmosphere with a weak public discourse and lately about immigrants' integration in society, while stakeholders and operators (such as migrants' associations and specialized NGOs) are left out of the dialogue about migration policies and legislation – the public consultation process is almost non-existent.... In Greece, laws are often formulated without input from key stakeholders. The Greek political system revolves around the major political parties.
>
> (Pavlou *et al.*, 2005: 16)

At least one migration policy activist interviewed for this research project argued that some of the responsibility for the inability to create consultative processes lay with the migrant lobby groups themselves, although it could also be argued that the formation and behaviour of these interest groups have actually been shaped from above. This research participant described two types of organization working on behalf of migrant interests in Greece.[30] On the one hand, the 'minority groups' occupy a space that is 'very crowded', since they are divided among themselves and there are many of them. Another interviewee pointed out the problem with respect to the Albanian community, which is, according to the activist, riddled with internal conflict.[31] On the other hand, the representative from the Hellenic League of Human Rights argued, there are non-governmental organizations which are 'typically Greek' in the way that they operate, being highly personalized and dominated by an elite with little mass membership. Each of these groups 'has its own agenda', sometimes guided by the views of a particular academic, and there is 'no co-operation' between the groups.

Yet the relationship between overcoming collective action problems such as this, often through the centralization of interest groups through the creation of an umbrella organization, and consultation with the state is a more complicated one than this analysis suggests. The other case studies show that the construction of state-initiated consultative and incorporative policymaking can play a role in strengthening and even centralizing interest groups. In a sense, the state plays a role in 'activating' interests. Examples discussed in previous chapters include the centralization of the fourth or community and voluntary pillar under the Irish social partnership process; the activation if not centralization of migrant groups through the work of ACIME in Portugal; and the creation of a national student body (FAIRE) to negotiate with both international organizations and the Portuguese state.

The overwhelmingly negative analysis of the state's attitude toward migrant advocacy groups in particular should be moderated by a discussion of very recent attempts to incorporate migrant organizations into policy discussions, albeit in an exceptionally piecemeal manner. In addition, two new institutions created at the government level have been able to provide a check on other state institutions, especially recently in the sphere of what are widely regarded as human rights abuses carried out in the name of combating illegality. While the media is often used for drumming up anti-immigrant sentiment in Greece, it can be useful for other purposes as well. In October 2005, a number of photographs were published in local newspapers of children and young adults mainly of Albanian descent and mostly in their early teens, detained in very basic conditions in what appeared to be adult prisons. The teenagers had generally crossed over the Greek border alone rather than with legal adults. A not so closed secret was that these photographs had been taken and released by a migrant rights' activist working in the Ombudsman's Office.[32] The second institution, established in 2002, is the semi-autonomous Hellenic Migration Policy Institute (IMEPO). Charged with researching the impact of government policy in this field, it has produced some of the first actual breakdowns of statistics collected as the result of the regularization processes for other initiatives. It has also been charged with offering policy advice on integration issues, which is fast becoming a heated topic in Greece, even if this has had little impact on actual policy outcomes as yet.

Furthermore, some attempt to provide a platform for consultation between migrant groups and the government has been made, even if that has occurred at the insistence of the migrant groups themselves rather than from within the state. The formation of the non-government Greek Migrants' Forum constituted the first step in this direction. According to this group, their first main task was to help 'organize' the migrant organizations themselves, who, as already noted, are especially disorganized and decentralized. The aim of the new organization was then to start working the immigration issue, and even issues of migrant integration, more centrally onto the political agenda by convincing individual politicians to take an interest. 'Changing the perceptions of politicians' would involve working through political parties, and most of the work of the Forum has been carried out through working with more liberal factions of PASOK. Members of the Forum regard it as a major achievement to have had PASOK recently alter its party policy to allow children of migrants born in Greece to gain Greek citizenship.[33] This approach further underscores the importance of political parties in Greece, which are so intertwined with the state that they are often indistinguishable from it, not least from the point of view of activists.

Partly as a result of these efforts and partly in order to parallel a series of Migration Dialogue meetings conducted at the EU level, two rounds of consultation had taken place between the government and migrant groups at the time that

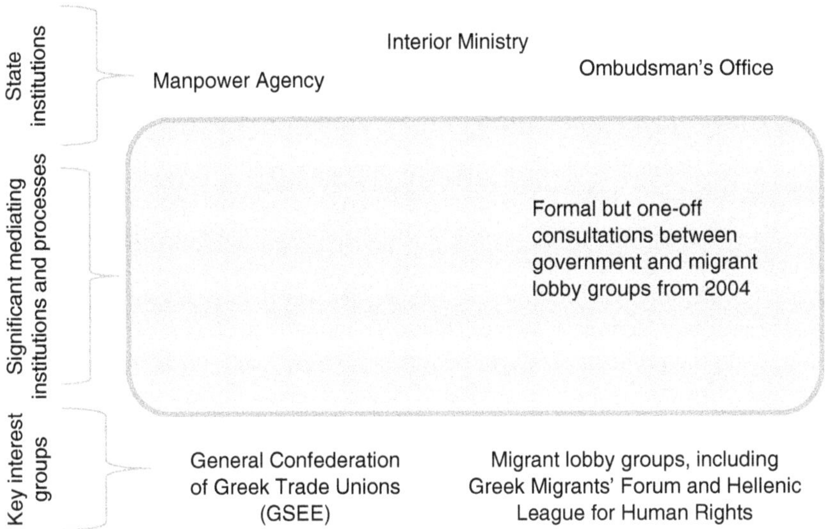

Figure 5.3 The zone of mediation in Greek immigration policy.

this research was carried out. The first consultation process, held in March 2004, almost did not happen due to resistance from the government. It appears that pressure from the labour movement helped change officials' minds, but the government chose to send low-ranking representatives who did not have much influence over policy in any case. A second dialogue was a little more successful in that it included representatives from all the main political parties, but still very few concrete policy proposals from the migrant organizations were taken up. Given the stage that Greek migration policy is still at, most of the discussion that has taken place within the confines of these dialogue processes centres on the ongoing problems associated with successive government regularization programmes. It is thus narrowed to technical problems rather than the negotiation over larger issues associated with overhauling the legal framework governing immigration and migrant integration that is so badly needed.[34]

These 'dialogues' held between the government and migrant organizations fall far short of the development of policymaking processes or institutions that balance functions of consultation and incorporation. Consultation, so far as it exists, is limited to negotiation between interest groups and *political parties* rather than bridging the gap between interest groups and the state. Given the dominant role that political parties play in Greek policymaking, perhaps it is unreasonable to expect anything else, yet there are additional reasons why the immigration dialogues do not constitute consultative and incorporative policymaking. According to the analytical framework outlined in Chapter 2, these dialogues have taken the form of one-off exercises in public consultation. Given that they are so short-term in nature, they do not really form part of a 'process' at all, and, because they are not institutionalized in any real sense, they are unable to provide the feedback loops that make interest group involvement in policymaking actually work in the long term.

The evolution of immigration policy

Greece's first attempt to deal with the new migration reality came in the form of a new Aliens Law in 1991, initiated and enacted by the New Democracy government. Its aim was apparently to control illegal immigration more tightly than it had been in the past but it carried over the provisions from previous legislation stating that the only way to import labour legally was to have potential migrants sign employment contracts in their home country. It made no provisions for dealing with the problem of illegal migrants in Greece and, furthermore, placed a number of restrictions on the access of undocumented migrants to public services, a feature that attracted a lot of attention from human rights campaigners both within and outside the country. In fact, law 1975/1991 emphatically states that Greece 'is not a country of immigration' (Papantoniou-Frangouli and Leventi, 2000: 950) even though by this stage it clearly was. This disjuncture between reality and policy response illustrates that the nation's 'self-perception as a country of emigration has left it unprepared for its new role as a country of migration.' It has thus 'operated the same restrictive policy on immigration for over 60 years, during which time it has been governed by a wide spectrum of political ideology' (Fakiolas, 2000). In short, a severely restrictive policy has survived several changes of both government and regime.

By the mid-1990s, it was at least obvious to some groups that this approach was not working. Chief among these was the GSEE, one of the few organizations that has regular influence in Greek politics so is able to act as a progressive force in this case, in marked contrast to the issue of pension reform discussed above. The task fell to the new PASOK government, which had started work on the idea of a 'one-off' regularization programme by 1995. This came to a head in 1997 when it was decided by government cabinet meeting that the proposed regularization programme would exclude applicants from Albania or any of the other countries sharing borders with Greece, government thinking being that this would only encourage more arrivals from the Balkan area. An uproar from migrant groups and organized labour did eventually cause the government to back down on this provision (Baldwin-Edwards and Fakiolas, 1999).

Law 2434 of 1996 laid the foundations for the first regularization scheme, a two-step process that would be put into effect by two Presidential Decrees in the following year. The first step would involve migrants already in Greece registering for a temporary residence permit, referred to as the 'white card'. A white card was generally granted provided migrants could prove that they had been residing in Greece for some time, had no criminal record, and were clear of infectious diseases. The registration period ran from January to May 1998. White card holders could then apply for 'green cards', given that they had worked legally at least from January that year. The work requirements needed to receive green cards, chiefly the length of time an applicant could prove that he or she had held down a job, varied by sector with more lenient provisions in agriculture for example. Two types of green card could be awarded: type A, valid for one to three years and type B, valid for five years. Committees of local labour authorities and other interested parties would be responsible for determining how long a green card would be granted for and how long it might be renewed for, meaning that a great deal of discretion was introduced into the system (Baldwin-Edwards and Fakiolas, 1999; Papantoniou-Frangouli and Leventi, 2000).

A separate Ministerial Decree set special procedures in place for Albanian citizens of Greek origin to apply for more generous residency permits. The country's tradition of special treatment for migrants who can prove Greek ethnicity is a unique and complicating factor in Greek immigration policy. Although Portuguese policy has a preference for migrants from Portuguese-speaking regions and Ireland has a policy of filling labour requirements from European Union countries, Greece is the only country in this set with an explicitly race-based component to its policy. This is driven less by concerns about migrant integration as it is in Portugal, since Pontian Greeks speak Russian or other languages and Albanian Greeks speak Albanian, than about maintaining racial purity. This harks back to the 'Megali' or 'Great Idea', popular in the early twentieth century and partially responsible for leading Greece into armed conflict with its neighbours, based on the concept of uniting all Greeks under a renewed Byzantium Empire. In concrete policy terms, a 1990 piece of legislation permitted ethnic Greeks to stay in Greece without any documentation, making this population indistinguishable from the illegal migrant one and confusing attempts to estimate how large it actually is. A 1993 policy laid down a process for members of this group to apply for citizenship, and, later in 2000, a system of special residency permits known as *'homogenei'* cards for ethnic Greek migrants was established (Baldwin-Edwards, 2004: 3–4).

According to official data, 373,000 applications were received for white cards under the 1998 regularization programme and out of 228,221 who then applied for the green card, 219,024 applications were approved. This means that a large number of white card holders did not apply for green cards, thus falling back into a status of illegality, and then a further possibly large number of short-term green card holders let their permits expire and did not renew them (Fakiolas, 2003a). Why? For a start, the regularization process was accompanied by a crackdown on illegal migrants and mass deportation, creating a climate of fear not exactly conducive to encouraging good relations between migrants and the authorities. Above all, however, the programme was hampered from the beginning by bureaucratic inefficiencies including understaffing which created long lines and delays in processing applications, so much so that deadlines were eventually extended by several months. Migrants also often had difficultly producing the required documentation and even in some cases understanding the process. In addition, the issue of affordability provided another barrier given that the fees in some cases were quite high and nationals from many countries were required to have documents officially translated into Greek.

In addition to those who did not apply during the 1998 regularization programme and those who lost their legal status shortly afterwards given the short-term nature of many of the permits given, the crackdown on illegality did not seem to work, and new migrants continued to arrive. This fact led to the passage of an updated immigration law in 2001 to replace the comprehensive Aliens Law enacted a decade earlier. Some of the most important provisions of the new law included the announcement of a second major regularization process; further measures to prevent illegal migrants from settling and an effort to strengthen border controls; a slight loosening of the provisions for family reunification; and a shift in responsibility for implementing immigration law from the Ministry of Labour to the Ministry for the Interior.[35] Initially, the legalization was due to happen over a short two-month period, but, due to a process that appears to have been even more marred by inefficiencies and delays than the 1998 effort, deadlines were again extended.

The 2001 regularization process granted successful applicants an initial six-month permit that would then have to be renewed for one year. This time, however, it was the requirements needed to gain that initial permit that attracted the most attention and caused the most problems, the main one being that migrants needed to show evidence that they had been in the country for at least a year prior to submitting their application. This could include an entry stamp on a passport or proof that an immigrant child had been enrolled in a Greek school for a year, or, most problematically, one year's worth of social insurance stamps as proof of payment into the state pension scheme. This last provision was muddied by the fact that, because many illegal migrants obviously do not pay social insurance, they were permitted to buy the required amount directly from the government during the legalization period. Since this could then be used as proof of residence, there is good evidence to suggest that it led to a new flood of migrants from neighbouring countries during the months that the regularization programme was in effect, only for the purposes of gaining legality (Fakiolas, 2003b: 129; Skordas, 2002: 43).

The fact that stamps could be bought, added to already very high application fees, meant that becoming legal was too expensive for some migrants. The slow pace at which applications were processed also acted as a deterrent to many. To date, no official data from the 2001 regularization scheme has been released, but unofficial statistics suggest that 220,000 permits were granted out of 368,000 applications (Baldwin-Edwards, 2004: 1–2). Because that again meant that many migrants had fallen through the cracks in the system, a third process was carried

Table 5.3 Major developments in Greek immigration policy

Year	*Policy development*
1991	New Aliens Law stating that Greece is not a country of immigration
1998	First regularization scheme
2001	Second major regularization scheme

out over 2004 in addition to the ongoing efforts to renew residency permits. Law 324 of 2004 gave a deadline of June 2004 for undocumented migrants and those with expired permits to apply, but little research on the success of this programme has yet to emerge. Implementation of processes designed for the renewal of residence and working permits continue to suffer. In addition, in 2005, a new immigration law was still in the process of being drafted. Again, this law was expected to include another regularization process with a restrictive labour market-driven recruitment scheme (Pavlou *et al.*, 2005: 5).

Greek policy responses to the new immigration challenge have generally revolved around efforts to regularize a portion of the large illegal migrant population that has grown since the mid 1980s. Most of the criticism of Greek immigration policy has thus centred on the failures of these efforts, as much in terms of their implementation as their design. Migrant advocacy groups argue that they would have helped the government avoid many of the bureaucratic inefficiencies associated with the legalization schemes, and they are probably correct in this. Alongside the bureaucratic problems associated with ongoing legalization processes, there is also plenty of evidence that corruption, especially in the police force, has further undermined policy implementation. However, it can also be pointed out that having a system designed almost entirely around ad-hoc and 'one off' legalization programmes is problematic in itself. In theory, Greece has a system of recruiting migrant workers from overseas in order to suit the fluctuating needs of the labour market. Yet this system, administered by the Greek Manpower Agency, is wholly ineffective. Based on annual breakdowns of sector-by-sector labour shortages, the number of migrants recruited through this system has remained at around 20,000 since it began in the early 1970s, and does not reflect either the number or character of the migrants who actually arrive by other means. In reality, there is no planning ahead in order to match migration policy to economic requirements, and, unlike in many other EU countries, the major piece of immigration law passed in 2001 makes no effort to recruit highly skilled workers, especially the technically skilled labour that is lacking in some sectors of the Greek economy.[36]

Overall, then, Greek immigration policy between 1990 and 2008 was mainly limited to, on the face of it, attempts to combat the steady flow of illegal migration into the country, first by tightening border controls and resorting to mass deportation, and second by reluctantly seeking to regularize the large number of economic migrants already in the country. Problems of migrant integration have so far failed to be reflected in concrete policy decisions and, overall, immigration legislation is not tied into a clear comprehensive assessment of the country's economic needs. Yet, at the same time, 'non-decisions' in the immigration policy sphere may also reflect a deliberate policy on the part of the state. As pointed out by both government and non-government actors during the course of the field research conducted for this book, having a large pool of illegal low-wage workers suits the interests of many, to the point where the favouring of illegal over legal, more expensive labour may be seen as a state policy objective.[37] In addition, due to the highly racialized and politicized nature of immigration policy in Greece, something which has only intensified since the economic collapse of 2008, any serious attempt at deep-seated reform is hampered. Because of a lack of the 'buffer' that a denser zone of mediation would provide, state actors again feel reluctant to tackle key issues head-on. That is also assuming that state actors actually *want* to overhaul immigration policy, an assumption that may not always in fact be warranted in this case.

Conclusions

This chapter has argued that patterns of interest group consultation and incorporation in Greece differ from those typically found in the mature Western European democracies, and that this has profound consequences for policy outcomes. In general, consultation is limited, but this does not mean that, in some cases, specific interest groups do not have significant leverage over public policy development. Several instances have been discussed in which necessary policy shifts, when governments actually recognized the need for them, became constrained by specific interest groups. The pattern varies across different policy areas according to the interests involved, but the relationship between the public sector dominated union movement and especially PASOK governments is particularly striking. Union resistance to policy innovation has occurred not only in the example of pension reform but also in the higher education field. Similarly, but in a different policy area, the development of policies for the reconciliation of working and family life has been constrained by the activism of 'large family' associations. In the case of immigration policy, the state has often seemed helpless in the face of widespread anti-immigrant sentiment and has been unwilling or unable to take the lead in overcoming such resistance to creating alternative channels for regular migration.

The weight of such organizations is difficult to understand unless we take a broader view of how interest group politics plays out in Greece. In mature democracies, the state avoids becoming a 'colossus with feet of clay' by constructing relationships that cannot be accused of being reduced to party politics and which are also so much more varied and broader based that the state cannot be judged to have been captured by certain interests.[38] It also provides a strategy for governments when they face particular pockets of resistance to certain new policy directions: they are able to build up alternative bases of support through the cultivation of relationships with other interest groups. Sometimes this entails real policy compromise, but this can only be achieved if there are established channels for doing so. This book thus emphasizes the importance of particular kinds of consultative and incorporative policymaking that centres mainly on the independent relationship built between interest groups and the state, regardless of which party is in power. But can political parties themselves provide alternative forms of consultative and incorporative policymaking, especially in a case such as Greece's where political party loyalties dominate so many aspects of political and social life? The problem in this specific case is found in the organization of Greek political parties. Greek parties can be highly mobilizational, PASOK in particular, but they are paradoxically elitist and not particularly democratically organized. In fact, this is not all that paradoxical if Greek political parties are likened less to Western European ones, which tend to have branches and other bottom-up elements built into their organization, and more to populist parties found elsewhere in the world. Political parties are used primarily as vehicles for mobilizing mass support rather than for aggregating societal interests as they are expected to do in mature democracies. The explanation for why party politics has developed in this way in Greece since 1974 might be found somewhere in Greek political culture, but, much more importantly for this analysis, can be considered as something of an authoritarian legacy. The particular democratization path taken in this case was so top-down in nature that the same set of pre-authoritarian political elites, and their associated behaviours, survived to shape post-authoritarian outcomes.

Notes

1 An interesting historical commentary on the challenges Venizelos faced, emphasizing foreign relations especially, is provided by Miller (1928/1929). A recent modern debate on the era is provided by Kitromilides (2006).

2 The unusual economic policies, at least for a military regime during the 'bureaucratic authoritarian' era, are emphasized by Bermeo (1995). Fishman (1990), in an important comparison of the three Southern European transitions of the 1970s, also finds Greece an in-between and less easy to classify case, although he eventually categorizes the Greek transition as emanating from the state but stresses how closely regime and state were intertwined in this case, given the direct role that the military played in governing at this time. My argument differs in that it considers the most important feature of the Greek colonels' regime to be that it was short-lived and actually *failed* to penetrate the state in such a way that it fundamentally changed the way it operated, allowing pre-junta political institutions and behaviours to be resurrected.

3 The original analysis of the problems experienced by the military regime in gaining any support at all is provided by Diamandouros (1986): 138–64. See also Woodhouse (1985).

4 The rapid nature of the transition is emphasized by Linz and Stepan (1996), 130–1.

5 Thanos Veremis, Interview with Author, Athens, 3 May 2010.

6 Sotiropoulos (1993) borrows the analogy from Nicos Mouzelis.

7 Eurostat 2003 from Labour Force Survey Data, Employment Rate by Sex, available at http://epp.eurostat.ec.europa.eu/portal/page/portal/statistics/search_database.

8 Interview with Maria Stratigaki, General Secretary for Gender Equality, Athens, 12 May 2010.

9 The term, applied to the Greek case, belongs to Matsaganis (September 2005). The relationship between the state and economic interest groups has also been described as 'disjointed corporatism', in which a pre-1974 state corporatist tradition has not yet been replaced by the kind of policy concertation that occurs elsewhere in Europe. See Lavdas (1997).

10 Interview with Manos Matsagnis, former government policy advisor 1997–2001, Athens, 11 November 2005. See also Sarikaki (2001), who makes essentially the same point.

11 The traditionally fragmented nature of women's lobby groups is detailed in Stamiris (1986).

12 Although the actual birth rate is 1.3 children per female, data shows that many Greek men and women remain single and do not have children at all, while most that do have children have on average about 2 per family. See Papadopoulos (1998), 47.

13 The best summary of this complicated array of benefits is provided in Matsaganis (2005b), 54–5, and the discussion in this paragraph is based on this.
14 The conservative–religious orientation of this organization pointed out above is not immediately obvious from the secondary literature but became a source of conflict during the late 1990s between these forces and the welfare modernizers. I owe much of the untold part of this story to Manos Matsaganis, who worked as a non-PASOK affiliated advisor to the Simitis government during the late 1990s. Interview with Author, Athens, 11 November 2005.
15 Maria Stratigaki, Interview with Author, Athens, 12 May 2010.
16 3 per cent of children aged under three were in formal care in 1993. Papadopoulos (1998), 50.
17 The uniqueness of the Greek language debate has been summed up rather succinctly by Grimm (1990: 85) 'Other countries, obviously, have bilingual problems, but Greece would appear to be the only nation which has created an artificial language and then forced it on itself'.
18 On students' (negative) attitudes to work while they are still studying see Dimtrio and Karaliopoulou (2005).
19 Grimm (1990: 73) describes the free education commitment as a 'welfare payout' to the upper classes. See also Giamouridis and Bagley (2006).
20 On the earlier period of second level but post-secondary school development of technical and vocational training see Paleocrassas (1987).
21 For further discussion on the reforms see Grant, (1986); Karmas *et al.*, (1988); OECD (1997), 58–9; Saitis (1988).
22 This is the general line of argument pursued in the OECD's national review of education for Greece conducted in 1997.
23 Interview with Thanos Veremis, President of the National Council for Education 2004–2010, Athens, 3 May 2010.
24 Kiprianos *et al.*, (2003), 151–2. Fakiolas (2000), 59, gives a similar number in relation to the labour force, putting the migrant percentage of that between 9 and 11 per cent of the labour force and over 25 per cent of wage and salary earners. The most complete report, based on incomplete sources, estimates the foreign population in 2004 at around 900,000 excluding EU nationals and ethnic Greeks who are treated differently under the law, and up to 1.15 million including this group. See Baldwin-Edwards (2004), 4.
25 For estimates of numbers of 'returning' ethnic Greeks see Cavounidis (2002), 47 and Kiprianos *et al.*, (2003), 150–1.
26 Cavounidis (2002), 51–2. The most complete analysis of the data collected from the regularization process is found in Baldwin-Edwards (2004).
27 On the impact of the 1998 and 2001 legalization schemes on migrant integration see Glytos (2005).
28 The incident is well-known in Greece. See Tzanelli (2006). On anti-immigrant tensions in rural Greece see Lawrence (2005).
29 Interview with Yannis Ktistakis, Hellenic League for Human Rights, Athens, 4 November 2005.
30 Interview with Yannis Ktistakis, Hellenic League for Human Rights, Athens, 4 November 2005.
31 Interview with Moáwia Achmed, Greek Migrants' Forum, Athens, 14 November 2005.
32 The individual in question revealed this to me himself.
33 Interview with Moáwia Achmed, Greek Migrants' Forum, Athens, 14 November 2005.
34 This discussion is largely based on an interview with a Senior Researcher for the Greek Ombudsman with expertise in immigration policy, Miltos Pavlou, Athens, 9 November 2005.

35 Details of the new law, especially provisions other that the regularization scheme which have received the most attention elsewhere, are comprehensively discussed in Skordas (2002).
36 Skordas, 'The New Migration Law' (2002): 46.
37 Anonymous Researcher with the Labour Institute of the GSEE, interview with author, 27 April 2010. Andreas Takis, General Secretary for Immigration Policy, Interior Ministry, interview with author, 28 April 2010. That the seeming contradiction between the stated aim of reducing illegal migration and actual tolerance can be explained by the 'needs' of Greeks employers is also highlighted by Triandafyllidou and Ambrosini (2011).
38 This is not the place to launch into a debate about whether or not all modern capitalist states are naturally beholden to business interests. Even if they are, the point here would be that some states are better at masking this than others. (Especially the 'consensual' democracies of Western Europe, to borrow Arend Lijphart's (1999) term.) On 'masking' see Althusser (1971); Offe (1984); Poulantzas (1978); Therborn (1980). On the structural dependence of the state on capital see Przeworski and Wallerstein (1988). For a non-Marxist interpretation of the problem see Lindblom (1982): 324–36.

References

Althusser, Louis, "Ideology and Ideological State Apparatuses", in *Lenin and Philosophy and other essays* (London: New Left Books, 1971), 121–73.

Bagavos, Christos, "Families in Greece: Policies, Challenges and Opportunities", General Monitoring Report 2004: Greece (European Commission, 2004).

Baldwin-Edwards, Martin, *Statistical Data on Immigrants in Greece: An Analytic Study of Available Data and Recommendations for Conformity with European Union Standards* (Athens: Mediterranean Migration Observatory, Panteion University for the Migration Policy Institute, 2004).

Baldwin-Edwards, Martin and Rossetos Fakiolas, "Greece: The Contours of a Fragmented Policy Response", *South European Society and Politics* 3, 3 (1999), 186–204.

Bermeo, Nancy, "Classification and Consolidation: Some Lessons from the Greek Dictatorship", *Political Science Quarterly* 11, 3 (1995), 435–52.

Burtless, Gary, "The Greek Labor Market", in Ralph C. Bryant, Nicholas C. Garganas, and George S. Tavias, eds, *Greece's Economic Performance and Prospects* (Athens and Washington DC: Bank of Greece/The Brookings Institution, 2001), 453–98.

Carlos, Monica P. and Laura Maratou-Alipranti, "Family Policy and New Family Forms: The Cases of Greece and Portugal", in Astrid Pfenning and Thomas Bahle, eds, *Family and Family Policies in Europe: Comparative Perspectives* (Frankfurt: Peter Lang, 2000), 49–69.

Cavounidis, Jennifer, "Migration in Southern Europe and the Case of Greece", *International Migration* 40, 1 (2002), 45–70.

Charalambis, Dimitris, Laura Maratou-Alipranti, and Andromachi Hadjiyanni, eds, *Recent Social Trends in Greece 1960–2000*. (Montreal and Kingston: McGill-Queen's University Press, 2004).

Close, David H., "The Changing Structure of the Right, 1945–50", in John O. Iatrides and Linda Wrigley, *Greece at the Crossroads: The Civil War and Its Legacy* (University Park, PA: Pennsylvania State University Press, 1995), 122–55.

Diamandouros, P. Nikiforos, "Regime Change and the Prospects for Democracy in Greece: 1974–1983", in Guillermo O'Donnell, Philippe Schmitter, and Laurence

Whitehead, eds, *Transitions from Authoritarian Rule* (Baltimore and London: Johns Hopkins University Press, 1986), 138–64.

Diamandouros, P. Nikiforos, "The Political System in Postauthoritarian Greece (1974–1996): Outline and Interpretations", in Piero Ignazi and Colette Ysmal, eds, *The Organization of Political Parties in Southern Europe* (Westport, CT: Praeger, 1998), 181–201.

Diamanti-Karanou, Panagoula, "Migration of Ethnic Greeks from the Former Soviet Union to Greece, 1990–2000: Policy Decisions and Implications", *Southeast European and Black Sea Studies* 3, 1 (2003), 25–45.

Ditch, John, Helen Barnes, and Jonathan Bradshaw, eds, *Developments in National Family Policies in 1996* (Luxembourg: European Observatory on National Family Policies, European Commission, 1998).

Dumon, Wilfried, ed., *National Family Policies in EC Countries in 1990* (Luxembourg: European Observatory on National Family Policies, European Communities, 1991).

Dumon, W. and T. Nuelant, *European Observatory on National Family Policies: Trends and Developments in 1992 Technical Annex* (Leuven: European Observatory on Family Policies, 1994).

Eurydice, *Two Decades of Reform in Higher Education in Europe: 1980 Onwards. Greece National Description* (Brussels: European Eurydice Unit, 2000).

Eurydice, "Country Report on Greece". Available at www.eurydice.org. Accessed October 2005.

European Union Industrial Relations Observatory Online, "The EU Parental Leave Agreement and Directive: Implications for National Law and Practice. Country Report: Greece" (1998). Available at www.eurofound.europa.eu/eiro/1998/01/study. Accessed March 2007.

Fakiolas, Rossetos, "Higher Education Financing in Greece", in Lyman A. Glenny, *Funding Higher Education: A Six-Nation Analysis* (New York: Praeger, 1979), 52–73.

Fakiolas, Rossetos, "Migration and Unregistered Labour in the Greek Economy", in Russell King, Gabriella Lazaridis, and Charalambos Tsardanidis, eds, *Eldorado or Fortress? Migration in Southern Europe* (Basingstoke, UK: Macmillan, 2000), 57–79.

Fakiolas, Rossetos, "Regularising Undocumented Immigrants in Greece: Procedures and Effects", *Journal of Ethnic and Migration Studies* 29, 3 (2003a), 535–61.

Fakiolas, Rossetos, "The Second Legalization of Illegal Migrants in Greece", *International Migration Review* 37, 4 (2003b), 1292–303.

Featherstone, Kevin, "The Politics of Pension Reform in Greece: Modernization Defeated by Gridlock", Paper presented to Conference of the Modern Greek Studies Association (Toronto, 16–18 October 2003).

Fishman, Robert M., "Rethinking State and Regime: Southern Europe's Transition to Democracy", *World Politics* 42, 3 (1990), 422–40.

Gavroglu, Kostas, "Certain Features of Higher Education in Greece and the Failure of the Attempts to Reform It", *Journal of the Hellenic Diaspora* 8, 1–2 (1981), 95–108.

Georges, Eugenia, "Abortion Policy and Practice in Greece", *Social Science and Medicine* 42, 4 (1996), 509–19.

Giamouridis, Anastasios and Carl Bagley, "Policy, Politics, and Social Inequality in the Education System of Greece", *Modern Greek Studies* 24 (2006): 1–21.

Giannarou, Lina, and Elena Karanatsi, "Strikes Stall College Studies for Foreigners", *Kathimerini* (26 February 2007).

Glytos, Nicholas P., "Stepping from Illegality to Legality and Advancing towards Integration: The Case of Migrants in Greece", *International Migration Review* 39, 4 (2005), 819–40.

Grant, Glen H., "University Reform in Greece: 1982 and After", *Journal of Modern Greek Studies* 4, 1 (1986), 17–31.

Greek Ombudsman, *The Greek Ombudsman's First Year as a Specialised Body for the Promotion of the Principle of Equal Treatment* [English version] (Athens: National Printing Office, August 2006).

Grimm, R. Eletherios, "Egalitarianism and Productivity: Rhetoric and Reality in Greek Educational Reform Since the Fall of the Military Junta in 1974", *Modern Greek Studies,* 6 (1990), 81–95.

Halkos, George and Dimitrios Salamouris, "Socio-economic Integration of Ethnic Greeks from the USSR: Obstacles to Entry into the Greek Labour Market", *Journal of Ethnic and Migration Studies* 29, 23 (2003), 519–34.

Hantrais, Linda, and Marie-Thérèse Letablier, *Families and Family Policies in Europe* (London and New York: Longman, 1996), 45–50.

Kalamatianou, A. G., C. A. Karmas, and T. P. Lianos, "Technical Higher Education in Greece", *European Journal of Education* 23, 3 (1988), 271–9.

Karmas, C. A., T. P. Lianos, and A. G. Kalamatianou, "Greek Universities: An Overview", *European Journal of Education* 23, 3 (1988), 261–9.

Kasimis, Charalambos and Apostolps G. Papadopoulos, "The Multifunctional Role of Migrants in the Greek Countryside: Implications for the Rural Economy and Society", *Journal of Ethnic and Migration Studies* 31, 1 (2005), 99–125.

Katrougalos, George S., "The South European Welfare Model: The Greek Welfare State, In Search of an Identity", *Journal of European Social Policy,* 6, 1 1996, 39–60.

Kiprianos, Pandelis, Stathis Balias, and Vaggelis Passas, "Greek Policy Toward Immigration and Immigration", *Social Policy and Administration* 37, 2 (2003), 148–64.

Kitromilides, Paschalis M., ed., *Eleftherios Venizelos: The Trials of Statesmanship* (Edinburgh: University of Edinburgh Press, 2006).

Kyriazis, Nota, "Women's Flexible Work and Family Responsibilities in Greece", *South European Society and Politics* 4, 2 (1999), 35–53.

Lavdas, Kostas, *The Europeanization of Greece: Interest Politics and the Crises of Integration* (Basingstoke, UK: Macmillan, 1997).

Lawrence, Christopher, "Re-Bordering the Nation: Neoliberalism and Racism in Rural Greece", *Dialectical Anthropology* 29, 4 (2005), 315–34.

Legg, Keith R. and John M. Roberts, *Modern Greece: A Civilization on the Periphery* (Boulder, CO: Waterview Press, 1997).

Liagouras, George, Aimilia Protogerou, and Yannis Caloghirou, "Exploring Mismatches Between Higher Education and the Labour Market in Greece", *European Journal of Education* 38, 4 (2003), 413–26.

Lianos, Theodore P., "Greece: Waning of Labor Migration", in Daniel Kubat, ed., *The Politics of Migration Policies: Settlement and Integration The First World into the 1990s* (New York: Center for Migration Studies, 1993, 249–61.

Lianos, Theodore P., D. Asteriou, and G. M. Agiomirgianakis, "Foreign University Graduates in the Greek Labour Market: Employment, Salaries and Overeducation", *Foreign Journal of Finance and Economics* 9 (2004), 151–64.

Lijphart, Arend, *Patterns of Democracy: Government Forms and Performance in Thirty-Six Countries* (New Haven, CT and London: Yale University Press, 1999.)

Lindblom, Charles, "The Market as Prison", *Journal of Politics* 44, 2 (1982), 324–36.

Linz, Juan J. and Alfred Stepan, *Problems of Democratic Transition and Consolidation: Southern Europe, South America, and Post-Communist Europe* (Baltimore and London: Johns Hopkins University Press, 1996).

Loukia, M., "Family Policy in Greece: Traditional and Modern Patterns", in W. Dumon, ed., *Changing Family Policies in the Member States of the European Union* (Luxembourg: European Observatory on National Family Policies, 1994), 87–104.

Matsaganis, Manos, "The Limits of Selectivity as a Recipe for Welfare Reform: The Case of Greece", *Journal of Social Policy* 34, 2 (2005a), 235–53.

Matsaganis, Manos, "Greece – Fighting Poverty with Hands tied behind the Back: Anti-poverty Policy without a Minimum Income", in Maurizio Ferrera, ed., *Welfare State Reform in Southern Europe: Fighting Poverty and Social Exclusion in Italy, Spain, Portugal and Greece* (London and New York: Routledge, 2005b), 33–83.

Matsaganis, Manos, "Inegalitarian Corporatism? Progressive Modernization and Pension Reform in Greece", Paper presented to the ESPAnet Conference (University of Fribourg, Switzerland, 22–24 September 2005).

Mavrogordatos, George Th., "Civil Society under Populism", in Richard Clogg, ed., *Greece, 1981–89: The Populist Decade* (Basingstoke, UK: Macmillan, 1993), 47–64.

Miller, William, "Greece Since the Return of Venizelos", *Foreign Affairs* 7, (1928/29), 468–76.

OECD, *Education in OECD Developing Countries: Trends and Perspectives* (Paris: Organisation for Economic Co-operation and Development, 1974).

OECD, *Educational Reform Policies in Greece* (Paris: Organisation for Economic Co-operation and Development, 1980).

OECD, *Reviews of National Policies for Education: Greece* (Paris: Organisation for Economic Co-operation and Development, 1982).

OECD, *Review of National Policies for Education: Greece* (Paris: Organisation for Economic Co-operation and Development, 1997).

OECD, *Education at a Glance* (Paris: Organisation for Economic Co-operation and Development, 2006).

Offe, Claus, *Contradictions of the Welfare State* (London: Hutchinson, 1984).

Paleocrassas, Stamatis N., "Technological Education in Greece", *Journal of Engineering Technology*. 4, 1 (1987), 5–11.

Panourgia, E. and K. Nenny, "On the Political and Symbolic Capital of Educational Reforms in Greece", *Modern Greek Studies* 6 (1990), 73–8.

Papadopoulos, Theodoros N., "Greek Family Policy from a Comparative Perspective", in Eileen Drew, Eileen Emerek, and Evelyn Mahon, eds, *Women, Work and the Family in Europe* (London and New York: Routledge, 1998), 47–57.

Papalexandris, Nancy and Robin Kramer, "Flexible Working Patterns: Toward the Reconciliation of Family and Work", *Employee Relations* 19, 6 (1997), 581–95.

Papantoniou-Frangouli, Maria and Kleio Maria Leventi, "The Legalization of Aliens in Greece", *International Migration Review* 34, 3 (2000), 950–3.

Pappas, Takis S., "Nea Demokratia: Party Development and Organizational Logics" in Piero Ignazi and Colette Ysmal, eds, *The Organization of Political Parties in Southern Europe* (Westport, CT: Praeger, 1998), 221–37.

Papstratis, Procopis, "Purging the University after Liberation", in Mark Mazower, ed., *After the War Was Over: Reconstructing the Family, Nation, and State in Greece, 1943-1960* (Princeton, NJ: Princeton University Press, 2000), 62–72.

Pavlou, Miltos, Irini Avramopoulou, and Leonidas Karakatsanis, *Current Debates in Europe: A Publication of the European Migration Dialogue – Greece* (Brussels/Athens: Migration Policy Group, 2005).

Paxson, Heather, *Making Modern Mothers: Ethics and Family Planning in Urban Greece* (Berkeley, CA: California Press, 2004).

Petmedisou, Maria, "Statism, Social Policy and the Middle Class in Greece", *Journal of European Social Policy* 1, 1 (1991), 31–48.

Poulantzas, Nicos, *State, Power, Socialism* (London: New Left Books, 1978).

Przeworski, Adam and Michael Wallerstein, "Structural Dependence of the State on Capital", *American Political Science Review* 82, 1 (1988), 11–29.

Putnam, Robert, *Making Democracy Work: Civic Traditions in Modern Italy* (Princeton, NJ: Princeton University Press, 1993).

Rigos, Platon N., "Greece: The Perils of Incorporation", in Marco Rimandelli ed., *Comparative Democratization and Peaceful Change in Single-Party-Dominant Countries* (New York: St. Martin's Press, 1999), 99–117.

Saitis, Christos A., "The Relationship between the State and the University in Greece", *European Journal of Education* 23, 3 (1988), 249–60.

Sarikaki, Alexandra, "Institutional Reactions Toward Low Fertility in Greece", Paper presented to The Second Demographic Transition in Europe: Euroconference on Family and Fertility Change in Modern European Societies: Explorations and Explanations of Recent Developments (Bad Herrenalb, Germany, 23–28 June 2001).

Seferiades, Seraphim, "Low Union Density Amidst a Conflictive Contentious Repertoire: Flexible Labour Market, Unemployment, and Trade Union Decline in Contemporary Greece", EUI Working Paper SPS N. 99/6 (Florence: European University Institute, Department of Political and Social Sciences) 1999.

Skordas, Achilles, "The New Immigration Law in Greece: Modernization on the Wrong Track", *European Journal of Migration and Law* 4 (2002), 23–48.

Sotiropoulos, Dimitri A., "A Colossus with Feet of Clay: The State in Post-Authoritarian Greece", in Harry J. Psomiados and Stavros B. Thomadakis, *Greece, the New Europe, and the Changing International Order* (New York: Pella, 1993), 43–56.

Sotiropoulos, Dimitri A., *Populism and Bureaucracy: The Case of Greece Under PASOK, 1981–89* (Notre Dame, IN: University of Notre Dame Press, 1996).

Sotiropoulos, Dimitri, "Administering the Summit: the Greek Case", in B. Guy Peters, R. A. W Rhodes, and Vincent Wright, eds, *Administering the Summit: Administration of the Core Executive in Developed Countries* (Basingstoke, UK: Macmillan, 2000), 176–95.

Spanou, Calliope, "Penelope's Suitors: Administrative Modernisation and Party Competition in Greece", *West European Politics* 19, 1 (1996), 97–124.

Stamiris, Eleni, "The Women's Movement in Greece", *New Left Review* 158 (1986), 98–112.

Stavrakakis, Yannis, "Religious Populism and Political Culture: The Greek Case", *South European Society and Politics* 7, 3 (2002), 29–52.

Symeonidou, H., "Family Policy in Greece", in W. Dumon, ed., *Family Policy in EEC Countries.* Report prepared for the Commission of the European Communities, Directorate General for Employment, Social Affairs and Education (Luxembourg: Office for Official Publications of the European Communities, 1990).

Symeonidou, Haris, "Social Protection in Contemporary Greece", in Martin Rhodes, ed., *Southern European Welfare States: Crisis and Reform* (London: Frank Cass, 1997), 66–85.

Therborn, Goran, *What Does the Ruling Class Do When It Rules?* (London: Verso, 1980).

Triandafyllidou, Anna and Maurizio Ambrosini, "Irregular Immigration Control in Italy and Greece: Strong Fencing and Weak Gate-keeping serving the Labour Market", *European Journal of Migration and Law* 13 (2011), 251–73.

Tzanelli, Rodanthi, " 'Not My Flag!' Citizenship and nationhood in the margins of Europe (Greece, October 2000/2003)", *Ethnic and Racial Studies* 29, 1 (2006), 26–49.
Vucinich, Wayne S., "Tragedy of Modern Greece", *Current History* 17, 8 (1949), 266–72.
Woodhouse, C. M., *The Rise and Fall of the Greek Colonels* (New York: Franklin Watts, 1985).

6 Portugal

This chapter argues that the reorientation of Portuguese family, higher education, and immigration policies around an economic development strategy for the twenty-first century occurred very unevenly between 1990 and 2008. Migrant integration policy, for example, was reoriented around the goal of 'social cohesion' more than in either of the other two national cases, yet immigration policy itself lagged behind that in Ireland in the extent to which issues such as how to attract highly skilled workers to the country were addressed. The following analysis shows that, where progress was made, a combination of two main factors was generally in play. First, some of the most creative Portuguese economic and social policies discussed in the pages that follow were initiated or developed by certain 'enlightened' individuals or factions of the national executive, meaning both elected government officials and bureaucrats. This is something that was clearly lacking in Greece. Second, interest group support or at least consent for these policies was then built up through mechanisms that were more incorporative than they were genuinely consultative. Interest groups were brought on board at a later date rather than treated as important sources of expertise at an earlier stage. In addition, these mechanisms tended to be constituted at a much lower level of the policymaking system and were less formal and ongoing than in Ireland. Although this limited the ability of interest groups to shape final concrete policy decisions, it did provide a channel for the manufacturing of consent, something which again was usually sorely lacking in Greece.

In addition, there are many areas in which the informal or loose nature of policy consultation in Portugal allows some groups far more opportunity to access policymaking than others. In general, academics, the legal community, and some other similarly elite groups are privileged over non-elite groups, though the scale of their influence depends on the precise issue area in question. This means that, when consultation occurs at the peak level, it is particularly 'segmented' across different policy areas. This is clearly so for higher education policy, where the Council of Rectors that governs public universities enjoys influence over policymaking equal to no other interest group. The only danger in this combination of elite-driven policy formulation, combined with the uneven development of low-level consultative and incorporative mechanisms and segmented high-level consultation with a smaller range of interests, is that it opens up the possibility that, even where policy developments appear in line with national requirements, they can still be out of touch with reality. As discussed in Chapter 3, consultation with interest groups matters not only because incorporation helps governments implement new policy frameworks but also because these groups can help governments better understand the policy problem in question. There are several instances discussed in this chapter where more consultation at an earlier stage of the policy process may have helped better match reality to policy response. These include the problematic privatization approach taken in the field of higher education from the mid-1980s, as well as how to make the new parental leave scheme deliver its desired results in the field of policies for work–life balance after 1996.

State–society relations and the policy-making tradition

Portugal is arguably the oldest nation-state in Europe, referring to the fact that, apart from a century of Spanish domination spanning the sixteenth and seventeenth centuries, its borders have not changed and the geographical area constituting the Western-most country in Europe has been governed from the area around modern Lisbon since the eleventh century. Until the recent arrival of migrants from former Portuguese colonies, this history ensured a relatively homogeneous population with regional flavours but not the divisions and emergence of distinct sub-national languages and identities that characterize its much larger neighbour. The Portuguese state has traditionally been very centralized, despite its colonial reach into Latin America, Asia, and Africa until the early 1970s. Traditionally fearful and suspicious of the Spanish and their influence, Portugal has rejected Spanish ways of doing things in favour of French language, culture, and, importantly for this analysis, legal traditions. The Portuguese admiration of the French legal and political system has assisted in the construction of a strong statist tradition that survived even late twentieth century democratization.

For much of its history, Portugal was ruled by a monarchy that benefited from Portuguese expansion from the sixteenth to the nineteenth centuries. This was finally ended by a liberal revolution and the creation of the First Portuguese Republic in 1910. The move towards liberal although still oligarchical democracy was, however, short-lived, when, after a fifteen-year period of political and economic instability, a military coup was staged in 1926.[1] While the outcome of this military intervention took a few years to take shape, it ushered in the rule of one of the longest lasting conservative dictatorships of the twentieth century. The transition to authoritarian rule was guided by António Oliveira de Salazar, first as finance minister in the new administration, and then as prime minister from 1932. A year later, a new constitution was enacted, defining Portugal as a corporative, single-party, and 'multi-continental' country, laying the basis for the *Estado Novo* (New State). There is much debate in the historical literature over whether or not the corporative and authoritarian tendencies of the *Estado Novo* constituted a fascist regime (Costa Pinto, 1995). Whether or not it was genuinely fascist is not particularly relevant here, but the emphasis placed on the top-down incorporation of social groups through a political party but also directly with the state through the labour relations system certainly is. The classic study of Portuguese corporatism (Schmitter, 1975) described the country as an 'ideal type' corporatist state, coming much closer to a pure corporatist system than is found anywhere else. Yet he also notes that this system only functioned as intended for a relatively short period of time and that, as new social groups and interests emerged that could not be controlled by corporatist mechanisms, these gave way to straight-out repression over time (Schmitter, 1975).

The tight control over society exercised by the Salazar regime during the 1930s and 1940s began to loosen in the 1950s, with increasingly contentious relations with the overseas colonies being a major precipitating event. Indigenous movements for independence emerged in Africa, especially Angola and Guinea-Bissau, eventually leading to the 1961 outbreak of war in Africa. India quickly moved to take back any of its territories still in Portuguese hands, while Portugal exported its men to fight to keep land in Africa. As the colonial wars dragged on, political tensions within the country began to build. The state responded by reforming and rearranging public administration in the late 1960s. Salazar resigned due to ill health in 1968 and was replaced by the reformist Marcello das Neves Alves Caetano, whose limited liberalization measures did not manage to ease social and political tensions. The *Estado Novo* was swept away by a (mostly) bloodless military coup on 25 April 1974, led by junior officers fed up with a long drawn-out and unpopular overseas war. This breakdown of authoritarian rule and the period of very slow and uncertain democratization that followed is referred to as a revolution, not only by the Portuguese themselves but also often in the academic literature. A couple of key features of the regime change justify this label, particularly the fact that it was accompanied, at least in the beginning, by mass social mobilization.[2] In addition, it had in its initial stages a strong Marxist–Leninist influence, imported by soldiers who had served abroad in the colonial wars and who absorbed both socialism and sympathy for Third World liberation struggles there. The economic and political changes, at least those intended by the immediate new regime, were also very radical: industries were nationalized, the colonies were given their freedom, and entire branches of the government were dismantled at the same time that others were expanded. The 1976 Constitution outlined a plan for the 'transition to socialism'.

Yet it is also extremely important to note that the transition from authoritarian rule had a number of 'top-down' elements that decisively shaped the path of democratization and democratic consolidation, in addition to any 'bottom up' revolutionary ones. In the initial stages of regime change, since it was not entirely certain that this would result in democracy at all, the importance of the military's role, and internal struggles within it, cannot be overestimated (Graham, 1993). This has special implications for political developments during the late 1970s and late 1980s, when social movements and popular uprisings gave way to a Portuguese desire for stability first and political democracy and European integration next. Socialism, so often associated with the Revolution of the Carnations as the events of 1974–76 became known, may never have even been favoured by the majority of Portuguese at all. By 1984, forces in favour of not only democracy but also capitalist development connected to European integration had won, marginalizing more radical elements.

Between 1974 and 1984, the Portuguese economy remained in turmoil and politics consisted of a quick turnover of provisional and then elected governments which tended to collapse very quickly. To sum up a long and complicated story, the radical left, itself split between hard-core Marxist–Leninists and socialists, was eventually sidelined in favour of social democratic forces. For instance, five different constitutional governments reigned between 1976 and 1979, reflecting a power struggle between the left and the 'right', although truly centre-right and conservative forces did not make much of an impact on Portuguese politics until a little later.[3] The major turning point occurred in 1982 when the 'Council of the Revolution' was abolished, meaning that civilian control over the military was finally achieved, and this was then reinforced by the 1984 Constitution which, among many other things, created constitutional courts. The 1983 election was won by the comparatively centre-right 'Centre Bloc', which comprised the Socialist Party (PS) and the Social Democratic Party (PSD), which later separately formed the two major national political parties. This coalition implemented a series of economic reforms aimed at stabilization and continued a programme of liberalization that had begun under the Sixth Constitutional Government elected in 1979. A key figure here is Prime Minister Aníbal Cavaco Silva, who instituted a series of wage pacts during the 1980s which formed the core of a weak neo-corporatist system.[4] The authoritarian corporatist system that framed relations between labour, business, and the state under Salazar was dismantled along with many other aspects of the pre-revolutionary state apparatuses. Because the period between 1974 and 1984 was characterized by state-led economic development, the tendency towards incorporation in policymaking, however, survived the revolution.

The legacies of the revolutionary aspects of democratization are otherwise reflected in the left-wing slant of Portuguese politics, including the fact that the two main political parties both claim attachment to a socialist tradition, named the Socialist and Social Democratic Parties even though they occupy centre-left and centre-right positions on the political spectrum respectively; that the contemporary constitution commits the Portuguese state to guaranteeing an extensive array of social rights; and that, in terms of actual outcomes, Portugal is the Southern European country which has moved the most towards universal health and welfare coverage, even if that coverage is still minimalist compared to other Western European nations.[5] Yet a backlash *against* the left and the initial attempt to implement a socialist project has been as significant an influence on public policy since the late 1970s as was the revolution itself. The swing between revolutionary and counter-revolutionary tendencies has aptly been referred to as the 'pendulum principle' with respect to the Portuguese case (Balsemão, 1986: 199) and is especially relevant to the privatization approach to higher education discussed below.

Although there is a strong tradition of studying the economic and sociological implications of public policies in Portugal, analyses of the Portuguese policymaking *process* are few and far between. Despite the fact that there are a number of comparative surveys of policymaking institutions and processes in developed, democratic, or European contexts that are quite comprehensive in nature, such works generally fail to include discussions of Portugal, or, for that matter, Greece. Where Southern European cases are discussed at all, Spain is usually offered as the example.[6] Is this because there is a bias against smaller and more peripheral European democracies, or is it because policymaking processes in Southern Europe do not fit easily into categories designed to describe the more open, and thus easier to study, processes and institutions found in the north? Or is it that there is an absence of anything that could even be described as an identifiable policymaking process in Portugal at all? It is quite likely that all three propositions are true. With respect to the last, it is quite clear that concepts such as 'policy networks' or 'triangles', designed to describe policymaking in Western Europe but especially the Anglo-Saxon world, do not really fit the Portuguese, or even more especially, the Greek situation. When 'Southern European' policymaking, or more often public administration, is the focus, it is usually in order to highlight what are regarded as the pathologies of the public administration in this set of countries. Southern European state bureaucracies are described as bloated, damaged by political party patronage, and overly legalistic, if not corrupt. The problem here is not only that this lumps all four of the Southern European cases together and obscures any differences between them but also that, by focusing solely on the continuation of problems *within* the bureaucracy, it does not tell us much about possible relationships between independent interest groups and the state.

Some studies of Portuguese public administration have attempted to take account of recent developments by considering the impact of a number of public sector-related reforms implemented during the 1990s. These attempted to devolve power from the centre to regional levels and to make public services more responsive to the needs of citizens. The reforms can also be seen as an exercise in modernization aimed at moving away from the overly bureaucratic state inherited from the Salazar era (Corte-Real, 2000; Luca and de Magalhaes Ilharco, 2002; Mozzicafreddo, 2003; OECD, 1996). Yet, while considered moderately successful, Portugal remains a highly centralized state, reflecting its Francophile tendencies, and also carries through certain features of the political and public administrative system that cause the 'Southern European' stereotype to ring true. Most important of these legacies is that (a) access to policymaking is still generally confined to an elite; (b) where broader participatory policymaking exists, it occurs at a relatively low level of the system and tends to be more incorporative than consultative; and (c) public administration is still highly legalistic. During the course of the field research undertaken for this book, I was told repeatedly that in Portugal, 'everything begins with the law'. This has implications for the policy and comparative politics researcher, since the way in which policies are researched locally is by reading the legal code governing that particular arena.[7] There are no discussion, Green or White Papers to consult; they simply do not exist or are else not made public. Such legal codes are written by policy elites, often with legal backgrounds, who may have remained insulated in the public service for their entire careers; are enacted by either legislative or executive decree; and are then implemented in a top-down fashion sticking (at least in theory) closely to the law. Moreover, public consultation over the content of legal frameworks is not generally considered to be especially important at the peak policymaking level, even if there is some demand for public consultation and input at the level of local politics.[8]

This follows on from the fact that, while Portugal may have been a hotbed of political protest, social movements, and participatory politics in the immediate post-revolutionary era, this was generally short-lived and limited to certain sectors. By the early 1980s, revolutionary politics was not conducive to the new goals of economic stability, capitalist development, and European integration. The point is not that the revolution did not make any policy impact but rather that this influence is best reflected in certain legislative commitments (such as the strong guarantee of gender equality in the post-revolutionary constitution), rather than overall changes in the way that the state interacts with interest groups and policy stakeholders. One pre-revolutionary legacy is that Portugal in many respects is still a 'dual society', where a highly educated elite enjoys privileged access to policymaking. Those with legal, engineering, economics and increasingly even social science training are especially well poised to influence policymaking, often through informal means. Another legacy is that although a robust *consultative* tradition is lacking in Portugal, it does have a relatively strong *incorporative* tradition that serves to bridge the gap between policy makers and policy stakeholders. Who is included in processes of policy incorporation varies according to the nature of each particular arena, as does the extent to which any genuine consultation occurs and at what level of the political system. Peak-level negotiations between labour, business, and the state are still mainly confined to industrial relations issues. More fragmented and lower level processes of consultation and incorporation are found especially in the family and immigration policy cases discussed below.

One of the key differences between the Portuguese and Greek cases is thus that Portugal has a much deeper history of interest group incorporation on the part of the state, whereas Greece's recent attempts have been confined to patronage administered through political parties. The Portuguese tradition is inherited from the state corporatist Salazar era, where interest groups were not only incorporated but also actually created by the state. In post-revolutionary times, political parties have remained a core vehicle for co-opting the leaders of civil society into parliamentary politics; the fact that Portugal does not have strong 'civil society' organizations or independent lobby groups can be attributed to the fact that political parties siphon off such individuals before they have a chance to create organizations of their own.[9] While party activists may argue that this allows them to influence politics directly, the tendency is not towards the development of an *independent* relationship between key interest groups and the state.

This is not to say that policymaking institutions and processes that have the potential to fill functions of both consultation and incorporation do not exist in this case. Rather, it is that, when they do, they are constituted at such a low level of the policymaking system and are confined to discussing such a narrow range of issues that they often have a very limited influence on actual policy outcomes. The best example here from the case study analyses which follow is the consultative body established by the Alto Comissariado para a Imigração e Minorias Étnicas (ACIME). One of ACIME's functions is to consult with migrant groups over policy issues and administer funding to them to support their activities. This is arguably the most progressive government initiative in the immigration policy field out of the three national case studies considered here. But ACIME only deals with issues of migrant integration and not with general immigration policy and there is no real parallel organization to deal with the issue of better tying immigration controls to labour market needs, which is where Portugal's problem currently lies in this field. In addition, migrant groups are dealt with primarily on an individual basis, and ACIME lists at least 100 different community organizations that it deals with. The relationship thus becomes more about funding the individual activities of these organizations thereby bringing them into 'the system' rather than about negotiating big policy issues with a centralized policy-oriented umbrella group. Again, incorporative characteristics seem to outweigh consultative ones.

Reconciling family and working life

Portugal is an unusual case when it comes to the development of policies for work–life balance because high rates of female workforce participation have been achieved without much support for families on the part of the state. This situation began to change in the late 1990s, with new legislative action in the field of parental leave and new resources for the development of childcare facilities. Where progress did occur, however, it was viewed through the lens of 'gender equality' rather than 'work–life' balance or the problems associated with declining fertility rates in an era of an aging population, and formulated and implemented by 'enlightened' bureaucrats rather than through negotiation with interest groups. This had some observable consequences for the substance of the policy shift. In recent times, the concentration of policymakers has been on such issues as paternity leave legislation rather than an overhaul of the childcare system or the type of high-quality flexibilization of working time that is increasingly the subject of efforts in this policy arena. Part-time work and job-sharing arrangements, for instance, are key components of this latter strategy, but are fiercely resisted by officials in the public administration for ideological reasons above all. More general problems associated with the development of policy through enlightened leadership rather than negotiation with and between interest groups is returned to in the conclusion to this chapter.

The policy problem

According to the highly influential analytical framework provided by Esping-Andersen that was summarized in Chapter 2, Portugal is somewhat of an outlier in the Western European context because it has maintained high rates of female workforce participation while generally belonging to the 'Southern European' family of residual and minimalist welfare states. Welfare regimes in Southern Europe tend to be patchy and less than generous in their coverage of the population, and fragmented and inefficient in their delivery. Welfare benefits are most often tied to occupational status, and a tradition of making welfare provision mostly an individual or family responsibility has been proven to increase the tension between family and working life (Ferrera, 1996; Flaquer, 2000; Martin, 1997). To this end, Greece, Italy, and Spain have especially low rates of female workforce participation as well as low birth rates even by European standards. By contrast, a majority of Portuguese women have a paid job, and most of these jobs are full-time. Portugal's rates of female labour force participation are closer to Scandinavian than they are to Mediterranean ones. Women took up paid work at what is in retrospect an astonishing rate especially after 1981. Female labour participation began at 19.0 per cent in 1970, increased to 29.0 per cent in 1981, then 41.3 in 1994 (Portugal, 1999: 237). Another way of underlining the increase in the rate of women entering paid work is to point out that while male employment grew by 93 per cent between 1981 and 2001, the increase in female workforce participation grew by 850 per cent over same period (Torres, 2004: 22). By 2000, the actual female participation rate had reached 60 per cent, higher than Germany at 55.9 per cent, and closer to the Swedish rate of 69.3 per cent than to Greece's at 41.2 per cent, Italy's at 39.6 per cent and Spain's at 40.3 per cent.[10] Furthermore, having children only mildly affects workforce participation in comparison to other countries; women tend to drop out of work for only a very short time after childbirth before returning to full-time paid employment.[11]

Yet, in calculations of benefit packages and overall state support given to families, Portugal has consistently been grouped at the bottom of the OECD in terms of generosity, along with Greece, Ireland, Italy, and Spain (Hantrais and Letablier, 1996). Welfare state development in general and family policy in particular was extremely limited during the Salazar era. Guided by a conservative ideology, most welfare responsibilities were devolved to the family. Furthermore, although the new forces that came to power after the revolution were convinced of the need to expand welfare provision, their ability to carry that through into practice was limited not only by the long-term underdevelopment of the economy as well as the short-term economic crisis of the late 1970s but also by the fact that it was a bad 'world time' to be attempting to expand welfare provision since most other OECD countries had started the process of cutting back theirs (Portugal, 1999: 236). In the family policy sphere, strategies for work–life balance did not go much beyond the existing child benefit scheme and some changes to maternity leave provisions until the 1990s. So despite post-revolutionary constitutional commitments to state provision of public services and a guarantee of gender equality that would also seem to suggest further intervention in this sphere, the Portuguese welfare state still retains a limited and familialist orientation even if it does not fit the 'Southern European' stereotype anywhere near as closely as does Greece.

While the data on female workforce participation might give the impression that Portugal looks more like Sweden or Finland than Spain or Greece with regard to gender equality, the reality is quite different. The universalist orientation of welfare state development and the gender equality driven component of family policy in Scandinavia has been surrounded by shifts in traditional ideas about gender roles, and, even more progressively, a greater sharing of unpaid household labour between men and women, and, more recently, talk of one-and-a-half income families in which both parents reconcile family and working life through part-time work, shorter working hours, or job-sharing (Esping-Andersen, 2002). Despite certain attempts to promote greater equality on the part of certain policy-makers, discussed more extensively below, this is not the reality for most Portuguese families. Recent time-use survey data finds that working Portuguese women on average labour outside the home almost as much as men, about 8.1 versus 9.0 hours per day respectively, yet these women also work an average of an additional 3.8 hours in the home compared to men's 1.3 hours (Torres *et al.*, 2004: 111).

Two questions arise from the fact of Portuguese exceptionalism. First, in the absence of much in the way of state services and benefits to help ease the tension between family and working life, *how* are the two actually reconciled? Second, if research proves that an absence of such services and benefits reduces female participation rates elsewhere, *why* have Portuguese women entered the labour force in such great numbers? This first question is much easier to answer than the second, which is much more contested and open to interpretation. While the following sections will discuss gaps in the provision of benefits and services for the purpose of achieving work–life balance in much more detail, it is quite obvious that it is not state intervention that allows Portuguese women to work both inside and outside the home. In fact, many would argue that the high female workforce participation rate is retained *in spite* of the enormous gaps in state provision and intervention that remain. In the absence of state provision of services such as affordable childcare, or government policies to encourage employers to offer flexible or even part-time working schedules, working mothers and fathers in Portugal rely overwhelmingly on the support of wider family networks. Childcare is clearly an even greater problem for solo mothers, especially in lower paid jobs and if family networks are lacking (Wall *et al.*, 2002). Not only is child welfare a concern in a situation in which much childcare is informal, there is in fact evidence that children are left home alone in Portugal more than they are in other OECD countries (OECD, 2004: 97).

With respect to the slightly more difficult question of why Portuguese women do engage so extensively in paid work outside the home at all, given the difficulties for childcare in particular that entering the paid workforce causes, there are a number of different and sometimes competing answers to this question. Academic analysts tend to stress economic factors that push or pull women into the workforce. Chief among the push factors is the fact of low wages in Portugal, something that was also emphasized by union officials during interviews conducted during the course of this book research.[12] Among the pull or 'demand' side factors, it has been suggested that Portugal's role in the international division of labour has played a major part (Cardoso, 1996). Although the workforce in Portugal is less stratified along gender lines than elsewhere in Southern Europe (Ferreira, 1998), there is a heavy concentration of female labour in certain sectors, such as clothing and footwear and cork processing, the last of which has traditionally been a very important industry for Portugal but is now operating in a tapering export market. Since the international competitiveness of these industries relies on cheap labour, and Portugal also has in fact an ongoing problem with the illegal employment of children in precisely these industries, women are pulled into employment in these sectors as well as being pushed by the need to supplement family income.

This is not necessarily the story told, however, by policy officials in charge of developing policies for work–life balance. In 2004, the OECD published a new volume in its *Babies and Bosses: Policies for Reconciling Work and Family Life* series that included Portugal as a case study. One main recommendation of the study was that the Portuguese state should remove structural barriers to part-time work in Portugal so that it became an option for parents attempting to resolve tensions between family and working life. I asked a senior policy advisor, also a key architect of the 1996 parental leave legislation detailed below, about the OECD's recommendations about the option of part-time work in Portugal and got a curious response. Portuguese women, in her opinion, chose to work full-time because it gave them power in society. They were 'not stupid' and knew that if they worked part-time instead of full-time they would lose their 'power and equality' in the workplace and would also have to take responsibility for the home.[13] That, given the feminist perspective self-consciously adopted by this senior official, may sound entirely reasonable, but one wonders how much 'power' women especially in low-paid unskilled or semi-skilled employment have in the workplace and over their labour conditions, whether they work full-time or part-time. The failure to bridge gaps between elite-level perceptions and the experiences of ordinary Portuguese families is heightened by the nature and limits of consultative policymaking in the field.

In summary, although Portugal was able to achieve comparatively high rates of female workforce participation, increasing from the mid-1980s, in the absence of comprehensive policies for the reconciliation of work and family life, the development of policies more specifically targeted at this policy remained important during the 1990s and 2000s. Not only was, and is, child welfare an ongoing concern, but the tensions between work and family life are likely to do very little to help combat long-term fertility decline, something which has begun in Portugal even if the situation has not been judged as dire as in Greece in particular. Recent academic research shows an increased anxiety among young people about the future, associated with delayed family formation and a perceived need to put work first (Guerreiro and Abrantes, 2004).

The role of consultation and incorporation in shaping policy responses

It has been noted that although there is a 'positive attitude of the state' in relation to gender equality in Portugal, this has not been translated into substantive measures likely to help women combine employment and family life due to its limited resources (Hantrais and Letablier, 1996: 133–4). This book argues that, although a lack of resources or, more accurately, a lack of resources combined with a minimalist welfare state tradition to build upon, has indeed hampered policy in this arena despite some recent improvements, the lack of consultative mechanisms within the Portuguese policymaking tradition is also problematic. The gender equality perspective is something that has been very much driven from above, giving rise to a number of important state institutions, some of which involve consultative and incorporative mechanisms but most of which concentrate on the implementation of formal rights and especially gender equality measures written into labour legislation.[14] Parallel institutions and processes have not developed in the family policy arena per se. This section gives an overview of policymaking institutions and processes in relation to work–life balance and family policy before the evolution of policy outcomes is discussed in the next.

The conservative approach to economic and social policy that marked the years of Salazar's dictatorship was, in theory, swept away by the regime's collapse in 1974. It has been noted in particular that the Portuguese Constitution introduced at the end of the 1974–1984 democratization period 'probably goes further than any other EU member state in conceptualizing the family as a fundamental social institution deserving support from the state' (Hantrais and Letablier, 1996: 27). Whereas the Irish Constitution does not promise much in terms of real material support for families, the Portuguese one certainly does, even if those promises have not always been realized. Article 67 of the contemporary constitution states that: 'The family, as a basic component of society, has the right to protection by community and the State and to the creation of all the conditions that permit the personal fulfilment of its members', before listing the specific ways in which the state is theoretically supposed to give that protection and support. These entail promoting 'the social and economic independence of family units'; establishing and guaranteeing access to child-care centres and other facilities for family support to include provisions for the aged; working 'with parents in the education of their children'; guaranteeing the legal right and 'technical arrangements' for family planning as well as 'regulating assisted procreation, in such terms as safeguard human dignity'; adjusting tax rates and welfare benefits in order 'to reflect family responsibilities'; and 'implementing an overall and integrated policy for the family' after consultation with associations representing families.[15]

More than anything else, however, the post-revolutionary constitution committed the Portuguese state to ensuring gender equality. This framed early attempts at making some of these ambitious promises a reality, but has equally influenced more recent policies aimed at reconciling family and working life implemented during the 1990s. For the purposes of the present discussion, however, it also gave rise to at least two important institutions that have had some impact on the development of policies for work–life balance even though they are not in fact responsible for formulating and implementing family policy itself. Not unlike Irish government efforts during the 1970s in response to EU pressure, the workplace was seen as the primary arena for pursuing goals of gender equality in the immediate post-revolutionary years. This initial approach is reflected in the institutional development that followed.

The Commission for Equality in Work and Employment (*Comissão para a Igualdade no Trabalho e no Emprego* or CITE) was established in 1979 and deals with complaints of discrimination in the workplace and adjudicates employment disputes. CITE is a tripartite organization overseen by the Ministry for Labour and Social Security and, in its early years, was chaired by the Director for Labour. During the period under present analysis, its current members were, on organized labour's side, both the centre-left *Confederação Geral dos Trabalhadores Portugueses* and the further left *União Geral dos Trabalhadores*, and on organized business's side, the *Confederação da Indústria Portuguesa* and the *Confederação do Comércio e Serviços de Portugal*. Overwhelmingly, the institution deals with complaints of unfair dismissal and is and always has been confined to the consideration of gender-based cases of discrimination. This specifically gendered focus of CITE was reinforced in an interview with a former chair of the organization, who was rather bemused by the increasing number of complaints presented to CITE on the basis of race or immigrant status, which is not within the institution's terms of reference.[16] Early cases presented to CITE tended to focus on issues of equal pay, with Portugal having an eye on joining the EU and the EU having passed a series of equal pay directives in the early to mid-1970s. More recently, cases have centred on issues such as pregnancy and breast-feeding. CITE's rulings are overwhelmingly in favour of the worker in the employment relationship. Even if this resulted in positive outcomes for working women, it should also be noted how narrow CITE's role is, and that few cases have yet been ruled on concerning issues such as the right to part-time work, flexi-time, or parental leave.

Similarly but with a much broader institutional role than the CITE, the *Commissão da Condicão Feminina* was established by decree law in 1977. This followed a 1975 conference that took place in the wake of the revolution on the status of women. The body was reconstituted in 1991 as the Commission for Equality and Women's Rights (*Comissão para a Igualdade e para os Direitos das Mulheres* or CIDM) under the responsibility of the Ministry of the Presidency. The CIDM has responsibility for inter-departmental coordination, producing the National Plan for Equality that is developed by all EU member states, and occasionally hosting consultative meetings with interest group stakeholders.[17]

Neither CITE nor the CIDM has direct responsibility for family policy, however, nor for the specific problem of developing policies for the reconciliation of work and family life, although much more recent research carried out of behalf of CITE has come to focus on such issues. There have been several attempts to create government departments with responsibility for this policy area, however, which are interesting in that they have received a considerable amount of attention from the EU as well as academic commentators. They are also interesting because they represent an early appreciation of issues surrounding work–life balance that has never been found in Greece and only appeared during the 1990s in Ireland. Yet it should also be kept in mind that family policy has usually been approached at the elite policymaking level from a social welfare/poverty relief perspective *or* a gender equality one, giving the debate a qualitative difference from the one that has been occurring at the European level.

The fullest albeit brief expression of state interest in conceptualizing and formulating family policy as a distinct arena of state activity occurred between 1980 and 1982. A State Office of the Family with a Secretary of State for the Family was established under Law 202/1980 and was followed by the 1982 creation of a Ministry of Social and Family Affairs which oversaw an Interministerial Commission on the Family, Cabinet of Studies and Projects for Family Affairs, a Director-General for the Family, and an Advisory Council on Family Affairs (Portugal, 1999: 238–40). The latter institution presumably had potential to combine consultative and incorporative functions. The explicit commitment to this policy area was abandoned, however, in 1983. There is not much analysis in the secondary literature to suggest why this abandonment occurred, but perhaps this policy area simply failed to remain a priority given that the economy had not

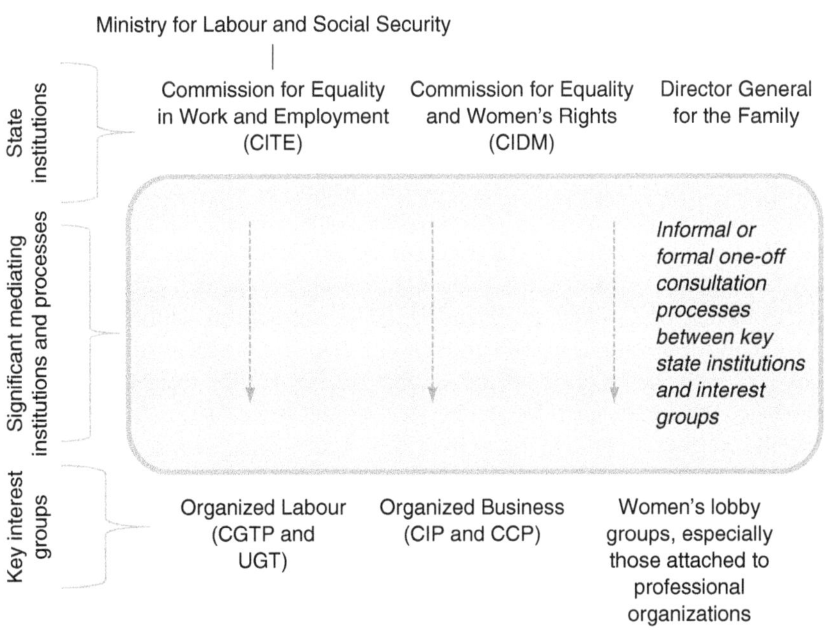

Figure 6.1 The zone of mediation in Portuguese work–life balance policy.

yet bounced back from its post-revolutionary period of crisis. The only institution to survive is the Director General for the Family, whose role is 'purely advisory' (Portugal, 1999: 40). This impression is backed up by the evidence presented below: policies for work–life balance especially, where they do exist, have not tended to stem directly from the efforts of this organization and certainly not any interest group consultation processes established by it.

A limited amount of consultation over family policy has occurred, in two basic forms. On the one hand, at the peak level, negotiations over issues of work–life balance happen in a minimalist way between trade unions and organized business as part of Portugal's neo-corporatist tri-partite industrial relations system.[18] The range of issues negotiated within this framework is very limited, however, and particular collective agreements only apply to particular occupations or industries. There is not much evidence of wider negotiations between economic players and the state over issues connected to this policy area, such as childcare provision or even paternity leave legislation, and Portuguese 'neo-corporatism' contrasts with Irish 'social partnership' in this respect. On the other hand, some consultative and incorporative mechanisms do exist in order to channel negotiations between other sorts of interest groups – parents' organizations and childcare providers for instance. However, in cases where this broader consultation occurs, it is generally at too low a level of the system to have genuine policy impact, and is non-binding and not particularly formal in nature.

As in the case of higher education policy discussed next, sometimes the only evidence of consultation between a broader set of interest groups and the state is found in a number of 'seminars' held pertaining to the issue. These fall into the category of one-off or short-term consultative processes discussed in Chapter 3, even where they are presented as part of an ongoing permanent consultative structure. Examples are one-off meetings held by the Consultative Council of Non-Government Organizations attached to the CIDM and seminars organized by the surviving Director General for the Family.[19] In both cases, there is a particularly high participation rate of academics compared to 'street level bureaucrats' or community workers, something that is not true of Irish policymaking. There is also no real evidence that these short-term efforts are able to function as part of a feedback structure on concrete policy decisions. In addition, an ongoing state Consultative Council for Family Affairs has representation from non-government organizations in the family policy field, but the focus of this body is on issues such as child protection rather than work–life balance. When I approached the organization for an interview about certain issues associated with work–life balance, representatives from the organizations stated that this fell outside their terms of reference.

Despite some evidence of ongoing relationships between interest groups and the state, however, this relationship is not very formal or else negotiations take place on such a short-term or low-level basis that it does not shape policy decisions in any serious way. Progress in the evolution of work–life balance policies has been achieved more through the individual actions of 'enlightened leaders' within the government or state bureaucracy, even if the main objective of many such leaders has centred especially on the promotion of gender equality for its own sake rather than as a means to increase the female labour force participation and/or fertility rates. A key enlightened leader of the push for gender-equality policy in the late 1990s expressed puzzlement that this researcher would even be interested in the role of non-state interest groups in shaping policy outcomes; in her opinion their influence and opinions did not matter and it did not matter that it did not matter.[20] How and why more robust consultative and incorporative institutions do matter is a theme returned to at the end of this chapter.

The evolution of policies for work–life balance

The commitment made in the Portuguese Constitution to assisting families has not always been consistently reflected in the expansion of services, benefits, or legal changes to facilitate work–life balance. One of the reasons for this is a lack of resources: Portugal remained one of the poorest EU members for the period under analysis here, and the Portuguese state has had a number of competing priorities in the social policy arena, to include a required investment in education discussed below. The development of stronger consultative and incorporative policymaking may not have helped change this situation, but it arguably would have done more to better match policy to the needs of families over the past two decades in particular. Three basic phases of post-revolutionary policy development subsequent to the establishment of CITE and the CIDM in the 1970s can be identified. The first, covering the 1980s, is marked by consistency with the past. Although there was an interest in expanding the level of services and benefits offered to working parents, apart from the establishment of CITE and its accompanying alterations to the labour code, much of this did not change from what had been offered before the revolution, being limited to child benefits and maternity leave legislation. By the early 1990s, interest in policies for work–life balance become more apparent, though still viewed through the lens of a gender equality or welfare perspective. The welfare perspective is reflected best in the attention to childcare facilities paid during this period. After the election of a Socialist government in 1995, parental leave guarantees were expanded. Third, in the era of budget restraint that characterized the period after 2001, attention shifted to increased targeting of the social welfare budget towards poorer working families.

The pre-revolutionary minimalist and familialist character of family policy under dictatorship did not preclude the existence of some state benefits and services before 1974, even if these were justified by the state's need to protect the family from the 'corrupt' ideologies of the outside world and certainly not aimed at reconciling family and working life (Amaro, 1994: 25). As in many other countries, including Ireland, family or child benefits and maternity leave legislation were the principal mechanisms for protecting families during the earlier period. A child benefit was first introduced in 1942 and, although not discussed much at all in the literature, was relatively high for much of the Salazar era in comparison even to Sweden and Finland in the early 1960s (Gautier, 1996: 74

Table 6.1 Major developments in Portuguese family policy

Year	*Policy development*
1922	First maternity leave legislation passed
1942	Child allowance/family benefit introduced
1977–1979	Establishment of institutions to address issues of gender equality – CITE and CIDM
1980–1983	State Office for the Family created (and then abolished)
1980	Maternity leave legislation brought into line with minimal European standard
1990–	Expansion of childcare supply through public contracting
1996–2001	Expansion and flexibilization of maternity leave provisions; introduction of non-transferable paternity leave
2003	Targeting of existing child allowance to poorer families

and 164). During the 1980s, Portugal was the only country in Southern Europe with a universal child benefit, even though that benefit was increasingly token in nature (Flaquer, 2000: 8). During the early 1990s, there was some discussion at the government level about better targeting the benefit to low-wage families, though this did not actually happen until a decade later (Ditch *et al.*, 1998: 217).

Maternity leave constitutes a second early arena of state activity, beginning in 1922 (Gautier, 1996: 52). Maternity benefits and pay during maternity leave have always varied according to social insurance contributions and plans, however, so that coverage has also varied widely. During the 1970s, legislation provided for nine weeks on full pay in some circumstances, which was raised to thirteen weeks in 1980, bringing Portugal into line with international commitments but far behind many other European nations (Lohkamp-Himmighofen and Dienel, 2000: 57). Finland and Sweden both provided for fifty-two weeks by 1985 (Gautier, 1996: 168). One study found that by 1991, one-off birth grants reached 75 per cent of mothers, nursing allowances reached 64.5 per cent, and maternity leave was taken up by 53 per cent (Portugal, 1999: 241). Because maternity and parental leave provided the major field of action for government policy in the field of work–life balance between 1996 and 2001, however, further policy changes are returned to shortly below.

By the beginning of the 1990s, attention had shifted to the important issue of the gap between childcare supply and demand. The Portuguese state relies heavily on contracting with the non-profit sector in order to try to meet demand, which is supplemented by a for-profit private sector and some pre-school education establishments controlled directly by the state. Like most countries, then, childcare is provided by a patchwork of organizations, and its affordability and availability varies according to geographic region and the age of a child in care. The consistent problem in Portugal over the period of interest here is the lack of available spaces, especially in the publicly subsidized sector, and especially for children aged under three. Some mobilization around the issue (but still mainly within the public administration) occurred during the 1990s and did result in an increase in public provision for children aged between three and six as a result.

A report of a seminar held by the CIDM's Non-Governmental Organization Consultative Council in 1991 laments the fact that while 50 per cent of children in the 0–3 age group had working mothers, only 11 per cent had access to formal care, even though there is a legislative commitment to the provision of care. The rate of coverage for the 3–6 age group was 35.6 per cent compared to 80 per cent for a 'majority of European countries (Comissão para a Igualdade e para os Direitos das Mulheres, 1991).

Efforts to expand childcare meant that the rate of coverage for the older age group had increased to 50 per cent by 1994. Yet much of this development occurred in institutions run by the Ministry of Education, the number of nursery schools in this category increasing from 2,141 with 49,820 users in 1985–86 to 3,049 schools and 72,428 users in 1993–94. It was pointed out at the time how little these schools contributed to the reconciliation of family and working life, however, since they generally opened for only five hours a day and closed for two hours during the middle of the day (Ditch *et al.*, 1996: 136–7). By 2004, participation rates for the 3–6 year old group had increased to 75 per cent, with an extension of hours, but only 22 per cent for younger children. This includes coverage by private providers that supplemented the not-for-profit and state sector, which is often very expensive in comparison to wages (OECD, 2004: 97). One curious aspect of Portuguese policy in this area is that, by law, parents had to pay full-time rates even for part-time use. A tax break is provided for childcare fees, but this has not usually been enough to offset the full-time rate requirement, providing a disincentive to part-time work (OECD, 2004: 20–1).

While some expansion of childcare provision occurred under the Socialist government of 1996–2001, most attention has focused on the parental leave scheme introduced at this time because of its unusual focus on paternity leave as opposed to general parental leave that is transferable between men and women. Maternity leave of 120 days can be transferred to the father after ninety days and spread out over one year on a part-time basis, but there are also two special sets of paternity leave, one of five days following the birth of a child and one of fifteen days over the period that maternity leave covers. Importantly, parental leave is paid, but it does depend on a worker's insurance contribution record so does not cover all cases. The logic behind the development of such policies was explicitly centred on the promotion of gender equality, specifically, changing the attitudes of Portuguese men toward childcare. According to one of the key architects of the reforms, transferable parental leave rights by adopting a gender neutral framework is 'a mistake', as is always targeting measures towards women as if they are the ones who are 'different'. To change the way men think about their role as fathers, rights have to be specifically and separately awarded to them.[21] Arguably, however, it is doubtful that Portugal's paternity leave legislation helps families cope with the tensions between work and family life over the long term. Fifteen to twenty days of paid paternity leave spread out over the first year of a child's birth, in addition to several other forms of partially paid or unpaid special leave for the care of sick children, for example, probably does not affect the choice to have children or to enter the paid workforce as much as some other reconciliation measures have the potential to do. As the recent OECD report noted: 'Portugal has a comprehensive child-related leave model but only few families can afford to make use of it' (OECD, 2004: 145). The cost of child-care, particularly for part-time work and multiple barriers to the use of flexible, reduced, or high quality part-time working arrangements are more likely to influence choices over family size (Erhel and Guergoat-Lariviere, 2013).

The centre-right government that came to power in Portugal in 2002 did so in the context of a developing budget crisis. During the late 1990s, the country had in fact expanded its social welfare commitments in general through the gradual expansion of a minimum income policy, widely discussed as a progressive move toward the provision of a universally applicable safety net and away from the occupational basis of welfare associated with the 'Southern European' model (Capucha *et al.*, 2005). The PSD–CDS government made no moves to overturn developments in the family policy arena made under the Socialists but did introduce a series of measures designed to target the family benefit and taxation structure increasingly to poorer and larger families. This resulted in about ten per cent of families losing the existing Child Allowance.[22] The overall climate for expanding policies for work–life balance, therefore, has been rather hostile over the past decade, a situation only deepened by the post-2008 economic crisis. Policymakers during the 1990s drove major changes in parental leave legislation, but major structural problems related to childcare and the lack of flexibility in relation to part-time work and family-friendly policies in the workplace are ongoing.

Higher education

Portugal's revolutionary regime from 1974 to 1976 and, subsequently, the country's democracy inherited a major problem in the form of an underdeveloped education system. The higher education system under the *Estado Novo* had been accessed only by a small elite and offered a narrow set of courses and programmes. Education policy from the late 1970s through to the 1990s aimed to increase participation but also diversity, first through the construction of a new public polytechnic system and several new universities, then later through the encouragement of the growth of private institutions of higher learning. These policies did increase participation, but their ability to increase the diversity of courses offered was rather more mixed. By the early 1990s, the attention thus shifted to the problem of how to increase the quality of higher education, a theme that carries through to the contemporary policy agenda, which is increasingly centred on how to enhance the reputation of the Portuguese education system abroad. There is a little more evidence for the use of consultative and incorporative policymaking strategies at the peak level here than there was in the family policy arena, at least in this later period. Genuine consultation is confined to a very narrow set of interests, namely an academic elite that tends to serve as both stakeholder and giver of supposedly neutral policy advice, a position that is unique to higher education policy. This is true everywhere, but, in other cases including Ireland, there have been at least some attempts to broaden participation in policymaking beyond this elite.

The policy problem

Nowhere is Portugal's inheritance of a 'dual society' as it made the transition to democracy more apparent than in the field of education. One of Europe's oldest and historically most prestigious universities is to be found here and intellectuals are both held in high regard and permitted a considerable influence in social and political life. Yet the country still suffers from having one of the most undereducated workforces in the developed world. As the following discussion will illustrate with respect to higher education, Portugal has done a lot of catching up in terms of expanding access to education at all levels over the past three decades. But it has also had much catching up to do. Under Salazar, access to basic education was limited for many, especially in rural areas, with primary school attendance for girls not made compulsory until 1960. Education suffered especially at the secondary level, beyond the initial six years of required attendance. During the 1969–1970 school year, 27.7 per cent of fourteen year olds were enrolled at school, compared to almost 50 per cent in Spain and around 90 per cent in a country such as the Netherlands (OECD, 1974: 30).

The long-term legacy of this has been a lag in literacy rates: by 1988 the illiteracy rate for those aged over fifteen still reached almost 18 per cent while those of most other Western European countries were approaching zero (Grilo and Rosa, 1988: 203). However, the 'dualist' nature of the education system is not only reflected in the undereducation of a large sector of the population but also in how well the elite has traditionally been educated. Revealing is the fact that although Portugal has the lowest proportion of the population aged 35–64 with a secondary school qualification in the OECD, bar Turkey, those who do manage to complete secondary school score very highly on literacy tests (Conceição and Heitor, 2005: 7–12). That class has traditionally mattered most when gaining access to education is particularly striking in light of the fact that gender provided no real barrier to members of the elite attaining university qualifications. By 1970, predating the revolution, 45 per cent of university students were female (OECD, 1974: 36). Given the discussion of Portuguese gender relations and female workforce participation presented above, perhaps that is not very surprising, but here it serves to further underline the extent of dualism and elitism in the education system that democratizing forces would have to deal with after 1974.

Prior to the early 1970s, higher education in Portugal was generally provided by a limited number of public universities while technical education was confined to the secondary level. The country's first university was established in the thirteenth century, eventually permanently at Coimbra, before parallel institutions were founded in the major cities of Lisbon and Porto in the mid-nineteenth centuries. An additional university for Lisbon was then established in 1930 and the Catholic University was founded in 1967. Apart from this latter institution, which did not really expand its teaching functions until the early 1970s, the provision of private education was limited to several art schools and conservatoires. At the beginning of the 1960s, 98.4 per cent of students in higher education were thus enrolled at public institutions, and 94.9 were enrolled at universities. The highly traditional universities that made up this system were divided into separate and distinct faculties, where courses aimed to give a five or six year degree in law, sciences, engineering, or medicine, for example, not a general education (da Cruz and Cruzeiro, 1995: 20–1).

As part of the much larger but ultimately failed attempt to modernize the *Estado Novo* in order to relieve some of the social pressures that eventually caused its downfall, an attempt to diversify the public higher education system was made on the eve of the revolution. This followed a decade of gradual expansion of participation in higher education that had occurred since the beginning of the 1960s, although this expansion was nothing like that which occurred a decade later. The 1973 plan included the intention to create several new universities and university institutes, particularly in regions such as the Alentejo and the Minho that had previously gone without their own, plus a new polytechnic system to offer more advanced technical training than had previously been taught at the secondary level, even though most of these courses taught by the proposed polytechnics would be at the sub-degree level. The programme was obviously put on hold as the result of the breakdown of the authoritarian regime, although elements of it carried through into the new administration's approach to higher education after 1974.

The policy problem from the late 1970s until at least the early 1990s was how to increase participation in higher education while containing costs to the state. This was achieved first through the creation of a polytechnic system and several new public universities but, most importantly for increasing participation, then through the stimulation of private provision. The latter strategy created a new set of problems that became the source of government attention from around 1994, namely the lack of quality control in the system and the failure of the privatization strategy to meet regional and labour market needs.

The role of consultation and incorporation in the shaping of policy responses

Although the argument of this book is that it is national patterns of policymaking that best explain outcomes and that there is a general consistency in the way that states deal with interest groups in each national case, there is some within-country variation that also needs to be explained. This is especially the case in Portugal, the difficult 'mixed' case. In short, there is somewhat more evidence for the development of institutions and processes established at the peak level for the purpose of the formal consultation (and incorporation) of key interest groups in the higher education field than there is in relation to policies for the reconciliation of work and family life and immigration. Although the range of groups consulted in any genuine way during the formulation of education policy is very narrow, and when attempts were made to expand the variety of groups consulted, their input was not always evident in concrete policy terms, that difference between policy areas deserves some elaboration and explanation.

Examples of consultative policymaking in Portugal in the field of higher education include the National Council for Education (CNE), founded in its present form in 1987 and responsible for consensus-building between education 'partners' over policy priorities and approaches. The CNE, however, is overwhelmingly made up of university professors and its work consists mainly of holding conferences and publishing research findings. In addition, a one-off 1996 Pact on Education, discussed in detail below and which guided or more accurately described the Socialist government's policy at the time, can be described as a relatively successful attempt to develop consultative and incorporative policy making in the sense that it committed policy 'partners' to a number of important policy goals. It was limited, however, in that it was initiated primarily by a single individual, the Minister of Education, and was short-lived. By far the most influential interest group, however, is the Conference of Rectors of Public Universities. Although there is a parallel organization to represent the public polytechnics, it is not as influential as the Conference of Rectors. In addition, there is an independent umbrella organization that represents the private sector, the Portuguese Association for Private Higher Education, but it does not have a formal relationship of the type enjoyed by the public sector representatives and has no clearly discernible impact on policy development.

Before further discussing some of the limits of consultative policymaking in the higher education arena in Portugal, it is worth exploring why there is more evidence for consultation happening at a national level in the case of education than there is in the other two policy cases. Part of the explanation lies in the nature of education policy itself, in light of what we already know about the Portuguese policymaking tradition. In some ways, interest group consultation and incorporation in the case of education policy are never as broad and do not need to be as broad as they do in the other two policy cases. Policies for work–life balance affect almost everyone, but only a small sector of the population at any given time is directly affected by tertiary education policy. The most crucial players are already part of the elite – the state, teachers as represented by their professional organizations, administrators of institutions of higher learning, and to a lesser extent, student associations. The interest of both organized labour and business is usually confined to the parts of the education system that aim at bridging the gap between schooling and work, such as apprenticeship systems. The fact that representatives from the most important groups belong to the educated elite anyway, along with the fact that the Portuguese policymaking tradition has always allowed plenty of room for intellectuals to move in and out of politics whether formally or informally, means that consultative and incorporative policymaking is more easily achieved in this field than in others. Put simply, the fact that intellectuals make up one of the key *interest* groups relevant to higher education policy helps produce this particular result. However, even the interests of intellectuals as a group are more often than not filtered through the Conference of Rectors rather than professional teachers' associations, for

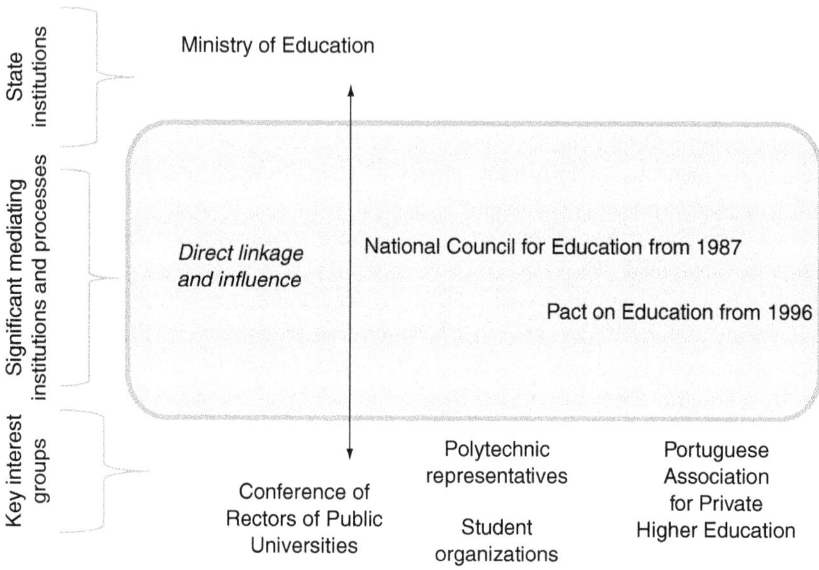

Figure 6.2 The zone of mediation in Portuguese higher education policy.

instance, when it comes to concrete policy decisions rather than the offering of research and general policy advice.

Attempts to broaden consultation with stakeholders beyond the special relationship enjoyed between a small selection of university administrators and the state are relatively recent and limited in the extent to which they are genuinely consultative, arguably thus leaning too far in the direction of incorporation. The consultative approach reflected in the 1996 Pact was something new for the formation of Portuguese education policy. The *Pacto Educativo Para O Futuro* consisted of a policy document supported by a consultative process involving the government and key stakeholders, including parents, teachers, and administrators.[23] It should be noted that its proposals applied not only to higher education but to education policy at all levels. The key document gives the impression, however, of consisting of a means to build support for a shift in government policy direction that had already been decided on, rather than of a genuinely consultative process. In this sense it can be contrasted with Ireland's public consultation process of the early 1990s, which took several years to complete and revolved around the publication of a Green or discussion paper rather than a 'pact' agreeing to a certain shift in policy goals.

By contrast, there is not much evidence that the decision to encourage private sector growth in the late 1980s discussed in detail in the following section had anything to do with any consultation with key interest groups in the field. What remains consistent across both decades in fact is that major initiatives actually resulted more from the interests and proposals of individual Ministers of

Education than from anything else. Specifically, Minister of Education Roberto Carneiro's commitment to stimulating private sector growth drove policy in the 1980s. Policy during the 1990s, aimed at improving quality and reining in parts of the system that appeared out of control, was steered by one Marçal Eduardo Grilo, Minister of Education from 1995 to 1999, and a prolific writer on education in Portugal, as witnessed in the notes to this chapter.

Opportunities for influencing the real detail of policy, however, even in the case of the Pact on Education, are very limited. There is a *qualitative* difference between the role of consultative bodies in the education field in Portugal and, for instance, in Ireland. Because the Irish policymaking tradition includes opportunity for the circulation of government discussion documents and formalized feedback on those documents, such as the Green and White Paper process which shaped education policy in the early to mid-1990s, consultation has been broader than in Portugal as well as more concrete. In Portugal, the work of the National Council on Education in particular seems to consist of academics joining together to give an opinion on an issue, rather than to formulate concrete policy proposals. This is witnessed by the fact that most of the documents published by this organization and available to the public consist of summaries of seminars where the main participants are academic experts on a particular issue. The Ministry of Education's 1997 *Autonomia e Qualidade,* published at approximately the same time as the Pact on Education, was presented more as a discussion document, but many of the proposals presented in it were already being implemented as government policy. Not only are the main contributors to the debate academics, but when attempts are made to broaden the range of interest groups involved, the process for providing 'feedback loops' in the case of government policy is not fully developed. It could be speculated that policymakers in Portugal do not see this as important, as the above discussion on policies for work–life balance clearly reveals in that case.

Some of these qualitative differences are spelled out by contrasting the responses of the heads of the national student organizations in Ireland and Portugal to similar questions about the extent to which they have gained representation through participation in national consultation processes and how they felt about the quality of that representation. The Irish student leader commented that because formal policy decisions are made at such a peak level, recommendations made by consultative bodies mostly involved tinkering with the edges or technical details of a policy decision since they have almost been 'pre-approved' by the government. Students' associations were not necessarily more disadvantaged here, however, in comparison to any of the other key stakeholders. Yet the Portuguese student leader argued that in his experience, although legislation actually spells out that student unions are supposed to be consulted over policy decisions, they are only ever included at the 'end point when the legislation is about to be passed as a token effort' which amounts to 'fast food student participation, because the students don't play any part in the actual cooking'. This is *different*, however, from the way that other stakeholders are treated since specific groups are included at a much earlier stage in the consultation process. The Portuguese student leader pointed in particular to the Council of Rectors, and the weight of the 'big traditional universities' at Lisbon, Porto and Coimbra who are dealt with on a one-to-one basis, compared to the smaller public institutions and representatives from the private sector.[24] Adopting the terms from the analytic framework guiding this book, student organizations in Portugal might be incorporated by being made to feel as if they have been included in state decision-making processes, but they have not been genuinely consulted.

The evolution of higher education policy

Education policy is one area in which the effects of the 'pendulum principle' of revolutionary and counter-revolutionary tendencies following the breakdown of Portugal's authoritarian regime and the at least temporary victory of the *Movimento das Forças Armadas* (MFA) discussed above can be clearly witnessed. The use by the MFA's leaders of the education system as a means by which to spread the ideology of socialism was demonstrated by the appearance of, among other things, literacy campaigns run by the MFA, worker's education centres, and the formation of student unions (Melo, 2004; Stoer, 1986: 60–8). Furthermore, the provisional government made two announcements immediately following the revolution aimed at turning higher education into a citizen's right rather than an elite privilege. First, virtually free access to the universities would be instituted. Second, the system of technical education that had been established at the secondary level and modified by the 1973 reforms would be elevated to the tertiary since it was believed that having a differentiated system such as this was responsible for perpetuating social hierarchy and removing this differentiation was part of 'democratizing' the education system. A prevailing view was that the old system of technical education at the secondary level was 'a socially devalued form of education' (Eurydice, 2000: 445). These measures resulted in an immediate increase of enrolments in higher education by 40.3 per cent between 1974–1975 and 1975–1976 (Cruz and Cruzeiro, 1995: 30). The difficulties that resulted from these actions, however, were predictable. Not only were many students unprepared for higher education and the university system in particular became overloaded without either resources to deal with the increase in numbers or the expertise to cope with teaching new sorts of students, but there was soon a realization that Portugal also needed to increase the technical skills of its workers and that a more adequate and varied technical or non-university sector was required.

By 1977 however, the revolution had reached its demobilization phase, during which a period of 'normalization' of the relationship between state and society set in. Post-revolutionary education policy until the mid-1980s thus consisted of the creation of a binary system of higher education but with far less explicit commitment to it than found in the Irish case. Policymakers recognized that the economy required an array of what is referred to as 'short cycle' technical courses that do not necessarily lead to advanced degrees but also wished to avoid the perpetuation of the 'dual society' through a differentiated approach to the university and non-university sectors. This ambivalent attitude toward the distinction between university and non-university higher education coloured state policy for at least the next two decades. Because of the enormous increase in demand that had placed pressure on the public universities in particular, a cap was placed on the number of enrolments in these institutions beginning with schools of medicine for the 1976–1977 year and then spreading to all programmes by 1978. After some uncertainty about how much of the old regime's 1973 plan to build new universities should be carried through, by 1980 there were nine public universities including 'university institutes' that were then turned into full universities a little later on, in addition to the pre-existing Catholic University and one additional private institution.

The decision to create a full polytechnic system was strongly influenced by the advice, and the loans that were tied to this advice, of the World Bank. The reliance on this funding and the role it played in stimulating the sector was emphasized to this author several times during the course of this research by different policymakers in the field. A 'secondary justification', however, was provided by the need to increase educational participation in the regions in order to enhance regional development. Under Decree Law 513-T/79, the 'short-cycle' system was referred to as Polytechnic Higher Education where the explicit objective was to fill gaps in manpower needs.[25] These institutions were thus conceptualized as tertiary ones, even if some courses provided not much more than basic technical training. The potential for 'drift' between the university and non-university sector and a lack of clear role for each became even more apparent during the 1980s.

The gap between the demand for and opportunities for access to higher education only began to be closed in the late 1970s through the creation of the polytechnic system. Further state interest in both broadening and increasing access opportunities was pursued in the 1980s along two distinct lines. On the one hand, the binary public system was consolidated, even if plenty of room was left for 'drift' between the university and non-university systems. On the other, an original if not unique attempt to encourage the private sector to fill gaps still left by the public system resulted in the partial privatization of higher education in Portugal. This latter strategy has been highly controversial and much debated and the main threads of that debate will be outlined below. First, the legal framework governing the public system needs to be discussed.

The binary distinction between the university and polytechnic sectors that had been adopted several years earlier was formalized in the 1986 Framework Law on Education. In line with the legalistic basis of Portuguese public policy in general, framework laws must state exactly what institutions *can* do, including with respect to aspects of their internal organization.[26] Conversely, if the legislation is silent on an issue it is assumed that this is something the institution *cannot* do. This means that autonomy must be formally *given* to institutions in precise areas of their operation, in sharp contrast to the Irish system in particular. Under the legislation, universities were given more autonomy than polytechnics, which were to report directly to the Ministry of Education, although university

Table 6.2 Major developments in Portuguese higher education policy

Year	*Policy development*
1973	Plan to create new polytechnic system and new regional universities, put on hold during revolutionary period
1974	Institution of open entry to public institutions
1977	Creation of public polytechnic system, with significant financial contribution from World Bank
1978	Introduction of *numero clausi* or cap on entrance to public institutions (overturning 1974 policy of free access)
1986	Framework Law on Education outlines binary structure of education system
1987	Beginning of privatization approach, with measures gradually introduced to stimulate growth of the sector
1987	Specialized Higher Education Courses (CESEs) introduced to allow polytechnics to award degrees higher than first-cycle *bachalerato* Abandoned 1997 and polytechs allowed to award the second-cycle *licenciatura*
1994	First law for evaluation/quality assurance introduced
1996–1997	Policy strategy outlined in the *Pact on Education* and *Autonomy and Quality*
1997	New Finance Law for higher education passed
1999	Portugal signs Bologna Declaration, leading to degree restructuring

autonomy was not strengthened until a decade later following the mounting criticism that Portuguese universities were not flexible enough to respond to changing international and labour market circumstances. The semi-autonomous consultative central body mentioned in the previous section, the National Council on Education, was also established under the 1986 Framework Law to offer advice to the government and to forge a policy consensus amongst representatives from the education sector.

As the previous chapter illustrated with respect to the Irish case, there are two ways in which a binary system can be established, and then kept in check if there is a self-conscious commitment to it on the part of policymakers. First, legislation can spell out the differences between the university and non-university sectors and force individual institutions to register with the state or in some way be 'approved' as one of the two types of institution. The 1986 Portuguese framework law basically does this. Second, once established, the binary nature can be reinforced through the qualifications framework. A qualifications system in which different types of institutions are permitted to teach different types of courses and where the state keeps a close eye on the content of those courses is often a thorn in the side for many individual institutions, but it allows the state to make sure that the overall logic of having a binary system is carried into practice. This is where Portugal's comparatively weak commitment to a binary structure is reflected most clearly, since changes within the qualifications framework implemented since the 1986 Framework Law was introduced allowed for a substantial 'drift' to occur between the two systems. Portuguese universities, the only real form of higher education until the late 1970s, have traditionally awarded a first-stage two-year undergraduate degree or *bachalerato* and a second-stage four- or more-year undergraduate degree referred to as the *licenciatura*. Postgraduate study was only carried out at the doctoral level until masters' degrees were introduced in 1980. Originally, in keeping with the short-cycle education supposed to be offered by the new polytechnics, the new institutions were permitted to offer the *bachalerato* only, but pressure over time and institutional drift eventually led to the implementation of Law 115 of 1997 which permitted the polytechnic sector to also award both the *licenciatura*, although only universities would still be allowed to award postgraduate degrees. The shift in emphasis through changes to the qualifications framework means that the original distinction made between the university and non-university sectors 'may not be as clear as the original planners intended' (Eurydice, 2000: 10).

From the perspective of this book the only problem with the drift of polytechnic institutes into providing something similar to what the university sector offers is that it often means that they fail to fill the objectives of meeting niche labour market requirements and providing the country with a highly technically skilled workforce overall. In order to 'elevate' courses to degree level, what were originally technical courses may become overly theoretical and book-oriented.[27] A similar point is made by a recent report on the diversity of course offerings in Portugal by the National Council for Education, which argues that, shortly after their establishment, the 'new universities' created in the regions and the polytechnic institutes seemed to fill the role intended for them, specializing in skills required for regional niche industries such as textiles or fisheries. However, over time a tendency evolved for the polytechnics and the new universities to 'copy' the universities in their course offerings, proliferating the number of social science, legal, and general business studies programmes offered in particular. The policy has resulted in institutional diversity but not so much in diversity of subjects and courses offered across the system (Conselho Nacional de Educação, 2002: 136). The path that the evolution of the private higher education system took from the mid-1980s has only intensified this problem.

By far the most important and interesting feature of the development of Portugal's higher education system from the mid-1980s is the privatization strategy adopted in the late 1980s. Government policy directed at stimulating the development of private institutions involved altering the access system to higher education, changing rules to allow professors to work in both the public and private sectors simultaneously, and the provision of subsidies to private providers (Amaral and Teixeira, 2000: 252–3). Despite initial achievements in establishing a new regional polytechnic system in the late 1970s, the country was only just emerging from an underlying economic crisis. The need to expand social policy across so many different areas could not even begin to be met by state finances. Privatization is thus often presented as the *only* choice policymakers had from the mid-1980s in order to expand participation in higher education.[28] Ideological motives, however, cannot be ignored. A key figure in the promotion of the privatization strategy was Roberto Carneiro, Secretary for State for Education in 1980–1981 and then Minister for Education under the first clearly centre-right PSD government of 1987 to 1991. Private education was promoted under Carneiro's leadership as a core tool of economic development, since he and others in the government believed that the private sector was naturally better at responding to 'market' needs so hoped that it would meet gaps in provision that still remained in the regions and in specific technical areas. Allowing the private sector to flourish was also considered an extension of democracy, moving away from the statist and overly bureaucratic model that had prevailed under the *Estado Novo* and may have in fact only been reinforced in the 1974–76 revolutionary period in which 'the public universities were used basically to teach Marxism'.[29]

The collective result of the growth of the public non-university sector but most clearly the private higher education system was an enormous increase in enrolments during the late 1980s and early 1990s. According to Portuguese government figures, the number of students in higher education increased from 83,000 in 1980, to 157,000 in 1990, and then rather astoundingly to 314,000 in 1995, doubling in the space of five years (OECD, 1998: 7). Much of this growth occurred in the newly created private sector, with enrolments in public institutions increasing by 40 per cent between 1987 and 1991, contrasting with a growth rate of 250 per cent in the private sector (Amaral and Teixeira, 2000: 53). Furthermore, as early as 1991, the actual number of students in the private sector outstripped those enrolled in public institutions the first time (Conselho Nacional de Educação, 2002: 102). By 1993, 25 per cent of young people between the ages of eighteen and twenty-four were participating in education, compared to six per cent for the 1974–1975 academic year (Grilo, 1995: 187). The private sector included anything from full private universities and polytechnics to small language schools, but became increasingly concentrated on the teaching of law, business studies, and social sciences.

Thus, the privatization strategy has been criticized on the grounds that it has failed in its explicit objective of responding to regional and labour market needs, and also with regard to the quality of education that the private sector has delivered. Although, in theory, new courses offered by private institutions are supposed to register with the state and in this manner be kept in check, the system has increasingly been described as 'out of control' since the mid-1990s since individual institutions have found ways to subvert the original policy's goals. First of all, the private sector has actually lagged behind the public sector in terms of serving regional needs, with private institutions becoming heavily concentrated in coastal urban centres already well served by the public sector. In fact, the public system actually arguably provides for better access to education in the regions, especially through the public polytechnics and the 'new universities' located in more traditionally isolated areas. In addition, the private sector has not tended toward the provision of technical and scientific education. During the 1998–1999 academic year, enrolments in courses in social science, law, and commerce accounted for 27 per cent of total places in the public sector, but 47 per cent in the private sector (Correira *et al.*, 2004: 463–4). This may not be as much due to demand as it is to the relatively cheap cost of courses in these subjects compared to science and information technology, for example.

There is also much scepticism about the quality of teaching in the private system, which is made up of everything from private universities and full polytechnics to small schools that provide short-term language courses. While some private institutions, most obviously the Catholic University, clearly provide high quality education, some argue that in 'most cases [private institutions are] little more than secondary schools of higher level, without a permanent and well qualified academic staff' (Amaral and Teixeira, 2000: 255). In fact, availability of qualified staff was one of the biggest issues confronting attempts to stimulate the private sector in the early 1990s: most academics already had permanent jobs in the public sector. The solution was that many of these took part-time jobs in the private sector in addition to their permanent jobs, a phenomenon described as the rise of the 'turbo' professor by the Portuguese (OECD, 1998: 13). The negative public perception of the private sector is also self-fulfilling since secondary school students generally opt for public universities as a first choice, public polytechnics second, and then private institutions last. This has muddied Portuguese policymakers' original intention to provide a binary system of education capable of producing both internationally competitive research and a technically trained labour force, since the public–private divide has perhaps become more important that the university–polytechnic one.

Partly as a result of the particular policy strategies pursued in the late 1980s, the main concern in the field of higher education shifted during the 1990s from expanding participation to quality assurance across both the public and private, and the university and non-university, sectors. A 1998 OECD review noted that teaching across the entire higher education system seemed particularly old-fashioned and out of date, with a focus on the rote learning of facts rather than interpretation and analysis (OECD, 1998: 15). To this end, a new law for evaluation of higher education was passed in 1994, introducing the concept of external reviews of individual courses and institutions for the first time. In line with the guidelines set down in the legislation, the Foundation of Portuguese Universities presented its first report in 1997, and the National Council for Assessment of Higher Education Institutions was created in 1998 in order to provide independent evaluation across the whole of system (Eurydice, 2000: 8).

This evaluation process was extended through the 1990s as part of a larger effort to take stock of and modernize the higher education system. Two documents are important here, namely the 1996 *Pact on Education for the Future*, and the 1997 government policy document *Autonomy and Quality* (Ministério da Educação 1996 and 1997. See also Grilo, 1996). The former document was supported by a consultative process involving the government and key stakeholders and represented something new in the field of higher education policy. As noted above, the *Pact on Education* applied to all levels of the education system, including a recurring reference to the need to build capacity for catering for lifelong learning into the existing system, the need to involve education 'partners' in policymaking and implementation, and the need to further 'democratize' the education system by further increasing participation. Specific concerns in the field of higher education included increasing attention to the financing of institutions especially with a view to increasing the degree of social assistance available to students from lower socio-economic backgrounds and to allow students 'choice' between the public and private systems, enforcing and deepening the system of quality assurance, carrying out a review of the existing access system to higher education, and a proposal to increase the number of places available in the public education system especially in science and technology courses.

This general set of commitments was then given effect in a number of different reforms, most of which are outlined in *Autonomia e Qualidade,* which was aimed more specifically at outlining government action in the higher education field. The document refers to a 'strategic triangle' for government policy, the three corners being the strengthening of institutional autonomy through decentralization of decision-making; changes in the way that institutions are financed; and the promotion of quality throughout the system. With respect to autonomy, Decree Law 170 of 1996 had clarified some specific issues, especially involving the power of institutions to create their own governing bodies. Decentralization of decision-making was also required in the sphere of access to education to give institutions more choice over which students were selected. Since the reintroduction of caps on numbers and following the introduction of a centralized access system in the 1980s, entrance to public education had evolved into one not unlike Ireland's 'points system' in which candidates rank six courses in order of preference after which placement is based on a combination of performance in secondary school and achievement in a standardized national entrance examination. With respect to quality, the new evaluation system would be extended and better control over the content of course offerings would be regained through the state's ability to register and deregister courses; the much-needed 'rationalization' of higher education, and steering it toward greater offerings in science and technology subjects, would be achieved through the accreditation system.

Aside from 1997 changes to the 1986 Framework Law on Education that provided for increased university autonomy, an important example of how some of these proposals and commitments were put into action was the new Framework Law for the Financing of Education that was also introduced in 1997. In the higher education arena, this legislation expanded social assistance to students from lower-income families. There are both parallels and differences with respect to the extent to which 'access' issues have been debated and addressed across the Irish and Portuguese cases. Chapter 4 showed how Irish authorities attempted to address the problem of ensuring equality of access according to income since at least the early 1970s, but how there has been a more recent shift of attention to other disadvantaged groups, such as mature students or those from ethnic minorities. This has been largely driven by concerns over labour shortages that have emerged since the mid-1990s. In Portugal, however, the focus on access remains largely confined to access based on parental income or class, and it has proved more an issue of academic concern rather than public debate.[30]

Academic concern translated into government action, however, under the 1997 law. Fees for public sector institutions have suffered a 'tumultuous history', staying stable since the late 1960s before being raised in 1992, lowered in 1996, and then raised again under the 1997 Financing Law to equal the minimum wage for all public undergraduate courses regardless of family income (Oliveira and Pereira, 1999: 112). A social aid system, however, had been introduced in 1993 to help financially disadvantaged students cover fees in the public system, to be administered at the institutional level. Eventually this was expanded to cover fees in the private system (although fee structures here vary widely, they are overall obviously higher than in the public system), and in 1997 a living expenses grant in addition to the government fee subsidy was introduced, as was the establishment of the National Council for Social Action (Ministério de Educação, 1998: 63). At the same time, as part of the other side of the effort to address quality concerns, apart from elevating the quality of teacher training and establishing an external assessment system, access was tightened through the introduction of minimum pass marks in national examinations for gaining access to tertiary education.

By the mid-2000s, the main topic of debate in Portugal, aside from ongoing clashes between student organizations and the state over course fees, was the country's commitment to the Bologna Declaration. The 1999 Declaration set off a process aimed at creating a higher education 'European space' to provide the continent with the basis for building a 'knowledge society'. In practical terms this means, most importantly, creating a system in which students can transfer credits more easily between different institutions across different European countries. This also entails some harmonization of national degree structures, meaning significant changes in the Portuguese case chiefly because undergraduate courses (counting both the *bachalerato* and the *licenciatura)* are comparatively long by European standards.

Although the Bologna process might seem to lie a little out of the scope of this book, it is important in Portugal because it has acted as a catalyst for deepening the commitment to quality assurance in particular, leading to several changes in the law in 2003. Increasingly it is recognized that in the new 'European space' of higher education, Portugal will have to compete for students and thus prove that its course offerings are internationally competitive. During the late 2000s, the existing quality assurance system of external reviews was dismantled, with a view to reconstructing it for the purpose of bringing institutions and those review systems itself in line with international standards (European Association for Quality Assurance in Higher Education, 2006). This has helped to deepen the debate, still largely between the state and the academic community at this point, about the need to tie the higher education system in more tightly to the needs of a high-skill, higher-wage economy. There is recognition that, in focusing largely on increasing the number of students enrolled in higher education, there has not been enough concentration of investment in specific areas of specialization.[31]

A couple of ongoing problems related to increasing the quality of higher education in Portugal are also worth mentioning, in part because of the attention they are currently receiving in the country. Apart from the ongoing troubles associated with attempting to rein in the private system so that it fills the sorts of gaps that it was originally designed to fill, the private system itself is in trouble. Portugal, as with all OECD countries, is experiencing a declining birth rate, which is beginning to be reflected in the number of students entering tertiary education. The population bubble that fuelled the growth of the private sector in the early 1990s is over, and it is likely that a number of institutions will not survive as a result (Amaral and Teixeira, 2000: 259). Some attention is also being paid to the 'quality' of students entering education. Portugal has a particularly high drop-out rate in higher education, suggesting that students are ill-equipped for tertiary studies (Conselho Nacional de Educação, 2002). This should perhaps direct the attention of policy-makers toward the secondary level, but also to the way that courses are taught at the third level. That latter issue is also important for addressing the needs of mature and returning students, since the long-term legacy of Portuguese under-investment in education is still reflected in the low skill level of Portugal's older working population.

Immigration

As discussed in previous chapters, Greece, Ireland, and Portugal were all traditionally countries of migration that have more recently had to come to terms with their new status as nations of immigration. As in the other two national case studies, getting to grips with the new situation has not been easy and, in Portugal, the problem has been complicated by a high degree of illegal migration, at least since the 1980s. In this context, a comparatively restrictive immigration policy has had to give way to a more realistic approach, first reflected in a series of one-off mass regularization programmes during the early 1990s. However, shifting to a more comprehensive legislative framework for regular legal migration has been slower and more difficult to achieve. Though increasing attention was paid during the 1990s and early 2000s to matching labour market requirements to migratory inflows, the trend generally was of large influxes of unskilled and semi-skilled labour, both legal and illegal, with little attention in the political debate paid to the possibilities of attracting skilled labour in order to stimulate new sectors of the economy. However, what makes the immigration issue in Portugal most interesting is the attention the state has paid to issues of migrant integration since the mid-1990s, and what this reveals about the relationship between interest groups and the state. While a lack of formal policy consultation and interest group incorporation may not have served Portugal particularly well when it comes to the consideration of strictly labour market issues, the informal and incorporative nature of policy consultation with migrant groups has played some role in allowing the country to address these issues. This is reflected institutionally: while the repressive and regulatory aspects of immigration policy are administered through the *Serviço de Estrangeiros e Fronteiras* (Foreigners' and Borders Service or SEF), migrant integration is dealt with by ACIME. ACIME was not only the product of the gradual and relatively informal incorporation of leaders of migrant communities and migrants' rights organizations into the political process, but performs an ongoing role in bringing such groups in civil society close to the state.

The policy problem

As in Ireland, Portugal's history of mass migration was shaped by a combination of political oppression and simply dire poverty. In the post-war period, to this was added a desire by many to avoid military service, which might have included many years fighting resistance in Portugal's African colonies during the 1960s. Policy until this time and especially under Salazar was dominated by attempts to regulate and stem mass emigration.[32] There is thus no real history of immigration in Portugal until the end of the colonial wars and the Revolution of 1974. Democratization brought efforts to strengthen the right to emigrate, with Article 44 of the 1976 Constitution guaranteeing freedom to both migrate and return. The pattern of Portuguese workers seeking work in Europe established during the 1960s was intensified during the economic crises of the 1970s that accompanied the country's rocky road to democracy, but this slowed during the 1980s as unemployment in Western Europe became a permanent part of the economic landscape.[33] On the other hand, and much more significantly, the seeds of Portuguese immigration policy for the next four decades were sown by the massive influx of *retornados* or 'returned ones', in effect refugees from the newly liberated African colonies of especially Cape Verde, Mozambique, Angola, and Guinea-Bissau. Since no official data pertaining to the 'return' of such migrants was ever collected, only estimates of the number of returning migrants are available. Based usually on census figures, these range between five hundred thousand to over one million (Carrington and de Lima, 1996: 334). This latter development is important for at least two different reasons. First, the *retornados* required much assistance from local communities in order to integrate them into Portuguese economy and society. Second, mass immigration and integration, especially by those who were actually considered Portuguese citizens even if born overseas and often racially and culturally different from the inhabitants of the Portuguese nation-state, in the long-run bred tolerance for immigration that is today measured in very little anti-immigration sentiment, if not always racial harmony (Machado, 1993).

Immigration statistics reveal a slowed but steady trickle of migrants from the lusophone or Portuguese-speaking countries through the 1980s with the return of political stability to Portugal, which carried through the 1990s. Added to that, the collapse of communism in Eastern Europe set off a new wave of immigration after 1989, this time from clearly non-Portuguese speaking countries and representing an entirely new phenomenon. The reporting of official immigration figures for Portugal is notoriously difficult because the data is complicated not only by the large number of illegal migrants who arrived during the 1980s and 1990s but also by the policy response favoured by Portuguese governments until very recently. Regularization schemes, as discussed in the Greek case, aim to legalize migrants already settled in the country and thus contribute to sudden jumps in numbers that do not necessarily reflect the sudden increase in the arrival of migrants. Added to that is the grey-area status of many individuals and families from Portuguese-speaking Africa who were not originally counted as foreigners resident in Portugal because they were officially considered Portuguese citizens until the break with the colonies occurred. This means that the increases in African immigration sometimes identified in the 1970s and early 1980s is thus partly attributable to some African-born residents already living in Portugal losing their citizen status.[34]

Despite these difficulties, it is worth reviewing the data in order to illustrate Portugal's transformation from a country of migration to a country of immigration. Between 1975 and 2001, the number of foreigners (legally) resident in the country had increased by an average of 7 per cent per year, fuelled not only by intensification of migration from Africa but also but the diversification of the migrant community to include Europeans, Brazilians, and eventually but noticeably Indians and Chinese (Pires, 2002: 152). In 1986, there were 86,791 foreign residents legally residing in Portugal, doubling to 190,896 in 1999, with major legalization efforts occurring between 1992 and 1996 (Fiolhais, 2003: 95–6). More detailed breakdown of immigration data is available after 1998, following not only increased oversight but also greater interest in the subject on the part of government and academia, which is measured in the increased research output on the subject after this time and especially that commissioned by the semi-autonomous *Observatório da Imigração.* Between 1998 and 2001, the acceleration of immigration from Eastern Europe began to be clearly reflected in the statistics, with an especially high number of resident permits issued to migrants from the Ukraine (Pires, 2002: 156). Yet census data from 2001 also reveals that African migrants still constitute the majority of the foreign resident population, at 56 per cent of the total, followed by migrants from the Americas at 24 per cent, compared to only 13 per cent from Europe overall (de Sousa *et al.*, 2004: 56).

The policy problem has thus been, on the one hand, how to create channels for the arrival of migrants without a pre-existing legal basis for doing so and, further, how best to tie policy into labour market needs. The vast majority of migrants to Portugal take up unskilled or low-skilled jobs, with no real corresponding effort to recruit high-skilled migrants as Ireland, for instance, has increasingly tried to do. On the other hand, the state has had to find ways to integrate new migrant communities, who are increasingly less likely to speak the language and know the customs of their host country. Portugal has actually achieved better results on the second score than on the first. The following section details how this has come about.

The role of consultation and incorporation in the shaping of policy responses

Portugal represents the most interesting and mixed set of approaches to immigration policy out of the three national cases compared in this book. While migrant integration policy is relatively advanced, immigration policy proper is not, and patterns of interest group consultation and incorporation also vary across the two different wings of immigration policy in a corresponding way. There is much more evidence for ongoing, if not always peak-level, consultation with interest groups, especially migrant organizations, in the integration policy arena than in the formation of labour migration policies. Chapter 3 identified organized labour, business, and migrant and human rights organizations as potentially important interest groups for the state to consult in the field of immigration policy. Traditional peak-level corporatist or Irish-style social partnership arrangements could provide one avenue for negotiating immigration policy between economic interest groups. While Portugal does have such a system, formal tri-partite negotiations have been much more limited to strictly industrial relations issues in Portugal than they have been in Ireland. The lack of formal lobby group pressure on the part of both organized labour and business in Portugal over immigration policy may be in part due to the ambivalent attitude of both sets of groups to the issue. The union movement is naturally wary of the possibility that low-paid illegal migrants may undercut the pay and working conditions of Portuguese workers, but there has also been considerable resistance on the part of professional organizations to the importation of skilled labour. Employer groups may formally favour the construction of legal channels for the importation of labour where skills gaps exist, but some businesses may also benefit from the exploitation of relatively cheap migrant labour.

Another possible reason for the lack of a robust national-level consultative process surrounding immigration policy is the fact that policy formulation and implementation is so splintered in this case. As will be detailed below, a *Report*

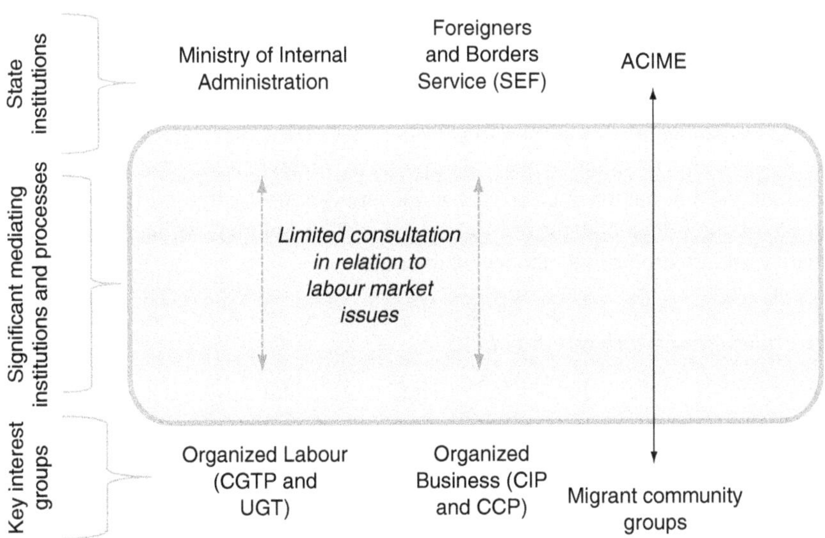

Figure 6.3 The zone of mediation in Portuguese immigration policy.

on Unsatisfied Labour Market Needs is regularly produced in Portugal, with primary responsibility for this aspect of immigration policy resting with the labour inspectorate. Yet most of the responsibility for administering immigration law resides with the Foreigners and Borders Service (SEF), which sees itself in primarily a technical role and is not a policy-making body. Policy-making in the field is housed in the Ministry of Internal Administration (MAI), but there is no special department dedicated to the formulation of immigration policy, and it is very unclear how the activities of the MAI are co-ordinated with those of the labour inspectorate. Many other countries with long histories of immigration have created distinctive immigration departments or ministries that combine the functions of these different institutions and provide a potential 'home' for coordinated policy consultation. This is something that is also lacking in the Irish case discussed in Chapter 4.

On the other hand, there is a very clear consultative and incorporative tradition being built in the field of migrant integration policy in Portugal, even if this occurs in a fragmented manner and at a low level of the political system. A dialogue between the state and migrant interest groups, chiefly through ACIME, seems to work well for the purposes of (a) distributing resources and information to migrant groups and, through those groups, individual migrants, (b) providing feedback to the state on how well certain anti-racist programmes or other sorts of integration policy are working, and (c) gaining the co-operation and support of migrant organizations by tying them in to the state through both (a) and (b). This last aspect shows the extent to which incorporation as much as consultation is at work. What the interface with migrant organizations in ACIME's structure does not provide, however, is an opportunity for input on wider aspects of immigration policy, especially that related to labour market needs and the recruitment of specific types of skilled labour from overseas. In fact, such topics would probably fall outside the interests of most of migrant organizations that ACIME deals with, considering that they tend to be based on cultural interests and concerned with basis integration issues.

The remainder of this discussion further underlines the correlation between the absence of consultative and incorporative policymaking and the lack of coordination that has characterized overall immigration policy on the one hand and the parallel development of migrant integration policy in an increasing consultative and incorporative manner on the other.

The evolution of immigration policy

Turning now to state responses to Portugal's new status as a nation of immigration, major changes have occurred in the field of immigration law and policy over the past two decades. These can be characterized as shifting slowly from ad hoc attempts to deal with the influx of migrants, and especially to the problem of illegality, towards a more comprehensive and coherent approach to labour migration that was still in the process of formation by the late 2000s. Until the early 1990s, when the problem of how to adjust immigration law to deal with the new immigration reality became more pressing, the framework for legal immigration into Portugal was laid out in Decree-Law 264-B of 1981. This outlined the process for applying for Portuguese residency, giving practically all institutional oversight to the *Serviço de Estrangeiros* (Foreigners' Service), which was soon renamed the *Serviço de Estrangeiros e Fronteiras* (Foreigners' and Borders Service or SEF). Applications for Portuguese residency could be made outside the country through overseas consulates or within Portugal through the SEF. Three types of residency authorization could be granted, varying from one-year renewable permits to permanent residency for those migrants who had already been living in Portugal for twenty consecutive years. In order to work legally, migrants were also required to apply for an additional working visa (Ferreira and Rato, 2000: 33–4). The 1981 legislation has been criticized on the grounds that it was largely repressive in nature, emphasizing conforming with Portuguese law above anything else when considering applications for residency. By apparently putting 'national interest', even political order, at the fore of immigration policy and using the same mechanisms for the control of the migrant population as before, the legal framework was 'imbued with the ideological principles of the previous regime'.[35] Probably much more importantly for this analysis, by making immigration largely a security issue, no connections were made between labour market requirements and the migrant population. At the same time and on a related point, legislation failed to take into account the new waves of migration to Portugal, particularly of the irregular variety, which were already beginning take place in the early 1980s. Estimates put the number of illegal migrants at around 70,000 or up to 30 per cent of migrants entering the country by the mid-1990s (Baganha, 2000: 86; Eaton, 1993).

Along with the increased problem of illegal migration, complying with the EU's Schengen Agreement also shaped changes to immigration policy during the early 1990s, which task fell to the centre-right Social Democrat (PSD) government that came to power in 1991. The Agreement posed a challenge for the Southern European countries overall, but most notably Portugal and Spain, since many West European nations argued during negotiations that the South represented the 'soft underbelly' of Europe when it came to immigration policy. In other words, these nations had, by tolerating a high level of illegality, created a climate in which they were likely to be viewed by irregular migrants as a backdoor route to the rest of Europe. Thus, the general direction of the PSD's immigration policy between 1991 and 1995 was to tighten up the existing legal framework to try to deal more fully with the problems of illegality and border security including the 1992–1993 restructuring of the SEF (Santos, 2004: 112). Asylum and refugee law was also tightened: although Portugal was never a recipient of large numbers of asylum applications, only forty-nine out of 457 applications were granted two years after the new regulations were implemented (Corkill and Eaton, 1999: 158–9). It is also interesting to note, in this specific context, how the 1990 Schengen Convention and the discussions surrounding it caused some degree of tension between Portugal and the Portuguese-speaking former colonies who had historically been extended a policy of 'positive

Table 6.3 Major developments in Portuguese immigration policy

Year	*Policy development*
1981	Decree-Law 264-B establishes limited framework for immigration into Portugal
1993	Decree-Law 59/93 re-enacts much of 1981 legislation but tightens security measures and strengthens role of SEF
1992–1993	First regularization campaign
1996	Second regularization campaign
1995	Establishment of ACIME
1998	244/98 provides for some new forms of labour migration, particularly with respect to temporary/seasonal workers and brings legislation into line with EU commitments
1999–2002	Major expansion of ACIME's functions
2001	New Immigration Act

discrimination' with regard to immigration matters (Santos, 2004: 110). Policy-makers thus had to negotiate between integration with Europe and the continuation of its relationship with non-European regions from which a proportion of Portugal's (unskilled) labour force was increasingly drawn.

At the same time that the legal framework governing border control, security, and asylum seeking was tightened, government policy began a long-term attempt to recognize and control the important role that migrant labour, and especially informal migrant labour, played in the Portuguese economy. The chief mechanism for achieving this was a series of regularization schemes, the first of which took place between October 1992 and March 1993 and aimed to formalize the status of the many migrant workers who had settled in Portugal since the 1980s, the main condition being the ability to prove Portuguese residency for a certain period of time. Although around 80,000 migrants applied under this scheme, only 39,166 were legalized, with three-quarters of these originally from Portuguese-speaking Africa. A large number of Brazilians were also granted residency, along with significant but much smaller numbers of Chinese, Senegalese, and Pakistanis. A further 35,000 individuals were legalized in 1996, aimed at covering those already in the country who had missed out on the earlier campaign, or whose permits had expired in the meantime (Baganha, 2000: 85).

As witnessed in Greece, the problem with regularization campaigns for countries with skills shortages such as Portugal, Greece, and to a lesser extent, Ireland, is that because they constitute a market-driven rather than state-led response to filling gaps in the labour market, they do very little to assist in the shifting of economic development strategies where the market fails to do so. In other words, regularization schemes attract or legitimize the arrival of unskilled migrants when a long-term strategy for economic development, assuming developmental goals are increasingly tied to a high-skill, high-wage strategy, requires the attraction of skilled labour. As the above discussion on education policy showed, Portugal still suffers from an oversupply of social science and humanities graduates and not enough highly skilled technical workers. Most OECD countries outside Asia suffer from skills gaps in the computing industry, for example, and Portugal is no exception here having done little to develop this important sector. This is not to say that Portugal has not benefited from the importation of unskilled labour or that these migrants do not fill a very important place in the Portuguese economy, but rather that an immigration policy based mainly on ad hoc legalization is probably not enough to match policy with development needs. Informal labour in the Portuguese case is overwhelmingly utilized in the construction sector, dominated especially by African migrants, and the service sector and more especially the restaurant trade, which is dominated by Brazilians. New migrant groups from Asia tend to engage more in small business ownership, whereas the new Eastern European migrants may arrive with more skills and yet may still drift into the service sector.[36]

Accompanying the 'extraordinary' legalization campaigns were further reviews of the existing framework governing regular or normal migration. While the challenges of European integration, especially the Schengen Convention and later the Treaty of Amsterdam which dealt with the principle of free movement within the European Union, had an impact on the policy debate from the early 1990s, these developments did not have a significant impact on actual legislation until 1998. Rather, the 1993 update of the regular process of applying for Portuguese residency substantially carried through the requirements of the previous framework established in 1981. Decree-Law 59/93 again outlined the conditions upon which residency permits were to be granted, allocating key responsibility for overseeing this process to the SEF. While much remained the same in the new law, some differences can be observed which amount to a gradual extension of rights to foreign residents. The new framework gave greater consideration to issues of family reunification and established a judicial process for the expulsion of migrants that had not existed before (Ferreira and Rato, 2000: 38–9). It also introduced the concept of a temporary working visa for the first time. These changes underline a growing concern for migrant welfare and integration issues that eventually culminated in the formation of ACIME.

The 1993 framework was then overturned, updated and re-enacted by Decree-Law 244/98, prompted mainly by the 1997 Treaty of Amsterdam and related European-level developments. By this time there had been a change in government, with the Socialist Party having been elected in 1995. While the political change this brought was most clearly reflected in the establishment of ACIME, discussed below, the 1998 legislation mostly carried through the provisions of Decree-Law 59/93 when it came to the treatment of non-EU citizens. Again, there was more attention paid to the issue of labour migration than there had been in the past, but very little attention paid to the deliberate attraction of skills and the rules regarding work permits remained cumbersome. A distinction was made between seasonal and non-seasonal work, where seasonal workers were permitted to enter the country for up to six months out of every twelve but were obliged to reside outside the country for those remaining six months. Other migrants were permitted working visas for a two-year period that could not be renewed from within the country, and a further distinction was made here between salaried workers, whose entry was permitted on the basis of a guaranteed job offer, and independent or self-employed workers. These provisions did not substantially alter the 1993 law (Ferreira and Rato, 2000: 46–8). EU nationals, on the other hand, were generally granted five-year renewable work permits, in line with European-level policy commitments.

By far the most significant development to occur under the Socialist government, however, was the establishment of ACIME. This state organ was initially constituted in 1995 and originally mainly limited to the work of one individual, the first High Commissioner, José Leitão. Two key interest groups joined forces with Socialist Party representatives in order to lobby for the creation of such a post: leaders of the lusophone African migrant community and left-leaning elements of the Catholic Church.[37] Commissioner Leitão was aligned with the latter and initially charged with creating a dialogue between various government departments and migrant communities on integration issues. It was widely judged within these circles that increased immigration had been accompanied by increased instances of racism, threatening Portugal's image as one of the more tolerant European societies. The role and functions of the High Commissioner were gradually expanded, first in 1999–2000 and again in 2002, eventually reconstituting the organization that had been built up around Leitão's work as the High Commission for Immigrants and Ethnic Minorities (ACIME).[38]

While the SEF's functions are largely repressive in nature, ACIME presents a softer side of the state to migrant communities. Significantly, the latter is legally bound not to report any of its activities including the identification of any illegal migrants to the SEF. Much of ACIME's expanded role concerns the provision of advice, through service centres, to individual migrants on access to state services. In addition to its relationship with the research organization, the Immigration Observatory, ACIME also oversees a Commission for Equality and against Racial Discrimination (CICDR) and an Advisory Board for Immigration Affairs (COCAI). The latter organization includes broad based representation including from the largest, Portuguese-speaking, migrant communities. ACIME is also responsible for administering a dedicated set of funds to support the work of migrant organizations, with which it has continuous contact. For the purposes of this book, this relationship ACIME cultivates with migrant organizations is the most interesting part of its work, but it should be noted that much of that relationship occurs on a one-to-one basis between individual migrants and the state body. Furthermore, many of the 'officially recognized' immigrant associations ACIME deals with, over one hundred in total, are primarily cultural groups. There is no centralized umbrella organization representing migrant interests, and representation is heavily splintered along ethnic lines.

Portugal's 1998 immigration legislation had continued to place restrictions on labour migration while governments attempted to deal with the problem of illegal migration through one-off, ad hoc regularization efforts. Soon after the 1998 legislation was enacted, however, it appeared that this combined strategy was not working since floods of irregular migrants continued to arrive, increasingly from Eastern Europe. Although several more major regularization programmes took place, a gradual shift towards developing a comprehensive labour migration framework can be observed after 2000. This represents a policy improvement in the sense that Portugal has begun to think more about how to match labour market requirements to migration policy, and yet there is a continuing absence of debate about the possibility of deliberately incorporating skills-based migration into the policy mix. It is the subject of academic discussion, but not much more.

A major departure occurred in 2001 with the passage of a new Immigration Act, which aimed to make the labour migration system more flexible at the same time that new rules to combat illegal migration were put in place. As the above discussion illustrates, the encouragement of legal migration is relatively new in the Portuguese context, and required substantial legislative review. In addition to the introduction of measures designed to streamline and speed up the application process for work permits, work visas could also be renewed from within Portugal for either a two-year period or an indefinite length of time. Those holding a work visa would also be permitted rights of family reunification, which had previously only been awarded to migrants with full residence permits, though family members were not themselves guaranteed work visas. The main innovation in this area, however, was to introduce a new type of permit that can be thought of as something in between a work visa and a full residency permit, the latter no longer requiring an accompanying additional work visa. These 'stay permits' would be valid for five years and constituted a more permanent system for dealing with the problem of illegality, since they may be issued to foreign workers living in Portugal regardless of how they initially entered the country. Eligibility rested on a written job offer from an approved employer and a series of security controls.[39]

The 2001 Act also paid some attention to the possibility of signing special agreements with non-EU countries to facilitate the importation of labour in order to fill gaps in the labour market. This is clearly a strategy long favoured by Portugal and its former colonies, since it seeks to maintain links through a shared language and culture at the same time that it meets economic need. It is also a way for the Portuguese state to balance its commitments to European integration at the same time as it satisfies those traditional ties. Further on this theme, a special regularization programme was carried out during 2003–2004 specifically for Brazilian workers. An additional general legalization scheme was also carried out during this period for migrant workers with proof of income and social security payments made in Portugal for the three months prior to applying (Fonseca *et al.*, 2005: 2).

The PSD government also intended to deal with illegal migration under the 2001 Act by targeting the employers of irregular labour, with the employment of illegal labour considered a crime for the first time. This again seemed to present a new approach in the Portuguese context. However, illegality remained and still remains a significant problem. In 2002, a change of government occurred, resulting in further work in this area and especially in response to the tightening labour market situation. Shortly after ascending to power, the PSD-led government's programme for the next term argued that the power of the state had been increasingly weakened in the past few years with respect to illegal migration and that security was an issue to be dealt with.[40] Shortly afterward, the 2001 Immigration Act was amended so that it was no longer possible to apply for working visas from within Portugal. This was intended to stop the very common pattern of overseas students and short-term visitors taking up paid employment before attempting to legalize their status through applying for a work visa. Reportedly, much of the push for a crackdown on illegal migration came from the SEF, perhaps left out on the cold during the term of the PS government and its preoccupation with integration issues.[41]

In general, the beginning of the twenty-first century witnessed a significant turn towards the consideration of labour market needs in the field of immigration policy. Not only was increased attention paid to the work visa system and the discouragement of irregular migration through the introduction of the stay permit, but, in theory, Portugal also maintained a formal quota system for the importation of labour during this period. This quota is set by a two-yearly publication of a government *Report on Unsatisfied Labour Market Needs* that is supposed to identify labour market gaps by sector. There are a number of problems with this system, however, reflected in the fact that in 2004, for example, the quota was set at 6,500, and yet, by 2005, only 4,500 applicants had been accepted. Many of these were already living in Portugal, rather than applying from outside the country. In other words, the system fails to recruit new workers from overseas and by becoming yet another means by which to regularize migrants already working in the country illegally, does very little to discourage illegal migration. Possible reasons for the failure of the quota system that have been identified include the complexity of negotiating the bureaucracy involved in using the system, especially for business; the ineffectiveness of the recruitment processes established through bilateral agreements with foreign countries; a mismatch between the real and predicted needs of the labour market; and inefficiency and possible corruption when it comes to administering the programme in overseas consulates (Esteves *et al.*, 2003: 3–4).

Furthermore, labour migration appears for the main part limited to the unskilled and semi-skilled variety, with little attempt to reorient the legal framework towards the attraction of foreign skilled workers. This might not be such a problem if the importation of low-skilled workers to work in low paid jobs permitted Portuguese workers to fill skilled positions, but this is not necessarily the case. Young Portuguese graduates, as in other small countries, are obviously likely to be attracted to higher paid positions overseas. As a recent report to an international working group on migration noted, the 'brain drain' debate that occupies such a prominent place in the debate over immigration policy in developed countries does not really exist in Portugal (Esteves *et al.*, 2003: 19). The same report also notes an actual resistance to the presence of skilled migrants in the Portuguese economy, for fear of competition with local professionals and young graduates. Similarly, in an article presented as a government-sponsored study on the issue, João Peixoto laments the focus of public attention in the migration debate on low skilled workers and how to avoid their marginalization and urges the government to reorient policy toward 'the deliberate recruitment of qualified professionals for certain sectors of the economy, such as information technology and health' (2002a: 65).

Conclusions

Portugal is, in many ways, the most difficult case study in this book to analyse. Policy success in Portugal is of a patchy nature, which can in part be explained by the fact that policymaking processes designed to bridge the gap between policymakers and stakeholders are established very unevenly across various arenas of state activity. Where such institutions and processes exist, they tend to be less genuinely consultative than effectively incorporative. Furthermore, they tend to be constituted at lower levels of the political system that they do in Ireland, meaning that they provide some channel for public or interest group input, but not in a way that can easily translate into policy detail or contribute to fundamental policy shifts. The discussion that follows also shows that although some extremely progressive and creative policy responses have resulted from decisions made from within the public administration without any serious input from policy stakeholders, these policy decisions often suffer because they do not reflect the reality of the problem as ordinary citizens experience it. Much of this contemporary pattern of state–society relations as reflected in policymaking institutions and processes is a result of legacies that actually precede the democratization process that began in the mid-1970s.

This chapter has argued that the uneven reorientation of Portuguese public policy around the needs of a high-wage, high-skill, knowledge-based economy is in part due to the fact that it has relied on the initiative of individuals or factions of the government and public administration more than it has on centralized negotiation between interest groups. This means that the extent to which Europeanized policy goals and values are embraced varies not only across time but also across different aspects of the same policy arena. Does it matter how policies are formed, so long as action is taken? There are at least two reasons why change through enlightened leadership without consultation with key interest groups is problematic. First, if policy development is dependent on particular individuals or political party factions, it is also vulnerable to change or stagnation once these individuals or factions leave the scene. This has been more clearly a problem for Portugal in the higher education field, where education pact-making as well as active policy development only occurred as long as one particularly enlightened Minister of Education guided the policy area. Second, especially relevant to the case of policies for work–life balance, a lack of insight from street-level policy experts may mean the policy fails to do what it is supposed to do. The Socialists' paternity leave legislation implemented during the 1990s is widely regarded as a particularly progressive move, but it is not clear that it will do very much to reduce tensions of work–life balance faced after the first year or two of parenthood. The problem of unintended consequences that is increased by a lack of consultation also appeared in higher education policy. The privatization approach pursued in the 1980s was informed by pro-market ideologies popular at the time but not by the consultation and incorporation of the higher education sector, including private institutions themselves. There is an additional third reason as to why policy change through enlightened leadership can prove problematic, although this is much more relevant to the Greek case and especially with respect to education policy, discussed in the following chapter: if policy decisions are made by enlightened leaders without the cooperation let alone active support of the key interest groups required to implement those policies, they can become unworkable. This represents a case of failure to incorporate as much as failure to consult. In Portugal, there is a tendency towards incorporation but much less genuine consultation.

Notes

1 On the collapse of the First Republic see Costa Pinto (2000) and Schwartzman (1989).

2 Especially in the agricultural Alentejo region, often considered the hotbed of Portuguese protest given that this was where the liberal First Republic was also declared. See Bermeo (1986). On mass mobilization as a necessary component of a 'social' revolution, see Skocpol (1979).

3 Good details of electoral outcomes during this period and the emerging party system are found in Ferreira and Marshall (1986); Bermeo (1987); Bruneau (1997); and Manuel (1996).

4 The pivotal document here is Cavaco Silva (1984).

5 On some of these legacies see Fishman (2003).

6 For example, see the otherwise comprehensive Rowat (1988), which includes a chapter on Spain.

7 When researching the formulation of policies for the reconciliation of work and family life, I was repeatedly directed to the *Codigo Laboral,* even though I was asking questions about *how* and *why* policies were made.

8 Local-level participatory decision-making is making a comeback in Portugal. See the special issue of *South European Society and Politics* 9, 2 (2004).

9 I originally owe this observation to Dr Fernando Luís Machado, a long-time student of immigration politics in Portugal, who points to a number of individuals from the former African colonies who had become activists for mainstream political parties rather than attempt to work through migrant rights' organizations. Virgínia Ferreira (2000) gives a slightly different explanation for the failure of independent women's organizations to develop, arguing that since rights were handed down from above in the wake of the revolution, women became accustomed to not having to fight for anything. Activists on women's issues whom I was directed to during the course of this research were either aligned closely to one of the main political parties or occupied permanent policymaking positions in the public service, or both.

10 From Eurostat data, see Table 2.4, this volume.

11 This point is made in OECD (2004), 18. In addition, very good data which proves the point can be found in Boeri *et al.*, (2005), 21, Table 2.6. This data shows very little variation in the take-up of part-time work by women in Portugal with children compared to those without children, in contrast to other European countries.

12 Interview with Odette Philipe, Equality Officer, General Confederation of Portuguese Workers, Lisbon, 20 October 2005. See Cousins (2000) for evidence that family incomes in Portugal are the lowest in the EU.

13 Interview with Maria Cuhna Rego, Senior Policy Advisor on Equality Policy 1997–2001, Lisbon, 5 October 2005.
14 The fact that the state's commitment to gender equality has never been matched by strong mobilization of Portuguese women is emphasized by Ferreira (2000).
15 English version of the Portuguese Constitution (revised 1997) at www.parlamento.pt/, Articles 67, Parts one and two.
16 Interview with Josefina Leitão, Former Chairperson of CITE, 7 October 2005. Much of the remainder of this discussion of CITE's role is informed primarily by this interview.
17 For example, during the early 1990s at least, a group known as the Consultative Council for the Commission for Equality and Women's Rights, which included a non-government organization wing, (Organizações Não Governmentais Do Conselho Consultativo da Comissão para a Igualdade e para os Direitos das Mulheres) appears to have been in existence. However, no policymaking official or Portuguese academic consulted in the course of this research mentioned such an organization or considered it important.
18 On Portuguese 'neo-corporatism' see Barreto and Naumann (1998); Campos and Naumann (2000); Quarternaire Portugal and Centro de Estudios de Economia Industrial do Trabalho e da Empresa (1997); and Royo (2002).
19 I have two specific cases with accompanying documentation held by these organizations and on which this analysis is based. Comissão para a Igualdade e para os Direitos das Mulheres (1991), and Director-Geral da Família (1989).
20 Interview with Maria Cunha Rego, Lisbon, 5 November 2005.
21 Interview with Josefina Leitão, 7 October 2005.
22 OECD (2004), 133. For details of the policy shift see Wall (2004).
23 Ministério da Educação (1996). See also Eduardo Marçal Grilo, *Intervenções 1: Política e Acção na árena Educativo.* Lisbon: Ministério da Educação [Portugal], 1996 for further discussion of the *Pact on Education.*
24 Interviews with the President of the Union of Students in Ireland and the Fórum Académico para a Informação e Representação Externa were conducted in Dublin on 28 April 2005 and in Lisbon on 26 September 2005 respectively.
25 Correira *et al.*, (2004). That concerns for regional development needs drove the creation of the public polytechnic system is emphasized in Conselho Nacional de Educação (2002), 101–2.
26 Interview with Pedro Lourtie, former Secretary of State for Higher Education, Lisbon, 1 October 2005.
27 This seeming natural tendency associated with system drift is something that has happened with the conversion of polytechnics to universities in Australia and the UK, and is one of the main reasons why Irish policymakers have continued to defend the rigidity of the binary system.
28 This was primarily the view put across in interviews with both Pedro Lourtie, former Secretary of State for Higher Education, Lisbon, 1 October 2005, and Eduardo Marcal Grilo, former Minister of Education, Lisbon, 12 October 2005.
29 Interview with former Minister of Education, Lisbon, 12 October 2005. On the ideological dimension see also Amaral and Teixeira (2000), 250.
30 For examples of academic research on the subject see Balsa *et al.*, (2001), and Ferreira de Almeida *et al.*, (2003). Both works are presented as investigations on the behalf of government departments.
31 Interview with former Minister of Education Eduardo Marcal Grilo 12 October 2005. See also Conselho Nacional de Educação (2004), which has an extended debate on Portugal's relationship to the 'knowledge society', and Grilo (2002).
32 On Portugal's history of emigration and the laws that attempted to control emigration under Salazar's *Estado Novo* see Rocha-Trindade (1993).
33 See the background discussion to emigration policy before the 1980s in Santos (2004), 17–18.

34 This complication in the data was helpfully pointed out to the author by officials at ACIME during a visit in October 2005.
35 Ferreira and Rato (2000), 36. My translation.
36 On the reliance of the construction sector on (informal) African migration see Mendoza (2003), and on the entrepreneurial strategies of the new migrant communities originating especially from Asia see de Oliveira (2004).
37 Much of my understanding of ACIME's creation and work comes from its own publications in addition to interview material collected on a visit to the organization with several different mid-ranking ACIME advisors and managers in Lisbon, 7 October 2005.
38 Since the Portuguese state does in general adopt an assimilationist model in migrant integration matters, however, 'ethnic minorities' is a euphemism for Portuguese indigenous gypsies rather than new migrant groups or second-generation migrant communities. Thanks are due to an ACIME organizer for pointing this out.
39 The details of the 2001 Act and especially the new stay permit system are discussed fully in de Sousa, (2002), 49–69.
40 Cited in Santos (2004), 105–06. The idea that the Portuguese state is unable to control inward migration is also put forward in Peixoto, (2002b), but Peixoto also argues that this is a problem increasingly experienced by all states, rather than the fault of any national policy regime.
41 The details of the SEF's involvement in policy formulation during this period is discussed in Esteves *et al.*, (2003), 7.

References

Amaral, Alberto and Pedro Teixeira, "The Rise and Fall of the Private Sector in Portuguese Higher Education", *Higher Education Policy* 13 (2000), 245–66.

Amaro, Fausto, "Portugal: Improvement of the Quality of Family Life", in W. Dumon, ed., *Changing Family Policies in the Member States of the European Union* (Luxembourg: European Union Observatory on Family Policies, 1994), 250–70.

Baganha, Maria Ioannis, "Labour Market and Immigration: Economic Opportunities for Immigrants in Portugal", in Russell King, Gabriella Lazaridis, and Charalambos Tsardanidis, eds, *Eldorado or Fortress? Migration in Southern Europe* (Basingstoke, UK: Macmillan: 2000), 79–103.

Balsa, Casimiro, José Alberto Simões, Pedro Nunes, Renato do Carmo and Ricardo Campos, *Perfil dos Estudantes do Ensino Superior: Desigualdades e Diferenciação* (Lisbon: Edicões Colibri, 2001).

Balsemão, Francisco Pinto, "The Constitution and Politics: Options for the Future", in Kenneth Maxwell ed., *Portugal in the 1980s: Dilemmas of Democratic Consolidation* (New York: Greenwood Press, 1986), 197–232.

Barreto, José, and Reinhard Naumann, "Portugal: Industrial Relations Under Democracy", in Anthony Ferner and Richard Hyman, eds, *Changing Industrial Relations in Europe*, 2nd edn (Oxford: Blackwell, 1998), 445–81.

Bermeo, Nancy, *Revolution in the Revolution: Workers' Control in Rural Portugal* (Princeton, NJ: Princeton University Press, 1986).

Bermeo, Nancy "Redemocratization and Transition Elections: A Comparison of Spain and Portugal", *Comparative Politics* 19, 2 (1987), 213–331.

Boeri, Tito, Daniela Del Boca, and Christopher Pissarides, eds, *Women at Work: An Economic Perspective* (Oxford: Oxford University Press, 2005).

Bruneau, Thomas, ed., *Political Parties and Democracy in Portugal: Organizations, Elections, and Public Opinion* (Boulder, CO: Westview Press, 1997).

Campos, Maria da Paz and Reinhard Naumann, "Social Pacts in Portugal: From Comprehensive Policy Programmes to the Negotiation of Concrete Industrial Relations Reform?", in Philippe Pochet and Giuseppe Fajertag, eds, *Social Pacts in Europe* (Brussels: European Trade Union Institute, 2000), 321–42.

Cardoso, Ana Rute, "Women at Work and Economic Development: Who's Pushing What?", *Review of Radical Political Economy* 28, 3 (1996), 1–34.

Carrington, William J. and Pedro J. F. de Lima, "The Impact of the 1970s Repatriates from Africa on the Portuguese Labor Market", *Industrial and Labor Relations Review* 49, 2 (1996), 330–47.

Capucha, Luís, Teresa Bomba, Rita Fernandes, and Gisela Matos, "Portugal – a Virtuous Path Toward Minimum Income?", in Maurizio Ferrera, ed., *Welfare State Reform in Southern Europe: Fighting Poverty and Social Exclusion in Italy, Spain, Portugal, and Greece* (London and New York: Routledge, 2005), 204–65.

Cavaco Silva, Aníbal A., *Pacto Social e Politica de Rendimentos* (Lisbon: Faculdade de Ciências Humanas da Universidade Católica Portuguesa, 1984).

Comissão para a Igualdade e para os Direitos das Mulheres [Portugal], *O Emprego das Mulheres e as Estucturas de Apoio às Crianças.* Seminar notes (Lisbon: Organizações Não Governamentais Do Conselho Consultativo da Comissão para a Igualdade e para os Direitos das Mulheres, 1991).

Conceição, Pedro and Manuel V. Heitor, eds, *Innovation for All? Learning from the Portuguese Path to Technical Change and the Dynamics of Innovation* (Westport, CT: Praeger, 2005).

Conselho Nacional de Educação [Portugal], *Diversificação e Diversidade de Ensino Superior: O Caso Português* (Lisbon: Conselho Nacional de Educação/Ministério da Educação, 2002).

Conselho Nacional de Educação [Portugal], *As Bases da Educação.* Notes from a seminar held 16th and 30th of October 2003. (Lisbon: Conselho Nacional de Educação, 2004).

Corkill, David and Martin Eaton, "Multicultural Insertions in a Small Economy: Portugal's Immigrant Communities", in Martin Baldwin-Edwards and Joaquin Arango, eds, *Immigrants and the Informal Economy in Southern Europe* (London: Frank Cass, 1999), 149–68.

Correira, Fernanda, Alberto Amaral, and Antonio Magalhes, "Public and Private Education in Portugal: Unintended Effects of Deregulation", *European Journal of Education* 37, 4 (2004), 457–72.

Corte-Real, Isabel, "Administrative Modernisation in Portugal", in Isabel Corte-Real, Koen Nomden, Michael Kelly, and Franck Petiteville, *Administrations in Transition: Modernisation of Public Administration in Four Countries: Portugal, the Netherlands, Ireland, and France* (Maastricht: European Institute of Public Administration, 2000), 1–26.

Costa Pinto, Antonio, *Salazar's Dictatorship and European Fascism: Problems of Interpretation* (Boulder, CO and New York: Social Science Monographs/Columbia University Press, 1995).

Costa Pinto, António, "A queda da Primeira República", in Nuno Severiano Teixeira and António Costa Pinto, eds, *A Primeira República Portuguesa: Entre o Liberalismo e o Autoritarismo* (Lisbon: Edições Colibri/Instituto de História Contemporânea, Universidad Nova de Lisboa, 2000), 25–46.

Cousins, Christine, "Women and Employment in Southern Europe: The Implications of Recent Policy and Labour Market Directions", *South European Society and Politics* 5, 1 (2000), 97–122.

Cruz, Manuel Braga da and Maria Eduarda Cruzeiro, *O Desenvolvmento de Ensino Superior em Portugal: Situação e Problemas de Acesso*. Lisbon: Instituto de Ciencias Sociais da Universidade de Lisboa for Ministério de Educação, 1995.

de Almeida, João Ferreira, Patrícia Ávila, José Luís Casanova, António Firmino da Costa, Fernando Luís Machado, Susana da Cruz Martins, and Rosário Mauretti, *Diversidade na Universidade: Um Inquérito aos Estudantes de Licentiatura* (Oeiras, Portugal: Celta, 2003).

de Oliveira, Catarina Reis, "Estratégias Empresarias de Origem Imigrante em Portugal: Oportunidades tnicas e Estruturais e Recursos Pessoais", *Sociologia, Problemas e Práticas* 45 (2004), 71–98.

de Sousa, Constança Urbano, "The New Portuguese Immigration Act", *European Journal of Migration and Law* 4 (2002), 49–69.

de Sousa, Eduardo, Helena Rato, and Maria João Mortágua, *Viagens de Ulisses: Efeitos da Imigração na Economia Portuguesa* (Lisbon: Observatório da Imigração, Alto Comissariado para a Imigração e Miniorias étnicas, 2004).

Director-Geral da Família, *Tempo para o Trabalho, Tempo para a Família*. Seminar notes (Lisbon: 1989).

Ditch, John, Helen Barnes, and Jonathan Bradshaw, eds, *Developments in National Family Policies in 1995* (Luxembourg: European Observatory on National Family Policies, European Commission/University of York, 1996).

Ditch, John, Helen Barnes, and Jonathan Bradshaw eds, *Developments in National Family Policies in 1996* (Luxembourg: European Observatory on Family Policies/European Commission, 1998).

Eaton, Martin, "Foreign Residents and Illegal Immigrants: os Negros em Portugal", *Ethnic and Racial Studies* 16, 3 (1993), 536–62.

Erhel, Christine and Mathilde Guergoat-Lariviere, "Labor Market Regimes, Family Policies, and Women's Behavior in the EU", *Feminist Economics* 19, 4 (2013), 76–109.

Esping-Andersen, Gosta, ed., *Why We Need a New Welfare State* (Oxford: Oxford University Press, 2002).

Esteves, Alina, Maria Lucinda Fonseca, and Jorge Malheiros, *EU and US Approaches to the Management of Immigration: Portugal* (Brussels/Lisbon: Migration Policy Group, 2003).

European Association for Quality Assurance in Higher Education, *Quality Assurance of Higher Education in Portugal: An Assessment of the Existing System and Recommendations for a Future System*. ENQA Occasional Paper N.10 (Helsinki, November 2006).

Eurydice, *Two Decades of Reform in Higher Education in Europe: 1980 Onwards. Portugal Country Report* (Brussels: Eurydice, Information Network on Education in Europe, 2000).

Fishman, Robert M., "Shaping, not Making Democracy: The European Union and the Post-authoritarian Political Transformation of Spain and Portugal", in Sebastian Royo and Paul Manuel, eds, *From Isolation to Integration: Fifteen Years of Spanish and Portuguese Membership in Europe* (London: Frank Cass, 2003), 31–46.

Ferreira, Eduardo de Sousa and Helena Rato, *Economia e Imigrantes: Contribuição dos Imigrantes para a Economia Portuguesa* (Oeiras, Portugal: Celta Editoria, 2000).

Ferreira, Hugo Gil and Michael W. Marshall, *Portugal's Revolution: Ten Years on* (Cambridge: Cambridge University Press, 1986), 209–14.

Ferreira, Vírginia, "Positive Action and Employment Segregation", in Vírginia Ferreira, Teresa Tavares, and Sílvia Portugal, eds, *Shifting Bonds, Shifting Bounds: Women, Mobility and Citizenship in Europe* (Oeiras, Portugal: Celta Editoria, 1998), 271–335.

Ferreira, Virgínia, "Sexualizando Portugal: Mundança Social, Políticas Estatais e Mobilização das Mulheres", in Antonio Costa Pinto, ed., *Portugal Contemporâneo* (Palto Alta, CA: The Society for the Promotion of Science and Scholarship, 2000), 180–212.

Ferrera, Maurizio, "The Southern Model of Welfare in Southern Europe", *Journal of European Social Policy* 6, 1 (1996), 17–37.

Fiolhais, Rui, "Imigração e Mercado de Tabalho em Portugal", in *Dimensão Social e Imigração* (Lisbon: Departamento de Estudos, Propectiva e Planeamento/Ministério da Segurança Social e o Trabalho [Portugal], 2003), 93–105.

Flaquer, Lluís, *Family Policy and Welfare State in Southern Europe,* Working Paper No. 185 (Barcelona: Institut de Ciències Polítiques i Socials, 2000).

Fonseca, Lucinda, Jorge Macaísta Malheiros, and Sandra Silva, *Current Immigration Debates in Europe: Portugal* (Brussels/Lisbon: Migration Policy Group, 2005).

Gautier, Anne, *The State and the Family: A Comparative Analysis of Family Policies in Industrialized Countries* (Oxford: Clarendon Press, 1996).

Lawrence S. Graham, *The Portuguese Military and the State: Rethinking Transitions in Europe and Latin America* (Boulder, CO: Westview Press, 1993).

Grilo, E. Marçal, "Ensino Formal e suas Condições", in Antonio Costa Pinto, *Portugal Hoje* (Lisbon: Instituto Nacional de Administração, 1995), 179–95.

Grilo, Eduardo Marçal, *Intervenções 1: Política e Acção na árena Educativo* (Lisbon: Ministério da Educação, 1996).

Grilo, Eduardo Marçal, *Desafios de Educação: Ideias para uma Política Educative no Século XXI* (Lisbon: Oficina do Livro, 2002).

Grilo, Eduardo Marçal and Manuel Carmelos Rosa, "The Contribution of Higher Education to Modernisation in Portugal", *European Journal of Education* 23, 3 (1988), 168–78.

Guerreiro, Maria dos Dores and Pedro Abrantes, *Incertas: Os Jovens Perante o Trabalho e a Família.* (Lisbon: Departamento de Estudos, Prospectiva e Planeamento, 2004).

Hantrais, Linda and Marie-Thérèse Letablier, *Families and Family Policies in Europe* (London and New York: Longman, 1996).

Lohkamp-Himmighofen, Marlene and Christiane Dienel, "Reconciliation Policies from a Comparative Perspective," in Linda Hantrais, ed., *Gendered Policies in Europe: Reconciling Employment and Family Life* (Basingstoke, UK: Macmillan, 2000), 49–67.

Lucas, Rui Afonso and João Francisco de Magalhaes Ilharco, "The Role of Public Administration in the Consolidation of Democracy in Portugal", in Randall Baker, ed., *Transitions from Authoritarianism: The Role of the Bureaucracy* (Westport, CT and London: Praeger, 2002), 151–65.

Machado, Fernando Luís, "Etnicidade em Portugal: O Grau Zero de Politização", in Maria Beatriz, Nizza da Silva, Maria Ioannis Baganha, Maria José Maranhão, and Miriam Halpern Pereira, eds, *Emigração/Imigração em Portugal* (Lisbon: Fragmentos, 1993), 407–14.

Manuel, Paul Christopher, *The Challenges of Democratic Consolidation in Portugal: Political, Economic, and Military Issues, 1976–1991* (Westport, CT: Praeger, 1996).

Martin, Claude, "Social Welfare and the Family in Southern Europe", in Martin Rhodes, ed., *Southern European Welfare States: Crisis and Reform* (London: Frank Cass, 1997), 23–41.

Melo, Albert, "The Absence of an Adult Education Policy as a Form of Social Control and Some Processes of Resistance", Licínio C. Lima and Paula Guimarães, eds, *Perspectives on Adult Education in Portugal* (Braga, Portugal: University of Minho, Unit for Adult Education, 2004), 40–63.

Mendoza, Cristóbal, *Labour Immigration in Southern Europe: African Employment in Iberian Labour Markets* (Aldershot, UK: Ashgate, 2003).

Ministério da Educação [Portugal], *Pacto Educativo Para o Futuro* (Lisbon: Ministério da Educação, May 1996).

Ministério da Educação [Portugal], *Autonomia e Qualidade: Documento Orientador das Políticas para o Ensino Superior* (Lisbon: Ministério da Educação, January 1997).

Ministério de Educação [Portugal], *Sistema Educação Português: Caracterização e Propostas para o Futuro* (Lisbon: Ministério de Educação, 1998).

Mozzicafreddo, Juan, "Descentalização Administrative e Inovação das Políticas Regionais em Portugal", *Sociologia-Problemas e Practicas* 41 (2003): 151–79.

OECD, *Education in OECD Developing Countries: Trends and Perspectives* (Paris: Organisation for Economic Co-operation and Development, 1974).

OECD, *Putting Citizens First: Portuguese Experience in Public Management Reform* (Paris: Organisation for Economic Cooperation and Development, 1996).

OECD, *Thematic Review of the First Years of Tertiary Education. Country Note: Portugal* (Paris: Organisation for Economic Cooperation and Development, 1998).

OECD, *Babies and Bosses. Volume 3: New Zealand, Portugal, and Switzerland* (Paris: Organisation for Economic Cooperation and Development, 2004).

Oliveira, Tania and Pedro Telhado Pereira, "Who Pays the Bill? Study Costs and Students' Income in Portuguese Higher Education", *European Journal of Education* 34, 1 (1999), 112–21.

Peixoto, João, "Os Mercados de Imigração", in Departamento de Estudos, Propectiva e Planeamento/Ministério da Segurança Social e o Trabalho, *Imigração e Mercado de Trabalho* (Lisboa, 2002a), 57–68.

Peixoto, João, "Strong Market, Weak State: the Case of Recent Foreign Immigration in Portugal", *Journal of Ethnic and Migration Studies* 28, 3 (2002b), 483–97.

Pires, Rui Pena, "Mudanças na Imigração: Uma Análise das Estatísticas sobre a População Estrangeira em Portugal, 1998–2001", *Sociologia, Problemas e Práticas* 39 (2002), 151–66.

Portugal, Sílvia, "Family and Social Policy in Portugal", *International Journal of Law, Policy and the Family* 13 (1999), 235–56.

Quarternaire Portugal and Centro de Estudios de Economia Industrial do Trabalho e da Empresa, *Labor Market Studies: Portugal* (European Commission, Luxembourg: Office for Official Publications of the European Unions, 1997).

Rocha-Trindade, Maria Beatriz, "Portugal and Spain: Culture of Migration", in Daniel Kubat, ed., *The Politics of Migration Policies: Settlement and Integration. The First World into the 1990s* (New York: Center for Migration Studies, 1993), 262–79.

Rowat, Donald C., *Public Administration in Developed Democracies: A Comparative Study* (New York: Marcel Dekker, 1988).

Royo, Sebastián, *A New Century of Corporatism? Corporatism in Southern Europe – Spain and Portugal in Comparative Perspective* (Westport, CT: Praeger, 2002).

Santos, Vanda, *O Discurso Oficial do Estado: Sobre a Emigração dos Anos 60 a 80 e Imigração dos Anos 90 à Actualidade* (Lisbon: Observatório da Imigração, Alto Comissariado para a Imigração e Miniorias étnicas, 2004).

Schmitter, Philippe C., *Corporatism and Public Policy in Authoritarian Portugal* (London: Sage Contemporary Political Sociology Series, 1, 6–11, 1975).

Schwartzman, Kathleen C., *The Social Origins of Democratic Collapse: The First Portuguese Republic* (Lawrence, KS: University of Kansas Press, 1989).

Skocpol, Theda, *States and Social Revolutions: A Comparative Analysis of France, Russia, and China* (Cambridge: Cambridge University Press, 1979).

South European Society and Politics 9, 2 (2004). Special issue.

Stoer, Stephen, *Educação e Mudança Social em Portugal 1970–1980, Uma Década de Transição* (Lisbon: Edições Afrontamento, 1986), 60–8.

Torres, Anália Cardoso, *Vida Conjugal e Trabalho: Uma Perspectiva Sociológica* (Oeiras, Portugal: Celta Editoria, 2004).

Torres, Anália Cardoso, Francisco Vieira da Dilva, Teresa Líbano Monteiro, and Miguel Cabrita, *Homens e Mulheres entre Família e Trabalh* (Lisbon: Comissão para a Igualdade no Trabalho e no Emprego, 2004).

Wall, Karin, "Developments in Family Policy in Portugal in 2003 (European Observatory on the Social Situation, Demography and the Family)", Working Paper 3–04 (Instituto de Ciências Socias da Universidade de Lisboa, 2004).

Wall, Karin, José São José, and Sónia V Correia, "Máes sós e Cuidados à Crianças", *Análise Social* 163 (2002), 631–63.

7 Conclusions and further reflections

This book started with the premise that the period between 1990 and 2008 presented both a series of challenges and a series of opportunities for highly developed democracies, within Europe as well as beyond. From the mid-1990s in particular, this was an age in which policy elites moved beyond the simplistic economic prescriptions that predominated in the 1980s and early 1990s, involving rolling back the state in favour of market forces. Concepts such as the 'knowledge economy' or, later and most pertinent to the European context, 'flexicurity', spoke to the need to shift to a high-wage, high-skill development strategy and managed to capture the imaginations of international and domestic policy actors. Whether or not this vision of the future carried with it a commitment to combatting the socio-economic inequality that began to deepen across the post-industrial world during the 1980s, ensuring that pockets of society did not get left behind as the result of technological and associated policy changes, depended on the precise mix of policies adopted at regional and national levels. The national case studies analysed here do show that overall development objectives surrounding the shift to a knowledge-based economy can be combined with social policy goals, such as increasing and broadening educational participation or assisting families in reconciling working and family life, although given external pressures such as international wage competition, these things are not always easy. Good examples of where such objectives have been combined include the programmes of the 'Rainbow Coalition' Government in Ireland of 1993–1997 and the Socialist Government in Portugal between 1995 and 1999. The question of whether this was a particularly good 'world time' for pursuing such strategies is returned to shortly.

The book has argued that the ability to take full advantage of the opportunities opened up by the influence of new ideas in the 1990s and into the 2000s depended, at least in part, on the existence of 'zones of mediation' in the three countries on which the analysis was concentrated. Having a robust tradition of policymaking that effectively combined functions of interest group consultation with interest group incorporation allows states to steer the overall policy direction armed with 'street level' expertise that members of non-government groups and organizations bring to the table, while, at the same time, makes it more likely that societal interests are kept onside during negotiations rather than becoming sources of opposition that stifle or block necessary changes. That story was traced through nine policy-level case studies across Ireland, Greece, and Portugal, all of which faced specific challenges in adjusting their overall economic and social policy frameworks around the needs requirements of the 'knowledge economy', given their traditional status as peripheral and comparatively underdeveloped countries located on Europe's western and southern fringes.

Chapter 2 argued that having a highly functioning labour market is integral to forging an economic development strategy for the twenty-first century, and that higher education and immigration policies and policy mechanisms for achieving work–life balance are just three important parts of the 'second tier' of ways that states can intervene in order to shape labour market outcomes. The choice of both policy and national case studies constituted one innovation in research design that frames the findings presented in this book. Importantly, even when political scientists do look at the ways in which state–society relations outside the realm of party politics structure policy outcomes, as this book does, they focus overwhelmingly on industrial relations or industry policy, the latter referring to the way in which states direct their economies toward certain modes of production. This is reasonable since these two policy areas constitute the first layer of the ways in which the state can influence labour market outcomes, but political scientists rarely extend their analyses to look at the second layer that is of particular interest here. The reason why this second layer of responses to labour market challenges is so interesting is that it involves a much broader set of interests, and interest groups. Studies of industrial relations and industry policy focus exclusively on the relationship between organized business, labour, and the state, whereas this research extended its analysis to include the role of university administrations and student unions, women's and charitable organizations, churches, and migrant rights organizations among others.

The choice to compare the national cases of Ireland, Portugal, and Greece was also unusual. Southern European countries are often grouped together, but both Greece and Portugal are generally under studied in the literature on European politics, and rarely are the two countries compared with non-Southern European ones on the basis of their size. Smallness matters especially when it comes to the study of responses to labour market challenges because small states cannot produce everything and fill a wide range of industrial niches in the same way that much larger states can. This means that governments need to help make national choices about which niche industries and services to develop and which labour market support structures are needed to support this development strategy. In addition, states with smaller populations also have much smaller pools of talent to draw on, making immigration and education especially important areas of policy attention. Ireland is a good choice of comparison with both Greece and Portugal because it too was comparatively undeveloped, poor, and struggling until the late 1980s. It also has some important points of difference from the two Southern European cases in terms of national political institutions, traditions, and culture, which serve to better pinpoint the importance of consultative and incorporative policymaking when it comes to the explanatory framework employed here.

The third main innovation of the analytical framework guiding the findings in this book is the attention paid to 'bringing the state back in' to the explanation of policy outcomes. The main focus is on the independent relationship between the state, defined as the executive branch of government but particularly the ongoing public administration, and interest groups. Policy study analysts look at this layer of institutions and processes that structure this relationship all the time, but it is a subject sometimes neglected by comparative political scientists whose focus is overwhelmingly on political parties and especially party system dynamics as reflected in legislative politics. The book does *not* argue that parties are somehow irrelevant to politics and even policy outcomes, because of course they do make a difference in both democratic and non-democratic circumstances. Rather, the argument is that we have to supplement the analysis of parties by looking at the sort of politics that occurs in a less explicitly political arena, since so much decision-making is in fact made in this space, especially when it comes to filling in the technical details of legislation. This may or may not involve the consultation and incorporation of interests, and the consequences of this have provided the main subject of this book.

At its most basic level of analysis, this book argues that there is at least a correlation between the extent to which policy outcomes in the three national case studies have been reoriented around the development goals of the twenty-first century and the robustness of zones of mediation in each case. Furthermore, as Table 7.1 illustrates, this correlation is relatively strong, explaining not only much of the difference between the national cases, but also between different policy areas or even aspects of policy areas within individual countries. Taking each of the national cases in turn, Ireland is the country in the sample that reoriented its policy framework the furthest between 1990 and 2008 as well as being the country that has developed the strongest consultative and incorporative policymaking processes and institutions. Chapter 4 argued that Ireland is advantaged in this respect because it has a longer democratic tradition than the other two cases, inheriting forms of consultative policymaking such as Green and White Paper public submission processes and commissions of enquiry in particular from British rule. Yet there is some variation in Ireland not only most obviously across time, but also between the three policy areas studied here. Across time, policymaking processes have becoming increasingly liberalized, moving away from a political tradition dominated by a single political party and its populist coalition in the form of Fianna Fáil and towards more open, formal, and peak-level types, the social partnership process being the most obvious new institution. At the same time, policy output has led to more successful outcomes, and especially in areas that both old and new forms of consultative and incorporative policymaking pay most attention to. Immigration policy was the least developed out of the three policy areas studied in the Irish case and it also happens to be the only area that became the subject of peak-level consultation between the state and interest groups only in the mid to late 2000s.

Table 7.1 The relationship between mediating institutions and policy adjustment

Policy Area	*Presence of Mediating Institutions*	*Principal forms*	*Quality of Processes and Institutions*	*Successful Policy Adjustment?*
Ireland				
Work–life balance	STRONG	Social partnership plus short-term commissions of enquiry	Peak-level, relatively formal, ongoing, involving wide array of actors	YES (albeit from minimal standards in recent past)
Higher education	STRONG	Social partnership plus large number of short-term commissions of enquiry and working groups	Peak-level, relatively formal, ongoing, involving wide array of actors	YES
Immigration	MEDIUM	Subject of social partnership agreements since 2000	Peak-level, relatively formal, ongoing and increasingly involving non-economic interest groups	MIXED (increasingly, although very belated)
Portugal				
Work–life balance	WEAK–MEDIUM	No real established channels outside gender-related state institutions	Informal academic influence predominates	MIXED (increasingly in some areas e.g. parental leave, but not in others e.g. use of part-time work or flexi-time)
Higher education	WEAK–MEDIUM	One-off Pact on Education	Mainly confined to elite actors, especially Council of Rectors	MIXED (much better policy results than in past but still behind Europeanized goals and standards)

continued

Table 7.1 Continued

Policy Area	*Presence of Mediating Institutions*	*Principal forms*	*Quality of Processes and Institutions*	*Successful Policy Adjustment?*
Immigration	MEDIUM (strong in integration, weak in immigration)	Integration through ACIME, minor influence of economic partners in tri-partite talks (opposition to skilled labour migration)	Incorporation of migrant interest groups, not paralleled in other aspects of policy development	MIXED (more in integration policy, much less in overall immigration framework)
Greece				
Work–life balance	WEAK	–	–	NO
Higher education	WEAK–MEDIUM	National Council on Education (ESYP)	Peak-level, relatively formal, but recent and not very inclusive	MIXED (some successes in late 2000s though too soon to assess full impact of reforms)
Immigration	WEAK	Sporadic, one-off consultations between political parties and migrant groups	Low level and minimalist	NO

Greek public policy is the least modernized, and Greek public policymaking is the least consultative and incorporative out of the three national cases. Despite more than three decades of democratization, politics and policy remains mostly an elite game. The result of this is that policymaking is highly politicized and even personalized, as is the public administration itself, consisting of the introduction of policy content often to satisfy the demands of client groups aligned with elitist political parties that have little or nothing to do with developmental needs or goals. Evidence of this is found in the frequency of complete policy reversals after changes in government or even ministers in charge of a particular policy area, rather than the gradual building of policy around a development strategy that can be witnessed in Ireland and even in Portugal. The tug-of-war over student subsidies and privileges in the case of higher education policy and over 'many children' benefits in the case of family policy are good examples. Even in Greece, however, there is some variation. The most successful example of where entrenched societal interests were able to be overridden and, to some extent, incorporated can be seen in the case of higher education through the work of the National Council of Education that managed to push through a series of reforms in the late 2000s, despite some extreme sources of opposition.

Portugal is the country in the sample with the most mixed set of policy outcomes and also in many ways the most complex policymaking tradition. Family policy has been partially oriented around new policy challenges, but interest group consultation and incorporation related to this policy arena has occurred at a very low level of the system or in a fragmented and informal way. There is no consistent tradition of consultative policymaking in the higher education field other than the ongoing relationship especially between the Universities' Council of Rectors and the state, even if there was a one-off attempt to introduce the idea of policy pact-making into the field in the late 1990s. Policy consultation and formulation is sharply splintered in the case of immigration between policies for the control of immigration itself on one hand and migrant integration policy on the other. There is much more evidence for ongoing policy consultation in the latter case than in the former, even though it can be argued that the forms of interaction between migrant groups and state agencies in this field are as much incorporative as genuinely consultative. Arguably also, although somewhat speculatively, the tendency of the Portuguese policymaking tradition toward incorporation is a phenomenon that has roots deep in a pattern of state–society relations that can be traced to the Salazar dictatorship if not before.

The correlation between policy shifts and the development of consultative and incorporative policymaking is thus reasonably clear. Two questions, however, remain. First, is there good reason to believe that the relationship is a causal one? Second, how much can policymaking traditions really explain policy outcomes, or are there other factors at play? Chapter 3 outlined the main theoretical reasons for believing that the relationship between the development of consultative and incorporative policymaking and the reorientation of development strategies is a causal one. On the one hand, consultation with policy stakeholders is important because stakeholders are also often experts in their field and highly functioning states rely on this information to fill in policy detail. To give a negative example from the case studies in which policy detail suffers from a *lack* of consultation, schemes for the regularization of illegal migrants in Greece have suffered badly because, even if formulated with good intentions in mind, their implementation has been marred by inefficiencies and even corruption, much of which could in fact be traced to their design. Some requirements of migrant workers were so unreasonable or impossible to meet under the scheme that it is more rational for those individuals to remain in Greece illegally than take part in the schemes. Migrant advocacy groups in Greece point out that many of these pitfalls could have been avoided if they had been consulted more and their views incorporated into legislation.

On the other hand, the incorporative aspects of policymaking institutions and processes come into play when there is marked divergence between the interests of different organized societal groups and between these groups and the state, necessitating policy bargaining over either the shorter or longer term. Compromise is more likely to be reached if there is a strong tradition of consultation and incorporation that not only facilitates bargaining but also gives a good reason for groups to voice their interests and concerns within the framework established by the state – rather than taking to the streets in protest or otherwise disrupting the overall policy direction pursued on the part of the state. An example of successful compromise in the Irish case is the strategy for promoting 'family friendly' measures in the workplace, agreed to through the social partnership process. Implementing compulsory measures through legislation was likely to alienate business interests, but a voluntary framework was able to gain support from the key players, organized labour and business in this case, the details of which are continually thrashed out within the context of social partnership.

The second major question concerns how *much* the presence or absence of incorporative and consultative policymaking can explain. Obviously, this variable or set of variables alone cannot explain everything and one additional factor especially stands out as a facilitator of policy change across the case studies analysed in this book. The independent role of what has been termed 'enlightened leadership' is particularly relevant to the Portuguese case and its importance here very likely has much to do with the peculiarities of this national case, traceable to the particular path the country has taken to democracy since 1974. While this book has argued that much in Portuguese politics did *not* change as a direct consequence of the revolution, especially the legalistic, top-down aspects of the national policymaking tradition, the sharp break with the past in terms of policy *content* in 1974 is clearly significant. To be more specific, the imprint of socialist ideology on constitutional and other legal commitments has given certain factions and individuals within political parties, but more especially the public administration, justification for pushing through particular reforms in a progressive direction at particular times. The best example drawn from Chapter 6 is the parental leave legislative package implemented with little interest group consultation but instead strident commitment on the part of several key senior bureaucrats. Not only were these particular state actors committed to pushing this legislation through, but explicit gender equality commitments made in the post-1974 Portuguese constitution and subsequent institutional development in the form of CITE and the CIDM arguably gave the actors something to 'hang' the initiative on. Note, however, how this example and the overall explanatory power of enlightened state leadership is specific to the Portuguese case.

Enlightened political leadership and the kind of constitutional and legal justifications found in Portugal, however, have clearly been lacking in the Greek case. Greece shares with Portugal some of the legacies of later socio-economic development, including the continuation of a 'dual society' in which policymaking is largely made and influenced by a highly educated elite. Notably, in both countries there is a high degree of overlap between the top-level public administrators and academia: academics are frequently seconded into the bureaucracy, something that is witnessed in the notes and appendix to this book. While I did not select potential interview subjects in any of these national cases by locating the authors of secondary works on the policy topics in question, my investigations eventually led to a number of academics who had been either temporarily or permanently integrated into the bureaucracy. In Greece, however, elite policymakers seem to see their own roles very differently from in Portugal, perhaps reflecting something fundamental about the democratic political culture of each country. Portuguese elites often could not understand my focus on interest group incorporation beyond trade unions and political parties, clearly believing that the 'correct' solutions to policy naturally came from within their own circles. Yet Greek policymakers were much more willing to use 'public sentiment' or interest group opposition as an excuse for policy inaction. In answer to one of my questions regarding the fact that Greece seemed out of step with much of the rest of Western Europe in that the state was not very proactive in the promotion of anti-racism measures, an immigration policy official argued that this would be 'paternalistic', which is generally something to be avoided.

Beyond a summary of findings from the case study analyses contained in Chapters 4 to 6, this conclusion now moves on to consider some of the broader implications of this book for students of comparative politics. In doing so, it highlights several major inter-related themes. First, I consider issues of generalizability in two senses: across space and across time. What lessons can the Irish, Greek, and Portuguese experiences offer other countries seeking to reorient their development strategies in order to address new economic challenges? The answer to this question points us towards consideration of the impact that long-term democratization paths and deep histories of state–society relations have on national zones of mediation. More complicated perhaps is the question of whether the utility of policymaking institutions and processes that effectively balance consultation with incorporation is relevant to the reorientation of development projects around the requirements of the knowledge economy specifically, or whether its importance is clear for *any* national reorientation of development goals regardless of content. Furthermore, what implications do the conclusions of this book have for understanding the relationship between democratic policy making and economic crisis? The introduction to this book began by underlining the fact that the nature of the post-2008 Eurozone crisis varied across the three bailout countries that provide its focus. That different developmental trajectories underpinned somewhat different reasons for the debt explosion across Ireland, Greece, and Portugal was made clear. In turn, the book then argues, these developmental differences have at least something to do with the zone of mediation, shaped as it is by national histories of state–society relations found in each case. However, what impact did variation in policymaking traditions for each of these countries have on how they coped with, and recovered from, the debt crisis?

Considering the first, and arguably the least complicated, of these issues surrounding the implications of this book's analytic framework and case study findings beyond the national cases that it considered, it is worth in particular looking across from where Ireland, Portugal, and Greece lie, toward Europe's new 'periphery', its Eastern fringe. Essentially, what the case study chapters in this book show is that even in the older of the 'newer democracies', including Greece and Portugal, the precise way in which a country broke with its authoritarian past can still have a major impact on its policymaking tradition today. Even in Portugal, arguably the 'third wave' democracy that broke most radically with its immediate past, authoritarian legacies remain in the way that state and society interact (Hite and Cesarini, 2004). Such authoritarian legacies are, of course, deeper in countries that have not only made the transition to democracy more recently but also have no 'pre-authoritarian' democratic legacy to resurrect or fall back on. Much of Central and Eastern Europe falls into this camp, where the corporatist structures established under Communism essentially prevented independent interest groups from developing, let alone zones of mediation in which they operate. The European Union, for its part, knows this very well, and has dedicated significant resources to activating interests – or at least civil society organizations – in this region (Parau, 2009; Petrovic and Solingen, 2005). Outside of Europe, including some notable Latin American examples, the Greek case study serves to illustrate how problematic democratic policymaking can become when political parties monopolize interest representation at the expense of all other channels.

Turning now to the second set of issues highlighted above, is the prior existence of a robust zone of mediation important for any democracy attempting to reorient its development strategy around any particular set of objectives, or were policymaking institutions that balance consultative and incorporative functions particularly or only important during the particular phase of development many post-industrial countries found themselves in during the 1990s and 2000s? The answer to this is two-fold: in a sense, both empirical and normative answers can be given.

On a theoretical plane, one of the perennial concerns held by students of comparative politics, political economy, and political sociology is the relationship between economic and political development. In the process of investigating this relationship, two separate, although not entirely unrelated, general observations have been made. The first is that, on average, certain levels of economic development are more likely to lead to democratic outcomes. This line of enquiry ranges from early modernization theory, to neo-modernization theory, to more recent, statistically sophisticated analyses that tend to produce more nuanced conclusions about the democracy–development relationship (Boix, 2003; Przeworski *et al.*, 2000). The second line of enquiry, more importantly for the conclusions to this book, proposes relationships between *particular* economic development strategies and *particular* national political regime types, including analyses of bureaucratic-authoritarianism; the historical connection between populism and import-substitution-industrialization strategies; the arguably authoritarian nature of many developmental states; and both older and newer iterations of rentier state theory (Chaudry, 1997; Kohli, 2004; O'Donnell, 1973; Ross; 2001). Something important to note here, however, is that, as rich and varied as this literature might be, the connection between certain economic development strategies and particular *authoritarian* regime types is generally the focus of study.

What about the relationship between different economic development strategies and specific phases of *democratic* development? Do market-oriented structural adjustment projects, for instance, tend to take place within the context of democratic deepening, in which interest group participation in policymaking is expanded, or are they more easily carried out if interest group participation in policymaking is restricted? Does full-scale regime change need to take place in order for us to observe such a connection, or are there more subtle transformations of political institutions and culture that occur within long-established political democracies that accompany major overhauls in economic development strategies, such as a shift from agro-export to service sector-led growth? Is democracy conducive to or indeed required by the shift to knowledge-based developmental strategies? At least initially, it would seem that even well-established democracies seem more willing to engage in reaching out to interest groups in good times, while there is indeed a tendency to want to limit their influence in bad. This appears especially relevant to the patterns observed across the OECD since the early 1980s. As discussed in Chapter 3, overall, policy prescriptions that dominated during the 1980s that involved rolling back the state in favour of market forces seemed also to encourage states to keep interest groups at arms' length in order to curb potential interest group 'capture' of the state in times of austerity. On the other hand, post-1990 interest in expanding state functions in terms of shaping labour market outcomes in order to meet the requirements of the knowledge economy, in particular, seemed to suggest the reincorporation of interest groups – easier to do perhaps, in comparatively good economic times.

Which brings us back to where this book started, with the debt crisis, international bailouts, and subsequent austerity packages forced on Ireland, Greece, and Portugal following the Global Financial Crisis (GFC) of 2008. Chapter 1 explained how, despite a number of structural similarities, there are some acute differences between these three economies and the way that the debt crisis unfolded in each. In particular, by the late 2000s Greece still exhibited some serious facets of underdevelopment that it had failed to address over the past twenty years. Portugal had gone further in terms of economic modernization, but it also had further to go given its starting point. Ireland had been as successful as a post-industrial economy can get in terms of growth rates, but its failures in terms of financial regulation in particular set the country back terribly in 2008. Yet because most of the fundamentals had already been put in place, Ireland was already set to recover much more quickly from the debt crisis than its Southern European counterparts by as early as 2010. Portugal struggled to get its economy back on track, showing positive growth in some sectors yet with a still fairly high unemployment rate, and was able to exit the bailout programme in May 2014. Meanwhile, Greece's six-year recession showed no signs of ending by the middle of 2014, and it remained unclear as to when its debt repayment targets would be met.

The nature of policymaking institutions and processes across the three countries helps explain not only how each country was positioned on the eve of the GFC, but also how and to what extent each has been able to work its way out of the debt crisis. Beyond the fact that Greece has the furthest to go in terms of restructuring its economy, Ireland the least and, as always, Portugal somewhere in between, the prior existence of mediating structures also conditioned the immediate crisis and recovery phase. The general line of argument I would make here is that not only does having a robust zone of mediation help governments flesh out policy detail and gain support from interest groups during times of state expansion, but mediating institutions and processes also help forge trust between players that helps states 'ride out', if not negotiate, tough economic times. The robustness of that zone of mediation, as discussed above, hinges on, or is one aspect of, the quality of democracy, something that varies markedly across the three countries in this and many other respects.

In Ireland, the public response to the bailout and subsequent austerity measures was surprisingly muted, lacking the backlash and certainly the protest activity observable across Southern Europe at approximately the same time. While there were political casualties of the crisis, especially in the ranks of long-time dominant Fianna Fáil, which had presided over the financial crisis, no major political instability resulted. While social partnership appeared to tilt on the brink of collapse several times following the events of 2008–2010, it also managed to act as a channel through which disputes between major societal actors could be managed. The *Towards 2016* partnership agreement negotiated in 2005–2006 had already deviated from the traditional three-yearly pattern in the context of increasing uncertainty about the future of economic growth. Because this took the form of a ten-year agreement, specific wage commitments only covered the first two years of its duration. Since renegotiations then took place during the midst of the crisis, securing agreement between the government and the social partners became more difficult, leading to the collapse of social partnership in 2009. Yet by 2010, austerity targets and overall policy goals were being negotiated through what became known as 'social dialogue', or social partnership in a modified form.

The political consequences of the bailout package in Greece were much more acute. Waves of strike action, social mobilization, and sometimes violent public protest met the rounds of austerity measures implemented between 2010 and 2012, leading to, among other things, the death of three bank employees after a building was fire-bombed during a protest in early 2010, and accusations of escalating police brutally through 2011 and 2012. Another wave of protests also took place in late 2013 as Greek leaders continually attempted to renegotiate the conditions of the bailout. Political polarization could also be observed: the era witnessed the rise of a new leftist political party, SYRIZA, but also the reassertion of neo-fascist groups whose violence was targeted at both migrant communities and leftist organizations of various kinds. What this shows is that Greece lacks channels not only for the forging of creative policy responses to new labour market challenges, but also those which are capable of seeing the country through difficult economic times. Tripartite corporatist mechanisms may exist to bring labour, business, and the state together, but the range of issues discussed here is apparently very limited and, much more importantly for this analysis, does not embrace a wide range of societal interests. Furthermore, such partial and segmented mechanisms are embedded in a political culture that is highly conflictual and a harder version of democracy that is resistant to compromise. The conclusions of this book do, however, offer some hope of breaking this cycle. If institutions shape behaviour, and behaviour and attitudes are the stuff of political culture, then the establishment of new institutions and processes in order to constitute a zone of mediation, creating a buffer between state and society, should be able to change that political culture over time.

Meanwhile, the Portuguese path through and out of the debt disaster and economic crisis was also marked by protest and social conflict, but not as deep nor as damaging as that experienced in Greece. Governments in the post-2008 era were marked by instability, including the calling of an early election in 2011 and a political crisis in mid-2013 leading to emergency measures to hold the ruling coalition government together. Yet this is a pattern that also preceded the debt crisis. Protest activity against austerity reached a height, belatedly perhaps, in 2011, partly as a result of a trans-Iberian backlash that began in Spain. At certain moments, however, the Portuguese path out of crisis has also demonstrated the country's strong incorporative tendencies, including inclusive cross-party talks between government, opposition, and organized labour and business, both at the height of the crisis and also in 2014 as austerity measures were coming to an end and the country looked ahead to its longer-term plan for economic and social development.

Normatively then, looking ahead to a potentially brighter future on Europe's Southern and Western fringe, and beyond that to other OECD countries in the process of reorienting their economic and social development strategies to meet the challenges of the twenty-first century, this book ends with a plea. Not only should policymakers consider the ways in which their own zones of mediation might help forge policies that are better suited to local needs at the same time that they incorporate as wide a set of societal interests as possible, but they should resist the temptation to shrink that zone of mediation in times of crisis – because it might just help them see their way through the next one.

References

Boix, Carles, *Democracy and Redistribution* (Cambridge: Cambridge University Press, 2003).

Chaudry, Kiren Aziz, *The Price of Wealth: Economies and Institutions in the Middle East* (Ithaca, NY: Cornell University Press, 1997).

Hite, Katherine and Paola Cesarini, *Authoritarian Legacies and Democracies in Latin America and Southern Europe* (Notre Dame, IN: University of Notre Dame Press, 2004).

Kohli, Atul, *State-Directed Development* (Cambridge: Cambridge University Press, 2004).

O'Donnell, Guillermo, *Modernization and Bureaucratic-Authoritarianism: Studies in South American Politics* (Berkeley, CA: Institute of International Studies, 1973).

Parau, Cristina Elena, "Impaling Dracula: How EU Accession Empowered Civil Society in Romania", *West European Politics* 32, 1 (2009), 119–41.

Petrovic, Bojan and Etel Solingen, "Europeanisation and Internationalisation: The Case of the Czech Republic", *New Political Economy* 10, 3 (2005), 281–303.

Przeworski, Adam, Michael E. Alvarez, José Antonio Cheibub, and Fernando Limongi, *Democracy and Development: Political Institutions and Well-Being in the World, 1950–1990* (Cambridge: Cambridge University Press, 2000).

Ross, Michael Lewin, "Does Oil Hinder Democracy?", *World Politics* 53, 3 (2001), 325–61.

Appendix

List of interview subjects

Ireland

(Anonymous) Member of Commission on the Family, 26 April 2005.
(Anonymous) Representatives of Union of Students in Ireland, 28 April 2005.
(Anonymous) Member of Commission on the Family, 5 May 2005.
(Anonymous) Policy Officer, Irish National Organisation for the Unemployed, 10 June 2005.
Deidre Carroll, Member of Family Policy Commission and Senior Civil Servant, 29 April 2005.
Denise Charlton, CEO of Immigrant Council, 30 May 2005.
Maria Cronin, Irish Business and Employers' Confederation, 17 June 2005.
Mark Field, CEO Irish Small and Medium Enterprises Organisation, 24 May 2005.
Paul Hannigan, Director of Letterkenny Institute of Technology, 15 June 2005.
Barbara Keogh, Irish Congress of Trade Unions, 23 May 2005.
Esther Lynch, Policy Officer of the Irish Congress of Trade Unions, 6 May 2005.
Catherine Murphy, Member of Parliament and Member of the Commission on the Family, 31 May 2005.
Brian Nolan, President of DIT, 24 May 2005.
Sean Regan, Community Workers' Co-operative (Community Platform Secretariat), 1 June 2005.
Dr. Don Thornhill, former secretary, Department of Education, and former head of the Higher Education Authority, 1 June 2005.

Greece

Moáwia Achmed, Coordinator, Greek Migrants' Forum, 14 November 2005.
(Anonymous), Education Policy Advisor, 28 April 2010.
(Anonymous), Researcher at Labour Institute, General Confederation of Greek Workers (GSEE), 1 May 2010.
Yannis Ktistakis, General Secretary, Hellenic League for Human Rights, 4 November 2005.
Manos Matsaganis, University of Economics and Business, Athens, and former political advisor to Simitis government 1997–2001, 11 November 2005.
Miltos Pavlou, Senior Researcher for the Greek Ombudsman and Hellenic League of Human Rights, 9 November 2005.
Sofia Voulgaraki, Greek Youth Council, 10 November 2005.

Thanos Veremis, Chair, National Council on Education, 3 May 2010.
Maria Stratigaki, General Secretary for Gender Equality, 12 May 2010.
Aliki Mouriki, National Centre for Social Research, 20 May 2010.

Portugal

Odette Felipe, Equality Officer, General Confederation of Portuguese Workers (CGTP), 20 October 2005.
Paulo Fontes, Fórum Académico para a Informação e Representação Externa, 26 September 2005.
Eduardo Marçal Grilo, Minister for Education 1995–1999, 12 October 2005.
Carlos Gonçalves, Borders and Foreigners Service (SEF), 7 October 2005.
Josefina Leitao, former head of Commission for Equality in Work and Employment (CITE), 7 October 2005.
Catarina Oliveira, *Alto Comissariado para a Imigração e Miniorias étnicas* (ACIME), 7 October 2005.
Maria Cunha Rego, former Secretary of State for Equality, 5 October 2005.
Pedro Lourtie, Professor of Mechanical Engineering at the Technical University of Lisbon and former Secretary of State for Higher Education, 1 October 2005.

Index

Page numbers in *italics* denote tables, those in **bold** denote figures.

For Product Safety Concerns and Information please contact our EU representative GPSR@taylorandfrancis.com
Taylor & Francis Verlag GmbH, Kaufingerstraße 24, 80331 München, Germany

www.ingramcontent.com/pod-product-compliance
Ingram Content Group UK Ltd.
Pitfield, Milton Keynes, MK11 3LW, UK
UKHW010957180926
475701UK00004B/417
* 9 7 8 1 1 3 8 5 0 4 8 9 9 *